DATA SCIENCE IN CONTEXT

Data science is the foundation of our modern world. It underlies applications used by billions of people every day, providing new tools, forms of entertainment, economic growth, and potential solutions to difficult, complex problems. These opportunities come with significant societal consequences, raising fundamental questions about issues such as data quality, fairness, privacy, and causation.

In this book, four leading experts convey the excitement and promise of data science and examine the major challenges in gaining its benefits and mitigating its harms. They offer frameworks for critically evaluating the ingredients and the ethical considerations needed to apply data science productively, illustrated by extensive application examples.

The authors' far-ranging exploration of these complex issues will stimulate data science practitioners and students, as well as humanists, social scientists, scientists, and policy makers, to study and debate how data science can be used more effectively and more ethically to better our world.

ALFRED Z. SPECTOR is a Visiting Scholar at MIT, who has innovated in large-scale, networked computing systems and provided research leadership to many. After beginning his career on the Carnegie Mellon faculty, he founded Transarc, and then led IBM Software Research. He was later Vice President of Research and Special Initiatives at Google and then CTO at Two Sigma Investments.

PETER NORVIG is a Distinguished Education Fellow at Stanford's Human-Centered Artificial Intelligence Institute and a research director at Google; previously he directed Google's core search algorithms group and NASA's AI efforts.

CHRIS WIGGINS is an Associate Professor of Applied Mathematics at Columbia University and the Chief Data Scientist at *The New York Times*. At Columbia he is a founding member of the executive committee of the Data Science Institute, and a member of the Department of Applied Physics and Applied Mathematics as well as the Department of Systems Biology, and is affiliated faculty in Statistics.

JEANNETTE M. WING is the Executive Vice President for Research and Professor of Computer Science at Columbia University and was the inaugural Avanessians Director of its data science institute. She is known for her research contributions in security and privacy, programming languages, and concurrent and distributed systems.

"This book provides an important view of the contextual landscape for data science: the context of related fields of statistics, visualization, optimization, and computer science; the context of a broad range of applications, together with an Analysis Rubric; the context of societal impacts from dependability, to understandability, to ethical and legal questions. These are critically important factors for any practitioner of data science to understand, and for others to be aware of in evaluating the use of data science."

— Daniel Huttenlocher, Massachusetts Institute of Technology,
co-author of *The Age of AI*

"As data science becomes a crucial element in momentous decisions of war and peace, as well as commerce and innovation, it is vital that it rests on sound foundations. This book is an important step forward in that regard, illuminating the context in which data science is practiced. It is essential reading for both data scientists and decision makers."

— James Arroyo, OBE, Director of the Ditchley Foundation

"Data science touches every aspect of our modern lives. This book digs into the practical, legal, and ethical challenges that result. It is the only book that's comprehensive in its consideration of the thorny issues arising from the broad application and unprecedented growth of data science. If you do data science, you should read this book."

— Michael D. Smith, John H. Finley, Jr. Professor of Engineering
and Applied Sciences, Harvard University

"This book will be essential reading for all data scientists and data teams. The self-contained text explains what students and practitioners need to know to use data science more effectively and ethically. It draws on the authors' years of experience and offers practical insights into data science that complement other books that focus on specific techniques. I'll be referencing and recommending this book for many years to come."

— Ben Lorica, Gradient Flow, host of *The Data Exchange* podcast

DATA SCIENCE IN CONTEXT

Foundations, Challenges, Opportunities

ALFRED Z. SPECTOR
Massachusetts Institute of Technology

PETER NORVIG
Stanford University, California

CHRIS WIGGINS
Columbia University, New York

JEANNETTE M. WING
Columbia University, New York

CAMBRIDGE
UNIVERSITY PRESS

University Printing House, Cambridge CB2 8BS, United Kingdom

One Liberty Plaza, 20th Floor, New York, NY 10006, USA

477 Williamstown Road, Port Melbourne, VIC 3207, Australia

314–321, 3rd Floor, Plot 3, Splendor Forum, Jasola District Centre,
New Delhi – 110025, India

103 Penang Road, #05–06/07, Visioncrest Commercial, Singapore 238467

Cambridge University Press is part of the University of Cambridge.

It furthers the University's mission by disseminating knowledge in the pursuit of education, learning, and research at the highest international levels of excellence.

www.cambridge.org
Information on this title: www.cambridge.org/9781009272209
DOI: 10.1017/9781009272230

First published 2023

A catalogue record for this publication is available from the British Library.

ISBN 978-1-009-27220-9 Hardback

Contents

Figures

Tables

Preface

Combine unprecedented scientific and engineering advances in computing with the aspirations, methods, and advances in statistics and operations research, and we get the field of data science, which broadly aims to extract insights or conclusions from data. Data science has come into existence due to rapidly increasing capabilities to collect, process, and learn from data, and then to apply what was learned with near- and long-term benefits.

Even though the term "data science" only began to be used widely circa 2010, it has had enormous effects on science, engineering, commerce, and society at large, and the field has explosively grown in vitality and impact by almost any metric: Educational programs in the field are blossoming, as is employment. Social networks, online shopping, streaming entertainment, internet search, new cancer treatments, many scientific discoveries, and semi-automated driving are not solely due to data science, but it plays a huge and central role in each. Most household name companies, whether in technology, pharma, logistics, finance, education, or another field entirely, are heavily based on data science techniques.

However, as the field has grown, so have public concerns about it, including, but not limited to the following:

- Economic and fairness impacts on people and institutions
- Potential and actual misuse of personal data
- Effects on harmony and governance
- Power consumption
- General mistrust

It seems every day we hear of a new concern garnering attention, whether well- or ill-founded. Perhaps this is unsurprising, as data science impacts so many aspects of life. Most innovations, no matter how good they are, have unintended consequences.

Data science's juxtaposition of opportunities and challenges gave rise to this book. By illustrating and exploring the complex issues, we aim to provide both students and practitioners the ability to use data science more effectively and more ethically. We offer a method for critically evaluating data science's applicability to particular problems, an extensive list of examples, and a detailed discussion of the technical, societal, and ethical challenges that data scientists must navigate.

Part I begins by delineating the field, explaining its historical roots in statistics, operations research, and computing. We then start a thread on ethical considerations in applying data science, which continues through later parts of the book.

Part II then describes more than 30 data science applications with three goals:

- Explaining aspects of how these applications work
- Illustrating the complexities in making them work *well*
- Introducing an Analysis Rubric that practitioners can apply to tease out those complexities when applying data science to new problems

Motivated by this Analysis Rubric, Part III delves into the technical, contextual, and societal challenges of data science, including privacy, security, the complexity in setting objectives, and many ethical issues.

Part IV describes societal concerns with the unintended consequences of data science, and then makes recommendations for ameliorating some of them. We summarize our major points in Chapter 20.

Our journey will intermingle topics in data science, its technological underpinnings, and related fields. In part, this is because data science arose through the confluence of diverse technical, scientific, and commercial advances. We believe this breadth is needed to explain how data science has become so important, how it solves problems, and what challenges exist.

As an example, topics like the growth in power of computation and computer security may not seem to be primarily data science topics. But vast computing capability makes data science feasible, while security issues force us to temper our enthusiasm with a deep consideration of risk. We were guided in choosing topics for this book by a desire to enhance our and our readers' understanding of data science and its future.

We do not duplicate textbooks on the theory and application of data science techniques, but instead address the breadth of data science, a field in which the revolutionary growth in computing coupled with advances in statistics and operations research is changing almost all aspects of society. We believe this material can be the basis for a full course, though we recommend adding supplemental case studies and analyses. We also believe this book provides important perspectives that are a useful addition to courses that focus on statistical, operations research, or computational techniques. We hope it will also be useful to technically oriented professionals wanting to apply data science to new problems. Finally, we have tried to make the material accessible to non-experts, particularly in public policy or business, who are interested in the benefits and challenges at the confluence of data science, technology, and society.

This is a fast-moving field, and we anticipate providing additional commentary, questions, and updates on the book's website, DataScienceInContext.com.

Alfred Z. Spector
Peter Norvig
Chris Wiggins
Jeannette M. Wing

Acknowledgments

We are deeply grateful to many who have given us specific advice and comments on this manuscript: Alfred Aho, James Arroyo, Robin Berjon, David Blei, Aaron Brown, Sarah Cen, Brenda Dietrich, Ulfar Erlingsson, Kaylee Fisher, Ben Fried, Alon Halevy, Mark Hansen, Reece Hirsch, George Hripcsak, Daniel Huttenlocher, Jon Kleinberg, David Konerding, Rhonda Kost, Aleksander Madry, Preston McAfee, Vikram Modi, Nicola Phillips, Calton Pu, Alexander Rodriguez, Roni Rosenfeld, Daniel M. Russell, Thomas Sakmar, Teymour Shahabi, David Shaw, James Shinn, Asher Spector, Benjamin Spector, Emily Spector, Billie-Grace Ward, Martin Wattenberg, Peter Weinberger, the spring 2022 students in MIT's class 6.S978, and several anonymous reviewers. We benefited greatly from the often extensive feedback we received, in part because the book covers such a broad collection of topics.

We are also very grateful to the following five people who improved the prose in this book: Nikki Ho-Shing worked on the transcription of co-author Alfred's 2015 talk, "Opportunities and Perils in Data Science," which was the book's initial seed (Spector, 2016); Cindy Bloch assisted in many ways – particularly by corralling our roughly 400 citations; Tom Galloway made two passes over our prose, suggesting thousands of improvements for readability, consistency, and comprehensibility; and Lauren Cowles, our editor at Cambridge University Press, and Geoff Amor, our freelance copy editor, had invaluable structural and editorial advice.

Co-author Jeannette thanks Armen Avanessians who endowed the directorship of the Data Science Institute at Columbia University, giving her the opportunity to explore data science in its breadth. We all thank the institutions at which we have taught and worked for giving us opportunities to explore and solve challenging problems.

Finally, we recognize the impact of our own teachers, and we cherish all the interactions we have had with students, colleagues, seminar attendees, clients, and user communities. We could never have written this book without them.

Any shortcomings in the book are due to us, not to any who have assisted us.

Introduction

The quantity of data that is collected, processed, and employed has exploded in this millennium. Many organizations now collect more data in a month than the total stored in the Library of Congress. With the goal of gaining insight and drawing conclusions from this vast sea of information, data science has fueled many of the vast benefits brought by the Internet and provided the business models that pay many of its costs.

Beyond the marvels of present data science applications, there are even greater breakthroughs on the horizon: semi-autonomous cars and trucks, and perhaps even fully autonomous ones; widespread precision medicine leading to longer and healthier lives; transformative improvements to education and the pursuit of science; new ways to pursue the humanities; and evolution in the workplace. There are new data science applications brewing in almost every field of human endeavor.

However, no new technology arrives without complications: Some of the complications are technological, based on challenges in both developing algorithms and then perfecting software and computer systems. For example, with so much data and processing capability, there are inevitably security, privacy, and reliability challenges. And, if applications of data science become as omnipresent as predicted, society needs the technologists to ensure they are rock solid.

Some complications are broader, relating to the very premise of using data to valuable effect. With mountains of data and correlations becoming available, we need to learn to cut through them to ascertain fundamental truths, not erroneous associations which may obfuscate the truth. Deeper risks arise when using data in decision systems; as new applications become available, and we can predict and optimize many outcomes, we must decide what we are really trying to achieve.

Some challenges are truly fundamental, as data science may change the operation of our society and impact our own humanness. We must come to grips with limitations on how much mechanistic advice and control we are willing to act on or even receive. As these systems alter our jobs and our socio-political systems, we will need to understand their effects and adjust in ways that we do not yet understand. Data science is affecting us already, and it may even challenge our notions of ourselves as the intelligent masters of our world.

Because of these very broad impacts, data science as a field has led to entirely new research agendas outside of its foundational fields of computer science, statistics, and operations research. Data science is also changing many other disciplines (e.g., how we think about and practice political science, but many more). There are also growing transdisciplinary relationships between data science and many of the humanities and social sciences.

This book's holistic approach to data science leads us through these topics:

- Part I, Data Science, provides a unifying definition of data science and sets forth the field's goals. It then provides a historical perspective on how data science arose from its foundational fields (statistics, operations research, and computing, metaphorically illustrated in Figure 1) and describes its relationship to the sciences, social sciences, and humanities. The historical story is an exciting one due to exceedingly rapid progress that has changed the course of technology, many domains of applicability, and even our society writ large.

Figure 1 This metaphorical braid shows the integration of the foundational fields, labeled S (statistics), OR (operations research), and C (computing).

- Part II, Applying Data Science, presents examples of data science applications from the domains of technology, commerce, science, medicine, and more. Based on our detailed exposition of six applications, the chapter develops a seven-element Analysis Rubric to help us analyze the relative ease or difficulty of applying data science to other applications. We then review 26 more applications against the Analysis Rubric. Some of these are straightforward; others gnarly but feasible; yet others nearly impossible. Almost all have unintended consequences that require care and thought. Figure 2 illustrates this part's flow.

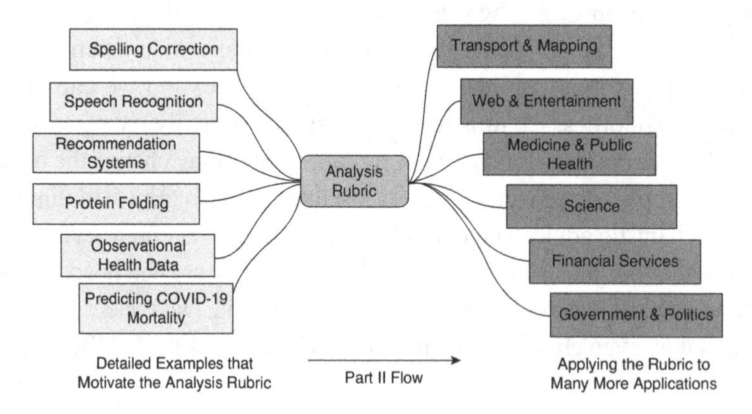

Figure 2 Part II introduces six applications, uses them to induce an Analysis Rubric, and then demonstrates its applications.

- Part III, Challenges in Applying Data Science, builds off the seven elements in the Analysis Rubric to present the technical, contextual, and societal challenges in making data science work well (this is illustrated in Figure 3). With care, users of data science can often navigate many of these challenges effectively. However, some are perilous and very difficult to resolve, implying that, in some cases, data science is simply not the right tool for the job. Part III is quite clear about the risks of the misapplication of technology.

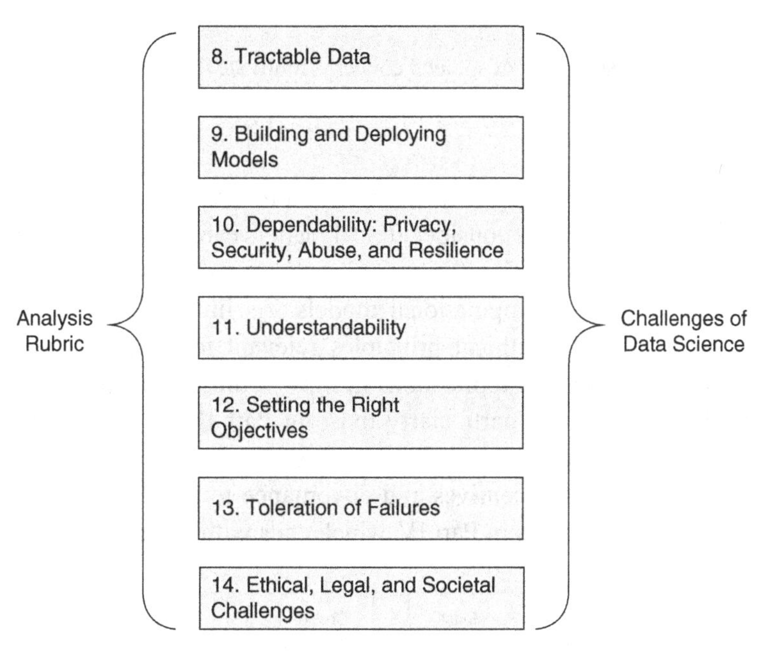

Figure 3 The Analysis Rubric's seven elements motivate the challenges in Chapters 8 to 14.

- Part IV, Addressing Concerns, describes many societal concerns regarding data science and its applications – concerns which in turn are influenced by Part III's challenges. It then discusses some approaches for mitigating these concerns while still allowing us to reap the rewards. In some cases, we make prescriptive proposals: For example, we recommend increasing data science education at the secondary school level and above, even if this means reprioritizing a little of the current mathematics curriculum and substituting more probability, statistics, and computing. In other areas, we only set forth some considerations that decision makers should take into account. Part IV's flow is described in Figure 4.

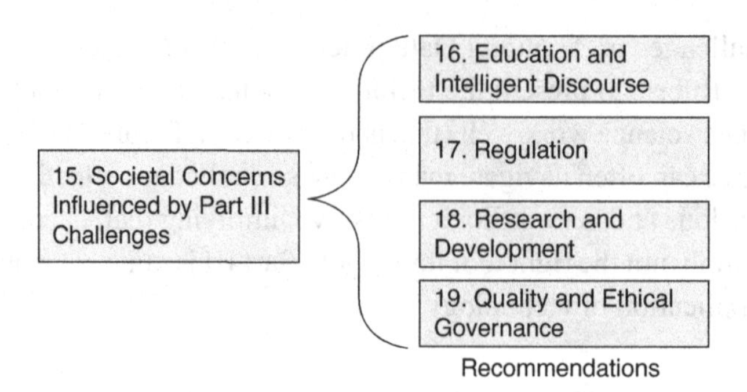

Figure 4 Part IV's summary of societal concerns motivate the recommendations in Chapters 16 to 19.

- An ethics thread flows through the book, with a focused section near the end of each part. Data science must consider ethical matters carefully because many data science applications have significant societal consequences and often rely on personal data to create computational models. As illustrated in Figure 5, the thread starts by defining ethical principles relevant to data science and then reviews some of the Part II applications in light of those principles. While most chapters of the book (and particularly those in Part III) present ethics-related issues, the ethics thread augments these discussions with the organizational challenges of balancing incentives and governance to achieve good outcomes. The ethics thread concludes in Part IV, which ends with three recommendations.

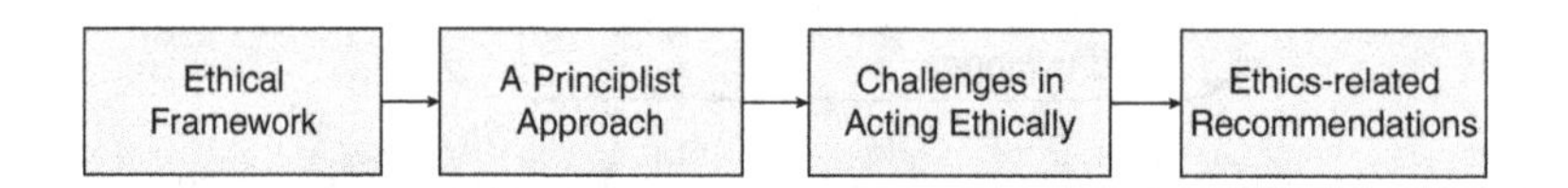

Figure 5 This figure illustrates the flow of the ethics thread, which spans Parts I to IV.

While the chapters build on each other, data science courses will vary in what examples from Part II they emphasize. Some readers may choose to omit Part IV (which bridges from the *challenges* of Part III to societal *concerns*), while others may wish to omit some of the technical details in Part II and Part III.

In all, this book's broad perspective on the field of data science aims to educate readers about the data science applications they regularly use, to apply that understanding to new applications, to more fully recognize the challenges inherent in data science, and to educate and catalyze thoughtful analysis, debate, and action to make data science ever more beneficial.

Part I

Data Science

This part begins with the goals, subfields, and history of data science. It continues by describing data science's broad applicability and a framework for ethical considerations. It concludes with five tables defining important concepts and terminology.

Chapter 1

Foundations of Data Science

This chapter first defines data science, its primary objectives, and several related terms. It continues by describing the evolution of data science from the fields of statistics, operations research, and computing. The chapter concludes with historical notes on the emergence of data science and related topics.

1.1 Definitions

Data science is the study of extracting value from data – value in the form of **insights** or **conclusions**.

- A data-derived insight could be:
  - a hypothesis, testable with more data;
  - an "aha!" that comes from a succinct statistic or an apt visual chart; or
  - a plausible relationship among variables of interest, uncovered by examining the data and the implications of different scenarios.
- A conclusion could be in an analyst's head or in a computer program. To be *useful*, a conclusion should lead us to make good decisions about how to act in the world, with those actions taken either automatically by a program, or by a human who consults with the program. A conclusion may be in the form of a:
  - **prediction** of a consequence;
  - **recommendation** of a useful action;
  - **clustering** that groups similar elements;
  - **classification** that labels elements in groupings;
  - **transformation** that converts data to a more useful form; or
  - **optimization** that moves a system to a better state.

Insights and conclusions often arise from **models**, which are abstractions of the real world. A model can explain why or how something happens and can be tested against previously unseen inputs. This is shown schematically in Figure 1.1.

Of course, scientists and lay people have used data and models for centuries. Today's data science builds on this usage. But it differs from classical data use due to the scale it operates at and its use of new statistical and computational techniques.

There is still no consensus on the definition of data science. For example, the *Journal of Data Science* in its initial issue says "By 'Data Science' we mean almost everything that has something to do with data"; Mike Loukides, co-author of *Ethics and Data Science*, says "Data science enables the creation of data products" (Loukides, 2011); Cassie Kozyrkov, Google's Chief Decision Scientist, says "Data science is the discipline of making data useful" (Kozyrkov, 2018). We believe our definition is consistent with other definitions and that it is usefully prescriptive.

If a retailer tracks a billion customer transactions, analyzes the data, and learns something that improves their sales, that's a data science insight. If the retailer then automatically recommends to customers what to buy next, that's a data science conclusion enabled by a model, perhaps one that uses machine learning.

Data science touches all of society. We will highlight many applications in transportation, the Web and entertainment, medicine and public health, science, financial services, and government. However, there are many others in the humanities, agriculture, energy systems, and virtually every field. In recognition of data science's cross-disciplinary nature, this book presents data science issues from multiple points of view.

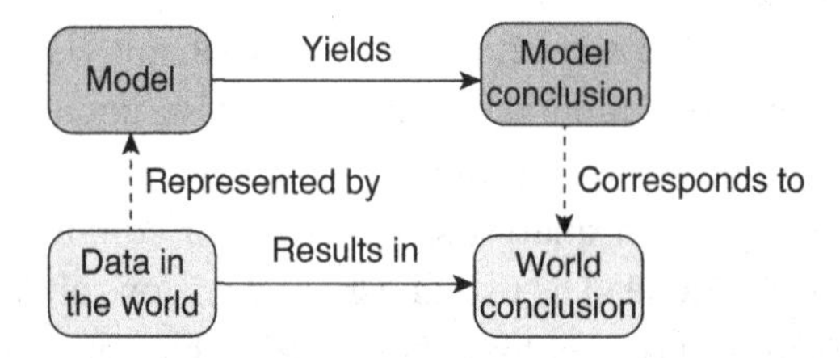

Figure 1.1 From data in the world, we build a model of some aspects of it, reason about the model to draw conclusions, and check that these conclusions correspond to what happens in the world. The better the model, the better the correspondence between the model's conclusions and the real world. Dashed arrows denote the mapping between world and model, and solid arrows are within the world or model.

1.1.1 Data Science – Insights

Data science offers insights by permitting the exploration of data. The data may show a trend suggesting a hypothesis in the context of a model that leads to useful conclusions – which themselves can be tested with more data. A trend might indicate that two (or more) things are **correlated**, meaning the variables are related to each other, such as smoking and cancer. A potential correlation is an insight, and a hypothesis that can be tested. The data may even suggest the possibility of an underlying **causal relationship**, which occurs when one thing causes another – smoking causes cancer, though cancer does not cause smoking. Or perhaps a conclusion is not obvious, but can be explored with many what-if analyses that also draw on more data.

Insights are facilitated by interactive tools that simplify this exploration and let us benefit from vast amounts of data without bogging down and missing the forest for the trees:

- Tools to help us gain insight start with data transformation, which converts units, merges names (such as "Ohio" and "OH"), combines data sources, and removes duplicates, errors, and outliers.
- Tools to automate experiments by providing integrated modeling capabilities that simplify creation, execution, exploration, and record keeping.
- Tools that offer interactive capabilities that guide us to non-obvious conclusions.

Pioneering data scientist John Tukey said "The simple graph has brought more information to the data analyst's mind than any other device" (Tukey, 1962), but modern visualization offers many other beautiful and useful ways to gain insight. However, graphs must be scrutinized very carefully for meaning.

As an example of a graph that provides some insight but that also leads to many questions, the scatter plot in Figure 1.2 shows the relationship between mortality and COVID-19 vaccination rates during the US delta variant wave. It shows four series of points representing different time periods ranging from delta's beginning mid-2021 to its late 2021 end. Each point represents the vaccination rate and number of COVID-19 deaths in each of the 50 states and the District of Columbia. We show **regression lines** for each of the four series of data – each line represents the linear equation that best fits the data. Critical analysis would be served with error bars for each data point, but this information was unavailable.

The 6-Sep-21 and 27-Sep-21 series data were from the peak of the wave, and they tilt strongly down and to the right, meaning that higher state vaccination rates were strongly correlated with lower death rates. The 11-Jul-21 and 16-Dec-21 regressions (beginning and ending of the wave) showed small negative slopes, but reports of the CDC's imprecision in vaccination reporting (Wingrove, 2021) sufficiently concerned us to demonstrate a good visualization practice by providing a prominent warning on the graph. Clearly, this data's association of vaccination rate on mortality declined after the delta wave crested. During the five-month period, the chart also shows that vaccination rates increased by about 13% (absolute).

This data and our prior understanding of vaccine biochemistry lead us strongly to believe there is an underlying causal relationship – that vaccinations reduce the risk of deaths. (The US Centers for Disease Control and Prevention (CDC) COVID Data Tracker provides even stronger evidence of a causal relationship (CDC, 2020).) However, Figure 1.2 does *not* provide conclusive insight, as there *could* be other explanations for some of the effects. States differ along many relevant variables other than vaccination rate, such as population age, density, and prior disease exposure. This is not a randomized controlled experiment where each state was randomly assigned a vaccination rate. The reasons the curve flattened at the end of the wave may not be because of reduced vaccine efficacy against the delta variant but rather because of the impact of behavioral changes, changes in the locale of the wave as it spread across different states, increase in immunity from prior exposure, waning vaccine efficacy over time, and the very beginning of the follow-on omicron wave.

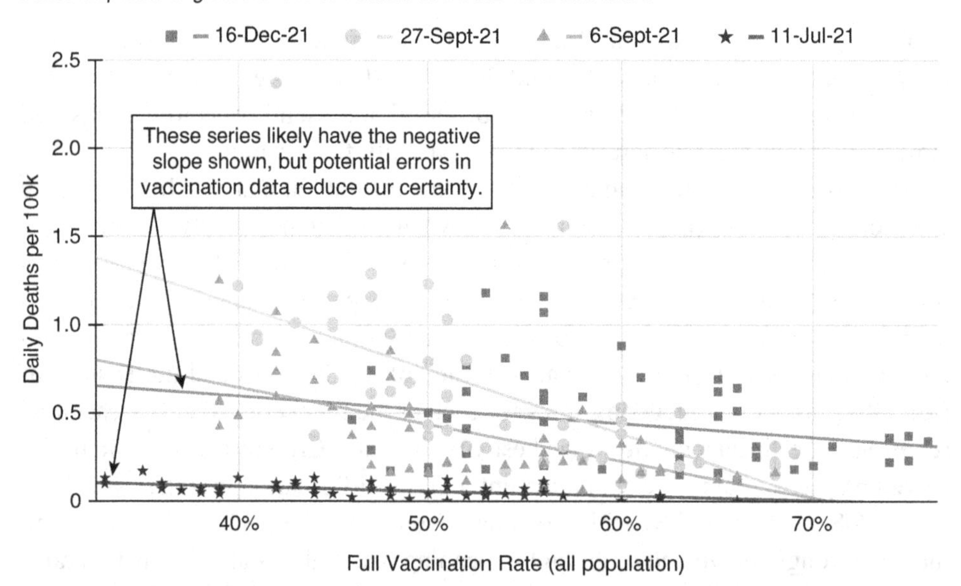

Figure 1.2 Each point shows the seven-day trailing average daily COVID-19 mortality of 50 US states and the District of Columbia plotted against their respective vaccination rates at the end of the time period. This data (though not this visual) was copied from the *New York Times* "Coronavirus in the U.S.: Latest Map and Case Count" during the period represented by this graph (New York Times, 2020). The *New York Times* itself gathered this data from government authorities, and this limited data was likely to be comparable across regions and time periods. US CDC data (not shown) reported state totals that vary from *New York Times*' data, but the trend lines are very similar.

A data scientist could gain further insight from the analysis of outliers. If not an artifact of the data, the twin 1.6 per 100k points that came from Florida, for example, may result from disease in the state's large at-risk elderly population. Data scientists could construct and evaluate many hypotheses from this graph using additional data and visualization techniques. But data scientists need to exercise caution about the quality of individual data points.

The US omicron wave, which followed the delta wave, showed a different regression line. While Figure 1.2 does not illustrate this, state per capita mortality and vaccination rates became positively correlated for a brief period in mid-January 2022, though just slightly so. There are many possible explanations for this, such as the specifics of the omicron mutation and the earlier arrival of the variant in vaccinated states. The reversal, and indeed this chart, reminds us to scrutinize data and visualizations carefully and to exercise due caution, recognizing the limitations of the data and its presentation. Section 11.4 discusses this topic further.

1.1.2 Data Science – Conclusions

Let's look at some examples of our six types of conclusions from the beginning of Section 1.1. Conclusions can be embedded in programs or serve to provide insight to a data analyst.

- **Prediction**
  - Predict how a protein will fold, based on its structure.
  - Autocomplete user input, based on the characters typed so far.
- **Recommendation**
  - Recommend a song, based on past listening.
  - Suggest possible medical therapies, based on laboratory results.
  - Show an ad to a user, based on their recent web searches.
- **Classification**
  - Assign labels to photos (e.g., "cat" or "dog").
  - Identify a bird's species, from its song.
  - Determine if a client is satisfied or unsatisfied, via sentiment analysis.
  - Label email as spam.
- **Optimization**
  - Find the optimal location to build a new warehouse based on minimizing supplier/consumer transportation costs.
  - Schedule product manufacturing to maximize revenue based on predicted future demand.

- **Transformation**
  - Translate a sentence from Chinese to English.
  - Convert astronomical images to entities.
- **Clustering**
  - Cluster together similar images of cancerous growths to help doctors better understand the disease.
  - Cluster email messages into folders.

Models that generate these conclusions may be **clear box** or **opaque box**. A clear box model's logic is available for inspection by others, while an opaque box model's logic is not. The "opaque box" term can also apply to a model whose operation is not comprehensible, perhaps because it relies on machine learning. Context usually clarifies whether opacity refers to unavailability, incomprehensibility, or both.

This book is filled with many examples of using data to reach conclusions. For example, Chapter 4 leads off by discussing data-driven spelling correction systems, which may *classify* words into correct or mispelled variants (perhaps underlining the latter), *recommend* correct spellings ("did you mean, misspell?"), or automatically *transform* an error into a correct spelling. Returning to the mortality insight discussion that concluded the previous section, we also discuss COVID-19 mortality prediction in greater detail, but we will see this is hard to do even when there is much more data available.

1.1.3 Scale

Some data science success is due to new techniques for analysis, and new algorithms for drawing conclusions. But much is due to the sheer scale of data we can now collect and process (Halevy et al., 2009).

As examples of the size of data collections as of 2021: There are 500 billion web pages (and growing) stored in the Internet Archive. The investment company Two Sigma stores at least a petabyte of data per month. YouTube users upload 500 hours of video per minute (Hale, 2019). The SkyMapper Southern Sky Survey is 500 terabytes of astronomical data; and the Legacy Survey of Space and Time is scheduled to produce 200 petabytes in 2022 (Zhang & Zhao, 2015). See Table 1.1, which describes the scale of data, with representative examples.

Data science grows rapidly because of a **virtuous cycle** whereby its impact leads to more data production (often from increased usage), more research and development and impact as the application improves, and then even more data. (While "virtuous cycle" is a commonly used term to describe this feedback loop, not all effects are beneficial, and we both recognize and discuss the cycle's negative effects as well.)

Table 1.1 *Scale of data and representative examples.*

Size			Example
10^3	kB	kilobyte	A half page of text, or a 32 × 32 pixel icon
10^6	MB	megabyte	The text of two complete books, or a medium-resolution photo
10^9	GB	gigabyte	An hour-long HD video, 10 hours of music, or the *Encyclopaedia Britannica* text
10^{12}	TB	terabyte	One month of images from the Hubble Space Telescope or a university library's text
10^{15}	PB	petabyte	Five copies of the 170 million book Library of Congress print collection
10^{18}	EB	exabyte	Twenty copies of the 500 billion page Internet Archive, or two hours of data at the planned rate of the Square Kilometer Array telescope in 2025
10^{21}	ZB	zettabyte	World's total digital content in 2012, or total internet traffic in 2016

The **World Wide Web** was developed in the mid-1990s. It resulted in a vast collection of informative web pages, and enabled the agglomeration of data about user interactions with these pages. The Web's extremely broad data led to novel consumer services and disrupted entire industries. Recommendation engines, as used at Amazon and eBay, became feasible (Schafer et al., 2001), web search continuously improved, and social networks emerged (boyd et al., 2007).

Big data refers to techniques for conceiving, designing, and developing vast amounts of information and operating systems that can gather, store, and process it. In 1994, the book *Managing Gigabytes* assumed that a gigabyte was big data. In 2021, a sub-$1000 laptop holds a terabyte of data, big data is measured in petabytes, and annual worldwide hard disk sales are measured in zettabytes.

Data science focuses on big data, but many of its techniques are equally beneficial for **small data**. Scatter plots and other visualization techniques often work better for a hundred data points than for a trillion.

Small and big data are often combined for a richer understanding. For example, a company with big data from website clicks might also recruit a few subjects for an in-depth user-experience assessment. They are asked questions such as: "What did you think of the user interface?" "How easy was it to accomplish this task?" "When you were trying to find the cheapest product, did you notice the 'sort by price' button?"

1.2 The Emergence of Data Science

Data science emerged from combining three fields. For the purposes of this book, we define them as follows:

- **Statistics** is the mathematical field that interprets and presents numerical data, making inferences and describing properties of the data.

- **Operations research (OR)** is a scientific method for decision-making in the management of organizations, focused on understanding systems and taking optimal actions in the real world. It is heavily focused on the **optimization** of an **objective function** – a precise statement of a goal, such as maximizing profit or minimizing travel distance.
- **Computing** is the design, development, and deployment of software and hardware to manage data and complete tasks. Software engineering gives us the ability to implement the algorithms that make data science work, as well as the tools to create and deploy those algorithms at scale. Hardware design gives us ever-increasing processing speed, storage capacity, and throughput to handle big data.

Some of data science's most important techniques emerged from work across disciplines. While we include **machine learning** within computing, its development included contributions from statistics, pattern recognition, and neuropsychology. **Information visualization** arose from statistics, but has benefited greatly from computing's contributions.

We will look at each of these topics in more detail, and then review the key terminology from them in Table I.1 to Table I.5 at the end of this part.

1.2.1 Statistics

Some of the key ideas from the field of statistics date back over a thousand years to Greek and Islamic mathematicians. The word *statistics* is derived from the Latin word for *state*. Statistics originally studied data about the state's tables of census data listing who is alive, who died, and who to tax, such as *The Statistical Account of Scotland* of 1794 by Sir John Sinclair (Sinclair, 1794). His inscription to the work is telling. Taken from Cicero, it argued that "to counsel on national affairs, one needs knowledge of the make-up of the state" (Cicero, n.d.). Even today, the perspective provided by the old tables is valuable: Sinclair's data, compared with current US Centers for Disease Control and Prevention data, vividly illustrates a 1000-fold decrease in childhood mortality over 250 years.

Soon after Sinclair published his accounts, statistics moved from just tabulating data to making **inferences**. For example, statisticians could count how many houses there are in a city, survey some to determine the average number of people per house, and then use that to estimate the total population. This estimate is an inexact inference, but much cheaper than an exact census of every household. Statistics, as it was understood in Sinclair's time, blossomed to become mathematical statistics, now focused on the mathematical methods that infer from the particular (e.g., a small dataset) to the general.

Work on inferencing began even earlier in physics and astronomy. For example, in the 16th century, astronomer Tycho Brahe collected detailed data on planetary positions. In 1621 Johannes Kepler analyzed that data, applied regression analysis to counteract errors, and wrote down the laws of planetary motion. The laws accurately predicted how the planets moved, but didn't explain why. That was left to Isaac Newton, who in 1687 showed that Kepler's Laws derived from the universal principle of gravitation.

In the early 1900s, statisticians such as R. A. Fisher developed methodologies for experiment design that made it easier to analyze experiments and quantify errors in fields such as sociology and psychology, where there is more uncertainty than in orbital mechanics (Fisher, 1935).

In a 2001 article, statistician Leo Breiman captured the (then) difference between the mindset of most statisticians and the emerging field of data science (Breiman, 2001). He argued that most statisticians belonged to a **data modeling culture** that assumes:

- There is a relatively simple, eternally true process in Nature (such as the orbits of planets due to the universal law of gravitation).
- Data reflects this underlying process plus some random noise.
- The statistician's job is to estimate a small number of parameter values leading to a parsimonious model with the best fit to the data (for example, assuming the model equation $F = Gm_1m_2/r^2$, estimating $G = 6.674 \times 10^{-11}$). The physicist, with the support of the statistician, can then examine the model to gain insight and make predictions.

Breiman contrasts this with the **algorithmic modeling culture**, which allows for complex and not as easily understood models (e.g., neural networks, deep learning, random forests), but which can make predictions for a broader range of processes. Making predictions in complex domains with many variables is the core of modern data science. While simple equations work exceedingly well in fields such as mechanics, they do not in fields like sociology and behavioral psychology – people are complicated. Breiman surmised that only about 2% of statisticians in 2001 had adopted algorithmic modeling, thus illustrating the need to broaden statistics and move towards what we now call data science.

Since the 2001 publication of Breiman's article, statisticians are now increasingly focusing on data science challenges, and the gap has diminished between algorithms and models. In part, this is because the scale of data has changed – 50 years ago a typical statistical problem had 100 to 1000 data points, each consisting of only a few attributes (e.g., gender, age, smoker/non-smoker, and sick/healthy). Today, these numbers can reach into the millions or billions (e.g., an image dataset with 10 million images, each with a million pixels).

In summary, statistics' and data science's objectives have become well aligned, and additional statistically inspired work will improve data science. Data science will undoubtedly pull both mathematical and applied statistics in new directions, some of which are discussed in the National Science Foundation (NSF) Report, *Statistics at a Crossroads* (He et al., 2019).

1.2.2 Visualization

Graphing has been relevant to statistics since at least the 1700s because it offers insight into data. William Playfair felt that charts communicated better than tables of numbers, and he published excellent time-series plots on economic activity in 1786 (Playfair, 1786). John Snow, the father of epidemiology, used map-based visuals to provide insight into the mid-1800s London cholera outbreaks (Boston University School of Public Health, 2016). Florence Nightingale, recognized as the founder of modern nursing, was also a visualization pioneer. In collaboration with William Farr, she used pie charts and graphs of many forms to show that poor sanitation, not battle wounds, caused more English soldiers to die in the Crimean War. Her work led to a broader adoption of improved sanitary practices (Andrews, 2019; Rehmeyer, 2008).

New approaches to showing information graphically have grown rapidly in the field of **information visualization**. Its goal is to "devise external aids that enhance cognitive abilities," according to Don Norman, one of the field's founders (Norman, 1993). Stu Card, Jock Mackinlay, and Ben Shneiderman compatibly define the field as "the use of computer-supported, interactive, visual representations of data to amplify cognition" (Card et al., 1999). These scientists all believed interacting with the right visualization greatly amplifies the power of the human mind. Even the simple graph in Figure 1.2 brings meaning to 204 data points (which include data from tens of millions of people) and clarifies the impact of vaccination on mortality.

Because of the enormous improvements in both computational capabilities and display technology, we now have continually updated, high-resolution, multidimensional graphs and an incredibly rich diversity of other visuals – perhaps even virtual reality (Bryson, 1996). Today, visualization flourishes, with contributions from multidisciplinary teams with strong artistic capabilities (Steele & Iliinsky, 2010; Tufte, 2001).

The resulting visuals can integrate the display of great amounts of data with data science's conclusions, allowing individuals to undertake what-if analyses. They can simultaneously see the sensitivity of conclusions to different inputs or models and gain insight from their explorations.[1] Visualizations targeted at very specific

[1] The Baby Name Voyager visualization (Wild Sky Media, n.d.) (see www.datascienceincontext.com/babyname) of the yearly popularity of US baby names convinced co-author Alfred that even a simple time-series plot, instantly displayed in response to user input, is very much more useful than the underlying tabular data.

problems in the many application domains addressed by data science can bring data science to non-data science professionals and even the lay public.

The public media regularly use interactive visualizations to reinforce and clarify their stories, for example, the vast number of COVID-19 charts and graphs presented during the pandemic. Computer scientists apply visualization in an almost recursive way to illustrate complex data-science-related phenomena such as the workings of neural networks. If successful, these visualizations will first improve data science and then visualization itself.

In addition to focusing on visuals, the field of visualization must also catalyze ever-improving tools for creating them. Some platforms are for non-programming users of data science in disciplines such as financial analysis and epidemiology. Other platforms are for programmers with sophisticated data science skills. In both cases, we can use data science to guide users in interactive explorations: suggesting data elements to join and trends to plot, and automatically executing predictive models.

A word of warning: Visuals are powerful, and so amplify the perception of validity of what they show. A timeline showing an occurrence frequency trending in one direction appears conclusive, even if the graph's points were inconsistently or erroneously measured. Pictures may evoke a notion of causality where there is none. Visualization's power is such that great care must be taken to generate insight, not spurious conclusions. For more on this, see Section 11.4 on "Communicating data science results."

We wanted to conclude this section by showing some compelling visualizations, but the best ones almost invariably use color and interactivity, both of which are infeasible in this black-and-white volume. Instead, we refer the reader to the visualizations on sites such as *Our World in Data* (Global Change Data Lab, n.d.) and *FlowingData* (Yau, n.d.).

1.2.3 Operations Research

While statistics is about making inferences from data, the field of operations research focuses on understanding systems and then creating and optimizing models that will lead to better, perhaps optimal, actions in the world. Applications are optimizing the operations of systems such as computer and transportation networks, facilities planning, resource allocation, commerce, and war fighting. This emphasis on optimization leading to action, as well as its problem-solving methodology, strongly ties operations research to data science.

Operations research was named by UK military researchers Albert Rowe and Robert Watson-Watt, who in 1937 and the lead-up to World War II were optimizing radar installations. Soon after, the principles and methods of the field were applied to business and social services problems.

In the 1800s, long before the field was named, Charles Babbage[2] advocated for scientific analysis to optimize public services such as rail transportation and postal delivery (Sodhi, 2007). Research by Babbage and by Rowland Hill led to the invention of postage stamps. With continuing growth in the scale of centrally managed societal systems and improvements in applied mathematics, operations research grew greatly in the 20th century. In part, this was due to its applicability to complex, large-scale warfare.

Operations research applies many models and mathematical techniques to a wide variety of application domains. For example:

- The **traveling salesperson problem (TSP)** tries to find the shortest route that lets a salesperson pass through each city that needs to be visited exactly once and then to return home (Cook, 2012). Operations researchers model TSP with a network (or graph) where cities are nodes and labeled edges represent the paths and distances between cities. Solutions need to consider that there are an exponentially large number of possible routes. Various techniques have been applied: *Dynamic programming* is elegant, provides an optimal solution, but only works well when there are a small number of nodes (Held & Karp, 1962). Hybrid techniques, which typically combine *linear programming* and heuristics, work better for larger networks, though they may only provide the approximate answers that many applications need (Concorde, n.d.).
- A **resource allocation problem** tries to achieve a project's goal at minimum cost by optimizing resource use. Consider a baker with a fixed supply of ingredients, a set of recipes that specify how much of each ingredient is needed to produce a certain baked good, and known prices for ingredients and finished products. What should the baker bake to maximize profit? Linear programming is often used for resource allocation problems like this.
- The **newsvendor problem** is similar to the resource allocation problem, but with the added constraint that newspapers are published once or twice a day and lose all value as soon as the next edition comes out (Petruzzi & Dada, 1999). The newsvendor needs to stock its papers by estimating the "best" amount, sometimes guessing from daily demand. "Best" here depends on the sales price, the unit cost paid by the seller, and the unknown customer demand. Estimating demand from data is tricky due to seasonal effects, the actual news of the day, and the simple fact that we never know true demand when supplies sell out. Could we have sold another 10, 20, or perhaps zero?
- An additional complexity is the more copies a paper sells, the more it can charge for advertising, so insufficient inventory also reduces advertising revenue. Thus,

[2] Babbage is most well known for having first conceived of the stored program computer, although he failed to build a working model.

if the optimization were to be done by the newspaper, there is a primary metric (direct profit on paper sales) as well as a secondary metric (total circulation). We will see examples of similar optimization trade-offs in the examples of Part II.

Operations research has a theoretical side, with a stable of mathematical modeling and optimization techniques, but it has always focused on practical applications. Its methodology begins with creating a model of how a system works, and often defining an objective function to define the goals. It continues with capturing the relevant data to calibrate the model, and results in algorithms that generate the best possible results. The field focuses on the rigorous analysis of results with respect to a particular model, and has expertise in simulation that is often used to calibrate or test optimization algorithms.

Traditionally, operations research operated in a **batch mode**, where there was a one-time data collection process, after which models were built, calibrated, analyzed, and optimized. The resultant improvement blueprint was then put into practice.

Today, we can continually collect data from a real-time system, feed it into a model, and use the model's outputs to continually optimize a system. This system could be a transportation network, pricing within a supermarket, or a political campaign. This **online mode** scenario (or **continual optimization**) became feasible when computer networks and the Web made real-time information broadly available (Spector, 2002).

Operations research techniques can be of great use to data scientists. As data science applications grow in complexity and importance, it becomes important to rigorously demonstrate the quality of their results. Furthermore, simulations may be able to generate additional valuable data.

In summary, operations research approaches are already infused in data science. Its objectives, models, algorithms, and focus on rigor are crucial to one of data science's most important goals: optimization. In return, data science's techniques and problems are driving new research areas in operations research, including reinforcement learning and decision operations.

1.2.4 Computing

The breadth of the field of computing has contributed deeply to data science. In particular, these five computing subfields have had major impact:

- **Theoretical computer science** provides the fundamental idea of an **algorithm** – a clearly specified procedure that a computer can carry out to perform a certain task – and lets us prove properties of algorithms.
- **Software engineering** makes reliable software systems that let an analyst be effective without having to build everything from scratch.

- **Computer engineering** supplies the raw computing power, data storage, and high-speed communications networks needed to collect, transmit, and process datasets with billions or trillions of data points.
- **Machine learning (ML)** makes it possible to automatically construct a program that learns from data and generalizes to new data. Its **deep learning** subfield allows these learned programs to transform input data into intermediate representations through multiple (deep) levels, instead of mapping directly from input to output.
- **Artificial intelligence (AI)** creates programs that take appropriate actions to achieve tasks that are normally thought of as requiring human intelligence. Robot actions are physical; other AI programs take digital actions. Most current AI programs use machine learning, but it is also possible for programmers to create AI programs using not what the program learns, but what the programmers have learned.

We are frequently asked to compare the fields of artificial intelligence and data science. One clear difference is that data science focuses on gaining value in the form of **insights** and **conclusions**, whereas AI focuses on building systems that take appropriate, seemingly intelligent actions in the world. With less focus on gaining insight, AI doesn't put as much emphasis on interacting with data or exploring hypotheses. Consequently, it pays less attention to statistics, and more attention to creating and running computer programs. Another key difference is that data science, by definition, focuses on data and all the issues around it, such as privacy and security and fairness. The kind of AI that focuses on data also deals with these issues, but not all AI focuses on data.

However, a clear comparison of AI and data science is complex because AI has come to have different meanings to different people: As one example, AI is often used synonymously with machine learning. While we do not agree that those terms should be equated, data science clearly has a broader focus than just machine learning. As another example, AI is sometimes used to connote techniques aimed at duplicating human intelligence, as in John McCarthy's 1956 introductory definition at a Dartmouth Workshop: "Machines that can perform tasks that are characteristic of human intelligence." While we again do not agree with the narrowness of this definition, data science has broader goals.

A major reason that computing has had such an impact on data science is that **empirical computing** augmented computing's traditional focus on analytical and engineering techniques:

- Computer scientists and programmers initially put their efforts into developing algorithms that produced provably correct results and engineering the systems to make them feasible. For example, they took a clear set of the rules for keeping a ledger of deposits and withdrawals, and they deduced the algorithms for computing a bank account's balance. There is a definitive answer that, barring a bug, can be computed every time.

- Empirical computing derives knowledge from data, just as natural sciences do. Science is built on results derived from observation, experimentation, data collection, and analysis. The empirical computing approach is inductive rather than deductive, and its conclusions are contingent, not definitive – new data could change them. Kissinger et al. frame a related discussion on AI (which, as practiced today, is empirical) and notes it is "judged by the utility of its results, not the process used to reach those results" (Kissinger et al., 2021). Below are example areas where the application of empirical methods led to advances.

Information retrieval is the study and practice of organizing, retrieving, and distributing textual information. It blossomed in the 1970s, as text was increasingly stored in digital form. Gerard Salton developed data-driven approaches for promoting information based on usage pattern feedback (Salton, 1971). For example, his system learned when a user searches a medical library for [hip bone], that [inguinal] and [ilium] are relevant terms. It also learned which results most users preferred, and promoted those to other users. These techniques played a large role in the development of today's web search engines.

A/B experimentation became pervasive in computing with the rise of the World Wide Web (Kohavi et al., 2020). Suppose a company detects that a page on their website confuses their customers. They perform an experiment by creating a version of the page with a different wording or layout and show it to, say, 1% of their users. If the experiment shows that the modified version B page performs better than the original version A page, they can replace the original page with version B. Then they can make another experiment starting from a new version B, and so on. Thus, whether done automatically or under human control, the website can continually improve. Notably, improvements lead to more usage, more usage generates more data, and more data allows for more site improvements. We will return in Chapter 14 to the benefits and risks of this classic virtuous cycle.

Problems with inherent uncertainty, such as speech recognition, machine translation, image recognition, and automated navigation, saw markedly improved performance as more empirical data was applied. Every day, billions of people use these improved applications, which are regularly enhanced via the analysis of data. Even systems programming – the software that controls operating systems, storage, and networks – has benefited from machine learning algorithms that learn patterns of usage and optimize performance.

The very usability of systems has been revolutionized by advances in **human computer interaction (HCI)**, which leverages experimental techniques to ascertain what user interfaces are both useful and natural. HCI's hard-won gains revolutionized computer use, moving computers from a specialized tool for experts to nearly universal adoption. We discuss many examples of the applicability of data science in Chapter 4 and Chapter 5.

Advances in computing hardware made the big data era possible. Transistor density has doubled every two years or so, as predicted by Gordon Moore in his eponymous Moore's Law (Moore, 1965). The first commercially produced microprocessor, the Intel 4004 from 1971, had 2000 transistors and a clock rate of 0.7 MHz. Modern microprocessors have 10 million times more transistors and a clock speed that is 10,000 times faster. Overall, computers in 2021 are about a trillion times better in performance per dollar than 1960 computers.[3]

Improvements in all computation-related aspects made systems cost *less* yet be *more* usable for *more* applications by *more* people. Increases in performance let more sophisticated algorithms run. More storage lets us store the Web's vast amount of data (particularly image and video), create powerful neural networks, and implement other knowledge representation structures. When the first neural networking experiments were done, they were limited by the amount of data and computational power. By the 1990s, those limitations began to disappear; web-scale data and Moore's Law facilitated machine learning.

This steady stream of research results and demonstrable implementation successes have propelled computing beyond its roots in theory and engineering to empirical methods. The pace of discovery picked up as Moore's Law provided computational, communication, and storage capacity; the Web provided vast data; and accelerated research in high-performance algorithms and machine learning yielded impressive results. Engineers have adapted to this change in computational style with new, fit-for-purpose processor and storage technologies. Key events in computing, illustrated by the timeline in Table 1.2, helped pave the way to data science.

Lest there be any remaining question on the importance of empirical computing, college student demand for data science courses and programs is on the rise worldwide. Berkeley's introductory data science course (Data 8) enrolled fewer than 100 students in the fall of 2014 when the course was first introduced. In spring 2019, enrollment had grown to over 1,600 students. At the same time, computer science students are increasingly specializing in machine learning, a core data science component. From co-author Alfred's experience leading intern programs at IBM, Google, and investment firm Two Sigma, machine learning internships started becoming popular in 2001 and have become the most asked for

[3] Consider that, if cancer treatment had kept pace with computation, the Earth would see much less than one cancer death per year. A trillion-fold difference is larger than the ratio of the combined weight of all the people in the US to a single pencil.

Table 1.2 *Key events in computing's contribution to data science*[*].

Year	Description	Person or entity	Paper or event
1950	The value of learning by a founder of the field of computing	Alan Turing	Computing machinery and intelligence (Turing, 1950)
1955	Successful application of learning to checkers	Arthur Samuels	Some studies in machine learning using the game of checkers (Samuel, 1959)
1965	The computational fuel: Moore's Law	Gordon Moore	Cramming more components onto integrated circuits (Moore, 1965)
1971	Early use of data in search	Jerry Salton	Relevance feedback and the optimization of retrieval effectiveness (Salton, 1971)
1982	Growth of use of data in computer–human interaction (CHI)	ACM: Bill Curtis, Ben Shneiderman	Initiation of ACM CHI Conference (ACM CIGCHI, n.d.; Nichols & Schneider, 1982)
1986	Reignition of neural network machine learning	David Rumelhart, Geoffrey Hinton	Learning representations by back-propagating errors (Rumelhart et al., 1986)
Early 1990s	Birth of the World Wide Web	Tim Berners-Lee et al.	Information management: a proposal (Berners-Lee, 1990)
1996	Powerful new data-driven technique for search	Sergey Brin and Larry Page	The anatomy of a large-scale hypertextual web search engine (Brin & Page, 1998)
Mid-1990s	Emergence of social networks	Various	Geocities, SixDegrees, Classmates, . . .
1998	Emergence of data in search advertising	GoTo/Overture	GoTo, renamed Overture and later acquired by Yahoo, launched internet search advertising
2007	Cloud computing: powering data science	Amazon	Announcing Amazon Elastic Compute Cloud – beta (Amazon Web Services, 2006)
2010	Growth in GPU usage for neural network processing	Various	Large-scale deep unsupervised learning using graphics processors (Raina et al., 2009)
2011	Demonstration of power of data on a gameshow	IBM	Jeopardy victory (Markoff, 2011)
2012	Practical demonstration of neural networks in image recognition	Alex Krizhevsky, Ilya Sutskever, Geoffrey E. Hinton	ImageNet classification with deep convolutional neural networks (Krizhevsky et al., 2012)
2012	Deployment of neural networks in speech recognition	Geoffrey Hinton et al.	Deep neural networks for acoustic modeling in speech recognition: the shared views of four research groups (Hinton et al., 2012)
2018	Demonstration of reinforcement learning in games	DeepMind: David Silver et al.	A general reinforcement learning algorithm that masters chess, Shogi, and Go through self-play (Silver et al., 2018)
2019	Large-scale, deep generative models	Various	BERT (Devlin et al., 2019), GPT-3 (Brown et al., 2020), Turing-NLG (Rosset, 2020), and other models

* This timeline places the birth of key technical ideas, important use cases, and necessary technological enablements. Note that the publication dates in the right-hand column may differ from the year of impact in the left-hand column.

specialization. At the major machine learning conference, NeurIPS, attendance grew eight-fold from 2012 to 2019, when 13,000 attended.

1.2.5 Machine Learning

Machine learning, a subfield of computing, is the field with the most overlap with data science. It can be broken down into three main approaches:

- **Supervised learning** trains on a set of (input, output) pairs, and builds a model that can then predict the output for new inputs. For example, given a photo collection with each photo annotated with a subject class (e.g., "dog," "person," "tree"), a system can learn to classify new photos. This task is called a **classification**; the task of predicting an output from a continuous range of numbers is called **regression**.
- **Unsupervised learning** trains on data that has not been annotated with output classes. For example, given a photo collection, a model can learn to cluster dog pictures together in one class and people pictures in another, even if it does not know the labels "dog" and "person." Internally, the model may represent concepts for subparts such as "torso" and "head." Such a model may invent classes that humans would not normally use. The task of grouping items into classes (without labels for the classes) is called **clustering**.
- **Reinforcement learning** builds a model by observing a sequence of actions and their resulting states, with occasional feedback indicating whether the model has reached a positive or negative state. For example, a model learns to play checkers not by being told whether each move is correct or not, but just by receiving a reward ("you won!") or punishment ("you lost!") at the end of each training game.

Another way to categorize machine learning models is to consider whether the model is focused on learning the boundary between classes, or learning the classes themselves:

- A **discriminative model** answers the question: "Given the input x, what is the most likely output y?" Sometimes this is explicitly modeled as finding the output y that maximizes the probability $P(y \mid x)$, but some models answer the question without probabilities.
- A **generative model** answers the question: "What is the distribution of the input?" Or sometimes: "What is the joint distribution of input and output?" Sometimes this is an explicit model of $P(x)$ or $P(x, y)$, and sometimes the model can sample from the distribution without explicitly assigning probabilities.

For example, if the task is to label the language in a sentence as being either Danish or Swedish, a discriminative classifier model could do very well simply by recognizing that Swedish has the letters **ä**, **ö**, and **x**, while Danish uses **æ**, **ø**, and **ks**. With a few more tricks, the model could correctly classify most sentences, but it could not be said to know very much about either language. In contrast, a generative classifier model would learn much more about the two languages, enough to generate plausible sentences in either language. Some generative models can answer other questions, such as: "Is this sentence rare or common?" However, a discriminative model, being simpler, can be easier to train and is often more robust.

As another example, if we trained models on images of birds labeled with their species, a discriminative model could output the most probable species for a given image. A generative model could do that, and could also enumerate other similar birds; or, if parts of the bird were obscured in the image, could fill in the missing parts.

The most common methodology for machine learning follows these steps (Amershi et al., 2019):

1. Collect, assess, clean, and label some data.
2. Split the data into three sets.
3. Use the first set, the **training set**, to train a candidate model.
4. Use the second set, the **validation set** (also known as the **development set** or **dev set**) to evaluate how well the model performs. It is important that the dev set is not part of the training; otherwise, it would be like seeing the answers to the exam before taking it.
5. Repeat steps 3 and 4 with several candidate models, selecting different model classes and tweaking **hyperparameters**, the variables that control the learning process.
6. Evaluate the final model against the third set, the **test set**, to get an unbiased evaluation of the model.
7. Deploy the model to customers.
8. Continuously monitor the system to verify that it still works well.

We will cover many applications of machine learning in Part II; here we introduce three major areas of use:

- **Computer vision (CV)** processes images and videos and has applications in search, autonomous vehicles, robotics, photograph processing, and more. Most current CV models are deep convolutional neural networks trained on large, labeled image and video datasets in a supervised fashion.
- **Natural language processing (NLP)** parses, manipulates, and generates text. NLP is used for translation, spelling and grammar correction, speech recognition, email filtering, question answering, and other applications. Most current NLP

models are large transformer neural networks which are pre-trained on unlabeled text corpora using unsupervised learning. Then, they are fine-tuned on a smaller and narrower task, often with supervised learning. As of 2022, NLP models are in a state of rapid improvement and are nearing parity with humans on many small tasks. However, they suffer from inconsistency, an inability to know what they don't know, and tremendous computational complexity.
- **Robotics** makes intelligent decisions on the control of autonomous machines and has applications in agriculture, manufacturing, logistics, and transportation. The forefront of robotics research relies on reinforcement learning, in which robots are trained by a combination of simulated and real-world rewards.

Machine learning has proven useful to all of these areas, but there are challenges, such as adversarial attacks, potential bias, difficulty in generating explanations, and more. These are discussed in Part III.

It is clear that machine learning and statistics have a large overlap with data science in goals and methods. What are their differences?

- **Statistics** emphasizes **data modeling**. Designing a simple model that attempts to demonstrate a relationship in the data and leads to understanding. It traditionally focused on modest amounts of numerical data (though this has been changing), and it is increasingly tackling other types of data.
- **Machine learning** emphasizes **algorithmic modeling**. Inventing algorithms that handle a wide variety of data, and lead to high performance on a task. The models may be difficult to interpret.
- **Data science** focuses on **the data itself**. Encouraging the use of whatever techniques lead to a successful product (these techniques often include statistics and machine learning). Data science operates at the union of statistics, machine learning, and the data's subject matter (e.g., medical data, financial data, and astronomical data).

Machine learning also distinguishes itself from statistics by automatically creating models, without a human analyst's considered judgment. This is particularly true for **neural network** models. In these, the inputs are combined in ways that lead to predicting outputs with the smallest amount of error. The combinations are not constrained by an analyst's preconceptions.

The **deep learning** subfield uses several layers of neural networks, so that inputs form low-level representations, which then combine to form higher-level representations, and eventually produce outputs. The system is free to invent its own intermediate-level representations. For example, when trained on photos of people, a deep learning system invents the concepts of lines and edges at a lower level, then ears, mouths, and noses at a higher level, and then faces at a level above that.

1.2.6 Additional History

The erudite mathematician and statistician John Tukey set forth many of data science's foundational ideas in his 1962 paper "The future of data analysis" and 1977 book *Exploratory Data Analysis* (Tukey, 1962, 1977). Tukey made a strong case for understanding data and drawing useful conclusions, and for how this was different from what much of statistics was doing at the time. He was two-thirds of the way to data science, missing only the full scale of modern computing power.

In 2017, Stanford Professor of Statistics David Donoho, in a follow-on piece to the aforementioned "The future of data analysis," made the case that the then-recent changes in computation and data availability meant statisticians should extend their focus (Donoho, 2017). His sketch of a "greater data science curriculum" has many places where statistics plays a large role, but others where computing and other techniques are dominant. These thoughts were echoed by others in a Royal Statistical Society Panel of 2015 (Royal Statistical Society, 2015). More recently, data science curricula such as Berkeley's effectively integrate these key topics (Adhikari et al., 2021; Spector, 2021).

Tukey used the term **data analysis** in 1962 (Tukey, 1962). The term **data science** became popular around 2010,[4] after an early use of the term by the statistician William Cleveland in 2001, the launches of *Data Science Journal* in 2002 and *The Journal of Data Science* in 2003, and a US National Science Board Report in 2005[5] (National Science Board, 2005). The term **big data** dates back to the late 1990s (Halevy et al., 2009; Lohr, 2013), perhaps first in a 1997 paper by Michael Cox and David Ellsworth of the NASA Ames Research Center (Cox & Ellsworth, 1997).

Related terms go back much further. **Automatic data** was used for punch-card processing in the 1890 US census (using mechanical sorting machines, not electronic computers). **Data processing** entered common parlance in the 1950s as digital computers made data accumulation, storage, and processing far more accessible.

While we associated A/B testing with the rise of the World Wide Web, its use is far older. In 1923, Claude C. Hopkins, who with Albert Lasker founded the modern advertising industry, wrote "Almost any question can be answered quickly and finally by a test campaign."

In 1950, Alan Turing laid out many key ideas of artificial intelligence and machine learning in the article "Computing machinery and intelligence" (Turing,

[4] The Google Books Ngram Viewer (Google Books, 2010), which samples the frequency of terms (or Ngrams) in the corpus of published books, shows a noticeable uptick circa 2010. See this: www.datascienceincontext.com /ngram-ds.

[5] Peter Naur used the term *data science* in his 1974 book *Concise Survey of Computer Methods* (Naur, 1974), but he was referring to issues of data representation. Later in his text, in a chapter entitled "Large data systems in human society," he referred to emerging political and ethical challenges.

1950). However, the terms themselves arrived a bit later: **artificial intelligence** was coined in 1956 for a workshop at Dartmouth College (Dartmouth, 2018) and **machine learning** was popularized in 1959 by IBM Researcher Arthur Samuel in an article describing a program which learned checkers by playing games against itself (Samuel, 1959). **Neural networks** were first explored in the 1940s and 1950s by Hebb (see Morris, 1999), McCulloch and Pitts (see McCulloch & Pitts, 1943), and Rosenblatt (see Rosenblatt, 1958). **Deep learning** (in its current form, for neural networks) was coined in 2006 (Hinton et al., 2006).

Chapter 2

Data Science Is Transdisciplinary

Data science's primary progenitors are statistics, operations research, and computing, but the sciences, humanities, and social sciences are also all part of its story for these reasons:

1. **New application areas.** Data science adds valuable techniques to a large and growing number of application domains, building on their unique data and preexisting capabilities. The combined capabilities of data science and domain-specific know-how can solve important scientific and social problems and have commercial value.
2. **Advancing data science.** Some domains possess advanced methods for dealing with their data. Data science benefits by incorporating these methods and then making them available for wider use. For example, the petabyte-scale datasets generated by experiments in physics, astronomy, and biology led to inventing new data science techniques.
3. **Building coalitions.** Data science operates in a societal context. Making sure we "get it right" requires partnerships which must include viewpoints from non-STEM (science, technology, engineering, and mathematics) domains such as sociology, law, economics, philosophy, and political policy. Good solutions can have great societal benefit, while poor ones can cause harm.

This chapter's title includes the term *transdisciplinary* to emphasize that data science has been able to achieve its theoretical, methodological, and practical results by combining the approaches of different disciplines to create a new field.[6] This combination is needed not only for data science's core disciplines, but also for its application areas and the fields that influence its proper use.

[6] *Multidisciplinary* is when different fields separately contribute their approaches to a problem. *Interdisciplinary* is when the approaches interact. *Transdisciplinary* is when a new field emerges from that interaction.

2.1 New Application Areas

We use two approaches to illustrate data science's broad applicability. First, we discuss data science's relevance to each economic sector. Second, we consider its relevance to academic research areas.

For the first approach, we divide the entire economy into major buckets, using the US Bureau of Economic Analysis's GDP Report as a guide (US Bureau of Economic Analysis, n.d.). Despite the data's US-centricity, the categories of economic activity are probably representative of most economies, and an analysis shows existing and growing data science roles in each one. Table 2.1 lists the categories and a few example data science applications for each.

While this book provides detailed examples from many of the areas, we have inevitably omitted some. Among others, we do not devote much attention to data science's many uses in national defense-related topics such as logistics, guidance and targeting, decision support, maintenance, or cybersecurity. We also don't discuss uses in precision agriculture, factory automation, building management, optimizing social service delivery, and so on.

For the second approach (relevance to academic research areas), we consider the role of data science in the various university education and research disciplines. Below, we discuss science, social science, engineering, and the humanities.

2.1.1 Sciences

The sciences have been a major source of data science use cases. As data becomes easier to use, scientific models have become more complex and highly tuned to real-world inputs. In some cases, data science has automated the process of creating models.

As an example, efforts to combat the COVID-19 pandemic show data science's increasing role in biomedical and social applications. Vaccine development and deployment could not have happened as quickly without pre-existing infrastructure, tools, and data ready to be used in a new situation:

- Genetic and protein structure databases and other tools for simulating structure facilitated the rapid decoding and promulgation of the underlying SARS-CoV-2 genetic structure.
- Tools were in place to manipulate this genetic data.
- Large-scale data management technologies were used to rapidly create, locate, manage, and monitor well-structured clinical trials.
- Logistics data and algorithms helped plan and control the complex supply chain for vaccinating large populations.

Table 2.1 *Components of the economy and data science applicability**.

Sector of US economy	Areas of data science applicability
Agriculture, forestry, and fishing	Precision cultivation and harvesting, fishery management, quality control, risk reduction
Mining	Predicting resource location, risk management, pricing
Utilities	Fault detection, optimized energy sources, production automation, predictive maintenance
Construction	Scheduling, logistics, optimized design and materials use
Manufacturing – durable goods	Quality control, production scheduling, automated design and manufacturing, customer support
Manufacturing – non-durable goods	Risk management, logistics, demand prediction, pricing
Wholesale trade	Inventory management, demand forecasting, logistics
Retail trade	Merchandising, advertising, pricing, upsell, loyalty programs, inventory management
Transportation and warehousing	Optimized routing, storage, pricing, tracing, safety monitoring, semi- and fully automated vehicles, yield management
Information	Advertising, audience engagement, content moderation, translation services
Finance and insurance	Risk assessment, portfolio construction, security, regulatory monitoring
Real estate, rental, and leasing	Construction, maintenance, property management, service automation
Professional, scientific, and technical services	Mapping and surveying automation, new software development tools, data-driven marketing, data-driven science
Management of companies and enterprises	Decision support of all forms, improved communications
Other administrative services	Employee hiring and scheduling, automated transcription, security monitoring, credit scoring
Education, health, and social assistance	Personalized education, remote health monitoring, disease diagnosis, social service delivery, fraud detection
Arts, entertainment, recreation, and food services	Personalization, pricing, upsell opportunities, automation, immersive experiences
Other highly diverse services	Fault diagnosis, dating services, locating civic needs, fund-raising
US national government – defense	Logistics, guidance and targeting, decision support, maintenance, readiness, cybersecurity, wargaming
US national government – non-defense	Tax audit, civic outreach, societal and economic monitoring
US state and local government	Maintenance operations, educational programs, criminal justice system, monitoring service fairness

* The first column divides the breadth of economic output into buckets. These come from the Bureau of Economic Research, which sources them from the North American Industry Classification System (NAICS) (US Census Bureau, n.d.). The second column is an eclectic list of data-science-enabled applications, either existing or soon to be likely.

On the other hand, our COVID-19 experience showed some data science weaknesses: in particular, limitations in our ability to draw conclusions from public health monitoring and prediction. We give examples of these and other weaknesses throughout this book.

Aspirationally, Turing Award winner Jim Gray proposed a new model for scientific research, which he termed *the Fourth Paradigm*, in a talk at a 2007 National Academies meeting. In it, he talked about how science can increasingly benefit from new tools and techniques for data capture, analysis, and communication/publication. Gray was first and foremost a computer scientist specializing in databases, but he became involved in projects at the borders of astrophysics, mapping, and computer science. This led to his advising scientists in many disciplines on their growing data-related problems. As captured and edited by colleagues at Microsoft Research (see Gray, 2009), Gray said:

> The new model is for the data to be captured by instruments or generated by simulations before being processed by software and for the resulting information or knowledge to be stored in computers. Scientists only get to look at their data fairly late in this pipeline. The techniques and technologies for such data-intensive science are so different that it is worth distinguishing data-intensive science from computational science.

Science is increasingly moving in this direction, particularly with the rapid growth in machine learning capabilities. As an example, scientists trained a neural network on thousands of molecules with known antibacterial properties. They then applied that network to a dataset of over 6,000 compounds with potential antibiotic activity. This approach quickly uncovered a potential new drug, Halicin, for treating certain antibiotic-resistant bacteria (Stokes et al., 2020). While this data-centric approach is capable of screening far more than 6,000 compounds, and preliminary laboratory studies showed positive results, this particular drug may well encounter roadblocks on the path to approval (Rees, 2020).

2.1.2 Social Sciences

Much of the social sciences involves gathering and analyzing data. In economics, this was traditionally confined to the subfield of econometrics, which Samuelson explained as enabling one to "apply the tools of statistics ... to sift through mountains of data to extract simple relationships" (Samuelson & Nordhaus, 2009). However, today, data science more broadly impacts all of economics. The related area of finance has been at the forefront of using large datasets and sophisticated predictive models in diverse applications. We present specific examples from economics and finance in Section 6.5.

In broader society, governments have always needed information about their populations. For example, at the most basic level, they need to count their people and collect taxes. They collect a great deal of other information as well; for instance, labor statistics, transportation statistics, and health data. From the other side, voters are interested in the results of pre-election polls. Polling agencies and social media platforms also collect a great deal of political and sociological data. More and more, information gathering underlies societal systems. We discuss some examples of political and governmental data science in Section 6.6.

In the future, perhaps all economic transactions will be digital, and physical currency will no longer be used. (China's early 2020s experimentation with a national digital currency may foreshadow this.) Economists may be able to measure and track all financial flows, and offer new mechanisms for economic governance. In a very ambitious proposal, data scientists and economists hypothesize that data science results could dynamically set tax policies to more efficiently balance revenue and equity objectives, as discussed in Section 6.5 (Zheng et al., 2020). A related, much simpler, present-day example is congestion pricing, in which highway tolls vary to reduce congestion and motivate use when there is extra capacity.

2.1.3 Engineering

Engineering disciplines abound with data science use cases, in both the design of new products and services, and the efficient operation of complex systems. For the former, data science and machine learning are the basis of GitHub Copilot, which assists programmers (Chen et al., 2021). Google researchers have developed a system that learns to do the physical layout of devices on computer chips (Mirhoseini et al., 2021). Civil engineers are likewise researching similar approaches to design far larger structures made of steel rather than silicon. Many engineering challenges, such as speech recognition, as discussed in Section 4.2 and Section 5.2, were practically unsolvable until we applied data-driven approaches to them.

In the domain of engineering operations, data, often directly provided by embedded instrumentation, can predict maintenance needs, provide early warnings of failures, and optimize system operations for applications, including cars, power grids, rails, naval propulsion systems, jet engines, and many more. Neural networks can classify work orders and optimize environmental and power systems. Continual anomaly detection is at the heart of many computer security systems, whether they are looking for operational failures or intrusions.

2.1.4 Humanities

In the humanities, applications have been slower to come into common use. The earliest days of computers did see occasional projects to connect digitized data with literature, art, and history. These early, one-of-a-kind, efforts all focused on single works. As large web-based archives of books and images were built, interest grew substantially in applying data science tools and techniques. Circa 2010, academicians began to recognize the opportunities (Kirschenbaum, 2012), and the US National Endowment for the Humanities launched its Digital Humanities Initiative. In 2009, the National Science Foundation (where co-author Jeannette was working at the time), in partnership with the US National Endowment for the Humanities, the Joint Information Systems Committee of the UK, and the Social Sciences Research Council of Canada, launched a "Digging into Data" challenge. It asked the question: "What could you do with a million books?"[7] It continues to this day, with 17 additional international partners.

Leveraging the millions of Google-scanned books, Google Research gave out awards in the digital humanities (Orwant, 2010), initially focusing on text analysis. J.-B. Michel et al. (including co-author Peter) used the Ngram viewer's frequency count of words or phrases in millions of books to gather insight on many societal or linguistic changes, ranging from the impact of censorship on books published to the rate at which irregularly conjugated English verbs change to become regularly conjugated (Michel et al., 2011).

Matt Connelly, circa 2015, created the History Lab Project at Columbia, which maintains the world's largest collection of declassified documents and lets researchers analyze them using data science techniques (Connelly et al., 2021). Legal scholars are analyzing the tens of millions of online court judgments released by China since 2014, to better understand the Chinese legal system and its rulings and consequences (Liebman et al., 2020). Many projects now geocode large numbers of records, placing people, historical events, or statistical measures on a map to provide insight or bring history to life. The Smithsonian Collections Search Center is an online catalog with 17.2 million records: "records relating to areas for Art & Design, History & Culture, and Science & Technology with over 6.6 million images, videos, audio files, podcasts, blog posts and electronic journals" (Smithsonian Institution, n.d.).

We could discuss many more applications in virtually every domain. We conclude this section by observing that data science's applications are broad and growing, while requiring the fusion of data science and discipline-specific capabilities to achieve their goals.

[7] A million books may not sound like a lot, but reading a book a day from birth to age 100 (give or take a day for leap years) amounts to only 36,525 books.

2.2 Advancing Data Science

As other fields address their data-related problems, they often end up making their own important contributions to data science. Necessity being the mother of invention, if a new problem requires a new capability, the field may be rapidly advanced.

A great example of a new capability coming out of physics is the World Wide Web. Sir Tim Berners-Lee created what became the World Wide Web to help the greater CERN supercollider research community communicate and collaborate. It turned out this was such a good idea that it rapidly caught on elsewhere and became a fundamental pillar of both data science and our everyday lives. As another example, many important technologies for efficient pattern matching came from computational biologists' need to match nucleic acid sequences. Finally, social scientists' need for census data is forcing consideration about making aggregations of data broadly and accurately available while still preserving privacy. We have a new understanding of privacy-preserving data aggregation – regrettably, one showing its difficulty.

Soon after the World Wide Web became available to the general public, online advertising became a big business. Advertising fees paid for the growth of many well-known internet services and also brought huge attention and money to data science. Deciding what ad to show to a viewer is a data science problem: there is data on what the current user is searching for and the pages they have been browsing, and there is data on what similar users have done in the past. Economists contributed by introducing data scientists to algorithmic game theory. Among other things, this helps determine what auction style is best for selling ad space, balancing interests of consumers, sellers, and web publishers.

2.3 Building Coalitions

Data scientists need to partner with many other disciplines to ensure their resulting work will be maximally beneficial, societally acceptable, or perhaps even legal. Here are six examples:

- **Philosophers** can help frame ethical considerations about data science work, including issues of privacy, free will, and fairness. These will be considered throughout this book, starting in the next section, as we lay out an ethical framework.
- **Lawyers, politicians**, and **political scientists** can help with the legal and policy issues relating to data stewardship and the governance of data-intensive applications. Public opinion can be strongly influenced by information publishing and recommendation systems.

- **Designers** and **psychologists** can help data scientists present aesthetically pleasing and accessible results that users find easy to understand and use.
- **Economists** (in microeconomics, behavioral economics, and more) bring economic modes of analysis to data science problems that can help achieve efficiency or fairness.
- **Sociologists** provide insights for new ways to study human behavior and social relationships using data from large digitally connected social networks.
- **Journalists** can aid data science's goal of explanation so it emphasizes truthfulness and is valuable to users and society. Computing a number or displaying a bar graph is not enough; the results need to tell a coherent and truthful story.

Chapter 3
A Framework for Ethical Considerations

Data-empowered algorithms are reshaping our professional, personal, and political realities, and they are likely to have an even larger effect going forward. However, as with all developing technologies, increases in impact inevitably give rise to unanticipated consequences. These challenge our norms for how we use technology in ways consistent with our values. Many scholars, educators, and technology companies refer to these as **ethical challenges**, building on the applied ethics tradition from basic sciences.

Some challenges are best met by inventing improved or more nuanced technological approaches. However, many challenges will still arise based on how we deploy technology as products, or how statistical analysis interpretations guide law and policy.

While the word *ethics* may imply a branch of somewhat obscure philosophy, the applied ethical tradition is about both defining ethics and designing ethical processes clearly enough to help guide good choices. In the case of data science, it is also to develop programs that make good choices.

3.1 Professional Ethics

Companies and professional societies, including the American Statistical Association (ASA), the Institute for Operations Research and the Management Sciences (INFORMS), the IEEE, the Association for Computing Machinery (ACM), and Engineers Canada have long had important and useful ethical codes addressing matters of personal conduct and technical execution (American Statistical Association, n.d.; Association for Computing Machinery, 2018; Engineers Yukon, n.d.; Institute for Operations Research and the Management Sciences, n.d.). These include principles such as honesty, impartiality, and integrity.

The introduction to the ASA's code (American Statistical Association, n.d.) observes that:

> The discipline of statistics links the capacity to observe with the ability to gather evidence and make decisions, providing a foundation for building a more informed society. Because

society depends on informed judgments supported by statistical methods, all practitioners of statistics – regardless of training and occupation or job title – have an obligation to work in a professional, competent, respectful, and ethical manner.

As the impact of statistics, operations research, and computing (and analogously, data science) has grown, many of these codes are being generalized to include broader societal considerations. Gotterbarn and Wolf write in a preamble to the 2018 ACM Code of Ethics that: "we find ourselves in situations where our work can affect the lives and livelihoods of people in ways that may not be intended, or even be predictable. This brings a host of complex ethical considerations into play" (Gotterbarn et al., 2018).

3.2 The Belmont Commission

In the human subjects research community, the *Belmont Report* is the central document of applied ethics in biomedical and behavioral research. In it, ethics is defined in terms of general principles (National Commission for the Protection of Human Subjects of Biomedical and Behavioral Research, 1978). The Belmont Commission met monthly for four years in response to the 1932–72 US Public Health Service Syphilis Study at Tuskegee, a morally and scientifically flawed medical experiment. By including commissioners from a wide range of fields, including researchers, lawyers, administrators, and philosophers, the organizers hoped to protect human subjects while balancing societal norms, legal constraints, and society's need for innovation.

Despite its roots in the human subjects research context, the report outlines principles that are sufficiently general to be a basis for a useful ethical framework for data science research and products. In Belmont, these principles are called "respect for persons, beneficence, and justice." In more detail, they were then framed as follows:

- **Respect for persons.** This means ensuring the freedom of individuals to act autonomously based on their own considered deliberation and judgments. Often summarized as informed consent, this principle also includes having sufficient transparency to make judgments and also defending the autonomy of those with diminished consent, e.g., children or those who may be coerced into making a decision.
- **Beneficence.** Belmont encourages researchers *not* to limit their thinking to "do no harm," but to maximize benefits and balance them against risks. Doing so requires careful consideration of the immediate risks and benefits as well as a commitment to monitor and mitigate harms as results occur.
- **Justice.** The consideration of how risks and benefits are distributed, including the notion of a fair distribution. Fair may not mean "equal" but rather that the risks

are borne by the populations who stand to benefit (and are not borne by populations who will not ultimately have access to the fruits of the research).

These principles are intended to be broad and therefore applicable to yet unenvisioned technology changes and their consequences. At the same time, they are intended to be sufficiently specific that communities can come to a shared, deliberative consensus as to their implied best actions. In other words, from general, common principles, a community derives more context-specific standards and instance-specific rules. For a technologist, these rules imply even more specific design choices in modeling or in data product development.

This principled approach to ethics does not offer a single all-encompassing checklist that one consults for an answer that is the same in all contexts. Instead, principles are, by design, in tension with each other. They provide a basis to ask specific questions, which often do not have a right or wrong answer, but illuminate the tension in a situation or between positions.

3.3 Belmont Application to Data Science

The breadth of data science's impact argues for applying Belmont-like principles to it. Numerous scholars (Fiesler et al., 2015), researchers, and technologists have suggested how these principles can guide applied ethics even in the context of data-empowered algorithms. They sometimes also argue for extending the principles to emphasize the impact on society at large (US Department of Homeland Security, 2012; Vitak et al., 2016). However, as Belmont frames them, the principles provide a common vocabulary for researchers, data scientists, product developers, and regulators with which to reach consensus.

As co-author Jeannette writes in her 2020 essay, *Ten Research Challenge Areas in Data Science* (Wing, 2020):

> The ethical principle of Respect for Persons suggests that people should always be informed when they are talking with a chatbot. The ethical principle of Beneficence requires a risk/benefit analysis on the decision a self-driving car makes on whom not to harm. The ethical principle of justice requires us to ensure the fairness of risk assessment tools in the court system and automated decision systems used in hiring.

Another voice in this area comes from the European Commission, the executive branch of the European Union. Their *Ethics Guidelines for Trustworthy AI* shows that the need for ethical frameworks in technological areas is recognized by world governments, as well as researchers and ethicists (European Commission High-Level Expert Group on AI, 2019).

We, of course, accept there are distinctions between data-science-oriented implications of Belmont and human subject research, in particular medical research. In medical research, the principles motivate standards such as **informed consent** (a process of disclosing risks and benefits to an individual before gaining approval) and **fair selection of subjects**.

However, the digital domain can have different standards that are also consistent with the Belmont Principles, often because algorithms initiate automated actions. Here are some example considerations:

- Informed consent is hard to achieve in our current digital environment. To use a digital product, users must click "I agree," most often without comprehending the long and complex terms of service authorizing software actions over an extended period. Barocas and Nissenbaum identify "complex data flows" such as in digital services as possessing what they term a **transparency paradox** (Barocas & Nissenbaum, 2014). They argue that information disclosure provided to users is so simple as to be incomplete or deceptive, or it is so complex as to be incomprehensible. Data scientists adhere best to informed consent by respecting user norms at a level of transparency that avoids deception or unfairness, while allowing more detailed auditing and critique (e.g., via appropriate technical documentation or open source).
- For software, the risk/benefit balance of beneficence includes thinking through unintended consequences. It also requires the humility to recognize how hard it is to anticipate all the ways people will experience or use a product. That requires a commitment to monitor and mitigate harms as they are revealed.
- Justice, in the context of data-driven products, includes ongoing assessment of their fairness (technical and otherwise) as well as their training datasets. Justice includes fairness, with the understanding that defining "fair," even in technical communities, can be subjective (Narayanan, 2018) and is not as simple as giving it the same meaning as "equal." Our norms of justice also include an understanding of addressing and redressing prior harms, where possible. We say much more on fairness in Section 12.3.

We use the Belmont Principles to organize the analysis of several case studies in Part II. We then address the challenges to aligning ethics with a university's or technology company's data scientists' operational process in Part III. Part IV contains recommendations on how to proceed in the future.

While the Belmont Principles are our ethical starting point, we recognize that applications of data science may also require the consideration of other ethical principles upon which societies are based. For example, the principles of justice of war (jus ad bellum) and the conduct of war (jus in bello) are relevant to data science applications in military domains (Moseley, n.d.). Furthermore, data science is a sufficiently new field that we may eventually need to identify new relevant principles for its ethics.

Recap of Part I: Data Science

Data science has advanced in large part by pooling techniques and goals from statistics, operations research, and computing. In turn, these fields have changed due to data's impact. Continual learnings from these fields and others are further improving data science. Data scientists increasingly must consult other disciplines to craft solutions that meet the needs of a broad coalition.

While data science does not solve all problems, it has already had extraordinary impact, with its full potential yet to be realized. With improved processing of ever larger amounts of data, data science will continue to grow in importance and performance. A field of study is in part defined by its most important terms, so we conclude this section by reviewing 16 terms we think are critical to understanding data science.

Table I.1 reiterates our introductory section's five key terms.

Table I.2 reiterates three key statistics terms that data science uses. Inference is absolutely central to almost everything in this book, and understanding correlation and causation and their differences is essential for effectively applying and understanding data science techniques and results.

Operations research contributes to the major data science focus of optimization as illustrated by the terms in Table I.3.

From computing, Table I.4 includes three key terms.

From our ethics discussion, Table I.5 describes three key terms motivating ethical considerations when applying data science.

Table I.1 *Key terms from the definition of data science.*

Data science	The study of extracting value from data, as insights or conclusions.
Insights	Understanding what may arise from a new hypothesis that can be tested against data, from an apt visual chart, or from interactively exploring a complex model of the data, or trying out different scenarios and seeing the implications.
Conclusions	Learnings from data science of the form of prediction, recommendation, clustering, classification, transformation, or optimization.
Model	A representation of a subject system – an abstraction that emphasizes key ideas about the system and ignores extraneous details.
Big data	A body of techniques for conceiving, designing, developing, and running systems that gather, store, and process vast amounts of information.

Table I.2 *Key terms from statistics.*

Inference	The process of drawing conclusions about the properties of a population or a system. Inference is often used to test a falsifiable hypothesis, which is one which can be disproven.
Correlation	The relationship between two variables. They could be positively correlated (e.g., if one goes up, the other tends to go up), or negatively correlated (e.g., if one goes up, the other tends to go down), or perhaps uncorrelated (e.g., like the outcomes of rolling one fair die and then rolling another).
Causation	The relationship where an intervention in one variable ("the cause") contributes to a change in the value of another variable ("the effect"). In searching for causal relationships, we are aided by a search for a mechanistic relationship between the cause and the effect, as in smoking's causal relationship with cancer, or the causal relationship observed by John Snow between drinking-water contamination and cholera. Often, an interpretable relationship requires knowledge of one or more intermediaries and a pathway; for example, water contamination causing water-borne pathogens, and these pathogens causing cholera. Excellent data science sometimes leads to understanding causation. However, often, experimentation outside the realm of an established body of data is needed to definitely determine causation. It bears repeating that correlation does not imply causation, but correlation is correlated with causation.

Table I.3 *Key terms from operations research.*

Optimization	The selection of actions or values needed to generate a most desired outcome, usually subject to constraints mirroring those in the real world. For example, finding the shortest travel distance path for visiting specified cities. Optimization may be subject to constraints, such as travel time between any two cities not taking longer than a specified value, or vaccination availability being subject to certain fairness constraints.
Objective function	Represents a precise statement of a metric on which different outcomes can be compared, where a better outcome has a better value (which can be higher or lower). Sometimes, this is very simple to state. For example, in manufacturing, one wants to maximize how many parts can be made with a certain quantity of raw material. Objective functions can also be limited by constraints, such as requiring equity across subgroups.

Table I.4 *Key terms from computing.*

Algorithm	A clearly specified procedure that a computer can follow to perform a task.
Artificial intelligence	The study and construction of programs that act intelligently. They achieve their goals by examining their inputs and then taking appropriate actions.
Machine learning	A process that uses data to create a model, which a program can use to reach conclusions.

Table I.5 *Key terms from ethics.*

Respect for persons	Ensuring the freedom of individuals to act autonomously based on their own considered deliberation and judgments. Often summarized as *informed consent*, this principle also includes having sufficient transparency to make judgments.
Beneficence	This emphasizes *not* merely "do no harm," but instead seeks to maximize the benefit from using data science both directly and for society at large. Doing so requires careful consideration of the immediate risks and benefits, as well as a commitment to monitor and mitigate new harms as results occur.
Justice	The consideration of how risks and benefits from using data science are distributed. This includes the notion of a *fair* distribution. Fair may not mean "equal," but instead that benefits accrue according to factors such as one's effort, contribution, merit, or need.

Part II
Applying Data Science

While we hope we have shown data science's wide and growing impact, we have yet to discuss how data science "works" and how it should be approached. From diverse examples, we provide an Analysis Rubric, illustrate its use in evaluating new data science applications, and also exemplify the use of the ethical framework presented in Chapter 3.

In this part, we address these questions:

1. *How does data science solve some real-world applications?* In Chapter 4, we present six examples that collectively give a good picture of how data science applies to a large range of applications. Some of our examples, such as spelling correction and recommendation engines, are part of everyday life. Others are at the forefront of science and illustrate great opportunities to improve health or gain new knowledge about the world.
2. *How can we determine if data science can help solve a problem?* In Chapter 5, we offer our Analysis Rubric, a way of characterizing data science applications along seven dimensions. We critically review our six example applications within the Analysis Rubric's framework, both to build understanding of it and to show the diversity of issues data science application developers must consider.
3. *How should we apply data science to new problems and is it likely to work?* In Chapter 6, we use the Analysis Rubric to evaluate 26 additional applications. Comparing applications to Analysis Rubric elements shows data science's trade-offs, capabilities, and limitations. Our applications are from many different domains, and range from straightforward to rather infeasible.
4. *How broad is the range of data science problems?* Given the 31 examples in this part, we expand on the perspective provided by Chapter 2.
5. *How can the ethical framework of Chapter 3 guide us through data science's inherent conflicts?* Armed with the principlist approach to applied ethics

advocated in Chapter 3, Chapter 7 shows how the Belmont Principles can be used to analyze data science applications' ethical challenges.

This part concludes by looking ahead to how the Analysis Rubric and ethical framework combine to motivate Part III's seven categories of data science challenges.

Chapter 4

Data Science Applications: Six Examples

In this chapter we present examples of what data science can do. For the technology, healthcare, and science-related examples, we define the problem and then show how to collect data, build a model, and use it to solve the problem.

We start with spelling correction, which is now so common that we hardly notice it. Its models are simple and its objectives are clear. We follow with speech recognition, which also has clear objectives, but requires considerably more complex models. In fact, speech recognition was considered a grand challenge problem in AI for decades. It only became widely practical circa 2012 when vast amounts of data and deep neural networks were applied to it.

Our third example, recommendation systems, may be the single most widespread use of data science. Recommendations have provided extreme value to companies and users alike, but setting their objectives properly is hard and subject to controversy. There are also many implementation challenges, which we will detail throughout this book. Of note, recommendation systems often make use of all six types of conclusions (prediction, recommendation, clustering, classification, transformation, and optimization) that data science offers.

Our fourth example, protein folding, predicts the shape of a protein just from the knowledge of its amino acid sequence. Progress in this grand challenge biochemistry problem was slow until 2020 when a broad ensemble of models using extensive protein databases were successfully applied. This problem differs from previous examples by the diversity and complexity of its modeling and its audience of scientists, not end-users.

Our fifth example is more general and presents the promise of using large quantities of individualized health data to learn about and improve human health. While we show the potential of data science in healthcare, we also illustrate the complexity of gaining meaningful results. Whether due to data quality, privacy, complex models, or the difficulties in determining causality, using healthcare records at scale is difficult.

The sixth and final example in this section is cautionary and relates to predicting mortality during the COVID-19 pandemic. Despite high stakes, high visibility, and a great deal of data, epidemiologists and data scientists have had very limited success in predictions beyond a few weeks.

4.1 Spelling Correction

People make spelling mistakes; about 1% of words in documents are misspelled, as are almost 10% of words in internet search queries. With the help of data science, word processors and search engines can address spelling mistakes in three ways:

- as a **classification** task – misspelled words are identified, perhaps with squiggly red lines;
- as a **recommendation** task – possible corrections are presented to the user to choose from; or
- as a **transformation** task – misspelled words are automatically replaced with corrections.

The **dictionary approach** to spelling correction, introduced in the 1970s, starts with a dictionary of correctly spelled words. Then, for each word in a document or query, check if it is in the dictionary, and, if not, the system can either flag it, make a recommendation, or correct it to the closest dictionary word. In this case, the phrase "dalmation dogs" might just be corrected to "dalmatian dogs," since "dalmatian" is the dictionary word closest to "dalmation" at only one replacement letter away.

However, the dictionary approach has limitations. There are many things a dictionary does not cover. It may not have the latest slang words, nor proper names, so it can't help with "covidiot," "Shia Saide LaBeouf," or "Huawei." A dictionary-based corrector will say that every word in "from me too you" is a proper dictionary word. Of course, "too" should be corrected to "to," based on the context. And finally, a dictionary approach is not sensitive to the fact that different input methods produce different types of errors. For example, typing on a standard keyboard often leads to misordered characters (like "teh caret") while dictation instead often leads to homophone errors ("the carrot").

Because of these limitations, spelling correction has shifted to **data-intensive approaches**. A common data source is a **corpus** (or body of written text) compiled from text published on the Internet. Although published text is not perfect – it may contain its own spelling errors – it has the advantages of showing words in context and of including new words as soon as they appear in the language.

An international company that deals with 100 different languages and multiple sublanguages (e.g., British and American English, formal academic prose, and text messages) might find it tedious to maintain a dictionary for each one. It is much easier to gather a relevant corpus for each new use case than to hire a team of lexicographers to produce dictionaries for them.

Deciding that "beleif" should be corrected to "belief" and "dalmation" to "dalmatian" is easy because no other words were just one transposition or one substitution away. Other cases are not so clear-cut. What should "teh" be corrected to? It is a transposition away from "the" and a substitution away from "ten," "tea," "peh," and a dozen other words. Deciding which is most likely depends on two factors.

1. What word did the author likely intend? Corpus data can tell us that "the," English's most common word, is very likely and "peh," the 17th letter in the Hebrew alphabet, is rare and thus unlikely. Corpus data can also use the context from surrounding words: "in teh first place" suggests "the," while "teh, Earl Grey, hot" suggests "tea," based on phrase frequency in the corpus.
2. How likely is the user to incorrectly type "teh," given the intended word? The corpus alone can't tell us, but we can create a model that says that similar-sounding syllables, such as "tion" and "tian," are often confused, as are adjacent letters on the keyboard, such as "h" and "n." The model can learn from user interaction. Every time the user accepts a suggested correction, we can add to a new database of [*typo* → *correction*] pairs. We will find that ["teh" → "the"] appears frequently, and ["teh" → "peh"] does not. This database can be personalized for each user. Or it could be anonymized and shared, so everyone contributes to it and gets better spelling correction suggestions.

How fast can we assemble this user-interactions database? Suppose a search engine processes a billion queries a day, and 0.0001% of them mention a new celebrity or product. This would be more than a thousand new examples every day! Lexicographers trying to do this manually could never keep up. Once a model is created, it can be shared by all users of a language with some minor variations; e.g., British and American spellers disagree on "colour" versus "color"; users in one city might refer to "Clark Ave" and in another to "Clarke Ave."

Spelling correction is a good application of data science for several reasons. It shows the usefulness of gathering publicly available data from one source to use for another purpose, as well as the ease of creating a new database from user interactions. Privacy concerns are relatively easy to address because personally identifiable data need not be retained. Making an occasional mistake costs little, because the user is still in charge and can correct it.

4.2 Speech Recognition

Automated speech recognition (ASR), sometimes called speech-to-text, is the task of transforming an audio spectrum to digitized text. It has been of enormous interest to technologists and the general public for decades due to its many use cases, including taking dictation, automating call centers, enabling hands-free voice interaction with computers or appliances, captioning videos, and motivating great robots in Hollywood movies (Juang & Rabiner, 2005).

Speech recognition is a much harder problem than spelling correction for several reasons.

- Speech is analog, and each person's speech is a little bit different, whereas every typist who transposes the "ie" in "belief" ends up with exactly the same result, "beleif."
- Speech has systematic variation due to different accents, mixed language, speech impediments, random variation due to background noise, and multiple people speaking at once.
- Speech has ambiguity due to homophones as well as the absence of capitalization and punctuation.
- Transcription errors can be distracting to users, but are usually not life-threatening. Risks related to errors could prevent ASR's use in applications where an error would cause great harm.

As with spelling correction, early approaches relied on expert linguists. They wrote rules to define several steps in the speech recognition process pipeline; from acoustic signals to phonemes, from phonemes to words, and from words to sentences. This pipeline let linguists contribute their knowledge about language, but because each component was defined independently, errors propagated between components without correction.

By 1980, the field had shifted to automatically learning a speech model from data. Like spelling correction, it used statistics of past frequencies to analyze novel speech sounds. IBM speech researcher Frederick Jelinek jokingly said, "Anytime a linguist leaves the group the recognition rate goes up" (Jurafsky & Martin, 2009).

For speech recognition, the data are parallel corpora of speech spectra aligned with transcripts of the spoken words. The most valuable data (and most expensive to produce) is aligned word-by-word, but models also use sentence-by-sentence aligned and non-aligned samples.

In the 1980s, only people with a compelling need for the technology were willing to deal with speech recognition systems' idiosyncrasies, which included a tedious training period. Continuing improvements were made year by year, but the real breakthrough occurred in 2009, when Geoffrey Hinton of the University of Toronto and two of his students demonstrated the effectiveness of deep neural networks for speech recognition (Mohamed et al., 2009). Research teams at Microsoft, Google, IBM, and other institutions immediately jumped on this approach, which quickly resulted in a pronounced performance improvement in commercial systems. The single change of introducing deep neural networks was more effective than all of the previous decade's work (Deng et al., 2013).

At first, the deep networks just replaced and improved individual components in the pipeline. However, by 2015, the whole pipeline had been replaced with an end-to-end neural network. One particular advantage of this approach was that early processing errors were carried forward in such a way that later parts of the network could correct the errors, in contrast to the error chains that linguists' pipelines allowed.

No two speech recordings are identical, but speech recognition systems can generalize, taking a novel audio spectrum and comparing it to its model of previously heard audio spectra, then outputting a transcript – even if the model had never heard that word sequence. With a good microphone, a careful speaker (with an accent sufficiently represented by training data), and minimal background noise, systems (as of 2022) make an error once every 30 or 40 words.

Just as in spelling correction, dynamic training can improve a speech recognition system's quality. Systems can learn to compensate for accents or microphone properties. They learn not only from recorded training data, but also from user-supplied corrections to system errors. As with spelling correction, a single system can be trained to recognize a hundred or more different languages.

We now use speech recognition for captioning videos, controlling home and automotive devices, and doing dictation – whether on computers, smartphones, appliances, or through smart assistants like Siri, Alexa, and Google Assistant. Speech recognition provides greater accessibility to hearing-impaired people, brings people of different cultures together with voice-to-voice translation systems, and perhaps even (someday!) will help call centers provide faster and better customer service.

In all, speech recognition quality has become so good that billions of people use it as an everyday part of their lives, so it now benefits from the virtuous cycle of increasing usage generating more data that improves quality and garners more usage. Like spelling correction, it's a good example of data science but one that is significantly more complex in many dimensions, including data gathering, modeling, breadth of application, and toleration of failures.

4.3 Music Recommendation

One of data science's most widespread uses is in recommendation systems. These systems recommend a user's next song, movie, book, app, or romantic partner. When someone browses a shopping site, the system suggests products they might like. On a news site or social network, they determine what stories to present to users.

Users depend on recommendation systems, because the Web has grown so large that no one can sift through all the available information on their own. Recommendation systems are also crucial to the Web's business model; better recommendations make for more subscriptions and purchases. Web advertising is in part a recommendation problem – one that must satisfy many different goals.

We focus on **music recommendations** as a representative example. With vast cloud-based music libraries at our disposal, including artists we have never heard of, recommendations truly help us find our way. How do we get recommendations of songs that we actually want to hear? The recommendation system builds a model from three types of data: a song's waveform, a song's metadata (title, artist, genre, composer, date recorded, length, etc.), and listeners' reactions. A "reaction" may be passively listening to the currently playing song, or it may be actively starting, skipping or replaying a song, or rating it with a star or a thumbs down.

A song's waveform can be analyzed for tempo, beat, timbre, and other factors. The system can recommend a song with similar features to songs that the user has previously liked or, for variety, perhaps recommend a contrasting song. The recommendations can be specialized for activity or time of day; perhaps fast, energetic songs for exercising, and slow mellow songs at the end of the day.

Metadata can be applied in many ways and even extended to permit creation of predictive, semantic relations between its entities. For example, a system could scan Wikipedia and other sources to learn that Telemann and Vivaldi lived at about the same time, Haydn taught Beethoven, Ringo Starr was a member of the Beatles, and Ramblin' Jack Elliott covered 24 Bob Dylan songs. If someone likes Telemann, Haydn, Ringo, or Dylan, they probably, respectively, also like Vivaldi, Beethoven, the Beatles, or Elliott.

User reactions help resolve the serious complication that different users should get different recommendations. There is no universally accepted "correct" recommendation in the way that there is a correct spelling of a word. Potentially every user needs a different recommendation model, rather than using a single shared model. This has two key implications:

- The system must ensure the privacy and security of each user's personal data.
- The data will be sparse. A large company with a billion users could gather enough data to build a good spelling correction system in a few days. But that is not nearly enough data to make good music recommendations. They would have billions of user reactions, but only a few for each user. A spelling correction system only has to learn about 100,000 words, but a large music recommendation system has to learn a billion users' preferences for each of a million songs – a quadrillion total preferences.

So, if a system has zero observations of a particular user reacting to a particular song, how can the system decide whether to recommend the song? The key is that it has many examples of *similar* users reacting to *similar* songs. The technique called **collaborative filtering** builds on this idea to examine the songs a listener has liked (or disliked), and compares them to every other listener's reactions. When it finds a similar history, the songs that the user likes can be recommended to each other listener.

To improve both efficiency and the ability to generalize, a system can group together both similar songs and similar users. A user might belong to groups for "cool jazz" and for "60s female Broadway vocalists." A machine learning system wouldn't know those groups by those names, but rather by their shared collection of numerical and categorical features. The important point is that when some group members agree on a new discovery, it becomes available to all the other group members. Many companies use collaborative filtering, with Amazon and Netflix particularly well known for it.

A second technique to address the "cold start" problem of new users (or new items) is to explicitly pose the recommendation problem as one of **stochastic optimization** or **reinforcement learning**. For example, in the domain of news, many techniques have been developed in the last decade for trying to find the right combination of attributes of the always-changing news stories, users, and their reading histories to maximize the click-through rate (Coenen, 2019; Li et al., 2011). These approaches balance the twin goals of enabling a reader to explore new stories while leveraging popularity.

Music recommendation methods are metaphorically similar to those that underlie quantitative approaches to investment management:

- Momentum investing based on understanding what others are doing is analogous to collaborative filtering.
- Fundamental investing based on knowledge of an investment's business is analogous to using semantic knowledge.
- Technical investing based on raw stock prices and market volumes is analogous to musical signal analysis.

Quantitative investment applications, like recommendation systems, can also learn from their success or failure and feed that back into future decision-making.

Our discussion of music recommendation systems shows that they may make use of all the conclusion types listed in Chapter 1 to make their own recommendation conclusion:

- They may *predict* what a user will like or not like.
- They may *cluster* users or songs into groups, to identify like elements or to do better collaborative filtering.
- They may *classify* songs by genre to make better recommendations or use the genre itself within the user interface.
- They may *optimize* customer satisfaction subject to meeting certain constraints, such as presenting sufficient new material or maximizing revenue.

- They may *transform* signals into a new form. For example, they may transform audio signals into a set of features to allow better comparison of music's sound.

Music recommendations are greatly differentiated from the previous examples by their diversity of models, types of conclusions, and the complexity of setting objectives. (See the case study of Pandora's approach as an example (Dorman, 2018).) Many model systems of this kind will be much larger, harder to maintain, and harder to debug. We will return to recommendations throughout this book due to their broad applicability, their financial importance, the challenges in setting their objectives, and their diversity of techniques they employ. In particular, Section 6.2 and Chapter 7 discuss news recommendations.

4.4 Protein Folding

A human protein is a stringy chain of amino acids connected in a specific order. As postulated by Anfinsen in his 1972 Nobel Lecture (Anfinsen, 1973), the identity and order of the amino acids determines a protein's shape. We also know that shape largely determines how the protein functions and what it does. Protein shapes can often be experimentally determined with techniques like X-ray crystallography, nuclear magnetic resonance, and cryo-electron microscopy. However, due to this work's time and expense, only about 100,000 protein structures have been determined out of the billions known to exist.

This motivates one of the greatest biochemistry challenges, the **protein folding problem**, which in part aims to predict the 3D structure of proteins directly from sequence data. More easily discovering protein structures would greatly benefit the life sciences, providing better understanding of many diseases and faster drug discovery. To calibrate the problem's scale, humans have 20 different amino acids and a protein is made up of tens to thousands of amino acids, and a protein could be in over 10^{100} possible shapes.

At first, scientists attempted to solve this structure prediction problem by building on fundamental physical principles. These so-called ab initio techniques provided some insight but proved computationally challenging for even the largest computers, peer-to-peer networks, and specialized hardware architectures. Levinthal's paradox contrasts the vast computational difficulty of ab initio modeling against how easily proteins fold in Nature. This disparity ("if Nature can do it . . .") has led many to believe there must be efficient approaches.

Such approaches have begun to appear based on models using (i) machine learning trained on known protein sequences and structures in combination with (ii) underlying physical principles. In 2020, at the 14th Biennial CASP (Critical Assessment of Protein Structure Prediction) competition, DeepMind's AlphaFold 2 software used such an approach and achieved results having similar quality to those using laboratory techniques (Jumper et al., 2021). Combining several types of deep network architectures, the system produces predictions in minutes to hours of GPU processing. While we don't know how well the results will generalize, AlphaFold 2's result is a clear turning point in the protein folding problem's nearly 50-year history.

In July 2021, DeepMind released all of AlphaFold 2's documentation, models, code, and training data for others to scrutinize, learn from, and use its capabilities. Alphabet, DeepMind's parent company, is planning to use its software to determine and then release hundreds of thousands of protein structures, with plans to grow this to over a hundred million. Importantly, also in July 2021, Baek et al. of the University of Washington released RoseTTAFold, a protein folding solution that used similar approaches, adding more credence to this form of modeling (Baek et al., 2021).

As good as these results are, there is still more to do. Time will tell how well data-driven approaches generalize to predicting multiple protein complexes or the shapes that occur from protein interactions. Also, they do not show the dynamic protein changes that might be seen using molecular dynamics (Shaw et al., 2010). As of late 2021, AlphaFold 2 has less accuracy at the sites where proteins bind with ligands. It is also unknown if data-driven approaches can predict protein shapes when there is no training data from evolutionarily related, naturally occurring proteins (Mullard, 2021). Finally, while its accuracy is approaching that of laboratory techniques, it can still be improved.

Nonetheless, AlphaFold 2's success, as well as that of other related work, is a concrete demonstration of data science's ability to leverage decades of experimentally derived data to advance biomedicine and health. The Oxford Protein Informatics Group published an informative summary post with more information on this (Rubiera, 2021).

We have included this example because it is a great example of a scientific application whose results will be used by scientists, not the population at large. It also relies on a very sophisticated collection of machine learning and other models, which have been trained on decades of painstakingly collected data. Even though its generality is not fully known, this protein folding solution will inspire other scientists and demonstrate that data-driven approaches are now a necessity in a scientist's toolkit.

4.5 Healthcare Records

Individual patient healthcare records, including test results, diagnoses, treatments, and their results, are increasingly digitized and available online. This could improve our ability to learn about disease prevalence in populations, different approaches to treatment, and other ways to improve human health. Vast amounts of data can be brought to bear; large healthcare institutions, such as the Kaiser Permanente Health System and the United States Veterans Administration, have circa 10 million enrollees. National systems have even more – the UK's National Health Service (NHS) has circa 58 million enrollees, whose data is made available for analytics purposes on the OpenSAFELY platform (OpenSAFELY, n.d.). An international collaboration, the Observational Health Data Science and Informatics (OHDSI), aims to make it possible to apply data from an international set of federated data stores. As of 2016, OHDSI had converted over 682 million patient records to a standard and comparable format. This included at least some information about an estimated 200 million patients (Hripcsak et al., 2015). Here are three illustrative results:

- A Kaiser Permanente study used machine learning on nearly four million patient records to train a predictive model to identify patients more at risk for developing HIV, and hence more likely to benefit from taking preventative medication (Marcus et al., 2019). Kaiser, as a very large integrated healthcare system, benefits greatly from its large unified data repository, making Kaiser's studies easier to do than most in the US healthcare system.
- The OHDSI database supported a retrospective study comparing two different common hypertension treatments across over 730,000 patients. It showed that the more highly recommended treatment is associated with more side effects (Hripcsak et al., 2020). This study does not yet prove the standard of care is wrong, but it does alert physicians to watch out for the side effects. It also increases the attention on an ongoing prospective controlled trial comparing the alternatives.
- During the 2020 focus on COVID-19 treatments, OHDSI's database and tools looked at two decades of records relating to the side effects of previous hydroxychloroquine and azithromycin uses. While there had been considerable hope that the combination of these two drugs would help treat COVID-19, the data showed troubling associations with cardiovascular problems, including ones resulting in death (Lane et al., 2020).

More generally, big data systems with many healthcare records enable visualizations and understanding of the natural history of disease and prevailing treatments. Researchers can then "design experiments and inform the generalizability of experimental research" (Hripcsak et al., 2016).

Another approach to using healthcare records at scale is based on crowdsourcing. An excellent use case is post-approval monitoring of new drugs to identify rare side effects that might not show up in more limited pre-approval trials. As an example, the US Centers for Disease Control created the V-Safe system to monitor post-COVID-19 vaccination side effects, using both text messaging and web technologies to increase coverage (CDC, 2021). With a potential patient base about four orders of magnitude larger than the populations in vaccine clinical trials, V-Safe aimed to provide very rapid information on vaccine reactions and low-prevalence risks. In late summer 2021, V-Safe was augmented to gather highly specific side-effect data from pregnant women, a particularly important subpopulation.

Within a one-month period ending January 13, 2021, 1.6 million US vaccine recipients (representing 10% of the total vaccinations given in the period) completed at least one survey. The rapidly available data allowed publication of both minor and serious reaction rates by mid-February (Gee et al., 2021). The survey showed a very small risk of serious adverse reactions, though about 80% of respondents reported pain at the injection site. The relatively high response rate reduced the risk of selection bias (though it is still possible), but V-Safe, like all crowdsourced systems, could be abused by individuals who register false adverse reactions – possibly to create fear, uncertainty, and doubt. In fact, the broader US vaccine adverse event reporting system has become considerably more politicized in the time of COVID-19 vaccine skepticism, and its data is increasingly being used out of context (Stecuła & Motta, 2021).

Results such as the preceding examples hide the complexity of doing such observational studies. Data needs to be sufficiently standardized, possibly across multiple sites, to be usable in combination. To support data gathering and use, there must be complex data management software that aggregates data while both preserving privacy and allowing for the transparency needed in scientific studies. When data is gathered from multiple sites, due attention must be paid to the risks of fraud. Sites are likely to anonymize or aggregate data prior to release, making validation more difficult.

Enormous attention must be paid to modeling. Observational studies are usually done with a hypothesis in mind, and there is inevitably pressure to show positive results. Even when these pressures are controlled, the complexity of the statistical analyses can lead to hard-to-find errors.

The privacy issues, particularly in systems like OHDSI which need to use cross-site data, are particularly challenging. Tools and methodologies are needed to let researchers evaluate the many possible correlations they identify and develop cost-effective approaches to prioritize the data gathering needed to shed light on causality. However, despite the frequent desire and need to do so, it is extremely difficult (and frequently impossible) to tease out matters of causality in observational studies.

As an example of where something went terribly wrong, well-regarded medical researchers published articles in May 2020 in two of the most prestigious journals using observational data from then-recent COVID-19 cases (Offord, 2020). One drew conclusions on the risks to hospitalized COVID-19 patients of common blood pressure medications, and the other on the risks of hydroxychloroquine (uncombined with azithromycin) as a treatment. However, the underlying data was not available for peer review, and the articles were eventually shown to be erroneous, if not fraudulent. Both articles were quickly retracted, but real damage happened when organizations briefly suspended research projects and modified patient treatment guidelines based on the work.

Many factors make observational studies challenging, but there are huge opportunities. The near-universal collection of healthcare records can suggest new hypotheses, support post-approval monitoring of new drugs, provide an interactive analysis platform for researchers to explore new ideas, catalyze new approaches for screening or preventing disease, and sometimes answer critical healthcare questions. However, frequently, issues of data quality and availability, modeling complexity, privacy and security, the difficulty in determining causal relationships, and more make these applications difficult. These challenges are discussed in much greater detail throughout Part III.

We've chosen the application of healthcare records at scale to illustrate the enormous opportunities in using observational data, but also the great challenges (e.g., scale, complexity, and potential for harm) to creating truthful insights and conclusions.

4.6 Predicting COVID-19 Mortality in the US

After the early reports of lockdowns and thousands of deaths in China, everyone hungered for predictions about SARS-CoV-2's impact in their own regions. In addition to informing the general public of expected risks, morbidity and mortality predictions could better guide institutions and governments to needed actions. Even better, if models could predict the effect of policy interventions (e.g., masks or levels of quarantine), they could help balance conflicting economic, social, educational, and health objectives. In the US alone, the COVID-19 Forecast Hub (COVID-19 Forecast Hub, n.d.) hosted more than 50 different predictive models, and there were numerous COVID-19 data science efforts elsewhere (von Borzyskowski et al., 2021).

In many ways, mortality prediction might seem a straightforward exercise. There was publicly available aggregate data: the number of COVID-19 positive tests, test positivity as a function of total tests, and number of deaths. There was also a growing understanding of disease transmissibility as it became clear that asymptomatic people spread COVID-19 through virus-laden aerosols. By the late spring 2020, there was initial data on seroprevalence of antibodies to COVID-19, which could be used to infer how many had been exposed to the disease. There were measures of mobility (as discussed further in Chapter 6) that showed the impact of quarantine regulations, and many more potentially useful features on which to base models.

There was also considerable modeling experience. Previous epidemiological modeling work dates back to Bernoulli's smallpox study in the 1700s (Dietz & Heesterbeek, 2002) and has continued to the present. There are many possible types of models, ranging from susceptible–exposed–infectious–recovered (SEIR) compartmental models (which are interpretable and based on our understanding of disease spread) to machine learning models (some simple, some using many features). Models were illustrated by excellent graphs and charts available in both the scientific literature and the press. These provided exploratory and explanatory insights to data scientists and epidemiologists.

The objective of this predictive modeling was clear, privacy issues were muted (since the data used for modeling is already highly aggregated), and many people would have accepted good predictions without needing an explanation. However, we do acknowledge that Cornell's COVID-19 modeling team emphasized the need for interpretability to increase the acceptance of campus health policies (Frazier, 2022).

However, modeling did not go smoothly for many reasons. First, data was lacking. In many countries there was reasonable data on the number of hospitalizations and deaths but insufficient testing to understand how many people were infected with milder cases. Changing testing availability also made data hard to compare across time intervals; i.e., the number of undiagnosed cases very early in the pandemic was much higher than at many other periods. Mortality was measured in different ways in different jurisdictions (e.g., co-morbidities led to inconsistent policies for attributing death), making that data noisy.

Furthermore, modeling based on reported cases is innately difficult. Infected people may harbor latent disease for a few days or longer before having symptoms, yet still be contagious. In fact, some infected with SARS-Cov-2 never had symptoms but still spread the virus. Viruses mutate, and transmissibility increased during the pandemic.

Popular behavior also changed greatly over time. This was due to changing perception of self-risk, governmental actions, and perhaps even as a direct or indirect result of model predictions on the public.

Finally, the available aggregated data did not match the actual subpopulations that arise due to the cultural affinity, employment, education, or shared circumstances that bind people together. Mortality in these subpopulations, where people differentially interact amongst themselves, can greatly skew societal averages, as happened, for example, in nursing homes at the beginning of the epidemic. Due to these and many other characteristics of the COVID-19 epidemic, modeling was problematic.

In an excellent comparative review, a community of 229 co-authors wrote a retrospective evaluation of 22 US COVID-19 mortality modeling efforts occurring from May to December 2020 (Cramer et al., 2021). The data on which the models were based varied. All but one used data on prior deaths, many used data on positive cases, and some included data on hospitalizations, demographics, and mobility data. A few models assumed that behavioral patterns might change during the modeling period, but most did not. Some models were based on the characteristics of disease spread (as in the SEIR approach mentioned previously), but most were not.

The paper's methodology compared model predictions to actual data, and also compared how accurate those predictions were to those made by a 23rd model – a naive baseline model with predictions based solely on past deaths. Against that baseline, about one-half of the models did better and about one-half did worse.

Cramer et al. (2021) observed that models with simple data inputs (e.g., positive case and mortality data) were some of the most accurate stand-alone models (which is vaguely depressing to this book's authors). An ensemble model, which equally weighted forecasts from all the available models, gave the best results for one-to-four-weeks predictions, with roughly one-third less error using the metrics of evaluators. While this seems like a very short period of prediction, it is still of value in terms of allocating treatment capacity to needy areas.

Longer-range forecasts had lower accuracy. Four-week-ahead forecasts had roughly twice the error of one-week forecasts; eight- to 20-week horizons had about five to six times higher errors. The longer-range forecasts, if better, would have been very useful in setting policies. Unfortunately, according to Roni Rosenfeld at CMU (one co-author of the Cramer et al. paper): "There were 4 major geo-temporal COVID waves in the US in 2020, and none of them was anticipated by any of the forecasts I have seen (ourselves included)" (R. Rosenfeld, personal communication to Alfred Spector, July 18, 2021).

If we reflect on the relatively poor results of these modeling efforts, they happened due to insufficient and erroneous data, the complexity of the necessary models, the changing nature of the disease, and feedback phenomena catalyzed, in part, by government actions. Rectifying these problems would be very difficult due to the logistics and privacy implications of gathering very fine-grained data and predicting public policy/societal responses. Furthermore, the virus's mutation may have stymied predictions in any case.

We concluded this chapter's examples with COVID-19 mortality prediction to show our humility in the face of very difficult problems. However, we do hold out hope that this data science application could significantly improve with more data and effort.

Chapter 5
The Analysis Rubric

This chapter defines the **Analysis Rubric**, which consists of seven major considerations for determining data science's applicability to a proposed application. While these considerations may not be fully understood at a project's inception, there needs to be a belief that answers will be forthcoming prior to completion. Three of these address requirements-oriented aspects ("for what or why") of data science applications, and three address implementation-oriented aspects ("how to"). The seventh addresses legal, societal, and ethical implications (ELSI[8]). Collectively, these considerations, or Analysis Rubric elements, cover the complex trade-offs needed to achieve practical, valuable, legal, and ethical results.

Implementation-oriented elements

- **Tractable data.** Consider whether data of sufficient integrity, size, quality, and manageability exists or could be obtained.
- **A technical approach.** Consider whether there is a technical approach grounded in data, such as an analysis, a model, or an interactive visualization, that can achieve the desired result.
- **Dependability.** Dependability[9] aggregates the following four considerations. Does the application meet needed privacy protections? Is its security sufficient to thwart attackers who try to break it? Does it resist the abuse of malevolent users? Does it have the resilience to operate correctly in the face of unforeseen circumstances or changes to the world?

Requirements-oriented elements

- **Understandability.** This means the approach must enable others to understand the application. Consider whether the application needs only to provide

[8] The acronym ELSI stands for "ethical, legal, and social implications." It was coined by James Watson in October 1988 as described in *ELSI: Origins and Early History* (Sankar, 2014). We will typically address these issues in a more operationally focused order that begins with legal issues, followed thereafter by societal and ethical issues.

[9] We devoted much effort before settling on *dependability* to aggregate privacy, security, abuse-resistance, and resilience. While *dependability* is often a generic term, this book will consistently use it as a placeholder for these four properties.

conclusions or if it will have to explain "why" it has rendered these conclusions. Will the application need to detail the causal chain underlying its conclusions? Or will it make its underlying data and associated models, software, and techniques transparent and provide **reproducibility** – that is, the ability for analysts or scientists to understand, validate, duplicate, or extend the results?

- **Clear objectives.** Consider whether the application is trying to achieve well-specified objectives that align with what we truly want to happen.
- **Toleration of failures.** Consider both the possible unintended side effects if the objective is not quite right and the possible damage from failing to meet objectives. Many data science approaches only achieve good results probabilistically, so occasional poor results must be acceptable.

Ethical, legal, and societal implications (ELSI) element

- **Ethical, legal, and social issues.** Consider the application holistically with regard to legality, risk, and ethical considerations. Many of the topics under "Dependability" or "Clear objectives" topics are relevant, but this holistic analysis is broader.

Many applications start with a **bottom-up approach**, focusing on implementation-related Analysis Rubric elements relating to data availability, a technical approach providing the necessary results, and techniques to provide needed dependability. This analysis then informs the requirements definition and influences its refinement.

Others require a **top-down approach**, first focusing on the requirements-oriented Analysis Rubric elements relating to understanding, clarity of objectives, and failure tolerance. This analysis then informs the implementation approach and influences its refinement.

Most commonly, the bottom-up and top-down approaches are mixed, and there is iterative flitting back and forth between different considerations. No matter what design approach is used, the ethical, legal, and societal implications must be considered throughout the design and analysis. They cannot be bolted on at the last minute, and they must be carefully reviewed before any effort is declared complete.

The Analysis Rubric is important to this book. It is illustrated in Figure 5.1, which summarizes its considerations in a graphic. The next six sections will make the Analysis Rubric more concrete by demonstrating its application to the six examples of Chapter 4.

5.1 Analyzing Spelling Correction

Spelling correction is a clear example of a really good data science application – as evaluation using the Analysis Rubric shows.

Data Science Analysis Rubric

Implementation-Oriented Elements			*Requirements-Oriented Elements*			
Tractable Data	Technical Approach	Dependability	Understand-ability	Clear Objectives	Toleration of Failures	Ethical, Legal, Societal Considerations

Dependability

Privacy	
Security	
Abuse-resistance	
Resilience	

Understandability

Explanation	
Causality	
Reproducibility	

ELSI Considerations

Legal	
Societal	
Ethical	

Figure 5.1 This graphic shows the seven top-level elements of the Analysis Rubric and the further breakdown of Dependability, Understandability, and Ethical, legal, and societal considerations.

- **Tractable data.** Anyone can easily collect an appropriate corpus of online text. A company already running a service can easily collect user feedback from spelling suggestions to verify which suggestions are good. There are "only" a few million distinct word tokens in any language, so individual word count data is relatively small. However, multi-word phrase data quickly grows in size – the Google Books Ngram project has a few hundred gigabytes of data for counts of phrases up to five words long.
- **A technical approach.** Section 4.1 outlined an approach to spelling correction in a search engine using word and phrase frequencies in the search corpus, together with user feedback from accepting or rejecting suggestions. The model is relatively simple, and a basic version takes just a few dozen lines of code (Norvig, 2009).
- **Dependability.** Spelling correction relies mostly on non-private data, so privacy and security are not major issues. However, privacy is always tricky, and a system that learns from an individual or institution should not expose confidential information (such as the spelling of code names) to outsiders. Erroneous corrections may occur, but the cost of a spelling error is low. Some care must be taken to prevent an attacker from spamming the spelling corrector with an incorrect spelling (perhaps to promote their brand name).
- **Understandability.** Users don't really care how spelling correctors work. Spelling correctors also don't need to understand a spelling error's root cause. Finally, a spelling corrector's internal operation can be opaque. Neither must its

inner workings be understandable nor must its logic and data be published. This is good, because the specific words each individual user types must be kept secret.

- **Clear objectives.** The clear goal is determining and providing the correct spelling. While a spelling corrector could correct "wheg" to many different words such as "when," "where," or "Whig," the correct spelling is what the user *meant* to type.
- **Toleration of failures.** While a spelling corrector should almost always do the right thing, almost all users are accepting if it does not correct a word's spelling or even guesses a word incorrectly, as long as the failure is plausible. However, even a rare failure that "corrects" words to become profane or otherwise objectionable would be unacceptable.
- **Legal, risk, and ethical issues.** Spelling correction would seem to have no legal issues and minimal risks (as long as it does not inappropriately suggest taboo words). Spelling would not seem to have ethical concerns, though Nicholas Carr questions whether automation of mundane things is harmful to us as humans (Carr, 2008), and Nick Romeo questions the impact of spelling correction, per se (Romeo, 2014). However, Romeo observes this type of concern is old, and references Plato's *Phaedrus*, which poses the question of whether even the written word might reduce people's memories and make them dependent. We think the advantages outweigh any disadvantages, and autocorrection could even teach us to spell.[10]

5.2 Analyzing Speech Recognition

Speech recognition has some similarities to spelling correction, despite it being a much harder technical problem.

- **Tractable data.** Speech recognition's most important data sources are the repositories pairing speech utterances (recorded waveforms) with correct transcriptions on which the system can be trained. These utterances may have been professionally spoken and transcribed or may have been mined from usage. While recognizing speech on behalf of a user, a speech recognition application may also consult repositories relating to local specialized word stores from the user's common vocabulary (such as personal or place names) and more. Just as in spelling correction, the repository may include user-provided corrections, for both improved overall speech recognition accuracy and better individual adaptation.

[10] A system could even remember the "meaningful" spelling corrections it has made for us, and periodically remind us of them, perhaps even teaching us with virtual flashcards.

- **A technical approach.** While data-oriented approaches have long been applied, the quality improvement brought by deep neural network recognizers made them the dominant approach. These systems initially used cloud computing and specialized hardware for the audio-to-text transformation step. This required complex engineering to efficiently transmit waveform data from a personal device to the Cloud and then to receive the resulting text. That round trip requires reliable communication (particularly for dictation), but now even cell phones can do many aspects of speech recognition locally, thereby reducing off-device processing.
- **Dependability.** When speech recognition systems collect utterances either for personalization or for their overall improvement, they must take great pains to protect those utterances. This is particularly difficult when the process uses human transcribers.[11] Depending on the application, speech recognition will make errors, as do even the best human transcriptionists. Many speech recognition systems learn from user feedback, such as user-supplied corrections, which makes them more resilient and adaptable, but also means they must protect against abuse in ways similar to spelling correction.
- **Understandability.** As with spelling correction, speech recognition need not be concerned with explanation, transparent reproducibility, or causality.
- **Clear objectives.** Here, the objectives are a bit more complex than spelling due to the need to consider differential accents, speech impediments, and multilingual speech. Speech recognition systems, if to be of broad utility, must consider word accuracy across an entire population. Furthermore, the objective may have occasional ambiguities, but usually the right answer can be understood from context.
- **Toleration of failures.** Speech recognition's failure tolerance depends on the application. In some cases, failures up to a certain rate are acceptable. However, in some situations, such as transcribing a judicial hearing, controlling a vehicle, or basing emergency response off of a 911 transcription, errors could cause substantial harm, necessitating mitigating techniques (e.g., manual checking). Thus, failure tolerance is application-dependent.
- **Legal, risk, and ethical issues.** Speech recognition creates minor risks except in critical safety applications. There is a privacy issue if speech recordings and/or transcripts are transmitted or stored. Therefore, many applications do speech recognition on-device without retaining recordings. There have also been controversies when humans have listened to speech utterances to do transcriptions to provide more training data. Machine-learned speech recognition models tend to

[11] There have been privacy concerns with speech utterances being sent to outside contractors for manual transcription, so speech recognition providers have had to both increase their disclosure to users and change their approach to manual transcription.

get more data and perform better for majority populations of speakers, and may perform poorly for subpopulations. Supporting these subpopulations is beneficial to all, and the balance of effort to do so is a fairness issue that must be considered.

5.3 Analyzing Music Recommendation

Recommendation systems are a broader data science application than our previous two examples. They have far more diverse uses, employ many more underlying techniques, and, while they focus on prediction, they may do many types of learning to achieve it.

- **Tractable data.** Music recommendations' underlying data sources are quite heterogeneous. Here are some example datasets that a music service would have available:
  - Recommendations and click data histories, indicating what was recommended and what was accepted and/or listened to.
  - A semantic information database about music, musicians, and musical periods. This can be compiled from many sources, ranging from record label data to Wikipedia.
  - Metadata about the music recordings and performances.
  - The music's audio tracks.

There have been millions of separate CD albums (Wikipedia contributors, n.d.). Assuming about 10 million albums at less than 100 megabytes per album (for, say, MP3 files), we have a corpus of about a petabyte of sound. As of 2021, this can be stored, albeit without redundancy, on a mere 100 hard drives!

- **A technical approach.** As described in Section 4.3, there are many approaches to creating successful recommendations, and they can be assembled into an ensemble to gain their collective value. Approaches to broader recommendations vary based on the specific application, but there are usually many available techniques. Often the choice is governed by how they address the objectives and need for understanding.
- **Dependability**
  - Systems that maintain a history of user interaction must very carefully protect it to prevent security or privacy problems. This is not so easy; Arvind Narayanan and Vitaly Shmatikov in the mid-2000s showed that even highly de-identified data from Netflix usage databases could divulge sensitive information (Narayanan & Shmatikov, 2007).
  - Resilience is not a great concern given that recommendations need not always be accepted, though there must be guards against really terrible (or jarring) recommendations that would be greatly disliked by a listener.

  - Music (and almost all) recommendation systems must include anti-abuse technologies, as bad actors can trick them into recommending something. Unlike with spelling correction or speech recognition, music recommendation systems may need to adapt to new data quickly, thereby being sensitive to easier-to-mount abuse attacks. This is a very considerable challenge for recommendation systems, and abuse-resistance may significantly impact what technical approaches are feasible.

- **Understandability**
  - A system may be required to explain why it has made certain recommendations to fulfill regulatory, or even contractual/audit, requirements. Even if there are no such requirements, users may still like knowing why a system thought they would like something, and might find that information educational. A system's implementers may also want to know this to help debug these complex systems, which gets harder to do as they combine more and more signals and approaches. When recommendations are based on an ensemble of algorithms operating on data from a huge user population, it may be hard to ferret out the relative contribution of any component. This is especially true if the system uses hard-to-interpret neural networks.
  - With respect to causality, why a user likes a recommendation is a truly complex matter. The ultimate cause may rest in neuroscience and be well beyond the capability of any system and its available data.
  - There is no reason for a music recommendation system to release its underlying data and models to others. There is no scientific result that others need to duplicate, though regulatory frameworks might require such release for other recommendations, e.g., in the realm of investment management. The Netflix data release mentioned under "Dependability" is a cautionary lesson.

- **Clear objectives.** The system's objective is to recommend tracks that a user then plays. However, there are shades of gray that make implementing a recommendation system very tricky indeed:
  - Should it try to diversify a user's listening repertoire and perhaps educate the listener?
  - Should it consider material's royalty costs? Notably, if there were a differential cost of material, as in movies or books, subscription services might penalize recommendations with high licensing costs, while à la carte services might recommend expensive items to make an increased profit.
  - Is a high proportion of accepted recommendations a good enough surrogate for listener satisfaction? Or could listeners – over time – become fatigued and

inattentive to the system, even though they have actively or passively accepted its recommendations?

- ◦ How much should a music recommendation system "throttle" itself? Some say good recommendation systems distract society from more important pursuits by enticing people to instead listen to yet more music. Other recommendation systems have similar concerns, perhaps enticing someone to read yet another novel or watch another cute cat video, or perhaps (more seriously) reinforcing an erroneous "fact."
- ◦ These and many more secondary considerations make music recommendations quite challenging, and Chapter 12 discusses these objective-setting challenges in much more detail.

- **Toleration of failures.** Music recommendations need not be "perfect," and a user may not heed a particular recommendation for many reasons. It probably is not even a goal that every recommendation be accepted, as users may appreciate bold or creative suggestions. However, recommendation systems need to walk the fine line between bold and jarring recommendations.
- **Legal, risk, and ethical issues.** Music recommendation has few legal issues and fewer risks than other domains (although, for example, it is crucial to be careful about recommending obscene lyrics to minors). However, there are many ethical issues relating to the type of recommendations made and their impact on individual listeners, their community, and the creator/artist whose success may be at the mercy of these algorithms. The fourth item under "Clear objectives" could easily be considered also an ethical consideration due to its need to balance rights and harms.

5.4 Analyzing Protein Folding

Protein folding does not provide direct consumer benefits, but rather intermediate results that scientists use to make other discoveries. This makes some Analysis Rubric elements easier to satisfy (e.g., no abuse), but increases others' importance (e.g., reproducibility).

- **Tractable data.** Data-driven approaches to protein folding build on many databases, for example, UniProt, which contains sequence data about millions of proteins, and the Protein Data Bank, which contains a global archive of experimentally determined 3D protein structures (wwPDB consortium, 2019). AlphaFold 2 requires many hundreds of gigabytes of such data as inputs. The extent to which the models can use raw, unprocessed data from these databases versus needing preprocessing (as in Section 8.2) varies depending on the details of their technical approach.

- **A technical approach.** In contrast to the spelling example, which has very simple models, the recently successful protein folding prediction uses some hard-coded techniques (e.g., for aligning related amino acid sequences) and several connected machine learning models (e.g., transformers (Vaswani et al., 2017)), which have only recently become understood. The technical approach also blends in physical constraints such as the triangle inequality and energy minimization.
- **Dependability.** There are few privacy, security, or abuse-resistance concerns for this application, although organizations may want to maintain confidentiality. Resilience is important, as scientists would prefer the highest-quality results independent of the precise protein being predicted or occasional input data errors.
- **Understandability.** Causality and explanation are not critical, as scientists already understand much of the underlying physics. Also, good structure predictions are more important than the explanation of how they were achieved. On the other hand, reproducibility is important for two reasons. First, others should be able to build on and improve the work. Second, scientists need to compare different protein folding prediction systems to learn their strengths and weaknesses. Even a cursory examination of the release packages of both AlphaFold 2 and RoseTTAFold shows the enormous amount of work data scientists must do so others can reproduce their results.
- **Clear objectives.** Protein folding's objectives are generally clear: accurately predict the correct structure. There is some leeway in how to handle near misses.
- **Toleration of failures.** Errors in protein structure can be tolerated if scientists know their likelihood and can estimate the costs of the extra work they cause. To minimize risk, scientists can often do experimental work to confirm predictions. Reproducibility allows others to find failures before they become more problematic and to suggest fixes.
- **Legal, risk, and ethical issues.** ELSI issues related to protein folding are minimal, though applying that knowledge (e.g., in diagnosing or treating disease) will result in many challenges.

5.5 Analyzing Healthcare Records

As we discussed in Section 4.5, there are immense opportunities to improve human health, but also many complexities. Applying the Analysis Rubric makes this clear.

- **Tractable data.** A vast amount of healthcare record data is kept at medical institutions, testing facilities, insurance companies, and other locations. However, the data is fragmentary, encoded in different ways, and recorded with differing degrees of accuracy. The data must be carefully guarded, due to both data privacy reasons and economic value. As an example of the complexity, a dictionary of different histologic test results alone fills a 388 page document (National Cancer Institute, 2022), and it represents a very small portion of the needed data definitions and standards!
- **A technical approach.** As healthcare records can be used in many different problem domains, technical approaches vary greatly. They center, however, on sophisticated methods informed by critical thinking (Schuemie et al., 2020). There are established best practices, sometimes implemented in standard libraries to reduce the effort in undertaking new research applications.
- **Dependability.** Privacy and security are of foremost concern, due to both ethical needs and legal protections of human healthcare data. As a result, institutions must control their own data carefully and not release it to others without careful safeguards, such as aggregation and anonymization (see more on the latter in Chapter 10 on Dependability). Abuse is not likely, but resilience is very important because errors, even if eventually uncovered by further experimentation, could be very costly.
- **Understandability.** The specific application determines what understanding needs to be provided. If the objective is prediction, as in the HIV-risk example, explanation may be needed. When retrospective, observational studies are used to learn correlations that would catalyze further study in clinical settings, there is a particular need to expose underlying assumptions and perhaps allow reproducibility (see Section 11.3). However, scientific reproducibility is complicated by the complex coding of data and privacy-related limitations on data dissemination. While it is very difficult to show causality from retrospective studies, many will want to use such studies to make healthcare decisions because no better information may be available. For example, by September 2021, the World Health Organization reported over 150 retrospective observational studies on COVID-19 vaccine effectiveness, and, despite limitations, their data was indeed used to inform vaccination policy (Sterne, 2021). (See Section 11.2 for more on causality.)
- **Clear objectives.** These applications usually have clear objectives, although, in the realm of prediction, balancing the likelihood of false positives and false negatives, and setting related thresholds may be difficult. Study design objectives may be open-ended when the goal is creating an interactive analysis platform for gaining insight, though there are statistical risks to this, as discussed in Section 11.4.2.

- **Toleration of failures.** For healthcare records, failure toleration varies. While many observational studies are used to create and hone hypotheses, it is quite important that the hypotheses are of sufficient value to warrant the cost of the ensuing and necessary confirmatory research.
- **Legal, risk, and ethical issues.** Health-related data is significantly regulated, as are study designs involving patient health records. The objectives must take account of compliance with these regulations. There can be great financial and reputational (not to mention safety) risks if data is lost or misused. Ethical issues frequently arise and are best illustrated with questions: Are different elements of society served equitably? If an observational study shows a potential risk to a patient or a population, should that risk be made known even if there is a lack of corroboratory evidence or uncertain potential harm? Should a study, of potentially great value, be undertaken knowing its reproducibility might be in doubt? We present more about these ethical issues throughout Part III.

5.6 Analyzing Predicting COVID-19 Mortality

We will be briefer in this sixth application of the Analysis Rubric, yet still attempt to provide additional color on this important, yet difficult, COVID-19 mortality prediction application.

- **Tractable data.** Data, particularly early in the COVID-19 pandemic, was late in arriving. It was inconsistent across time periods and populations, occasionally erroneous, and very incomplete. COVID-19 modeling certainly did not have location, diagnosis, or health data on individuals or even small subpopulations. Much greater detail (e.g., universal GPS/Bluetooth location tracking and reporting) might have greatly improved modeling capabilities, but would have had unacceptable privacy implications in many societies. Compare and contrast data availability for this application with that for recommendation systems, which have vast amounts of personal, highly detailed click data to make individual recommendations.
- **A technical approach.** There was no shortage of technical approaches, ranging from SEIR models based on disease transmission dynamics to autoregressive machine-learned ones. Some worked well for near-term modeling (e.g., for a period of weeks), but none worked well for longer-term modeling. As suggested above, vastly more data would have made this a very different, and likely more tractable, modeling problem.
- **Dependability.** Privacy and security were not concerns for modelers, but these issues are at the heart of why detailed data was not collected on individuals or

subgroups. Abuse wasn't a problem, mostly because there was no crowd-sourced data. Models were reasonably resilient for near-term projections, but not long-term.

- **Understandability.** Some models were based on disease transmission dynamics. These were explainable and naturally suggested causal relationships. Others were not. To the extent that models would be used to make important public policy decisions, explanation was crucial. The researchers who created the models referenced in the aforementioned Cramer et al. (2021) paper provided for scientific reproducibility.
- **Clear objectives.** The primary objectives were clear. First and foremost, this was to predict the mortality rate from COVID-19, though there was some definitional ambiguity in classifying the cause of death. Secondarily, it would have been excellent if models could have predicted what would happen under different policy assumptions, such as the impact of school openings. While Cramer et al. did not explicitly evaluate model performance for these goals, they are even harder predictions to make, and it is unlikely the models could shed much light on them.
- **Toleration of failures.** Failures are problematic, as they would be expected to have very significant effects on human behavior.
- **Legal, risk, and ethical issues.** There are few, if any, legal issues. The risks of poor forecasts are very real due to their serious impacts on health and welfare.

5.7 The Analysis Rubric in Summary

This chapter illustrated the breadth of considerations for effectively applying data science to a problem.

- **Tractable data** and a **technical approach** are necessary. Implementations must also include a significant focus on **dependability (privacy**, **security**, resistance to **abuse**, and **resilience**). These latter issues may be even more complex than what some might consider the "core" data science.
- Data science applications that must provide **understanding** (for **explanation**, determination of **causality**, or release of data and algorithms to enable **reproducibility**) have added implementation complexity. Many data science techniques do not easily support such objectives.
- While in many cases a data science application's **objectives** may seem clear, when considered in depth, they are hard to pin down, especially given possible unintended consequences. Recall the term **objective function** from operations research. Can we develop objectives with the precision connoted by this term?

- Data science techniques frequently work only probabilistically. If an application cannot **tolerate failures**, the challenges may prove insurmountable.
- Finally, data science applications can cause substantial problems, especially if incorrectly specified or implemented. The Analysis Rubric element covering **legal, societal, and ethical issues** must be very carefully weighed.

Chapter 6
Applying the Analysis Rubric

In this chapter, we pivot towards taking the view of a team building new data science applications. Their work begins when someone creates a concept for a worthwhile and plausibly achievable technique, product, or service. Goals may range from scientific pursuit to commercial gain. They may be motivated by the need to solve an existing problem or by a novel way of extracting information out of an existing data source.

Following conceptualization, the design process typically continues with further analysis and refinement of the initial idea, often with its decomposition into more solvable subcomponents. All of this has the ultimate goal of creating an implementation that delivers value. As we mentioned in the beginning of Chapter 5, most design approaches mix bottom-up and top-down thinking. There are many methodologies for designing new products and services (or even experiments), but they are a topic for a separate book. We recommend the classic *The Design of Everyday Things* by Don Norman (Norman, 2013), who we mentioned earlier as founder of the field of visualization. He can also be credited with moving computer science towards the empirical approaches that truly made computers much easier to use.

Whatever design approach is chosen, teams can realize value from the initial concept by applying the Analysis Rubric to ensure sufficient attention is paid getting the data science right. We now illustrate its use in 26 applications in six different domains, as listed in Table 6.1 through Table 6.6. More naturally solvable problems are towards the top of each table, and more difficult ones towards the bottom.

In the tables:

- A tick does not indicate that the Analysis Rubric is *easily* met, just that there is a path towards satisfying it. For example, web search has working technical solutions, but implementing them requires enormous creativity and labor. (We admit to there being considerable nuance in our assignments of ticks, so there is room for educational dialectic and disagreement.)

Table 6.1 *Transport and mapping applications of data science.*

Transport and mapping applications	Tractable data	Feasible technical approach	Dependability	Understandability	Clear objectives	Toleration of failures	ELSI
Traffic speed	✓	✓	Feasible, but risks	✓	Subtle challenges	Individual but not system-wide	✓
Route finding	✓	✓	Feasible, but risks	✓	Nuances and potential externalities	No egregious errors and not system-wide	A few ELSI issues
Level-5 (fully autonomous) cars	✓	Feasibility unproven	Resilience challenge	Explanation likely needed	Difficult challenges	Great safety required	All difficult

- A table element's few words cannot fully address an application's difficulties in meeting an Analysis Rubric element.

Some applications have considerable prose explanations, but in the grand tradition of "The proof is left to the reader," some descriptions are sparse. The more cursory ones, however, provide a greater opportunity to think through how we filled in the table rows with ticks and other annotations.

6.1 Transport and Mapping Applications of Data Science

Traffic speed estimation (Table 6.1) is a relatively straightforward data science application of great interest to drivers. Starting with implementation-oriented rubrics, data comes from cell phones that know their own location and are networked to data-processing cloud-based servers. The technical approach is based on a system knowing a cell phone's location at the beginning and end of some time interval. With that information, the system can compute the average speed by dividing the distance between those locations by the length of the interval. If captured from enough cell phones, the average data accurately reflects the speed of traffic on a stretch of road.

Privacy and security risks are minimal since this application need not use any identifiable cell phone or owner data. Anything identifiable is extraneous and can be discarded. The implementation resists abuse because spoofing requires physically manipulating many cell phones' locations. However, even this application did prove hackable when a Berlin artist put 99 cell phones in a slow-moving wagon in February 2020 and generated fake traffic jams on Google Maps (Bonifacic,

2020). This undoubtedly reminded the product team to protect against very close proximity, nearly identical location signals. Finally, the algorithm is extremely simple and functional, although it cannot differentiate between a road nobody happens to be driving on and a closed road. This is a **corner condition**, and most computer applications have them. To deal with this, the system designers could add additional data such as road-closing data from municipal or state websites or simply not report traffic speed on roads with insufficient data.

The application is also straightforward in the sense that it has no real need to provide explanation, show causal relationships, or provide reproducible data to others. Failures are tolerable, because the estimates are so much better than nothing. Also, drivers are aware of the likely limitations, since traffic can unpredictably and rapidly change due to an accident, inclement weather, or some unusual event.

The objectives are reasonably clear, but there are nuances to consider. Should the system show the current traffic speed, or should it show the traffic at a predicted arrival time? Should it show traffic speed relative to a road's speed limit (green might mean traveling at the speed limit) or perhaps versus the expected traffic speed (green is pretty good for rush hour)? These are relatively minor differences, but such details need precise definition, the data needed for implementation must be available, and the comparisons must be added to the software.

As for the ELSI review, there seem to be few problems. However, some might be concerned that providing traffic speed estimates tends to make driving easier, consequently reducing the appeal of mass transit. There is potentially some significant risk if the application fails completely, particularly as the driving population becomes more dependent on it.

Overall, this application seems quite straightforward and it is labeled with mostly ticks in the table.

Route finding is a related problem, listed to illustrate its much greater technical challenges and the unexpected complexity of objectives. Addressing the approach first, a classic operations research method would model roads as a network and algorithmically compute a shortest path based on predefined parameters such as speed limits and distances. A data-driven approach might only look at what others have done and use their successful paths (that is, paths that take the least amount of time or fuel for given start and end points). Actual approaches combine analytical techniques from the operations research's graph models with dynamically changing vehicle experience data.

There are many possible enhancements a design team can consider in this combined approach. With real-time data, how should the model (or routing algorithm) adapt when a traffic accident occurs? Should a model be calibrated with historical delay data as of when a route was requested or at a vehicle's predicted arrival time in a particular area? Should the directions account for feedback, that is, the impact on future traffic of current drivers following new traffic directions? How can a direction-finding system include creative driver paths taken from the history of travel – combining these driver-found solutions with those proposed by a model? Route-finding systems are increasingly using these hybrid approaches.

While an *obvious* goal is to minimize delays, property owners on quiet side streets might not want them used as overflow capacity for major highways. While not addressing this particular issue, Google (in the spring of 2021) added new possible objectives to its navigation system so users can prioritize safer or more fuel-efficient routes.

There is also the question of priority. Is a system first-come, first-served, or should buses, trucks, multiple-occupant, or lower-emissions vehicles, or even higher-paying vehicles, have priority?

From a failure perspective, small errors are fine, but it is not fine to direct a vehicle onto a one-way road against traffic or to send a vehicle onto a road that is closed. Furthermore, the complete breakdown of vehicle routing systems is growing problematic as drivers become increasingly dependent on them. Breakdowns could occur due to application failures, cloud infrastructure failures, attacks on the GPS system, etc., though there is enormous redundancy built into each component.

Level-5 (fully autonomous) cars are a complex application that incorporates many data science components built from many kinds of datasets and technical approaches.

Self-driving cars need to process and act on many forms of data representing road networks, lanes, interchanges, danger areas, traffic bottlenecks, etc. Bespoke sensing activities (such as Google or Bing street mapping cars) and car-mounted sensors can provide much of what is needed. Important data can also be gained from the many vehicles that have accurate location data. As we have observed, vehicular location data is extremely useful in showing traffic speed, but geotraces can be of even greater use for training autonomous driving models.

Self-driving cars can clearly incorporate machine learning techniques, which have proven very successful in object recognition. Examples include detecting curbs, stop signs, bicycles, or turning vehicles. Autonomous vehicles also need to learn how human drivers react to the sight of such objects and many other driving situations.

This application has significant dependability requirements. While privacy issues are not particularly different from other applications that know user location, there are significant security issues. If bad actors gain control, individually or collectively, cars (which some liken to two-ton projectiles) can do great damage. Some people might even try to bait (or, perhaps, abuse) a self-driving car into behaving improperly. Algorithms must be resilient in the face of many unanticipated conditions. They must respond appropriately to human drivers and their often iffy driving habits.

The objectives are difficult to get right. As two examples, consider first balancing arrival time versus risk tolerance, then determining right of way in complex situations. Autonomous vehicles may need to provide explanations for their actions, especially if they get into an accident with property loss or injury. In particular, they may need to justify their action as the best possible under the circumstances. While no systems (humans) are perfect, self-driving cars are very intolerant of failure. Many errors have extreme legal, ethical, and financial risks.

We don't know if present approaches are sufficient to allow for Level-5 Automation (fully attention-free self-driving cars in all conditions) (US Department of Transportation, n.d.). However, they almost certainly will allow autonomous cars to operate under specific conditions (Level 4) with better safety than cars with human drivers. However this plays out, data-science-based techniques will continue to make driving safer for all.

6.2 Web and Entertainment Applications of Data Science

There are many data science applications on the Web, in part because they are so natural given the large bodies of data stored and accumulated from users. Because of our familiarity with them and the previous web-related applications of spelling correction, speech recognition, and recommendation engines, our explanations of the examples in Table 6.2 are more succinct. In particular, news and video recommendations are similar to music recommendations, although they have more profound ELSI considerations.

Identifying copyrighted material became important when video sharing on the Web became prevalent in the 2000s. If sites could do this, they could then offer copyright holders the opportunity to take down or perhaps monetize their videos. When Google purchased YouTube, it quickly confronted the copyright problem and developed ContentID, a matching system. It uses machine learning to match uploaded content to previously registered (and provided) copyrighted material. A match triggers a notification to the copyright holder and makes the alleged infringer ineligible to receive advertising revenue. The objective is clear: to reduce copyright infringement.

Abuse is the biggest implementation challenge, as copyright infringers can attempt to camouflage material or bad actors can claim copyright they don't

Table 6.2 *Web and entertainment applications of data science.*

Web and entertainment applications	Tractable data	Feasible technical approach	Depend-ability	Understand-ability	Clear objectives	Toleration of failures	ELSI
Identifying copy-righted videos	✓	✓, but not foolproof	Abuse	✓	✓	✓	✓
In-session video game personalization	✓	✓	Abuse	✓	Balance tricky	✓	Ethics, financial
Targeted or personalized ads	✓	✓	Privacy, security, abuse	✓	Difficult	✓	Legal, risk, ethics
Video recommendations	✓	✓	✓	✓	Ambiguity	✓	Complex
Web search	✓, but voluminous	✓, but very many techniques	Privacy, security, abuse	✓	Significant nuance	Certain failures serious	Legal, risk, ethics
News feed recommendations	Fake news	Diverse challenges	Resilience, abuse	Increasingly important	Significant nuance	Certain failures serious	Legal, risk, ethics

possess. To deal with abuse, YouTube has a dispute resolution system with human oversight. As a truly unanticipated result of ContentID, police officers sometimes play copyrighted music to prevent recordings by bystanders during confrontations from being posted to YouTube (Schiffer & Robertson, 2021). The inclusion of that music makes it very likely that copyright holders will ask for the video be removed.

Otherwise, implementation is straightforward. The application is reasonably tolerant of failure, as uploaders or copyright owners can dispute the automated system's answers and request human arbiters make the final decision. The system appears to be in conformance with legal structures and has few ethical concerns.

In-session video game personalization can utilize game and player data to make video games more compelling, and perhaps more addictive as well. This is most feasible with games that have probabilistically occurring events (a certain card being dealt) or when the computer is a player. The data and technical approaches exist. However, there are dependability (in particular, abuse) challenges, hard-to-define objectives, and ELSI issues, e.g., relating to how addictive a game should be. There will be more on this, particularly in Chapter 12.

Targeted or personalized ads is one of data science's most prevalent web applications. Targeted ads may be shown when someone searches the Web, shops online, or views entertainment or news sites. This application has some commonality with recommendation systems, as its goal is to place (or recommend) an ad that meets some goals. Ads have been a primary revenue source for many internet companies, which try to make *personalized ads* beneficial to these four different constituencies, which are also illustrated in Figure 6.1:

- The **consumer** viewing the ad, who wants to see pleasing, relevant, and useful ads.
- The **publisher**, such as a periodical, a video site, or a blogger, who receives revenue for providing ad space and viewership. They want ads that maximize revenue but don't detract from their site's value.
- The **advertisers** who place ads to enhance their image or to sell products. An advertiser often desires a particular target audience so it can customize its ads, making them more effective.
- The **advertising platform** that coordinates the matching: the "right" ad for the "right" user on the "right" site in the "right" context. The advertising system makes a commission based on the value of the ads placed or clicked-on, how many people see or click on an ad, or perhaps even how much they buy. In some

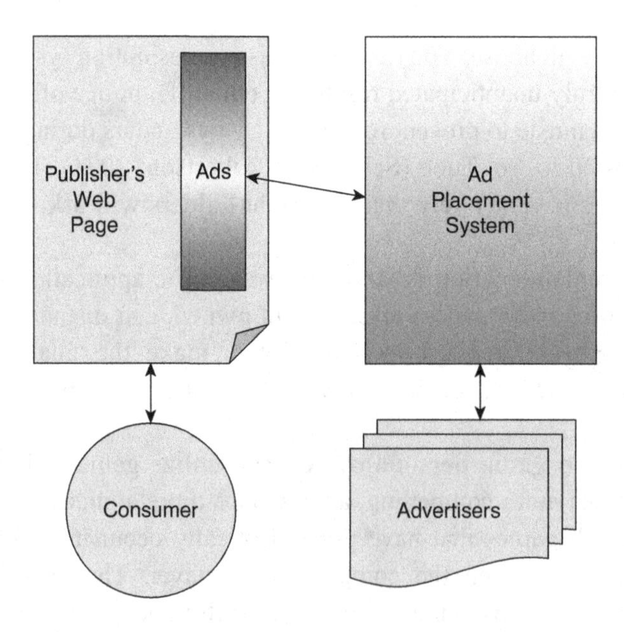

Figure 6.1 Advertisers bid to have their ads inserted into publishers' web pages; an ad placement platform chooses the best ads to be shown to each consumer.

instances, such as search and social networking advertising, the ad placement system and the publisher may be the same.

Vast amounts of data are available for ads personalization, with its type depending on the particular situation. Data may include geographical location, recently viewed websites, purchases, and (in the case of closed systems such as search engines or Facebook) detailed information on interests or searches. Advertisers have data that powers systems that provide automated recommendations on advertising budgets, keyword selection, and ad placement. Recently, there has been considerable evolution in how to gather data, due to public and regulatory concerns, and it seems likely that the role of web cookies will decline.

There are many technical approaches for generating a recommended ad from that data, often based on machine learning based using deep neural networks. Requirements must inform the technical approach, because users, advertisers, and publishers will tolerate only some mistargeted advertisements.

The engineering complexity of a personalized ad system is very high. Once appropriate ads have been identified, online auctions direct ads to the buyers who find the space most valuable. For any given query or page view, the potential ads must be identified and the auctions run so quickly that the user does not notice any delay in page load. Advertising systems may need to handle thousands of queries per second.

Perhaps targeted advertisements' greatest implementation challenge relates to dependability concerns. In part, this is due to the significant privacy and security issues when vast amounts of personal data are applied to a problem. As further discussed in Section 10.1, not only does the data need to be protected from disclosure, it cannot be used in ways a user would feel are spooky. However, increased privacy protections could also decrease competition, as discussed in Section 10.1.5. In addition to privacy issues, the vast amounts of money associated with advertising systems invite financial and other forms of abuse.

Turning to the requirements rubrics, advertising can be opaque, with little need for explanation. But there is the complex question of how to balance the needs of the consumer, publisher, advertiser, and advertising system. For example, should near-term site revenue or long-term customer satisfaction be optimized? How is revenue allocated between the publisher of the site showing the ad and the system brokering the advertisements?

Ethical, legal, and societal considerations also come into play in setting objectives, for example:

- If the objective were solely to maximize clicks on an ad (in the near term), deceitful ads that practiced "bait and switch" would be truly overwhelming.

- If the objective were only to sell a product or maximize economic activity, there would be no limits on advertising. But protecting consumers is also a concern: advertising of medicines is carefully controlled, and much of the world has banned cigarette ads, optimizing health over economic activity.
- To reduce foreign influence on political systems, there may be laws that restrict political ads paid for by foreign entities.
- Even more generally, some argue that ads elicit consumer behavior not in consumers' true self-interest. Ads encourage consumers to overindulge in alcohol, tobacco, and unhealthy food, or to spend beyond their means. Nobel Prize-winning economists Akerlof and Shiller in their book *Phishing for Phools* suggest regulation (Akerlof & Shiller, 2015).
- Advertising payments may support the creation and display of harmful content, or the ads themselves may be harmful even if not illegal.
- There are financial risks if the ads are not seen by actual potential customers due to insufficient system-wide abuse prevention.

Chapter 12 addresses the challenges in setting objectives, and Part III, in aggregate, addresses many other challenges. Despite them all, data-science-driven advertising has been a very powerful addition to commerce and benefited the public by paying for much of the growth of highly popular and useful web services.

Web search makes the Web's vast agglomeration of data easily accessible to users. We expect search to *locate* websites possessing desired information, to *navigate* to a specific website, to *return* an answer, or perhaps even to *perform* a transaction, such as finding a route from city A to city B (Broder, 2002). Web search engines are critically important because they are a frequent gateway to the Web.

Web search, like music recommendation, relies on three broad sources of data:

- **content** – the words on a page and the concepts behind them;
- **metadata** – facts about the page, the reputation of the website hosting the page, and facts about the links to this page; and
- **user reactions** – popularity of a page in general, or as an answer to a specific query.

Abuse is a significant problem. All webmasters want their websites to be ranked highly, and some achieve high rankings by providing quality content. But some "web spammers" try to abuse the system by creating fake web links and manipulating the system in other ways. Search engines need to stay on top of each new type of manipulation and reward good content, not manipulation. Some complex issues arise in setting objectives:

- Search objectives may be subjective and conflicting: Designers need to consider how to arrive at answers for political queries and what balance of results should be presented. Should the website's response speed influence the ranking? Should a search engine try to return search results from multiple sites? Should search engines provide answers when they can, or restrict themselves to returning page links?

- Many ethical questions that impact the objectives also arise, such as: What focus should there be on the source's likely veracity? Should the searcher's pre-existing views be taken into account?

Failure tolerance is complex. When search engines return links to web pages, the searcher knows that some links will be excellent, but others may not be. Thus, search engines are tolerant of some forms of failures. For example, most users will understand if the query "cataract" returns information on eye diseases rather than waterfalls, and refine their search accordingly. However, users may not tolerate other types of errors. For example, a search engine's reputation would decline greatly if even a small percentage of its results were truly atrocious.

For example, in 2004 a Google search on "miserable failure" returned "George Bush" due to Google's then-inability to prevent a kind of abuse, termed a "Google Bomb." For this reason, many search engines use algorithms, tuned with considerable human labor, to prevent very poor results. This reminds us that data science approaches should consider rare downsides and mitigate the effect of bad actors.

Video recommendations and **news feed recommendations** are important data science applications that share some characteristics with music recommendations as described in Section 4.3 and Section 5.3. Both build off of similar techniques, but there are two key differences:

- The scope of their corpora varies. As presented, music recommendations focused on a relatively constrained corpus as defined by the music publishing industry. However, video and news feed recommendation applications have far larger and more irregular corpora, particularly if there is user-supplied content. Publishers are highly motivated to have their content viewed, and they sometimes go to extreme lengths to game recommendation systems.
- The individual and societal impact of video and news content is far greater. While all content creators want their content to be seen, many who post video or news stories have significant political goals and go to considerable efforts to achieve them. Recommendation engines have their own complex goals (e.g., perhaps to moderate content or suppress fake news) that are both challenging to define and to meet.

Because of these two differences, all of the Analysis Rubric elements are more complex to satisfy. We will discuss these applications' many challenges in Part III and summarize some ethical issues relating to news recommendations in Chapter 7.

6.3 Medicine and Public Health Applications of Data Science

Table 6.3 lists several such health applications, supplementing the two presented in Chapter 4 and Chapter 5. We will discuss three briefly, but devote more attention to disease diagnosis, genome-wide association studies (GWAS), and understanding the cause of a disease.

Table 6.3 *Medicine and public health applications of data science.*

Medicine and public health applications	Tractable data	Feasible technical approach	Depend-ability	Understand-ability	Clear objectives	Toleration of failures	ELSI
Mobility reporting by subregion during quarantine	✓	✓	Tricky privacy	✓	✓	✓	Perhaps, ethics
Vaccine distribution optimization – when limited supply	✓	Plausible ✓	✓	"Why" is needed	Numerous, conflicting	✓	Ethics
Identify disease outbreak from aggregated user inputs	✓	Plausible ✓	Abuse, resilience, privacy	Explanation, reproducibility	✓	✓	Perhaps, ethics
Disease diagnosis	Training data difficult to obtain	✓ for some diseases	Resilience	Reproducibility, explanation, possibly causality	Agreeing on error rates	Wrong diagnoses very harmful	Legal, risk, ethics
Genome-wide association study	Difficult to obtain	Complicated by confounders, complexity	Privacy, security	Reproducibility, explanation, possibly causality	Agreeing on error rates	✓	Ethics
Understanding cause of a disease	Difficult to obtain	Complex	Privacy, security	Reproducibility, explanation, possibly causality	Agreeing on error rates	✓	Ethics

Mobility reporting was introduced by Google in 2020 during the early COVID-19 quarantines and used individuals' location data to chart regional movement trends over time. Its reports were broken down not only by region but also by categories such as retail and recreation, groceries and pharmacies, parks, transit stations, workplaces, and residences (Google, n.d.-a). Google engineers felt these reports would show society's acceptance of government recommendations, and perhaps catalyze safer behaviors or better governmental responses (Aktay et al., 2020). These were referenced by over 2,000 scholarly papers as of September 2021.

The application uses similar data to the traffic speed application of Section 6.1, though mobility reporting needs to solve much harder privacy issues. After all, its objective is to report on travel patterns, but to do so without divulging anything that could be used to infer private information about any individual or to exacerbate societal divides.

In addition to Google, other organizations introduced tools that showed changes in mobility. Apple introduced a tool based on counting the number of requests made to Apple Maps for directions, stratified by mode of transportation. Facebook provided mobility data based on the number of geographic tiles an individual moved to, relative to a baseline. Other datasets were also used as a proxy for mobility (Nuño et al., 2020).

Vaccine distribution optimization involves balancing a truly wide variety of competing objectives against the likely operational success of achieving rapid vaccine uptake. Objectives might include minimizing mortality, supporting childhood education or economic activity, ensuring caregivers stay safe and willing to work, demonstrating fairness across multiple subgroups, being politically expedient, and many more.

Models must take into account the likelihood of supply or distribution constraints (e.g., refrigeration), the predilection of subpopulations to accept vaccines, the likelihood that vaccines prevent disease transmission, and even the effects of influencers – who might not themselves be a priority but might positively influence others. There are many papers evaluating different strategies, for example, this one by Bubar et al. (2021). Modeling approaches for reducing vaccine hesitancy would seem to be particularly difficult.

Identifying disease outbreaks using crowdsourced data has potential value. However, we defer this discussion to Section 11.3 on reproducibility challenges, to allow us to focus on the problems created by this application's opaque nature.

Disease diagnosis represents an opportunity to use large-scale training data and machine learning to provide new diagnostics. While there have been specific tests for diseases since at least the late 1800s, when Gram staining started using stains to classify bacteria, it is ever more possible to create new classifiers using neural networks on new forms of sensor data. Data diagnostic tests of many varieties, including X-rays, MRI (magnetic resonance imaging) scans, and multispectral cameras, can then be classified to carry out or aid diagnoses (Shen et al., 2017). In fact, there are now published reports indicating that some techniques are approaching human capabilities (Esteva et al., 2017; Nabulsi et al., 2021).

Privacy and security issues can be minimized by anonymizing training data and protecting patient imagery and diagnoses the same way as healthcare data is protected. There is little likelihood of abuse, but resilience is very challenging, as errors are very problematic. False negatives (or underdiagnosis) result in untreated disease, and false positives (or overdiagnosis) cause patient anxiety, financial costs, and potentially unnecessary treatment. See Section 11.4.4 for more on false positives.

Reproducibility of results is certainly needed and seemingly feasible. Explanation and causality would be very beneficial for acceptance by both medical professionals and patients. Unfortunately, achieving these is difficult, particularly if the primary technique is machine-learned image classification.

While the objective appears clear, its complexity relates to the toleration and distribution of errors. While human doctors are imperfect, data science approaches must nearly always make the right call. Society at large and its legal frameworks are likely to hold automated systems to a higher-than-human standard.

Medical regulations, as well as the liability and ethical considerations relating to errors and the associated financial risks, make the ELSI element rife with complexity.

Genome-wide association studies (GWAS), according to Francis Collins, the former long-serving leader of the US National Institutes of Health, are defined in this way: "A genome-wide association study is an approach used in genetics research to *associate* specific genetic variations with particular diseases. The method involves scanning the genomes from many different people and looking for genetic markers that can be used to predict the presence of a disease. Once such genetic markers are identified, they can be used to understand how genes contribute to the disease and develop better prevention and treatment strategies" (Collins, n.d.; Eisenstadt, 2017). For example, GWAS has been used to show an association between certain variants located in the FTO gene and an increase in the energy-storing white adipocytes (fat cells) that contribute to obesity (Claussnitzer et al., 2015).

Strictly speaking, GWAS refers to the gathering of genomic mutation data and associating that with a label of interest (e.g., disease state). However, a typical published GWAS study will not only use these data as the basis for a scientific result, but also augment them with other qualitative and quantitative research. This includes the stratification of the population and researchers' domain expertise in order to suggest not only correlations, but also ideally mechanistic or causal associations. This is both to reduce the risk of time-wasting, expensive, spurious results and to speed the translation of positive results to treatments.

More generally, diseases may have many contributing causes (genetic predisposition, and specific exposures and patient activity over a long period), making the underlying analysis even more challenging. Causal sequences may be very long, with some stimulus A influencing B1 and B2 in the same way; B2 influencing C; and C influencing D (say, mortality). By just looking at correlations, it would be easy to conclude that, if B1 were somehow controlled, D might also be controlled, but this would likely not be true. B1 is not in the causal chain, and also is a **confounder**, a non-causal correlate only associated with disease. Section 9.1 and particularly Section 11.2 have further discussions on causality.

Against the data Analysis Rubric element, GWAS requires genomic and phenotypic data for sure. It may also need to contain other information about individuals, such as age or race. They may also need historical information covering diet, exercise, environmental risks, stress levels, and communicable disease exposure, as these can trigger gene expression. There may be strong reasons for the data to represent a complete cross-section of the society being studied. Health data is often imprecise, inaccurate, and incomparable across health centers or populations, and is subject to many regulatory protections. All of this makes its use difficult.

Even if all the data were available, a GWAS study might require an exceedingly complex model. This is due to the possibility of delayed impacts (e.g., hereditary, late-onset Parkinson or Tay–Sachs disease), complex causal pathways, and the previously mentioned risks related to confounders.

Relating to the dependability Analysis Rubric element, health-related data science applications require laser focus on minimizing the risk of public exposure of private data. They must use the anonymization and encryption techniques described later in this book. In the case of genetic data, exposure not only affects individuals, but may also adversely affect their relatives.

GWAS results almost always trigger much additional work to pin down causality and find therapeutic agents, so great care in engineering and statistics must be taken to minimize the risks of errors. False positives are particularly prevalent. A positive association, if not carefully promulgated, can result in useless or even harmful effects. However, systems may not need to pay too much attention to abuse unless there is significant crowdsourcing of information.

At a minimum, systems need to show their evidence for associating particular genomes, and perhaps other factors, with disease. It is impossible for a system to decree "trust me." The biomedical sciences strongly value peer review, so GWAS studies would be under great pressure to publish the methods, the data, and the detailed semantic understanding needed for its use. However, this is always difficult given the underlying data's ownership and privacy issues and the complexity of the analysis.

GWAS has reasonably clear high-level objectives, though there may be ambiguity in seeing the right threshold of association versus complete explanations to minimize wasted downstream efforts.

There are laws, some with significant financial and other penalties, governing how research data is used. Others govern how human research subjects both are informed of risks and have to consent to participation. There is significant risk to researchers, to their institutions, and to human participants should problems occur. The Belmont Principles address many of the relevant ethical issues.

Understanding the cause of a disease represents a tremendous opportunity for data science. It has the ability to aggregate information on disease incidence and on a growing number of underlying, potentially causative factors, including, though certainly not limited to, genetic information.

However, gathering the needed breadth of consistent and comparable data faces considerable challenges. Truly measuring and recording all the potential disease-causing factors would have to deal with extreme privacy and security issues. Measures already in place to protect such data add significant complexity to medical research data science applications (Institute of Medicine of the National Academies, 2009) and even more measures might be needed. Abuse is unlikely to be an issue, but resilience is important. The technical approach may be very difficult due to the breadth of the problem. Among other things, many factors (e.g., environmental ones) may take years or decades to cause disease.

Objectives are clear. Failures are acceptable if they are not too likely or costly and if results can be independently confirmed.

In the category of understandability, scientists need reproducibility to validate results. Beyond our previous medical examples' need for explanation, this application is (by definition) trying to show causality to enable development of good public health measures, prophylactics, or cures. For example, for many years, correlation between coffee drinkers and cancer implicated coffee as a carcinogen. But researchers eventually concluded that coffee consumption was correlated with cigarette smoking, and smoking turned out to be the "smoking gun." See Section 11.2 for more on causality. Applying data science to understand the causes of disease is challenging across all Analysis Rubric elements.

6.4 Science-Oriented Applications of Data Science

As discussed in Section 2.1 and Section 4.4, data science can be of enormous value to science. At a minimum, it can provide the intuition for creating more and better hypotheses. It can also generate new knowledge and contribute to understanding causality. In this section, we discuss two more examples of using data science in the scientific realm (see Table 6.4).

Determining the historical temperature of the universe is a scientific application that has confirmed the universe has warmed 10-fold by some metrics (Chiang et al., 2020; Williams, 2020). Scientists have determined this by amassing data from the Sloan Digital Sky Survey (SDSS) and the European Space Agency's Planck Infrared Astronomical Satellite. As background, every day the SDSS accumulates 200 gigabytes of data, all of which is eventually made public, so there are no privacy or security issues. More than 5,800 scientific papers using this data have been published.

In this case, scientists gathered two million spectroscopic redshift (measuring the speed at which celestial objects are moving) references from the SDSS and combined these with sky intensity maps (which indicate temperature). Since objects moving faster are further away, and their measurements are from longer ago, the scientists thus had a technical approach for measuring the change in temperature over time. In this instance, the scientists' deep theoretical understanding lets them apply big data and get their desired results. There was no problem with reproducibility because the astrophysical data was publicly available and the scientists could publish their models.

Weather or earthquake prediction are data science applications based on different physical principles, though, like the astrophysics example, they center around forecasting. Weather predictions are now useful enough that we rely on

Table 6.4 *Science-oriented applications of data science.*

Science-oriented applications	Tractable data	Feasible technical approach	Dependability	Understandability	Clear objectives	Toleration of failures	ELSI
Determining the historical temperature of the universe	✓	✓	✓	Reproducibility	✓	✓	✓
Weather or earthquake prediction	Insufficient sensor coverage	Very complex problem	✓	Explanation, reproducibility, causality	✓	Some harmful	Risk

them daily, but earthquake prediction has achieved only limited success. For somewhat distant earthquakes, systems can provide seconds of advanced warning since electronic broadcasts travel faster than seismic waves.

For weather forecasting, it has been demonstrated that more sensor data, such as temperature, pressure, and/or wind data, at more locations, improves forecasting. Seismologists believe this may also be true in their domain. Weather prediction models are hugely complex, and small errors in the measurements or the models can cause large changes in the predictions. Furthermore, small differences in an event's location (e.g., the exact path of a tornado) can result in very different effects.

For earthquakes, modeling is at a very early stage, though hopefully machine learning approaches will prove useful (The Economist, 2022b). For new data science approaches, scientists will want reproducibility to verify the results. If data science leads to new scientific results, providing explanation or demonstrating causality may also be important. If society were to become dependent on earthquake predictions, ELSI Analysis Rubric elements could be of considerable importance. The risk from mistakes could be considerable, in both economic and human costs. However, at least these scientific examples have no privacy risks.

6.5 Financial Services Applications of Data Science

The financial services sector is a huge part of the economy. In the US, it contributes about 10% to GDP and includes sectors such as banking, investing, insurance, lending, and more. Prediction problems abound because of the enormous value in knowing a future interest rate, an equity or bond price, the likelihood of a claim or a default, or even a customer's real identity. Good predictions strongly reward those who can make them, encourage safe practices because of insurance pricing incentives, and may benefit society at large by guiding capital to areas of higher returns.

To support prediction models, companies and governments are capturing ever-growing amounts of data, including detailed information on customers, businesses, markets, and financial transactions. Some countries, such as India and China, are pushing hard for almost all transactions to be digital to enable easy capturing of almost all financial data.

Very large datasets coupled with statistical and machine learning techniques are already used to evaluate individual investments, create portfolios of those investments, and analyze their risk under varying assumptions. Data science applications may provide insight to analysts and portfolio managers who then apply their own discretionary judgment. Alternatively, algorithmic investors might also use them to draw conclusions and execute investment choices, as described by the book *Inside the Black Box* (Narang, 2013). Recently, consumer finance has been affected by automation with the advent of "Robo Advisors" providing individual investors automated investment advice.

Data science is also used to detect fraud and to ensure compliance with anti-fraud regulations, such as "know-your-customer" identification rules. Its tools predict health, mortality, and property/casualty risks, and thus contribute to pricing insurance policies. Data science helps predict customer wants and needs, thereby better tailoring marketing campaigns and recommendations.

However, even with voluminous data, many of the financial services' data science problems are hard to solve. Much of the data requires immense processing to make it comparable. Some data, such as stock prices, must be available nearly instantly. Furthermore, in some finance applications, market dynamics can rapidly change and invalidate previously useful predictive models.

Almost all financial services problems use confidential customer data, and so have significant privacy and data security risks. There are also security risks beyond data loss, because bad actors or nation states have motivation to spy on or attack individual institutions or the financial sector at large. Below, we'll say a few more words on each element of Table 6.5.

Table 6.5 *Financial services and economic applications of data science.*

Financial services and economic applications	Tractable data	Feasible technical approach	Dependa-bility	Understand-ability	Clear objectives	Toleration of failures	ELSI
Stock market investment selection and trading	Depends on approach	Complex, but there are successes	Depends on approach	✓ opacity may be acceptable	✓	Certain failures intolerable	Legal, risk, ethics
Underwriting/ pricing of property/ casualty insurance	✓	✓	Privacy, security, abuse, resilience	Explanation	Competing objectives	✓	Legal, risk, ethics
"Know-your-customer" warnings for financial entities	✓	✓	Tricky privacy, security	Explanation	✓	Some, not all	Legal, risk, ethics
Country-wide economic prediction	Insufficient data	Feasibility unproven	Privacy, security, abuse, resilience	Explanation, reproducibility, causality	✓	Probably	Legal, risk, ethics

In **stock market investment selection and trading**, data scientists with specialized finance-related knowledge, called quants, modelers, or researchers, choose datasets and create models that recommend trading financial instruments to construct profitable portfolios. These activities are often referred to as **quant trading** or *algorithmic approaches to investment*.

Much of the vast and diverse quantity of data has low predictive value. Market-oriented prediction problems are game-theoretic in that other profit-seeking players may change the financial situation before one can profit from a prediction. In high-speed trading domains, predictions are made and acted on in microseconds.

In addition to the most obvious task of **forecasting** a tradeable entity's price at some future time, quants consider numerous other factors, including the following:

1. The market impact of the trade itself. If a firm is buying or selling a large amount of something, buy orders tend to raise the price and sell orders have the opposite effect. This **slippage** results in a lower trade value.
2. The way the trade should be executed. The proper setting of the size and timing of orders can benefit the prices paid or received.
3. The portfolio optimization so that its individual components' aggregated value has a higher likelihood of achieving investor goals.

There are many approaches to creating prediction and optimization algorithms. Earlier algorithms were based on statistical regression, but today they increasingly involve machine learning. Models are validated by back-testing them on historical data and forward-testing them on simulated future scenarios.

But it is difficult to know how well the simulations will correspond to the actual future. Model development is challenging because investors want to (a) maximize expected returns, (b) avoid big negative swings, and (c) have some resilience to unforeseen circumstances, such as significant changes in investor sentiment. Certain quant challenges, such as price forecasting, are particularly prone to such changes in sentiment, while others, such as trade execution, are less so. When sentiment changes are rapid and broad, they are called **regime change**, a topic that Section 9.1 addresses in more depth.

Algorithms do not have to provide insight as to why they work, though investors would certainly prefer to know. Objectives are usually quite clear. Poor results have some degree of acceptability, since investment returns are known to be probabilistic. However, certain types of errors require regulatory disclosure that cause both reputational and financial risk. For example, firms cannot exceed certain ownership limits on securities or commodities, and they must disclose errors they make. Most investment activities are highly regulated, meaning many seemingly predictive models may be off-limits, with serious legal risks for violations.

There are ethical risks, for instance, in achieving justice. Specifically, data science makes it possible to create products that lure naive investors while giving professional investors opportunities to achieve high returns from mining their data and mistakes. This can result in potentially undesirable wealth transfers.

Underwriting/pricing of property/casualty insurance is a data science problem with a long history dating back to antiquity. The 17th century saw increasing use of math and data in evaluating risks, with the actuarial profession being formalized in the mid-18th century. Today, vastly more data is available for predicting risks and pricing insurance policies, but it is often hard to assemble. Additionally, regulations may prohibit using certain data, such as zip codes for property/casualty insurance or gender for automotive insurance (because using them could lead to unfair bias).

Technical approaches abound, given large amounts of historical data and since, for insurance, the past is usually a predictor of the future.[12] The heavy dependence on individual client data may cause even greater security and privacy challenges than it does in investment management applications, and approaches must be resilient in the face of unexpected behavior. Abuse typically relates to guarding against false claims or fraudulent representations during application processes.

Objectives are quite complex and must balance at least all of the following:

- pricing decisions that will win customers;
- expected profitability margins;
- overall risk to an insurer of specific portfolios (given an insurer may not want too many eggs in one basket); and
- equitable treatment of subpopulations.

Insurance typically cannot use opaque approaches due to needed regulatory reviews. As with investing, losses are inevitable, but certain failures are unacceptable. Legal and ethical issues abound, certainly when considering the pros and cons of different regulatory regimes. As an example, European Union (EU) regulations require auto insurance products not to consider gender, though young men and young women drivers presumably have differential risk.

Know-your-customer (KYC) compliance regulations are part of anti-money-laundering laws to prevent criminal money management use of the financial system. KYC obviously begins with the ability to accurately identify a criminal. This may be more accurately determined by the pattern analysis of activities than from what an account application states. With vast amounts of transactional data

[12] While the past is *usually* a predictor, climate change could increase property claims, and increased human lifespan could be increasing costs for insurance such as long-term care insurance.

available, both hard-coded algorithms and machine learning approaches to clustering and prediction can be applied to warn about suspicious behavior.

We need transparency since regulators want to know financial institutions are applying proper due diligence. Guarding against abuse is what this is all about, and this anti-abuse system is itself subject to abuse! Inevitably there are major legal, risk, and ethics challenges. For example, KYC systems will inevitably have occasional false positives that point a finger at innocents. Thus, it is ethically crucial for different subpopulations to be treated fairly. Additionally, automated systems require human appeals channels to resolve problematic results.

Country-wide economic predictions might be better made using the torrent of data and techniques used by financial services firms. While this is in the tradition of econometric forecasting, predictions might be more timely and accurate if guided by far more real-time data.

In 2009, Varian and Choi wrote about using aggregate information on Google Search traffic to better predict sector activities (e.g., retail or home sales) that are material to an economy as a whole (Choi & Varian, 2012). The trend towards using more data has continued (Einav & Levin, 2014), and in 2021 *The Economist* summarized its growing importance in "The Real-Time Revolution" (The Economist, 2021b).

Perhaps, as economies are increasingly digitized, individual transaction data could be utilized for more timely and specific economic prediction and, perhaps, more accurate and effective governmental interventions. One can almost, in a science fiction sense, envision a world where policy makers have a large real-time economic dashboard with economic controls and predicted impacts of all changes. It is not our goal to invent such a system, but rather to map such an application against the Analysis Rubric.

Trying to use all economic transactions would result in a truly huge amount of data. The needed models would be very complex and hard to test, in part because an economy has so many different possible configurations and is affected by so many different stimuli. As with investment optimization, changes in consumer or business sentiment may cause regime change and render existing models unpredictive. Dependability issues are extreme; there are the risks of exposing all citizens' transaction data, security attacks that cause economic warfare, and the resilience problem of the "Oh no, we forgot to include that!" effect, as well as many others.

Opaque systems that are neither reproducible nor comprehensible are probably unacceptable. For example, economic policy makers would find it very hard to act on economic predictions to change interest or tax rates without first understanding them. While it is easy to find correlates with economic growth, causality, especially over the long term, is hard to show. Forecasting would seem to have clear objectives, but there would be difficulty in determining the requisite granularity and necessary accuracy. While forecasting will always be imprecise, some failures would have catastrophic effects affecting entire nations. There is no end to the legal and ethical risk.

We end this section on financial services by noting its data science applications are continually evolving with the growth in data, computational capability, and machine learning. The final example was more of a grand challenge research problem pushed to the limit. But there is no doubt that the increasing amount of data coming from the economy's digitization will lead to significant changes in economic forecasting.

6.6 Social, Political, and Governmental Applications of Data Science

Governments provide diverse and critical services to vast numbers of people. Operating at scale, there is great opportunity to sense opinions, needs, successes, and outcomes, and to optimize results. Possible uses range from political campaigns to operations of state agencies and include the domains of economics, health, education, and more (see Table 6.6).

Table 6.6 *Government service and political applications of data science.*

Government service and political applications	Tractable data	Feasible technical approach	Dependability	Understandability	Clear objectives	Toleration of failures	ELSI
Targeting in political campaigns	✓	✓	Privacy, security, abuse	✓	Competing objectives	✓	Legal, ethics
Detect maintenance needs	Insufficient sensor coverage	✓	Security, resilience	✓	Complex due to prioritization	Certain failures intolerable	Legal, risk, ethics
Personalized reading tutor	✓	✓	Privacy, security, abuse, resilience	Explanation	✓	✓	Legal, risk, ethics
Criminal sentencing and parole decision-making	✓ but may be hard to assemble	✓	Resilience	Explanation, reproducibility	Conflicting	Individual freedom and societal welfare	Legal, risk, ethics

Targeting in political campaigns refers to the interest that political candidates have in knowing what positions appeal to voters, which communication channels to use, and even what exact words to use to disseminate their positions. Furthermore, candidates do not want to waste resources either in areas they are sure to win or in those which are hopeless for them. In systems where candidates need to fund-raise, data science is critical for helping candidates focus their messages as well as the target audiences to raise the most money. For better or for worse, big data allows candidates to truly slice and dice populations and send out targeted messages to best appeal to fine-grained constituencies (Nickerson & Rogers, 2014).

Significant amounts of data are already available. In the US, data begins with voter registries from which campaigns can get voting rolls (including party registration) and historical data on when individuals have voted, though NOT for whom they voted. Political parties and both not-for-profit and for-profit entities augment this data with additional individual and aggregate district data. For example, campaigns commission polls to learn voter positions and interests.

The application space is broad with many applicable clustering and prediction techniques. For example, campaigns predict the likelihood of sympathetic voters within a small region and then target voter registration drives to those regions with mostly sympathetic voters. There are the usual privacy and security issues with some personal data, though campaigns can buy recommendations from others and possibly avoid directly holding too much data. Abuse is increasingly likely, even by nation-state actors seeking only to create chaos.

Given Western democracies' extreme focus on elections, election-related data science is a fertile area for seeing how objective functions vary:

- Candidates may have different goals at different times. During a primary, they need to maximize votes from members of their own party. During the general election, they need to maximize votes across a more politically diverse electorate. Data scientists on a campaign may suggest that a candidate's approach and messaging vary accordingly.
- An individual vote's value may differ depending on the voting district. A vote in a contested district is far more important than one from a safe district. The fluidity in changing voter perceptions makes this challenging.
- Fund-raising may try to either maximize total funds raised, or perhaps demonstrate a broad-based groundswell of appeal by receiving many small donations.

Political campaigns may well accept opaque systems, and certain failures are both likely and acceptable, given the application's inherent uncertainty. There are legal regulations on campaign operations, but the biggest ELSI challenges are ethical. Candidates need to balance their own views on what is "right" with increasingly explicit recommendations on what positions the electorate wants them to take. Data science may also tell a candidate that one part of the electorate wants them to take position A, while another part wants the opposite position B. This leaves a candidate to decide whether to take no stand, to choose one stand, or possibly to take different stands with different audiences. While candidates have always had to make such complex decisions, data science quantifies them and makes them explicit.

We briefly cover the next two topics:

Detecting maintenance needs is a considerably more mundane application than targeting in political campaigns. Data science can make it possible to provide early warnings of potential failures based on data from vibration, corrosion, and other failure precursor instrumentation or from crowdsourcing from cameras or vibration sensors on vehicles (Eriksson et al., 2008). These warnings are important because it's both safer and more cost-effective to identify and fix problems prior to failure than after.

Depending on the specific application, there are a variety of models to use this data, taking into account structural, failure, and risk properties. Remember, though, there is always the challenge of balancing false positives with false negatives. Also, bad actors might try to interfere with a systems operation to cause societal harm. Maintenance officials must understand this application's objectives and coverage to avoid complacency leading to undetected errors and catastrophic failures.

As our next example, we turn to the domain of **education**. While there are many possible examples, ranging from school budgeting to student/class scheduling to personalized learning, we focus on the latter.

For subjects taught to most students, such as reading and writing, there are vast amounts of pupil data to work with, and it might be possible to create customized education that better motivates students and is more effective. In the 1980s, researchers such as Benjamin Bloom showed that students learn best with an approach known as **mastery learning** – studying a subject at their own pace until mastery is reached (Bloom, 1984). Having an individual tutor to guide each student has been prohibitively expensive, but systems that gather individualized data may make it possible.

Personalized reading tutors are a good place to start. Already, there are online reading tutors for early childhood education that provide compelling material and immediate student feedback based on individual interests and level of mastery. Online reading education could be extended to additional populations, as data science techniques could categorize vast amounts of reading material. Systems could learn from a large student population's signals, such as engagement or comprehension. Their prediction abilities could reduce boredom from repeating known materials or the confusion caused by excessively fast-paced instruction.

Student data collection is a serious concern from a privacy and security perspective. However, resilience would seem the biggest dependability problem if optimization techniques can fail. As in healthcare, widespread adoption of educational innovations may require proof of success in small, controlled trials. This makes explanation and reproducibility of high importance.

Reading education's exact objectives are often unclear and vary by region and over time. There are also debates on how best to teach the subject. This makes it hard to create applications that can be deployed widely, which reduces both available funding and data. Failures are harmful, and education involves significant ethical issues. Applying the Belmont Principle of beneficence, we must carefully balance the benefit and risk to a student's educational progress when replacing a known approach with an automated tutor. Educational solutions must benefit many students, so balancing benefits is challenging.

Criminal sentencing and parole decision-making is our final example. Data science applications in this area might provide judges with decision aids for use during pre-trial detention, criminal sentencing, and parole assignment. These tools could enable judges to make decisions more consistently and lessen the variability of human judgment. They could better ensure consistency by a single judge over the course of each day or over an entire judicial tenure. Better yet, they could ensure some degree of consistency across judges in the same or different jurisdictions. For example, tools could mitigate "serial position effects," the widely studied biases that may influence judicial decisions based on when a case is scheduled (Plonsky et al., 2021). Ideally, individuals with similar criminal histories who commit the same crime in similar circumstances would be treated similarly, which is called **algorithmic fairness** (Dwork et al., 2012).

Today, US courts are using such tools, though some researchers have shown that the risk assessment tools are statistically biased (Eckhouse et al., 2019). However, other researchers have shown that using data-driven decision aids can reduce bias and increase accuracy of pre-trial decisions (Kleinberg et al., 2018). There is more detail on this in Section 12.3 on Fairness.

In principle, the needed data is available. In practice, though, different jurisdictions may collect different types of data and differently code/format what they have. Data can be incomplete and noisy, and data collected for the same individual can be inconsistent. Moreover, many criminal justice systems still use manual processes, so much data may still be only on paper. Data must be balanced in the sense that it will not lead to unfair treatments for any population. Once sufficient data is available and processed to be comparable, we can apply straightforward statistical models, from logistic regression to deep learning.

An algorithmic decision-making tool's failure can have disastrous and potentially long-term consequences. Choosing to develop and deploy such tools demands consideration of the ethics and societal risks, not just the statistical challenge. Denying bail or parole to a low-risk individual can have mental and economic consequences for the person and his/her family. Granting bail or parole to a high-risk individual could lead to another crime. We will refer back to this example in Chapter 7, and also have more to say on it in the context of fairness in Section 12.3.

Chapter 7

A Principlist Approach to Ethical Considerations

In this chapter, we describe how the ethical framework we introduced in Chapter 3, based on the Belmont Principles of respect for persons, beneficence, and justice, can be applied in the context of data science. This principlist approach to ethics attempts to provide a shared analytic framework and vocabulary to help communities and teams resolve difficult questions. Principles are most useful when broad enough to be comprehensive and capture, rather than ignore, the tensions that make questions of "right" and "wrong" so difficult.

As the Belmont Report states: "the objective is to provide an analytical framework that will guide the resolution of ethical problems," however, "these principles cannot always be applied so as to resolve beyond dispute particular ethical problems." That is, our goal is not to provide a universal yes-or-no algorithm for ethics. Rather, it is to guide ethical decision-making so it provides practitioners and stakeholders a shared understanding of a decision-making process and logic.

To illustrate, we chose five of Chapter 6's use cases to explain with respect to the Belmont Principles: criminal sentencing, newsfeed recommendation, vaccine distribution, mobility reporting, and insurance underwriting. The three principles are not ranked in importance, and each example may not have concerns related to all three. As in the context of Belmont's original deliberations, "beneficence" includes not only individual harms and benefits but also those of society at large.

The observation that a data science application may not satisfy each Belmont Principle does not necessarily mean we advocate discontinuing the application. Vaccine mandates, for example, would prioritize public good over individual autonomy. The complexity of this balance is reflected in US law: "Since Jacobson v Massachusetts (1905), the judiciary has consistently upheld vaccination mandates" (Gostin et al., 2021), while there are COVID-19 vaccination decisions that show nuance. The original Belmont Report similarly notes of principles that: "at times they come into conflict" and "cannot always be applied so as to resolve beyond dispute particular ethical problems." Instead, they are meant to "provide an analytical framework that will guide the resolution of ethical problems."

Here are applications of the Belmont framework's three principles to some of the examples in Chapter 6.

7.1 Criminal Sentencing and Parole Decision-Making

As discussed in Section 6.6, algorithms for criminal pre-trial, sentencing, and parole decisions are fraught with ethical challenges.

- **Respect for persons.** All stakeholders' autonomy would be challenged if such algorithms were opaque: defending attorneys lack understanding of how decisions are made now, and defendants who may become incarcerated lack understanding of how their actions may be scored in such an automated decision system. The transparency paradox discussed in Chapter 3 thwarts complete information. Instead of over-explaining technical subjects or under-explaining (which can lead to deceptive or unfair practices), proponents of increased use of automated decision systems can adopt a "tiered" approach (Bunnik et al., 2013). This would involve explaining the basic concepts in plain language while providing extra detail to those who want increased transparency. Another concern is the likely event that algorithmic approaches do not provide interpretability. The answer to "why" a decision is rendered is both important and perhaps not answerable.
- **Beneficence.** The claimed benefits of using such algorithms, such as efficiency and uniformity, must be explicitly evaluated with respect to their impact on many parties and performance versus existing human approaches. These include defendants, potential parolees and other stakeholders, including the judiciary, the criminal justice system, and society writ large. For example, algorithms may be trained to minimize expected errors against a test set (e.g., prior decisions by human judges). However, this training may not minimize the total number of future crimes, the total expense of the justice system, or other more beneficial, societal goals.
- **Justice.** Biases resulting from deploying algorithms for criminal sentencing and parole decision support – e.g., different model outputs for demographically different defendants with similar criminal data – is the subject of ample research and journalistic inquiry. Many of these inquiries argue, via statistics as well as case studies and interviews, that some are benefiting relative to others. Also, perfectly accurate models trained on biased data perfectly reproduce these biases. As discussed in Section 6.6, the use of data science in algorithmic sentencing and parole decisions catalyzed research discussions on the multiple ways to quantify fairness (Pleiss et al., 2017). We discuss this in more detail in Section 12.3.

In short, this example includes a variety of data science and societal challenges. The ethical considerations are clear, with reduced accountability, serious risk of harm to individuals and society, and opportunity for amplifying unfairness and injustice as applied to individuals. However, there could be enhanced judicial uniformity and possibly other benefits. Aside from ethical considerations, different stakeholders (defendants, lawmakers, members of the judiciary) might have extremely different notions of what objective an algorithm is to optimize.

7.2 News Feed Recommendations

As discussed briefly in Section 4.3 and Section 6.2, news feed recommendations are considerably more challenging than music recommendations. News corpora vary in size and quality, as well as the motivations of those who add to them. News also has a much greater impact on individuals and society.

- **Respect for persons.** Informed consent is challenged when news recommendation algorithms are opaque. The transparency paradox is exacerbated given their complexity, which prevents even their designers from fully understanding the resulting technical systems. A widely discussed example of informed consent was Facebook's 2012 "Emotional Contagion" automated news feed experiment, published in the *Proceedings of the National Academy of Sciences* in 2014 (Verma, 2014). In this experiment, Facebook users' news feeds were experimentally manipulated to amplify posts of positive or negative sentiment. Subsequent posts by those users were then used to quantify whether the algorithmic changes caused subsequent increased or decreased happiness. Section 12.4 has more detail on this.
- **Beneficence.** These algorithms can indeed inform and delight when delivering content that optimizes engagement through joy and surprise. However, they can also create filter bubbles (Section 12.4.2) or amplify fear or hate, leading to a radicalizing "rabbit hole" (Alfano et al., 2018). The complexity of content ranking algorithms, and the unpredictability of their impact on users' well-being, is driving companies to spend more time investigating unanticipated ways content recommendation may lead to harm. Of course, they also have to develop ways to mitigate these effects (Wells et al., 2021). We need long-term studies, where users' behavior is observed for several weeks or months, for developers to know the impact of a news feed's content recommendation algorithm.
- **Justice.** Without question, algorithms affect different societal groups in different ways, leading to many considerations of fairness. Some impacts are benign (perhaps, a propensity for a subgroup to get sports entertainment recommendations), while others reinforce societal problems.

We have chosen this example because there has been increasing societal reliance on algorithmic news feeds. This has led to increased public scrutiny. The complexity of the algorithms prevents designers and readers alike from understanding what content and world view is being amplified. As to harms, the attribution of benefit and risk to these algorithms is debated daily in the press, by researchers, by companies doing news recommendations (including their own researchers), and by lawmakers and regulatory agencies.

7.3 Vaccine Distribution Optimization

Distributing a vaccine with supply, logistical, and vaccine hesitancy constraints is a truly complex problem, as briefly discussed in Section 6.3.

- **Respect for persons.** This is a concern, as societies increasingly pressure and even mandate that vaccine skeptics be vaccinated. If vaccines were outright forced, vaccination would violate the principle of informed consent. Society-level rationing also reduces individual autonomy.
- **Beneficence.** Beneficence's role in vaccine distribution, particularly since both the supply and distribution channels may be limited, is extremely difficult to know in advance. The coupling of optimization and health policies requires complex trade-offs, e.g., between supporting opening schools or reducing disease in prisons or assisted living facilities. Here, a commitment to beneficence includes adjusting distribution policy as supplies and health policies change and as the effects of a distribution policy become evident.
- **Justice.** At the individual distributor level, whether state or private, appointment booking mechanisms have varied usability and interface complexity. The technology divide may contribute to a "vaccine divide" among those with and without the technology access to secure vaccine appointments. The digital divide may correlate with demographic divides and could result in unfair outcomes.

We have included this example because of its widespread importance and serious ethical complexity. Even though data-driven models are needed to optimize vaccine distribution, ethics are of paramount importance in this example, and balancing objectives is particularly complex.

7.4 Mobility Reporting

The Google team that showed aggregate regional movement trends was cognizant of the need to preserve individual location privacy and effectively used differential privacy techniques to protect that data. (See Section 10.1 for more on differential privacy.) However, even if individual privacy is preserved, using geographical data gives rise to ethical issues worthy of consideration.

- **Respect for persons.** Neither any individual nor Google would have contemplated in advance that anonymized location data would be used for this purpose. However, Google's anonymization policy is explicitly written to allow Google wide latitude in the use of anonymized data (Google, n.d.-b). On the one hand, users might be surprised, given how few users read the policy. On the other hand, opt-in would have greatly reduced the likely effectiveness of this application.
- **Beneficence.** Correlations between who is mobile and how disease progresses offer societal benefit for informing health policy. However, there may be implications to individuals, even if identities cannot be inferred from published mobility data. For example, mobility data could be correlated with widely available demographic data and reinforce stereotypes or create societal divides. This same effect could occur in many other applications that aggregate anonymized individual data.
- **Justice.** Since mobility data is often gathered via smartphones, it risks being skewed towards those users. This requires a careful analysis of the policy's efficacy and impact based on such data. Sampling bias is discussed more in multiple places in Part III.

We used this example to show there are ethical concerns beyond the most obvious one, which is privacy. It shows the subtle issues a design team must navigate even when the primary goal is to produce an information system intended to benefit public health and policy.

7.5 Underwriting/Pricing of Property/Casualty Insurance

Ascertaining risk to enable better selection pricing of insurance policies is a traditional application of data, and it is significant given how important it is to people. As discussed in Section 6.5, data can be applied to many aspects of the problem space.

- **Respect for persons.** Availability and pricing of insurance should be based on the specific risks of an individual application, not exogenous factors which may not be related. Opaque algorithms which set loan policies and insurance rates for individuals challenge the concept of informed consent, as neither applicants nor insurance regulators may be able to determine the rationale for an underwriting decision. Some who particularly need insurance (e.g., those in fragile economic circumstances) have diminished autonomy, possibly meriting increased protections against hard-to-understand or deceptive terms and conditions.

- **Beneficence.** Increased use of more personal data can itself affect the risk-taking behavior of individuals or groups. For example, high penetration of insurance and low reimbursements could drive practitioners out of a medical subfield, causing societal harm. Insurance's increased use of personal health information could also motivate individuals to avoid useful health diagnostic tests, thus causing societal harm due to a lack of preventative testing or even increased disease transmission.
- **Justice.** Such algorithms can reinforce societal bias, e.g., if they are accurately trained to reproduce biased human insurance underwriting decisions, they would constitute a form of "digital redlining." Data could facilitate the creation of new, finer-grained risk pools (e.g., assigning people with genetic predisposition to disease), thereby increasing differentials in insurance costs. This unequally distributed harm illustrates the Belmont Report's multiple meanings of justice, "in the sense of 'fairness in distribution' or 'what is deserved,'" to quote the original.

We include this example to illustrate how a mechanism that pre-dates digital computation can, by including far more data and complex algorithms, risk amplification of already present harms and injustice.

To close, we refer back to Gottenbarn and Wolfe, who state, "... every decision requires us to identify a broader range of stakeholders and consider how to satisfy our obligations to them. A primary function of the Code is to help computing professionals identify potential impacts and promote positive outcomes in their systems" (Gotterbarn et al., 2018). While they are talking about computing and the ACM Code, their quote is also consistent with our principlist approach to ethics. It underlies our view, as demonstrated with this section's five examples, that ethics must be considered as many types of decisions are made. We believe that doing such analyses against a set of principles, like the Belmont Principles, (1) reminds data scientists to think about difficult challenges, (2) acts as a check on significant errors, and (3) motivates practical improvements.

Recap of Part II: Applying Data Science

Reaching the end of Part II, we hope our detailed discussions of the initial six examples and the somewhat more cursory discussions of 26 more have been enlightening.

- While we have not surveyed all possible applications, we hope we demonstrated data science's valuable potential in domains ranging from research to entertainment to medicine to commerce to finance to government, and more. In many cases, we also explained a bit of their "how-to" and demystified how many applications operate.
- We showed that data science is often applied in different ways to multiple subproblems of an application. For example, in a video streaming application, we illustrated copyright identification, video recommendation, search, and advertising. Video streaming could also benefit from additional applications of data science, such as for closed captioning, language translation, summarization, and more.
- By our repeated referral to the Analysis Rubric, we illustrated seven important considerations in applying data science to a problem. We believe that examining an application in detail against the Analysis Rubric elements teases out its design's hard parts.
- Whether contemplating a new data science application or evaluating an existing one, careful consideration of data science's unique and complex aspects is essential. While the Analysis Rubric elements are of necessity listed in a particular order, we fully recognize that the application of the Analysis Rubric may be done in a more bottom-up or top-down way, depending on the application.
- Our analysis shows a few applications to be straightforward, many to be challenging, and some to be very hard or perhaps presently impossible. When difficulties occur, they are usually because:
  - Data capture of sufficient quality and scale is impossible for some reason.
  - Existing technical approaches are insufficient.
  - The cost of achieving dependability is too high.

- Opaque approaches in either sense of the term are insufficient; furthermore, there may be a particular need to prove causality.
- Objectives are in dispute.
- Failures are essentially intolerable.
- Insurmountable difficulties arise from the ELSI criteria.

Finally, we resumed our ethics thread. We explored how the principles set forth in Chapter 3 can guide us when applying data science to gnarly problems.

All of this sets the stage for Part III, a considerably deeper discussion of data science challenges.

Part III

Challenges in Applying Data Science

In Part II we explored many data science applications, some quite natural and others very challenging, and we presented the Analysis Rubric to guide our evaluations. This part discusses the challenges that arise from the Analysis Rubric elements, mirroring the order in which they were previously presented:

If we are to achieve the maximal benefits while minimizing risks, we need to understand these data science challenges. Our goal is to provide a coherent survey of these topics, recognizing that, individually, most of them are sufficiently involved to be the subject of numerous books.

Part IV

Chapter 8

Tractable Data

In advising companies on using machine learning, your authors have found that many companies are initially excited because they have the necessary data. But they are also apprehensive about the mathematical complexity of building a machine learning model. With experience, they often realize that model building may be the easy part; the hard part is establishing and maintaining a data pipeline to manage the data throughout its life-cycle.

In the early 2000s, IBM Research worked with a large chauffeur service to optimize car scheduling, capacity management, and crew assignment. Optimization opportunities were just becoming tractable due to the availability of accurate vehicle location data and distributed computing systems. This first appeared to be a great and rewarding project for IBM's applied mathematicians, who did indeed make the project a success. However, in the end, they weren't so happy. They felt they spent most of their time doing mundane engineering, rather than applying their sophisticated mathematical knowledge. In the words of a recent article, "Everyone wants to do the model work, not the data work" (Sambasivan et al., 2021).

We will consider some of the challenges in generating, collecting, processing, storing, and managing data, following co-author Jeannette's data life-cycle model (Wing, 2019). Other authors use the term **ETL (Extract, Transform, and Load)** for the process of making data useful for a specific application. We mostly defer the crucial issues of data privacy and security to Chapter 10.

8.1 Data Generation and Collection

Data can come from different types of sources:

- **Instrumentation.** The chauffeur service used data from GPS sensors. In Part II we saw other examples, such as the Sloan Digital Sky Survey's use of telescopes, health sensors, and infrastructure instrumentation. Self-driving cars use an array of sensors, including accelerometers, cameras, radar, and lidar. As the Internet of Things connects more devices, ever more data will become available.

- **Users.** Users may explicitly add data, as the dispatchers did in the chauffeur example, or they may implicitly contribute data, as do shoppers when they click on a recommendation. Making it easy and natural for users to create data is part of quality data science. This is not just user-interface design – it is more of an application design problem to ensure users want to participate and create quality data. Users naturally have privacy concerns with collecting their data; we cover that in Section 10.1.
- **Third parties.** Existing data may be readily available, e.g., from publicly available web data. Alternatively, data can be licensed or new data can be commissioned from another party. There are complexities in defining the terms of use and liability, the exact technical requirements, and the pricing model. Data science applications at scale require sophisticated procurement or licensing operations much like what is needed for managing a manufacturer's supply chain.

In case of failure, there must be a plan for alternative data sources, especially for systems requiring high availability. In a nutshell, data does not often grow on trees, at least not ones with easy-to-reach branches.

In addition to data sources, there must be secure and reliable transmission paths that can handle the volume. There may need to be redundant communication channels so a channel's failure doesn't lose or excessively delay data. Data may need to be compressed or encrypted. In some applications, such as scientific instruments gathering petabytes of signal data, it may be necessary to just sample the data and discard the rest.

8.2 Processing Data

Data may need to be checked and cleansed in many ways. To reduce the likelihood of receiving erroneous information, applications must screen incoming data for errors. This is very challenging, however, for it is extremely difficult, if not impossible, to determine whether unexpected, incoming data is erroneous, or indicative of a significant change. Data may need to be recoded for internal use or for consistency or comparability (e.g., the same standard units of measure). Broadly, the colorful term for all these data processing steps is **data wrangling**. Beyond these steps, data may be compressed or encrypted to increase performance, decrease storage costs, preserve confidentiality, or comply with data licensing commitments.

For example, in quantitative investment management, there are enormous data pipeline issues. Stock splits require consistently adjusting stock prices, dividends, and holdings at the precise instant a split occurs. The regular and extraordinary issuance of dividends and corporate spin-offs further require continuing adjustments to make data comparable across time periods. Stock indices periodically change their membership. Finally, the thousands of tradeable entities – and vastly more if one considers bonds and derivatives – have some degree of flux and require normalization before we can use even simple things like stock prices or volumes.

Beyond these normalization steps, converting data into useful signals for a data science application may require sophisticated techniques. These may be machine learning systems unto themselves, but, at minimum, there are likely large numbers of available language or processing libraries to transform incoming data into useful elements. The challenge of deciding how to transform the incoming data is discussed in the next section.

Data may be very private and those handling it need to be good shepherds, instituting strong privacy and security measures. (Again, see Section 10.1 and Section 10.2 for these.) For now, suffice it to say that legal and ethical requirements may impact the data pipeline and the operation of data science services.

- A data scientist working on email spam detection typically is not allowed to read any customer's email. Instead, the company might create its own email accounts and try to attract examples of spam messages. It might also ask its employees to donate mail messages for use in spam-fighting research.
- Licensing agreements might restrict data use only to selected people or for particular uses. This may force the use of restrictive storage and audit systems to both control usage and prove that it has been compliant.

Another example is the fight against child pornography. One might think that internet service companies could just match any uploaded photos against a library of known child pornography. However, they cannot do this, because it is illegal to store this material. Thus, in the US, they instead have a library of fingerprints (or, in computer terminology, hash values) of illicit images obtained from the National Center for Missing and Exploited Children (NCMEC). They then fingerprint uploaded images, look for matches against this library, and report them to NCMEC.

When there is little data, machine learning systems generally do not work well; indeed, there is a reason the terms "big data" and "machine learning" frequently go together. Thus, a voracious need for data is often machine learning's first challenge. For example, if it had very few labeled images from which to learn, image identification would not be a success. Fortunately, image processing applications are global in nature, and there is generally no training data shortage, though there is a risk that limited data from some populations could create fairness issues (see Section 12.3 on Fairness). The large amount of data may still be difficult to gather and expensive to process, but it is demonstrably feasible for organizations of sufficient scale.

However, the state space in some domains is so very large it may be impossible to gather a large enough dataset. For example, so many different events influence economic growth, inflation, and unemployment rates that it is very difficult to gather enough historical training data to create macroeconomic models. The amount of training data relative to the diversity of possible economic situations is just too small.

8.3 Data Storage

The sheer quantity of data may also be a challenge, requiring sophisticated techniques to distribute storage over many networked sites (for reasons of performance and reliability) while still eliminating data redundancy and storing only useful information. Data compression techniques, analogous to those that reduce the storage size of photos or videos, help greatly. On the other hand, regulations require many industries to keep vast amounts of historical detail, making it problematic to delete anything. From an operational perspective, infrequently accessed data is often stored on low-cost, archival media that may be difficult and expensive to access. This may even be deliberate to reduce the risk of lost data, but these storage mechanisms add to the complexity of deletion and may delay how long data is maintained after someone requests its removal.

There are many different technologies with which to store data. Certain database systems may optimize storage performance at the expense of retrieval (say, for rarely read data used for audits). Others may facilitate highly flexible queries (say, for data exploration). Yet others may support reliable, high-frequency updates to fine-grained record data (say, for recording purchases). These are but a few of the possibilities.

Difficult engineering-oriented decisions must also be made to store data in the right locations to minimize storage costs and latency of access, and – if needed – to ensure data availability when there are storage, server, or network issues.

Beyond these engineering issues, there are also regulatory issues constraining decisions on data storage. We discuss some of the privacy issues in Section 10.1, but many countries also have data residency laws that confine data to being stored within a country's borders. These may well be at odds with efficiency, and they generate complex questions; for example, the legality of short-term, out-of-country, data caching.

In addition to data, storage systems must also store **metadata**, or data about the data. In particular, if an organization has multiple datasets, it needs to have a data catalog to make data easy to find and available. An approach called **datasheets** has been proposed to standardize metadata that describes what a dataset is and what it can be used for (Gebru et al., 2021).

The data catalog itself contains, in essence, the organization's data DNA, and thus is valuable in itself, and requires security measures to prevent misuse or data theft. For example, in an investment firm, even knowing the firm uses certain economic data would tip off competitors.

One kind of metadata is **data provenance**, the data's "chronological history of creation, ownership, and chain of custody" (Ellison et al., 2020). Provenance is helpful when there are questions about the data: perhaps a model is performing poorly, and it turns out that, due to a bug, the data collected on a certain date is faulty. With proper provenance, that small slice of faulty data can be deleted and the model updated. Without provenance, all the data is tainted. Provenance is necessary when dealing with legal requirements: there are many regulations regarding what personally identifiable information can be used for what purposes, so it is not enough to have the data; organizations must track when and where the data originated, and what permissions have been granted. In 2022 the Coalition for Content Provenance and Authenticity (C2PA) released a technical specification for data provenance.

8.4 Data Quality

As we have mostly looked at engineering-related data challenges, let us consider the problem of non-erroneous, but still problematic, data. With so much data, errors are likely to creep in. Data may be incomplete. And, for all the effective wheat, there is also much chaff. Most simplistically, the late 1950s computing adage of "garbage in, garbage out" is true. While some big data approaches tolerate very noisy data, most applications require data to meet certain criteria to obtain good outcomes. Here are some specific data quality issues:

- Data may have statistical bias. One key problem is **selection bias**, such as in survey results. Those who bother to complete a survey are often unrepresentative of the whole population. Records of crime frequency may be biased, because they track only reported crimes, not all that are committed. We discuss many more biases in Section 11.4.4.
- It's very challenging to combine similar data from multiple datasets, because data may be coded with different underlying assumptions. For example, in multi-site medical studies, one might assume data is comparable, but hospitals in different regions may measure or code data very differently.
- Big data techniques can hide underlying problems. For example, Tina Saey, a *Science News* reporter, got interested in the microbiome and had her gut bacteria

analyzed. Her February 2015 article described how she had two different companies analyze her bacteria and got back different data (Saey, 2015). At the time, understanding the impact of gut bacteria was of very high interest, so her article was very illuminating. It showed research models weren't as inconsistent as they seemed. It was just when others tried to replicate results, they were using differing and erroneous input data.

The impact of data quality is well illustrated in a controversy relating to Eran Bendavid et al.'s spring 2020 study to determine the percentage of people who had contracted COVID-19. As reported in a medRxiv preprint (Bendavid et al., 2020), the researchers sampled Santa Clara County, California, residents, tested them for antibodies to the 2019-nCoV virus, and found that about 1.5% had them. After adjusting for differing population demographics between the sampled and county populations, they extrapolated that 2.8% of the population at large had those antibodies. They further adjusted their estimate upward taking into account test sensitivity, and they arrived at a seroprevalence rate about ~50 times larger than what was then known and, hence, a much lower infection fatality rate.

However, their result led to considerable controversy. This was, in part, because the antibody tests could report up to about 1.5% false positives, leading to doubts that the conclusions were sufficiently certain. The Bendavid study may also have had challenges adjusting for selection bias. The Andrew Gelman Blog had months of back-and-forth discussion, with Gelman's thoughts summarized in an article in the *Journal of the Royal Statistical Society* (UK) (Gelman & Carpenter, 2020).

Regardless of the correct conclusion, this example illustrates the challenges in sampling and properly framing the results to accommodate the available data. Whole books have been written on *sampling* (Lohr, 2021) and the broader topic of *experimental design* (Box et al., 2005; Fisher, 1935; Peirce, 1883), a topic to which we will return in Section 11.2.1. We note in closing that Bendavid et al. eventually published a similar, but revised, version of their initial work (Bendavid et al., 2021).

One final concern is that learning from today's available data may create a kind of inertia based on today's actions and norms, even if they are not what we ultimately want to persist. We observe, metaphorically, that *learning from the present may imprison the future*.

In 2015, Amit Datta et al. wrote one of the first articles about this. They showed that advertising systems might automatically place ads in periodicals aimed at a certain subpopulation, thereby denying some opportunities to another population (Datta et al., 2015). They specifically noted that click rates on certain ads might normally be higher for one gender than another. It would then be natural for ad selection algorithms to use this information to bias ad presentation on properties more likely to interest that gender. If those ads were for higher-paying jobs, a data science approach to ad recommendations could unintentionally perpetuate an existing societal tendency. This article was influential and helped influence data science to increase its focus on fairness, which we discuss in Section 12.3.

8.5 Appropriate Use of User-Generated Data

We feel we cannot end this chapter on data without a brief discussion of privacy. We presage some of the topics of Section 10.1 with a list of thought-provoking engineering and policy challenges that many applications need to answer:

1. How can we reliably ensure privacy throughout the data acquisition, storage, and use life-cycle?
2. What mechanisms would allow users to know what data is stored, control with whom their data is shared, retrieve their data, and retract rights to it?
3. Under what conditions may data science applications use an individual's data in confidentiality-preserving ways?
4. If a user retracts data access rights from a service, what happens to its anonymized aggregate summaries based in part on that user's data?
5. What is the balance between individual rights and confidentiality-preserving use of data for scientific, civic, law enforcement, national security, or commercial uses?
6. How do applications and users balance the value that accrues from user data?

While much of data science today is concerned with machine learning, application design, and all manner of policy issues, this section has illustrated classic and new data management issues associated with the data itself. Whether engineering, normalization, careful statistical analysis, or paying due attention to data sensitivity, *engineering the data pipeline is often the most time-consuming and labor-intensive* part of new data science applications.

Chapter 9

Building and Deploying Models

Machine learning models have proven to be effective at solving a wide variety of real-world problems. But it can be difficult to develop and maintain these models. By their nature, they are not 100% effective, and producing a good model is an art. This section describes some of the issues.

9.1 Theoretical Limitations

One week into a new job, co-author Alfred was using gesture-typing to let his then brand-new assistant know he would call later "when I'm in the car." The text produced, which was "I'll call you when I'm on the can[13]," was embarrassing. Also, his automatic message transcription system once mistakenly interpreted an extraneous sound as a "5," leading to this confusing transcription: "My number is area code (626) 523 8023. Once again, that number is (562) 652 3802 free."

Traditional software engineers have a methodology for eliminating bugs in systems that deal with clear-cut correct answers. But in applications like speech recognition, the problem is that there is inherent **uncertainty**. For some inputs, even the best experts disagree on what the right answer is, so any model will necessarily disagree with some expert answers at least some of the time. The challenge is to build an overall usable and robust application, even though it may make occasional errors. Part II illustrates that error tolerant applications are much more likely to be amenable to machine learning solutions, and Chapter 13 discusses the challenges of dealing with uncertainty.

A second problem is that the world changes. A system trained on yesterday's data may no longer perform well tomorrow. Technically, we say most machine learning systems assume that the data-generating process remains **stationary**, meaning the

[13] For any reader not knowing the meaning of this circa 1900 idiom, suffice it to say it was embarrassing.

relationship between inputs and outputs remains constant over time – or at least close to constant. There are places where this works well:

1. Cats evolve slowly enough that an image recognizer trained on existing cat images still works well on new cat images – even for cats yet to be born! "A cat is a cat is a cat."
2. A listener who likes hip-hop music is unlikely to suddenly switch their preference to classical, nor will the classical listener suddenly switch to country.

However, there are many applications where the world does change. This is a problem, because a machine learning model trained on past data only continues to work if the future data resembles the past. When there is any change in the distribution of data over time, we say the process is **non-stationary**. When that non-stationarity has an effect on the variable we are trying to predict, we call it **concept drift**. There are several kinds of change to look out for:

- **Sudden change.** In finance, the past is often a great predictor of the future . . . until something significant changes – such as an economic panic. The finance world calls this a **regime change**. After the regime change, the old models no longer work. Many stock market models became less predictive at the onset of COVID-19 because the rapid onset of the pandemic changed consumer and investor behavior in previously unseen ways. As another example, a highway accident will instantly break all the predicted arrival times of a traffic-routing application.
- **Periodic change.** Purchase patterns exhibit seasonality – people buy mittens in winter and swimsuits in summer – and a model that does not include the time of year as an input will exhibit concept drift. Other patterns occur with weekly and daily periods.
- **Gradual change.** An online retailer may find that a certain fashion is a top seller. However, over time its popularity begins to fade and a new favorite emerges. Recommendation systems need to keep up with these changes, balancing how much they rely on past data with how much they should concentrate on the present.
- **Adversarial change.** In game theory, we know that one player's actions will change other players' actions. Applications such as email spam filtering are game-theoretic in this sense. A company can build a near-perfect spam filter, but as soon as spammers notice that their mail is not getting through, they invent new, previously unseen patterns of spam mail.
- **Sampling change.** It may be that events in the world have not changed, but the data that is collected has. For example, customers might still be buying the same things, but a new rule for opting-in to cookie tracking may change the slice of data that is collected. As another example, in 2000 Google expanded the range of books included in their Books Ngram Viewer. This made the tool more useful for the average consumer, but harder for scientific researchers to compare results

before and after 2000. This would be an example of non-stationarity without concept drift.

It is vital to continuously monitor a deployed system to watch out for any unexpected changes, and to correct for them by updating the model.

A third problem is that it can be difficult to specify exactly what we want a machine learning system to do – *what we want to optimize*. Yes, we want a speech recognition system to minimize the words that it gets wrong. But that's not quite the right metric, because the embarrassing mistake that happened to Alfred should receive a larger penalty than an innocuous mistake. It is easy to measure the word error rate, but hard to measure the embarrassment of serious mistakes, and thus hard to minimize them.

One place this shows up is in search engines. While it is important to provide great results in the top positions, it is even more important to avoid a terrible result there. One bad result might lead to a news article seen by millions of readers hurting the search engine's reputation. Therefore, search engine teams must understand the full distribution of answers, not just the average number of good results.

In finance, optimizing a portfolio's return is a great goal. However, investors also like bounds on how much the value of their portfolio will vary so they can sleep at night. Risk-adjusted returns are a critical financial concept (Chen, 2021), so machine learning approaches must include a careful analysis and mitigation of risk. Chapter 12 will return to this problem of setting the right objective.

Machine learning is a fast-moving field, and new models can emerge faster than our understanding of them. In particular, we don't yet have a full understanding of where and when deep learning systems will work well. In general, we know deep learning networks can approximate any computable function well, but we don't know for sure what the right network architecture is for a particular problem. We have techniques to search through the space of possible networks but no guarantees about how long it will take. We also know that searching through parameter space is only guaranteed to find a locally optimal solution, not a globally optimal one. Fortunately, for many problems, most locally optimal points are almost as good as the globally optimal ones.

As a related problem, not understanding how some machine learning systems work makes it difficult to augment them with other semantic knowledge. How does a system developer of a complex neural network instruct it with additional common-sense knowledge? For example, we might want to tell it, "You labeled this photo a wolf, but it is actually a Siberian Husky dog; wolves are typically larger than this" or "Don't recommend pork to someone observant of Kosher food rules."

Many of these theoretical challenges have been fundamental to statistics. As data science expands to high-stakes fields like biomedicine, health policy, and epidemiology, statistics needs to keep up with the ELSI challenges around privacy and fairness. Statistics is also focusing on the mathematical challenges of understanding and creating the high-performance algorithms appropriate to massive datasets and inferencing that can be done on multiple distributed machines. Statisticians are expanding mathematical analyses to study error not only as a function of the number of observations but also as a function of the number of processors or computational operations.

Finally, statistics also contributes important techniques that can aid us in ascertaining causality. Causality is important for scientific understanding and to answer both forward-looking "what-if" questions and historical counterfactual questions. However, creating models that show causality is very challenging, as strong correlation *may* indicate a causal relationship but most certainly does not offer proof. We will continue this discussion in much greater detail in Section 11.2. A 2019 NSF Report entitled *Statistics at a Crossroads*, representing the views of a number of well-known statisticians, contains an additional, compatible viewpoint on the challenges of statistics (He et al., 2019).

9.2 Inductive Bias

There is a myth that machine learning is completely objective – the data determines the results, with no human intervention. That is a myth, in part because the process of collecting the data involves subjective choices by humans (as covered in Chapter 8), and also because the training data, no matter how plentiful, only covers a finite number of inputs. A learning algorithm can **memorize** the examples it was trained on, but when given an input it has never seen before, it must **generalize**. Some assumptions must be made to guide this generalization; this is the **inductive bias**.

It is important to note the distinction between **social bias** and inductive bias. Social bias is the unfair treatment of one class of individuals, an unfortunate effect that we need to eliminate (as covered in Section 12.3). Inductive bias is a necessary part of any learning, machine or human.

Consider the top row of Figure 9.1. The same training set of 15 data points is shown in each of the four boxes. Each box also shows a line representing a different model that is fit to the data. These four models are:

- **a linear model** showing the straight line that comes closest to all the data points;
- **a nearest-neighbor model** in which each new point is assigned the value of the closest point in the training set;
- **a cyclic model** that combines an overall linear trend with cyclic variation; and
- **a polynomial model** of degree 13 which fits the data almost perfectly.

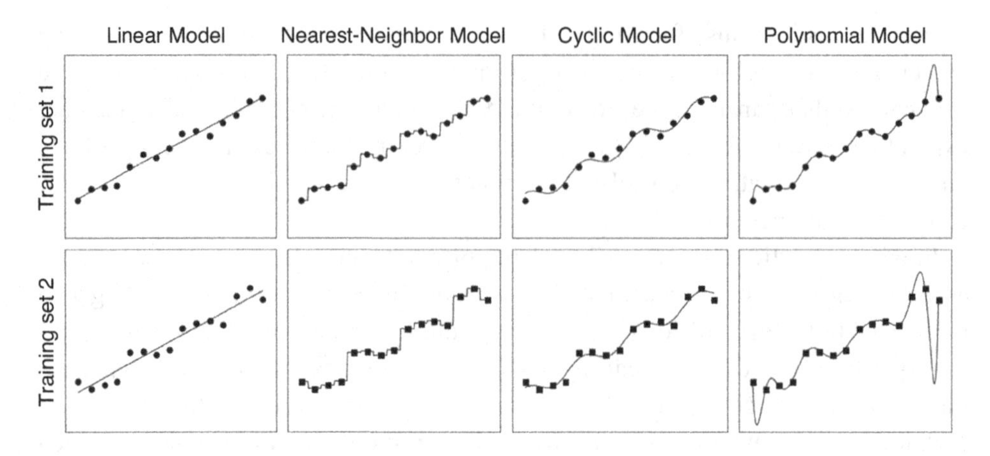

Figure 9.1 Fitting models to training data (synthetic data generated by the authors).

Which model is best (out of the four shown, or any other)? The answer to that question is not contained only in the data points themselves; it is also in what we know about the data. The linear model is a good choice if, say, each data point represents the mass and volume of a chunk of the same metal. The slope of the line would then be the density, which all chunks have in common. The nearest-neighbor model makes sense when we have a lot of data but little knowledge about it, except that we expect similar inputs to have similar outputs. The cyclic model is appropriate for traffic data to a website that is steadily becoming more popular, but suffers a lull every weekend.

The polynomial model appears to suffer from a problem called **overfitting**. We can see that by comparing the two rows of Figure 9.1, which represent two different training sets, each sampled from the same distribution of data points. The linear model looks the same with both training sets, but the polynomial model is quite different, with large spikes in different positions. The model has high **variance**; a small change to the training data makes a big change to the model. That means the model is unreliable. In this case, the root problem is that the polynomial has too many parameters, which allows it to fit the input's noise instead of the real underlying pattern.

To deal with overfitting, we can use a simpler model with fewer parameters. Or we can constrain the parameters to have values that are smaller in absolute value so that the function is smoother, without the large spikes. **Regularization** is a procedure that enforces this; we evaluate a model's goodness not just by how well it fits the training data, but also by how "simple" the model is. A version called **L_2 regularization** works well for polynomials.

Ensemble models, in which the predictions of several component models are combined, are another effective way to avoid overfitting. The ensemble technique called **bagging** trains multiple complex models on different training sets. The randomness in the training tends to smooth out the spikiness in individual models.

The linear model appears to be **underfitting** the data. The model captures the overall increase as we go from left to right, but a straight line is incapable of capturing any variation from that (whereas the cyclic model is capable). We need to loosen the overly strict inductive bias by allowing a less-constrained model (such as the cyclic model). In some cases, but not here, reducing the amount of regularization also counters underfitting.

The ensemble technique called **boosting** overcomes underfitting by training a sequence of simple models. Each model is focused on correcting the mistakes made by the previous model.

As another example, if a model makes the overly strict assumption that the input comes from a normal distribution, it has difficulty handling data where outliers occur more frequently, as Taleb (2007) states in *The Black Swan*. Real-world distributions are often quite different from mathematically tractable ones. Furthermore, some systems are just chaotic, such that a rare event can throw off the best of analyses. Regrettably, COVID-19 has been one of these rare events.

There are many ways to impose an inductive bias. Computer vision systems are built with an inductive bias for translational invariance – seeing a cat in one position of the image should generalize to seeing the same cat moved over a few pixels. Convolutional neural networks enforce this bias, because they treat every part of the image in the same way, at least in the initial processing.

In genomics, biologists believe that only a small number of genes are involved with each disorder or trait. Good genomics models should learn to pick out only the few important genes. The technique of **L_1 regularization** forces many parameters to become zero, thus imposing the inductive bias for selecting just the right genes and ignoring others.

Statisticians distinguish between models based on the number of parameters in a model. In a **parametric model** there are a fixed number of parameters, such as the three parameters a, b, and c in the equation $y = ax^2 + bx + c + ?$, where ? represents random noise. A learning algorithm applied to (x, y) data points can quickly find the best fit for these parameters, requiring only a small amount of data. A parametric model imposes a strong inductive bias that is appropriate when some known theory suggests the right equation to use. For example, if the data points describe locations of a ball in flight, we have a physical theory of gravity that tells us the path will be a parabola (absent air resistance).

In a **non-parametric model** the number of parameters is not fixed, and can grow without limit as more data is added. For example, the nearest-neighbor model retains every data point as part of the model. Non-parametric models have less inductive bias – make fewer assumptions – and let the data speak for itself. So they could learn to describe the non-parabolic flight of a ball that was influenced by air resistance and wind. But they typically require more data to learn well, because there are fewer limits on what the model can be. Popular non-parametric models include neural networks, decision trees, and nearest-neighbor models.

The choice of model class is the most important choice to be made, but there are also choices in how to search through the model class to find the best model instance. Techniques like regularization, dropout, early stopping, weight sharing, and pruning can be used to guide the search to a model that nicely balances bias and variance.

This section has tried to show that a data scientist has to use good judgment to arrive at a model that is appropriate to the problem at hand. In all but the most trivial problems, the model will be an abstraction of reality that leaves something out. The data scientist's task is to find models that don't leave out anything important. As the statistician George Box said, "All models are wrong, but some are useful" (Box, 1979).

9.3 Practical Considerations

There are practical concerns in keeping a machine learning application up and running properly. We have mentioned the data challenges, but the large scale of some systems may pose additional challenges:

- data acquisition (when it is arriving at, say, 100,000 items per second);
- data storage (of petabytes or exabytes);
- data processing (of trillions of floating-point operations per second, or "teraflops");
- power consumption (of 100 megawatts for a large data center);
- personnel (many skilled people needed to design, build, and operate the system); and
- privacy, regulator system integrity, and availability requirements that add to the engineering complexity of big data systems.

Since the dawn of the computer age, Moore's Law (the ability to reduce the size of transistors geometrically and thus increase computing power) has let us overcome scale issues if implementers could just wait for the development of a new generation or two of systems. However, while we will still shrink transistors for quite a while and cram more onto a single chip, it's harder and harder to make the transistors switch faster and to make easy improvements in cost-effectiveness.

However, computer architects at Apple, NVidia, Google, Intel, and elsewhere are coming to the rescue with specialized computer architectures aimed at machine learning problems. Google built its Tensor Processing Unit (TPU) Version 1 in response to a concern that "people searching by voice for three minutes a day using speech recognition DNNs (deep neural networks) would double our datacenters' computation demands" (Jouppi et al., 2017).

Operations research has a history of dealing with large-scale problems. Its practitioners now see increasing challenges arising from new applications, increased scale in data and computation, and the combination of their field's traditional approaches and newer data-driven ones (CCC (Computer Community Consortium), n.d.; Van Hoeve, 2014). The expansion of applications to problems in healthcare, the smart grid, and other areas generate not only scale, but also the need for real-time answers, increased resilience, and reduced uncertainty.

An example large-scale problem is the World TSP (Traveling Salesperson Problem), in which the goal is to find the shortest route that visits each of 1,904,711 cities around the world (World Traveling Salesman Problem, n.d.). As we have observed in the route-finding example of Section 6.1, navigation systems combine multiple approaches to produce their results. However, the general topic of how best to combine models that use both operations research techniques and machine learning is a great challenge.

Of course, not every data science problem is at the petabyte/petaflop scale. Small companies and academic labs run smaller machine learning experiments using GPU clusters or rented data-center time. Some applications run on "edge" devices where the data is gathered, either for privacy reasons or because it is inefficient or difficult to transfer the data. These applications, though typically smaller in scale, are still complex to manage and run. Their challenges relate to minimizing expenses, reducing data scientist overhead, managing experimentation, and more.

Some machine learning applications are deployed as stand-alone systems that make autonomous decisions (such as recommending a video to view). But other systems are just part of a decision-making team, such as a computer vision system that analyzes X-ray images and makes a diagnosis that human doctors then take into account in creating a treatment plan. In such systems it is important to optimize the overall decision-making quality, not just the accuracy of the machine learning system's recommendations. Chapter 11 examines how to make machine learning systems interpretable and explainable, so that human experts can best use their advice. Kleinberg and colleagues examine how to integrate a machine learning system into a decision-making framework (Kleinberg et al., 2018), and others have added to this line of work (Vodrahalli et al., 2022).

Chapter 10
Dependability

To be accepted by society, data science applications must perform properly for a wide variety of users in a wide variety of circumstances, with few, if any, critical errors. For example, demonstrations of self-driving cars in controlled circumstances have impressed many. However, they are not yet widely deployed because they do not work well in all circumstances.

Making systems dependable may take more time and effort than collecting and analyzing their data. This is particularly true for consumer-facing websites, mission-critical applications, and almost all healthcare and financial applications. In this section we address the four aspects of dependability: **privacy**, **security**, **resistance to abuse**, and **resilience**.

10.1 Privacy

Most people feel that their personal data – such as medical records, school grades, and browsing history – is private, and maintaining their privacy is important. However, the topic of privacy is more complex than just maintaining confidentiality, and we distinguish five areas of concern that people have about their personal data:

1. **Collection.** What data should an organization be allowed to collect about me, either by asking me questions, recording my online actions, or using sensors such as GPS, cameras, and health monitors? What consent do they need to ask me for, and what do they have to tell me about what they are collecting? Which organizations do I trust?
2. **Storage.** Where, how, and for how long should they be allowed to store my data? What guarantees do I have that the data will not leak?
3. **Confidentiality.** My data should not be shared with others without my permission. But I will want to share social media with my family and friends, medical records with my doctors, and financial records with my trusted advisors. Can

I count on my applications to protect my data? Will I be able to change my sharing preferences when I want to?

4. **Usage for self.** How can the organization use my data to benefit me? I may appreciate it when I get a localized restaurant recommendation or an accurate personalized spelling correction, but I may find it creepy, manipulative, or annoying to get products recommended to me when I am not interested. Do I have control over how my data is used for these purposes?
5. **Usage for others.** Data can be anonymized and aggregated so that it creates value for many people without breaching confidentiality. For example, many small inputs from different users combine to create a better spelling correction system for everyone. Combined anonymized medical records from many patients lead to a new and improved treatment. Many simple "yes" or "no" census answers provide an accurate picture of society. On the one hand, most people participate in this kind of data sharing because the result is beneficial to all. On the other hand, users may be concerned if they feel that their data is contributing to a societal ill, that they are not fairly compensated for its value, or that their confidentiality might be breached. How can I know if allowing this use of my data will truly be beneficial to others and not be harmful to me?

Over the years, philosophers, political scientists, and legal experts have contributed to privacy debates. Consequently, privacy is a very rich domain, but this book considers it somewhat narrowly: from the perspective of data science applications, companies offering them, individuals who use them, and governments that may regulate them.

The rules governing privacy may arise either from a formal or informal contract between the user and the provider of a data science application, by societal regulation, or both. Helen Nissenbaum, in her theory of privacy called **contextual integrity**, argues that we have expectations of what constitutes an appropriate flow of information. Anything outside of those expectations constitutes a violation of privacy (Nissenbaum, 2009). For example, we expect our priest or lawyer to keep a conversation in confidence, but that a reporter or police officer need not do so. These expectations evolve over time as technologies and cultural expectations change.

Privacy can no longer be an afterthought. It is a key and complex part of product design. For example, co-author Alfred had a project at Google that required over a year of analysis to be sure it was free from privacy risks and hence launchable. All institutions that handle sensitive data need to have policies for assessing and mitigating privacy risks.

10.1.1 Privacy versus Usage Rights

Data may be collected from a user explicitly (e.g., when the user answers a questionnaire, contributes a medical specimen, or fills out a form) or implicitly (e.g., from clicking on a link, from the location of the user's mouse on a screen (Navalpakkam & Churchill, 2012), or the GPS location of a phone). In the specific context, what rights do the user and the collector have with respect to this data?

Regulatory frameworks such as the European Union's General Data Protection Regulation of 2016 (GDPR) mandate that explicit user consent is required to gather certain types of information (European Parliament and Council of the European Union, 2016). In addition, there must be a disclosure of the rationale for the collection and the data's intended uses. The GDPR is more modern and influential than the US Federal Trade Commission (FTC) Fair Information Practice Principles (FIPP) of 1998 (US Federal Trade Commission, 1998), although they have considerable overlap.

These regulatory frameworks specifically call out **personally identifiable information (PII)**. Clearly, a user's name, home address, and Social Security number are PII. But, for some information, there is less clarity, and standards are diverging across political boundaries. For example, a user's internet address is considered PII in Europe, but not in the US. Some particularly **sensitive personally identifiable information (SPII)** may have even greater protections since its compromise would "result in substantial harm, embarrassment, inconvenience, or unfairness to an individual" (DHS Privacy Office, 2017).

The scope of regulatory and contractual privacy requirements increasingly covers not only the direct disclosure of personal information, but also other ways in which personal data may become available. For example, regulations seek to prevent the disclosure of aggregated data if statistical analyses can be used to infer personal information.

Privacy goals can conflict with using data to benefit individuals and society. The 1996 US Health Insurance Portability and Accountability Act (HIPAA) tries to balance the privacy and the value of data by assuring "that individuals' health information is properly protected while allowing the flow of health information needed to provide and promote high quality healthcare" (Office for Civil Rights (OCR), 2008). However, many researchers say HIPAA slows progress by making it harder to do some types of medical research. For example, if researchers get permission to use X-ray images to test one hypothesis, they may need to return to the subjects and ask permission again to use the images on a variant. Even the privacy-focused GDPR acknowledges the need for balance (European Parliament and Council of the European Union, 2016):

> The processing of personal data should be designed to serve mankind. The right to the protection of personal data is not an absolute right; it must be considered in relation to its

function in society and be balanced against other fundamental rights, in accordance with the principle of proportionality.

Patients want control over their own health information, but are often willing to share when it benefits themselves and others. The popular website PatientsLikeMe.com (www.patientslikeme.com/) lets patients with rare conditions discuss their case and find possible treatments.

While GDPR is relatively clear on how it regulates PII data, its rules about using anonymized aggregated data are complex and subject to interpretation (Ducato, 2020). That leads to nuanced challenges about implicit data gathering that often occurs when someone uses a computer application. User actions generate data that could be very valuable in making better recommendations, either privately for that user, or aggregated and anonymized and shared across users. However, regulators and users may have concerns even when data is anonymized.

To date, major websites have adopted a pragmatic approach to privacy. They have taken into account their own goals and technological capabilities, along with changing consumer views and governmental requirements. While they continue to depend on aggregated data and recommendations to make their systems work and provide profit, as of 2022 they have been offering users more protection and control over their data. Some sites have long allowed users to download or delete their data. Extending these capabilities, Google in 2011 launched Google Takeout with which users could download and/or delete the breadth of their Google data (Google, Inc., n.d.). Facebook (Facebook Help Center, n.d.), Apple (Apple Support, 2019), Twitter, Microsoft, and other companies now provide similar services, especially after 2018 when they were mandated by GDPR's Article 20, Right to Data Portability, and the Data Transfer Project was founded (Data Transfer Project, n.d.). These facilities are meant to prevent users from being locked in to one vendor. However they also constitute their own security risk. If an attacker gets access to an account, a single request downloads all the data to the attacker.

Some question whether companies should pay users for their data. However, Tim O'Reilly argues in the article *Data is the New Sand* that data should not be thought of as a valuable commodity (like oil), but as a plentiful, cheap, common resource (like sand)[1] (O'Reilly, 2021). The numbers back up his argument. For example, in 2019 Facebook had costs and expenses per user (for data centers, salaries, etc.) of about $19, taxes of $2.50, revenue of $29, and profit of $7.50. Some of the value is no doubt due to data that users generate with their clicks and other feedback. One could ask whether each user should receive a portion of the $7.50 profit, or if they are already getting enough compensation from the free service? In hypothetical

[1] Two additional reasons why "Data is the new oil" is a bad analogy: (1) Oil is consumed when it is used, whereas data can be reused, replicated, and shared. (2) Oil is fungible: oil from Texas or Saudi Arabia or Russia is all traded in one global market and can be used anywhere while most data is highly specific to localized use.

auction experiments, users self-report that they value the use of Facebook at over $1,000 per year, suggesting that they are already getting a favorable deal (Corrigan et al., 2018).

Other websites are also highly valued. In experiments by Erik Brynjolfsson and colleagues, users say that they value internet maps at $3,000/year, email at $8,000/year, and search engines at $17,000/year (Brynjolfsson et al., 2018). Even if these self-reported amounts are exaggerated, much lower ones would still serve to highlight the value of these free (advertising-supported) services. Nonetheless, some companies' high valuations create a perception they should share their wealth with consumers.

The medical ethics community has considered what compensation human subjects should receive for clinical trial participation (Pandya & Desai, 2013). On the one hand, medical scientists would like to offer compensation to subjects exposed to the risk of discomfort. On the other hand, compensation may induce poor and otherwise vulnerable populations to take increased risks.

One well-known case is Henrietta Lacks, who was treated for cancer in 1951 (Skloot, 2010). It was found that her cancer cells would live and continually reproduce in the lab while previous cell specimens had died within days. Her cell line was cultured and medical scientists used it to make dozens of scientific discoveries (National Institutes of Health, Office of Science Policy, n.d.). The case reflects poorly on the era's lax medical ethics: She was not asked for consent to use her cells; and her cells were labeled as "HeLa" cells, a privacy violation that led to her name becoming known. Of less clarity is the fact that she and her estate received no compensation. Her cells certainly had great scientific value, but many scientists would argue it was years of hard work and advances by many others that created the breakthroughs.

In addition to personally identifiable information, there are regulations to protect commercial **intellectual property (IP)**. Consider a cloud storage vendor that stores clients' intellectual property. Typically, a contract specifies penalties if the vendor exposed this sensitive IP. (See the liability discussions in Section 13.2.) However, the vendor might want to negotiate for some rights to the data:

- The right to monitor the storage growth rate and to use that data to predict future demand and have sufficient resources ready to go. The cloud vendor would argue this is mutually beneficial.
- The right to share or sell aggregate storage growth statistics. This could be valuable to disk drive manufacturers and investors in the industry. There is minimal risk to the client in sharing it, since it only reveals how many terabytes were consumed.

- The right to seek value from the IP itself, either by reselling it (sharing profits with the client) or making it public. Sites such as GitHub operate under this model. They host for free an unlimited amount of source code as long as that code is publicly viewable. This makes the site more attractive to other customers. There is a storage fee for customers who want their code to be private.
- The right to train a machine learning model using the data. Continuing the GitHub example, the company's Copilot tool, which autocompletes computer code based on a GPT-3 deep learning model, is trained at least in part on publicly accessible GitHub repositories. Gmail's Smart Compose and Smart Reply are similarly trained on a large body of email, though their outputs are carefully restricted to prevent leakage of either privacy-sensitive or otherwise valuable data (Chen et al., 2019). Both GitHub and Google Cloud customers can request that their data not be used for training purposes.

10.1.2 Balancing Corporate, Individual, and Government Concerns

Corporations offering data science applications, their customers and users, and their governments may clash over several matters.

Governments have decided they have a role in providing privacy protections, and that individuals should not navigate these difficult issues on their own. The GDPR and other frameworks mandate rules relating to data collection, storage, deletion, disclosure, and more.

Societal interests may derive from believing privacy is a universal right that must be protected. For example, in April 2021 the European Commission proposed draft regulations that would restrict biometric identification, such as facial recognition, in public spaces by private companies. In reaction to growing societal concerns and the unclear regulatory environment, Facebook decided to shut down their use of facial recognition in November 2021.

Governments may also want to protect residents who cannot make informed decisions. This includes those who might be coerced into providing permissions they regret. Also, society may feel that some collective uses of data should be controlled no matter what individuals may desire. Clearview AI's facial recognition product, which has been trained on billions of publicly available images on the Web, illustrates the impact of large-scale data aggregation's uses and concerns (Knight, 2021). This is a complex topic addressed more in Chapter 12 and Chapter 14.

Many regulations focus on data retention. Regulations may mandate that no personally identifiable data should be stored for longer than a certain period, and prescribe penalties for data disclosure. The risk of penalties has a powerful effect on companies. For example, in 2008 when Google announced the first Google Health product, the penalties for health record disclosure were steep enough to catalyze a pre-launch privacy and security audit. This led to a re-implementation of the underlying data storage system to encrypt all patient data both at rest and in transit to greatly reduce the risk of data leaks. Some countries mandate that certain types of data be stored only in-country, so that it is subject to their legal apparatus. EU countries and US companies are engaged in considerable give and take on this.

In some cases, governments seek to violate individual privacy for society's greater good. Law enforcement wants access to phone/email communication records and location data for criminal suspects, to decrypt suspect's encrypted data, and perhaps gather biometric identification data. Even the most liberal Western governments argue that search warrants can apply to private data. The US Constitution's Fourth Amendment limits searches to those that have "probable cause" and that are "particularly describing the place to be searched." There is active debate over exactly how those standards apply to private computer data. These debates reached a crescendo in 2015 on the topics of US NSA or FBI metadata collection (endpoint information on phone calls or chats) and the pros and cons of robust, on-device encryption of user data on iPhones, versus agency access through a backdoor.

Also, telephone companies like AT&T also receive many requests for data, as do the large internet technical companies (AT&T, 2022; Google, n.d.-c; Microsoft, n. d.). In the first half of 2020, for example, Microsoft and Google reported they received requests by governments for data on 50,000 and 250,000 accounts, respectively. Roughly 30%–40% of the Microsoft and Google requests came from US governmental entities, mostly local law enforcement. About a quarter of these requests were **geofence warrants**, which ask for the identity of any users whose phone indicates they were near a crime scene when it occurred. There is debate over whether such searches are unconstitutionally broad, but law enforcement use of them increased rapidly from 2018 to 2021.

Companies offering data science applications must navigate complex waters, given the conflicting desires of user communities, the often unclear and changing governmental regulatory regimes, and the contradictions between government regulations in the multiple locations in which a company operates. It seems reasonable to expect a continually changing landscape of laws and regulations as governments try to keep up with changing norms, while data science practices both catalyze and adapt to change. See Section 14.1 for more.

Some of the most challenging trade-offs relate to how much data to collect and retain. Data science's earliest practitioners reasoned that collecting and storing data was purely an asset. Therefore, storing lots of raw data provided the utmost flexibility for any future data science applications – "if some data is good, more is better!"

As an example, it might not seem necessary to log and retain every transaction's exact time and internet address. But a comparison of present and historical activity patterns can uncover suspicious activity (a cyber-attack, credit card fraud, or other abuse), either forensically or in real time.

As another example, Google used search log data for its Flu Trends application, which was available for about five years. Based on crowdsourced search term frequencies, it reported the severity of flu outbreaks with initially promising but ultimately disappointing accuracy (Ginsberg et al., 2009; Lazer & Kennedy, 2015). See Chapter 11 for more details. Similarly, Microsoft used Bing search logs to detect previously unknown adverse drug reactions (White et al., 2014). As mentioned in Section 6.3, Google used its history of individuals' location data to chart societal movement trends over time.

Despite the benefits of retaining all available data for possible future use, there is a growing recognition that data can also be a liability. GDPR Article 5 expresses a **principle of data minimization**: "Personal data shall be . . . limited to what is necessary in relation to the purposes for which they are processed" (European Parliament and Council of the European Union, 2016). Many privacy advocates believe a system should discard data unless it is already known to be necessary, as a system cannot leak what it does not have. In many cases, compliance with privacy standards will mean that data collected for one purpose cannot be used for a different one. Data science implementers have come to realize that there are costs to holding onto more data – bookkeeping costs in recording and tracking its provenance and the potential for fines, lawsuits, and reputation loss if data is mishandled.

While most data leaks occur because of security failures, as discussed in Section 10.2, limiting disclosure of confidential information is subtle due to many policy issues. As examples, how do individuals easily and safely authorize or revoke a system's right to share their personal information with others? How fine-grained are the authorizations and how long should they last? Consumer advocates want users to have fine-grained control over their data. However, consumers don't want to be bombarded with too many questions.

If a user forgets their password, how should one balance the ease of recovering account access against an attacker's ease in gaining unauthorized access? Should individuals be informed if the government demands access to their private data? Interestingly, this last answer is partially government limited, as certain information requests, at least in the US, are themselves confidential. (See the previous footnote on national security.)

Companies need prudent and clear policies around maintaining confidentiality. In 2012, Target was criticized for using customers' purchase histories to predict likely pregnancies (Duhigg, 2012). Target made two mistakes. First, they mailed pregnancy-related marketing materials in packages that revealed the potential pregnancy to anyone who glanced at the package, violating the "for self" restriction. Second, many customers found these recommendations creepy ("How did Target know?"). Finding the line between creepy and acceptable is complex; it probably would have been fine to mail a diaper ad post-birth.

10.1.3 Technologies for Privacy

While privacy's social, legal, and policy issues are thorny, there are promising technologies that address specific privacy concerns. We will cover seven:

- **Access control** determines who can see data.
- **Encryption** obscures data even when it can be accessed.
- **Differential privacy** provides guaranteed limits to what can be learned about any individual in a dataset by carefully adding noise.
- **Federated learning** lets each user keep their data on their own device, but for all users to share what machine learning derives from that data.
- **Secure multi-party computation** provides cryptographic guarantees of privacy.
- **Secure enclaves** provide hardware-based guarantees.
- **Homomorphic encryption** allows queries against an encrypted dataset.

In online data's early days, privacy was not a priority, and privacy protections were certainly insufficient. In a practice called **de-identification**, personally identifiable information such as names, Social Security numbers, and street addresses were removed from datasets, with the expectation that the datasets could then be released for research purposes without risk.

In 2002, Latanya Sweeney demonstrated that this was insufficient. If the mentioned fields are removed but birth date, gender, and zip code remain, then 87% of the US population could be re-identified. Sweeney identified then-Massachusetts Governor William Weld's hospital admission data by conjoining state medical records and motor vehicle records (Sweeney, 2002). As we mentioned in our analysis of recommendations in Section 5.3, in 2007 Netflix was criticized when they released an anonymized dataset of customer movie rankings. It turned out that people who give a supposedly private Netflix movie rating sometimes gave a publicly viewable rating on IMDb at about the same time. Researchers used this to re-identify some of the Netflix users (Narayanan & Shmatikov, 2008).

Consider a utility company that wants to publish aggregated smart meter data, such as a neighborhood's average household energy usage, but must ensure it doesn't reveal any individual customer's usage. If the only available information was a large neighborhood's single average, there would be no problems. But when multiple queries are allowed, it quickly becomes possible to compromise privacy.

For example, if someone makes the two queries, "average energy usage for homes in zip code 12345" and "average energy usage for homes in zip code 12345 using less than 200 million BTUs per year," and if from different data sources we know the number of homes in the zip code and that customer X is the only one likely to be using over 200 million BTUs, then customer X's exact usage is exposed. Researchers have proven that there are only two ways to protect against such attacks: Either don't allow such queries, or limit the kind of queries and add carefully controlled *noise* to the results. In other words, don't give the exact average, but rather an approximate average (Dwork & Roth, 2014).

Access Control

Access control is a mechanism for limiting who can see data. Each dataset has a list of the only users allowed to access the data. Corporate employees should receive access to sensitive data only after training on privacy-preserving procedures. The **principle of least privilege** says they should have access only to what data they strictly need. Usually, access will be to anonymized aggregated data products, not to the original raw data.

An employee with multiple roles should use the least-privileged role that gets the job done to minimize risk of inadvertent errors. All access should be logged and audited, and, for the most sensitive operations, multiple people should be required to simultaneously approve access, and alerts should be sent whenever access occurs. That way a single rogue employee can't break privacy. Unfortunately, the continual overhead of fine-grained access control is real, and it can result in reduced communication and collaboration. Computers holding especially sensitive information may be completely isolated from the Internet (an "air gap") or may have limited, carefully vetted access paths.

Individual consumers bear some of the burden of managing access controls. Every time an app is installed, it asks for a set of permissions, and consumers should attend to these. However, these permissions are often hard to understand, and often the only alternative is to not use the app. Careful consideration needs to be paid as to how best to explain to users what their choices mean, whether to have defaults be opt-in or opt-out, and how frequently to ask users questions.

Encryption

Encryption is the process of altering data so its true meaning can only be restored with the correct decryption keys. That shifts the burden of privacy from a large dataset to a smaller collection of keys. Sensitive data should be encrypted both when at rest (stored on disk) and in transit (transmitted between computers). The most sensitive data might stay encrypted even when in use (during computation), with homomorphic encryption or secure enclaves.

It's easy to forget how much has changed since the Internet's earliest days. In 1995, Netscape introduced **HTTPS (HyperText Transfer Protocol Secure)** over **SSL (Secure Sockets Layer).** It was used for passwords and financial transactions on the Web, but was not commonly used to protect user data. Most web data still traveled over the insecure HTTP protocol or improperly configured versions of HTTPS. Only since about 2013 (due in part to the Snowden revelations about government surveillance of internet traffic) has most network communication been encrypted. As of 2021, most traffic now uses SSL's successor, **TLS (Transport Layer Security).**

Differential Privacy

Differential privacy allows the release of summary statistical information about a dataset while maintaining the confidentiality of individuals within it (Dwork, 2008). For example, hospitals use differential privacy to share medical information about the expected course of a disease, without compromising the privacy of any patient.

The key insight is this: If an individual's data is not in a dataset, then that information cannot leak when statistics are published. Therefore, we should only answer queries such that there is a vanishingly small probability that the querier can distinguish between the answers they get when an individual is or is not in the dataset. Differential privacy is a way of figuring out the minimum amount of noise that must be added to the data while guaranteeing a vanishingly small probability of revealing confidential information.

Recently, using Census 2010 and other public data, the Census Bureau itself exactly re-identified nearly 50% of participating individuals using just block, sex, age, race, and ethnicity information. Motivated by the legal requirement that the Census keep personally identifiable information confidential for 72 years, Census 2020 adopted differential privacy for the public release of census results. However, scaling this idea to the breadth of the Census has run into some practical problems, e.g., small subpopulations being affected more than larger ones, and logistical inconsistencies because of rounding fractional numbers to the nearest integer (NCSL, 2021). Whether differential privacy works sufficiently well for this application is yet to be seen.

Federated Learning

If data can be a liability for the company that holds it (due to leakage risks), then never holding the data eliminates the risk. Suppose a company develops a speech recognition app that runs on users' phones. To ensure privacy, no users' voice recordings are transmitted to the company. A machine learning algorithm could run on the phone, continuously learning and improving performance for that one user. That's an example of "use of data for self." The goal of **federated learning** is to allow this improved performance to be shared by all users, making this "use of data for others" without actually sharing any of the data.

Federated learning's trick is for each phone to transmit back to the company the machine learning model parameters it has learned, but not any data. A company-controlled computer then combines all users' parameters and broadcasts them back out, so everyone gets an improved model. If users are worried that their individual parameters might be intercepted, a technique called **secure aggregation**, where random numbers are added to each parameter value, can be used. The sum of the random additions cancels out to zero, so the aggregation is accurate, even if each contribution is obscured.

Of course, even though each user's voice recordings remain secure on their own device, users may still be concerned that information about their recordings could be reverse-engineered from the model parameters. For many domains, such as voice recognition, this risk may be adequately addressed by increasing the number of users over which aggregation is performed. However, in general, to completely eliminate this privacy risk, it is necessary to add random noise that does *not* cancel out to zero. This can be done either by users' themselves, or as part of the aggregation, in a manner that guarantees differential privacy of the model parameters.

This raises the question of how to trade off local storage versus cloud storage. If data never leaves a personal device, then individuals are no longer at risk of a data center breach, but they have an increased risk of data loss if their personal device is lost, stolen, or damaged. The threat of search warrants and other law enforcement requests remains no matter where the data is stored, but overly broad requests are more likely to target big companies.

Secure Multi-Party Computation (SMC)

Suppose multiple parties each hold some data, and they want to compute a function over its aggregation while still keeping their individual data private. For example, say that a group wants to compute their average salary without disclosing any individual salary. This is easily done if they all trust a third party. They tell their salary to that third party and it then calculates the average and reports back.

Doing this without a trusted third party motivates the technique of **Secure Multi-Party Computation (SMC)**. It relies on the difficulty of breaking cryptographic primitives. Input data (e.g., each person's salary) is encrypted and a "garbled" circuit computes over these encrypted values and publicly outputs a decrypted result for all parties.

In 2008, the Danish beet auction used SMC with 1200 participating bidders (Bogetoft et al., 2009). In 2015, the Boston Women's Workforce Council partnered with Boston University to determine if there are wage disparities based on gender in companies in the Greater Boston Area (Lapets et al., 2016). In 2017, Google and Mastercard used SMC to determine which ad clicks resulted in credit card purchases, without divulging any individual's identity or history (Ion et al., 2017). SMC is practical and scalable (Kamara et al., 2014) when the computation is restricted, for example, computing an average or computing the intersection of two sets, such as two customer lists.

Secure Enclaves

Another approach to guaranteeing data security is specially designed computing hardware. Modern CPUs have instructions that define a private memory region, called a **secure enclave**, whose contents cannot be read or written by any process outside of that enclave, including the operating system itself. An enclave protects its data by encrypting it in storage and decrypting it only when a processor assigned to the enclave uses it. Enclaves enforce computation over encrypted data in use, strengthening the previously discussed use of encryption at rest and in transit. Getting secure enclave technology right has proven very challenging, as there are many forms of attacks to analyze and counter.

In 2015, Intel introduced Software Guard Extensions (SGX) in its Skylake micro-architecture to support secure enclaves. AMD and IBM followed with their own variants in their respective EPYC and S390 processors. Apple's M1 chipset uses a secure enclave for touch ID. Major cloud vendors provide secure enclave-enabled services.

Homomorphic Encryption

Encryption makes data more confidential, but does not protect it against those who hold its decryption keys. This leads to the question of whether a cloud provider could hold data, but not have the keys? **End-to-end encryption** using traditional methods can be employed if the cloud provider is merely storing data. However, the cloud provider will not be able to process it, for example, to retrieve all files containing the words "sales report" and "EMEA." Those words won't appear in the encrypted files, nor will their encrypted versions, because strong encryption methods do not encrypt words one-by-one.

Homomorphic encryption lets certain computations take place on encrypted data. For example, a user can give encrypted search terms to the cloud provider and it could retrieve files containing those words, without the provider knowing what the search terms are or what words are in the files. The breadth of possible computations goes beyond search, but still has significant limitations.

The mathematics for homomorphic encryption was developed in the 1970s. However, initial versions were impractical as the needed computations were trillions of times slower than unencrypted computation. In 2009, Craig Gentry's Ph.D. thesis (Gentry, 2009) spread virally in the mathematics and computer science communities. His approach was only thousands of times slower, not trillions. While still too slow for most use cases, it is sufficient for others, and cloud providers are taking notice. Amazon, IBM, Google, and Microsoft all offer fast variants of homomorphic encryption as part of their cloud offerings, but there are still significant limitations on their use.

10.1.4 Location Data

Our cell phones know their own location quite accurately, and thus know their owner's. Cell phones receive signals from Global Positioning System (GPS) satellites, WiFi hotspots, and cellular towers, and can estimate the distance to their known positions. When signals are unavailable (e.g., inside some buildings), a built-in inertial measurement unit measures accelerations to compute location changes.

Location data is crucial to many key smartphone functions, such as direction-finding and physical fitness apps. If we search for "Vegetarian Restaurant," we expect our phone to show us nearby restaurants. Fitness applications typically depend on knowledge of our running, hiking, or bicycling paths to estimate our workouts and share them with others. Parents may get rights to track younger children's location, providing peace of mind while giving the children more autonomy to roam.

Anonymous aggregation of location data can produce real-time traffic reports and measure the popularity of different destinations. The previously mentioned Google COVID-19 Community Mobility Reports, based on cell phone location data, help health officials track the effectiveness of social distancing measures.

In all these aggregation applications, great care must be taken to not disclose any individual's location. Individuals could experience embarrassment if revealed to be someplace they shouldn't. Businesses could lose strategic advantage if known to be meeting with a potential partner.

Even aggregate information can cause problems. In 2017, an International Security student noticed the Strava fitness-tracking app was revealing concentrations of GPS jogging tracks made by users in remote areas of Syria, Yemen, Niger, and Afghanistan (Sly, 2018). Clearly, soldiers were making these tracks and inadvertently revealing their locations. Strava did nothing wrong; they displayed anonymized tracks for opted-in users who hadn't realized this compromised military security.

Using location-dependent apps is a clear individual benefit, though there are risks as well. Sometimes terms are not clearly specified, or there is an opt-out arrangement rather than opt-in, and a user unintentionally shares information.

There is also a **chain of trust** issue where users may be happy sharing with an entity, but not sure whether that entity will in turn share their data with a less trustworthy entity – perhaps someone they are not even aware of. In 2021 a company called X-Mode created a software library for simplifying access to location data on phones. For example, a Muslim prayer app with nearly 100 million downloads used X-Mode's library to remind users when to pray based on the phone's location. But the library sent location data directly to X-Mode (not to the app makers who incorporated the library) without users' permission. It is not clear what X-Mode did with the data. As a result, Google and Apple banned all X-Mode-using apps from their app stores (Tau, 2020).

Any time data is recorded, there is always the chance that it may be leaked or requested by a law enforcement agency. In general, society agrees that catching criminals is a good thing, but if requests are too broad ("show me everyone whose phone was within a mile of this address on this day where and when a crime occurred"), then many innocent people may be subject to harassment from authorities.

10.1.5 Unintended Consequences of Privacy

One unintended consequence of a strong privacy regulation focus is that it may force companies to control information more tightly – by prohibiting external use, even of aggregated information. This may further increase the corporate push to vertically integrate, thereby reducing the benefits of information sharing and of competition. Sharing scientific data, particularly health-related, raises analogous problems, making multi-center projects more difficult. "Democratizing data" is a worthy goal, but it must be weighed against privacy risks.

Every time a company delegates responsibility to subcontractors, it incurs an additional security risk. Using cloud computing services makes some delegation almost inevitable, with cloud vendors arguing their exceptional investments in security and privacy reduce risk. But delegation can still lead to problems. For example, a 2020 data privacy breach at many not-for-profits was due to a security breach at Blackbaud, a vertical cloud vendor that provided their automation technologies (Davis, 2020). The 2016 Facebook/Cambridge Analytica scandal, discussed in more detail in Section 11.3, also happened in part because Facebook delegated data rights to a party who violated them.

The complexity of meeting privacy regulations may be sufficient such that they increase barriers to entry in markets, further favoring incumbents (Layton, 2019). Just adhering to data take-out and deletion rules can be hard for a small organization. In July 2020, North Dakota Representative Kelly Armstrong noted European GDPR privacy regulations had had a negative effect on competitive ads marketplaces, since Google was no longer making certain data public due to privacy concerns (Rev, 2020). Decisions by Apple, Google, and others are ending the use of third-party cookies. While this increases privacy, it could adversely affect third-party players in the online advertising industry.

A notable privacy versus security challenge is illustrated by the TOR Project (TOR Project, n.d.). Among other goals, TOR aims to provide anonymity for its users in surfing the Web and communicating, yet it also facilitates criminal behavior.

A privacy versus safety challenge arises in the fight against child pornography, which was discussed in Section 8.2. While most internet services proactively scan for illicit photos, maximal privacy guarantees argue against this. For years, there seemed to be little debate that this was the right thing to do.

However, in 2021, Apple, which had been a vocal privacy supporter, announced it was undertaking these scans in a new manner that could eventually be used to scan photos that only resided on user devices. To quell concerns, Apple published a lengthy Q&A and stated that it was proposing to only scan photos stored in its iCloud service (Apple Inc., 2021). Privacy advocates then persuaded Apple to delay its plans. As of early 2022, the plan has now gone back to the drawing board to better tune competing objectives.

The more barriers there are to using information and sharing data, the harder it is for institutions to apply data science and reap its rewards. If medical institutions could share patient records, then we could build better machine learning models for diagnosis and treatment. For example, finding patients with similar mammograms to determine the best course of treatment. HIPAA prevents this data sharing, further disadvantaging smaller clinics.

As another example, many (including co-author Alfred) believed that location tracing applications on mobile phones, possibly fusing GPS and Bluetooth proximity data, would have helped reduce COVID-19's spread (Spector, 2020; Wymant et al., 2021). However, the perception of privacy risks in the Western democracies was often hard to overcome. While the necessary apps were written, they were rarely used, though there were exceptions (e.g., Finland). Kai-Fu Lee argued that reduced regulation and less societal concern over privacy gave Chinese institutions advantages over others (Lee, 2018). However, since Lee's book was published, Chinese policy has been evolving, so time will tell how this finally plays out.

10.2 Security

Computer security is concerned with protecting systems from "unauthorized access, use, disclosure, disruption, modification, or destruction in order to provide confidentiality, integrity, and availability" (NIST, n.d.), Computer security addresses issues in storage, processing, and communication.

Security is related to privacy because of the shared concern with undesired data disclosure. Many privacy problems reported in the news are actually security breaches. Examples include the following:

- The 2015 break-in to the US Office of Personnel Management, which exfiltrated data from millions of background checks of people seeking government security clearances (Gootman, 2016).
- The 2017 breach of over 100 million Equifax customer records (Wang & Johnson, 2018).
- The 2020 breach of Blackbaud, which revealed philanthropists' personal data (Blackbaud, 2020).
- The 2021 breach of 40 million T-Mobile customers' data, which exposed Social Security numbers (T-Mobile, 2021).

Beyond protecting confidentiality, computer security also covers attacks that interfere with a system's correct operation, such as malicious code insertion, denial of service, or ransomware. Security is truly hard for many reasons including these:

1. Political and economic motivations for bad actors.
2. The complexity of computer systems.
3. The fallibility of programmers and systems operators.
4. The sad truth that attackers are often as talented and well funded as defenders.
5. The asymmetry of the security challenge, where defenders must secure every door, while attackers need only find one way in.[2] Even one vulnerability can allow inserting code in a system that acts as a vector for all manner of additional harm. In late 2021, the Log4j vulnerability, in a package which many Java programs depend on, again demonstrated this risk (Apache, n.d.).

[2] We note that defenders do gain some leverage because fixing an important security vulnerability can eliminate the possibility of multiple specific attacks.

Passwords for controlling access are commonly the first line of security defense, but are problematic. They can be leaked or phished.[3] Common passwords can be guessed. Unusual passwords can be forgotten. For added security, it is best practice to use all three of:

- something known, like a password;
- something possessed, like a hardware token or a phone[4]; and
- something biometric, like a fingerprint, retinal scan, or voice match.

The process for retrieving a forgotten password can't be perfect, and will sometimes grant invalid access or deny valid access. It is also good practice to set up contingency plans so friends or family can access data if the user dies or is incapacitated.

Security is also a cat-and-mouse game; new mechanisms, new attacks by bad actors, and new defensive countermeasures are constantly being tried out. Data science applications are inviting targets, due to their importance, and breaches have serious repercussions. For society to trust these applications, they must be secure.

The National Academies 2007 book *Toward a Safer and More Secure Cyberspace* (National Research Council, 2007) contains a statement of security goals known as the **CyberSecurity Bill of Rights**. Table 10.1 lists these goals and annotates each one with its implication on data science (*in italics*).

The good news is that many governmental entities, organizations, and individuals recognize the challenges and have improved computer security. However, the risks remain high. The CSO's 2021 survey indicates that a majority of organizations suffered economic damage from security incidents, 28% said PII (personally identifiable information) was stolen, and 12% suffered "massive" economic loss (Knorr, 2021). Because of this, 71% of organizations plan to increase their security budget. Security implementation challenges include:

- Safe user authentication mechanisms, given human propensity to cut corners, such as reusing passwords and the prevalence of bad actors tricking users into providing credentials and/or access to them.
- Preventing and recovering from ransomware attacks.
- Using audit data and other real-time signals to detect attacks or other breaches in a way that does not add additional risks, such as divulging confidential information.
- Encrypting data and managing encryption keys in easy yet secure ways. As mentioned in Section 10.1, encryption is a key to privacy and the future of

[3] A Google Blog post in 2019 (Pullman et al., 2019) reported there were four billion username/password pairs that were unsafe due to data breaches!

[4] The phone's hardware-protected secure element provides more security than retrieving a code from an SMS message.

Table 10.1 *Security challenges in data science: CyberSecurity Bill of Rights (goals and* implications).

I. Availability of system and network resources to legitimate users.
Data science applications have become critical to society, and harm may result when they are not available.

II. Easy and convenient recovery from successful attacks.
*Nothing is perfect, so systems need to recover. Consider the increasing number of ransomware attacks such as the 2020 attack on the Garmin fitness tracking device and app. The attack took that application down for days, and Garmin reportedly paid a $10 million ransom to get back online (*Porter, 2020*).*

III. Control over and knowledge of one's own computing environment.
Users need to understand, trust, and have control over their computing environment, including their data, whether it's on their phone, computer, or internet services. Many users do not understand the available privacy and security settings in user interfaces that are time-consuming to learn.

IV. Confidentiality of stored information and information exchange.
This is central to preventing information leaks and shared with concerns of privacy.

V. Authentication and provenance.
Users need to prove their identities to systems in convenient and secure ways. If not convenient, the mechanisms will not be used. If insecure, systems will mistakenly divulge data to imposters. Furthermore, users should understand the provenance of their accessed data, which better enables understanding and interpretation (or perhaps outright rejection) of it.

VI. The technological capability to exercise fine-grained control over the flow of information in and through systems.
Data flows and storage must be controlled within data science applications and the entities controlling them. For example, data science applications must be locked down in ways that prevent programmers, data scientists, or administrators from either mistakenly or maliciously divulging data.

VII. Security in using computing directly or indirectly in important applications, including financial, healthcare, and electoral transactions, and real-time remote control of devices that interact with physical processes.
Each of these domains is potentially privacy-sensitive, mission-critical, and regulated. They must balance innovation versus resilience (see Section 10.4) and preserve confidentiality, while allowing the needed transparency of operation to regulators and law enforcement.

VIII. The ability to access any source of information (e.g., email, web page, file) safely.
Users of data-science-enabled systems need to be confident that they can access information privately and without fear of corruption, regardless of location, communication network, or device.

IX. Awareness of what security is actually being delivered by a system or component.
Users benefit from understanding the security properties of systems they use, including but not limited to data privacy, thereby letting them make cost/benefit trade-offs.

X. Justice for security problems caused by another party.
Users will be more confident in data science applications if they believe bad actors will be punished and that there is due process that could compensate them for actual harm.

hardware-based encrypted-computation mechanisms, such as secure enclaves.

- Verifying and operationally maintaining the correctness of vast amounts of computer software, particularly when it includes possibly opaque externally written software libraries.
- Protecting against nation-state malfeasance aimed at infiltrating and sabotaging organizations that operate data science applications.
- Creating policies and procedures for operational and regulatory responses to failures if and when they occur.

Regrettably, there are no simple solutions to these issues. First, security revolves around people. Second, computer systems consist of many complex and diverse components of unclear provenance. The breadth of security problems has convinced co-author Alfred that computer security is computing's greatest challenge.

10.3 Resistance to Abuse

In the early days of computer networks, the user base was a small homogeneous community of computing researchers, students, and teachers. Like the residents of a small town, they trusted each other and felt no need to lock their doors. MIT's 1967 ITS time-sharing network allowed anyone to use it without a password or account. The benign nature of these early days provided a false sense of security.

With a million-fold growth in the user population of network systems,[5] developers of systems must remember that a significant number of users may be bad actors. Small-town trust has disappeared, and nefarious actors have moved in – everyone from teenagers making a little mischief, to professional criminal rings, to political movements willing to play dirty tricks, to terrorist operations, to nation states with billion-dollar cyber-warfare budgets. Defending against the most sophisticated attackers has been an enormous challenge that is still not fully understood or controlled. Facebook has removed more than a billion fake accounts per quarter since late 2018 (Statista, n.d.).

We define **abuse** as using a computer system outside of its rules of behavior, usually with the goal of subverting its proper operation and achieving some disruptive, profitable, political, or nihilistic end. Whereas security attacks involve

[5] The *Arpanet Directory* of 1978 (SRI International et al., 1978) had 4,000 individuals listed in it, contrasted to the billions who use the successor Internet today.

deliberate efforts to compromise programs and data, abuse is committed without any security penetration. Regrettably, there are many examples:

- Advertising click fraud was an early case of widespread abuse. To produce advertising revenue, some advertising property holders, who were paid per ad click, would build and deploy bot networks that clicked on ads to generate revenue. In effect, they manufactured fake data (i.e., clicks). In response, advertising systems developed anti-abuse systems to detect and discard this data.
- Search engines rank pages among factors including the page contents, the links to it, and the clicks it receives. An industry of "white hat" search engine optimization attempts to make pages better by improving these factors. There is also a shadow "black hat" industry that attempts to trick search engines without actually improving pages. Because of this, mechanisms to thwart abuse have long been essential.
- Online marketplaces like Amazon rank products in part by user reviews. This has led to fake reviews falsely promoting a product, or falsely putting down the competition.
- Facebook, Twitter, and others have had to contend with advertisers who hide their national identity and publish propaganda-style content. This behavior violates policies and laws limiting foreign interference. Even when a large percentage of such attacks are successfully defended against, those that get through are harmful.
- Facebook mistakenly let abusers steal a half billion users' personal data via a vulnerability in the "contact importer" tool. If an uploaded contact list included a Facebook user's phone number, then Facebook completed the contact entry with that user's data. Abusers uploaded contact lists with random phone numbers.
- Microsoft's chatbot, Tay, was taught hate speech in less than one day through repetitive hate-speech messaging to it (Lee, 2016). The chatbot was metaphorically a parrot, which regrettably learned all too quickly and well.

Deep fakes use computer-generated images, audio, or video that seem to portray a real person doing or saying something that they did not. Machine learning advances have increased the ability to create these fakes and made them more realistic. Advances have also enhanced our ability to detect deep fakes, leading to another cat-and-mouse game (Greengard, 2019). Techniques of data provenance, mentioned in Section 8.3, could be a partial solution, as they might deter abuse and let viewers know the chain of creation of what they are watching or listening to. Some camera manufacturers now offer hardware that helps prove authenticity.

All computer systems are vulnerable to abuse. However, data science applications are doubly vulnerable since both programs and data can be attacked. There are three subcategories of data attacks: **adversarial data attacks**, **data poisoning**, and **model stealing**.

In an **adversarial data attack**, the attacker crafts an example specifically to trick a machine learning program into giving a wrong prediction. Consider an image recognition program that takes images as input and outputs labels such as "panda" or "gibbon." With access to a model's exact parameters, an adversary can start with, for example, an image of a panda. They then mathematically determine the minimal number of pixels to change so the model will label it as "gibbon."

The necessary changes are often surprisingly small.The top part of Figure 10.1 shows that the resulting adversarial image does not look like a half-panda/half-gibbon. To the human eye, it is imperceptibly different from the original panda image.

The bottom part of Figure 10.1 shows that the human visual system is not immune to misinterpreting small changes in an image. The dots in the corners of the squares fool the eye into thinking the straight lines are not straight.

The first adversarial attacks were tailored to fool one specific machine learning model. Recent attacks are more robust; a single adversary can fool multiple different models. Successful adversaries can be made from 3D printed shapes

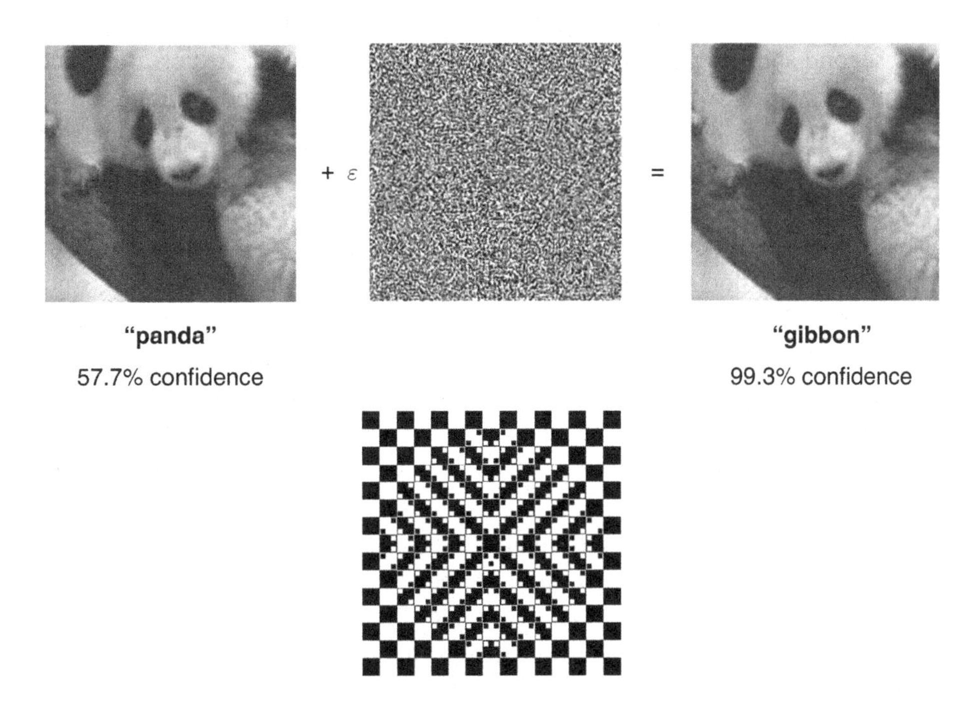

Figure 10.1 Top: Changing a small number of pixels yields an adversarial image that is mis-labeled by a deep neural network. From Goodfellow et al. (2015), used by courtesy of the authors. Bottom: An optical illusion that fools humans. Image copyright Akiyoshi Kitaoka, used with permission from www.ritsumei.ac.jp/~akitaoka/.

photographed at different angles, or by adding small amounts of graffiti to road signs to confuse self-driving cars (Gitlin, 2017). Similar adversarial attacks also work in speech recognition and natural language understanding.

Previously, it had been widely accepted that small changes to an image would lead to small changes in the probabilities of each label. It turns out this is not the case for deep neural network models. In these high-dimensional nonlinear models, it is easy to find cases where two examples are close to each other in the input space, but are assigned different labels by the model.

Several steps can partially mitigate adversarial attacks:

- Train on more images from a wider variety of situations.
- Generate synthetic images with a rendering program that can produce variants with different rotations, blurring, textures, color tinting, and backgrounds.
- Keep the details of the model secret. This makes it harder for an attacker to be sure of success, but many attacks work against a wide variety of similar models.
- Defend against adversarial attacks as part of the development process, and retrain using the successful adversarial images as additional data.

Even with these defenses, we can't guarantee protection against adversarial attacks.

The second subcategory of data attacks is **data poisoning**. Adversaries feed a training machine learning system bad data, resulting in a model vulnerable to future attacks. This can be a problem for any system that accepts data from users.

For example, an email system lets users label their emails as spam or not spam. It then uses those labels to train a machine learning model. Attackers can open multiple accounts, flood them with their own spam messages, label them as not spam, and there's a good chance the model will accept their subsequent messages as not spam. Similarly, the Tay chatbot suffered from data poisoning.

To mitigate data poisoning, it is important not to let any one group contribute too much data to a model. Monitoring may detect when an attack is underway, and regression testing can show if the attack succeeds in changing the system's predictions.

The third subcategory is **model stealing**. Attackers do not disrupt a system's operation, but make enough queries to it that they can either reproduce the underlying model and steal it or they can determine if the model uses particular data, thereby compromising privacy. A strong defense against stealing a model's training data is not to have a single model, but rather to train and deploy an ensemble of models. Private Aggregation of Teacher Ensembles (PATE) is one such ensemble training method (Papernot et al., 2018).

To summarize, any valuable data science application is a potential target for attackers, and defense against abuse is needed. First, when designing applications, developers must keep abuse defense in mind.[6] Second, developers must invest in abuse prevention, which could be more costly and time-consuming than creating the application. Prevention techniques include:

- defensive thinking (imagining what an attacker could do);
- minimizing feedback to attackers (don't tell them when they're getting closer);
- limiting the attack surface (e.g., by rate-limiting queries);
- planning for managing incidents and emergency responses; and
- monitoring for anomalies (even if potential attacks cannot yet be identified).

Anomaly detection paid off when Bitcoin prices rose in 2017. Various actors started using Google Cloud servers to mine for Bitcoin. It wasn't profitable to pay for the servers, so attackers used stolen credit cards, phishing, and other attacks to gain access. Monitoring systems detected changing usage patterns for cloud computing, and Google analyzed what was happening, shut down illegitimate use, and warned clients with compromised accounts.

As with all computing, abuse techniques will continue to evolve, as will anti-abuse measures in response.

10.4 Resilience

Resilience refers to a system's ability to metaphorically bend, compress, or stretch so as to continue to function under stress, to rarely crash, and to recover quickly after a failure. Also, they must produce anticipated results under challenging circumstances. We say "anticipated" to indicate perfection is not required, but results should be within expected ranges.

Resilience is most important for critical infrastructure, such as power and water systems, and life-and-death situations, such as in clinical systems. More mundanely, we are becoming increasingly dependent on data science applications – ranging from our phone and email contacts database, to our communications infrastructure, to automatic map routing. Since we rely on them, they must be resilient.

Co-author Alfred recalls visiting a major medical center circa 2010 and seeing that patient bed assignment was done on a whiteboard. The team knew the manual process was suboptimal, but believed it would work in almost any scenario. They could not tolerate the risk and liability if computer systems failed. Possibly it was an excuse to not automate the system, but their system did indeed need to function even under dire circumstances.

[6] This lesson is apparently still hard to fully learn; at the very hour this paragraph was receiving its penultimate revision, a new Slack feature was immediately subjected to abuse and had to be disabled (Statt, 2021).

Co-author Peter recalls arriving at Heathrow airport to find that the terminal had no power. Happily, everyone boarded and departed on time even though the computers were down. This was a great example of a computer system so resilient it could operate even without computers. Someone had the foresight to plan for a power outage, to have paperwork printed offsite, and to train personnel to carry out the procedures to use these paper backups.

The Boeing 737 Max crashes in 2018 and 2019 showed a lack of resilience in a data-centric control loop added to overcome flight instability due to retrofitting very powerful engines in an older airframe. With the control loop in operation, the plane is more efficient and easier to fly than its predecessors, with the key proviso that the airspeed sensors would report the correct airspeed.

However, the 737 Max's design was susceptible to just one sensor's malfunction, so a single failure could make the plane nearly impossible for some pilots to control. This resulted in catastrophic crashes in 2018 and 2019, followed by two years of the aircraft's grounding. Interestingly, this problem was solved properly in the 1970s on the Space Shuttle (Spector & Gifford, 1984). Boeing engineers mistakenly (i) made their system overly dependent on data from sensors that proved unreliable and (ii) did not properly prepare pilots to seize manual control during a failure.

In retrospect, engineers overly optimized for fuel economy and time to market at safety's expense. While this may seem a bit far from many data science examples, it is a perfect example of the challenges of achieving resilience; the needs for data redundancy, graceful degradation, and sufficient preparation for manual override.

Resilience suggests there should be no single point of failure, but this often conflicts with a desire for optimality. Consider scheduling pickups for an Uber/Lyft-like service. If requests for all services were to flow through a single system, it could compute the optimal schedule, minimizing wait times and miles driven. However, a single failure could disrupt all service. Instead, if different computers schedule competing services, each service might have slightly longer wait times, but single failures would cause less global disruption.

The Irish Potato famine of 1845 is, in part, traceable to a lack of resilience. Farmers overwhelmingly planted the "Lumper" potato variant because of its high yield even in poor soil. This was optimal for years, but Lumpers were vulnerable to water mold which wiped out much of the crop. The famine would have been less severe if there had been more crop variety.

In general, systems should take care to leave some buffer between their normal operation and their theoretical maxima just in case something goes wrong. Pre-COVID-19, the Internet was provisioned with extra capacity to support streaming video – which proved essential for the widespread video conferencing needed during the pandemic. In 2008, the global financial system had insufficient buffers, resulting in a debt-induced recession. Regulations were written that try to fix this.

Tom DeMarco calls this buffer "Slack" in the 2001 book with that title (DeMarco, 2002). Companies that focus on optimizing labor productivity turn out to do worse than companies that build in some slack. For example, firms can employ extra employees so no one burns out, order extra supplies to prevent ordering delays, and support extra projects that might slightly delay the main project, but could eventually lead to even more valuable ones.

Perhaps the most well-known failure due to lack of resilience was the 1940 Tacoma Narrows Bridge disaster. Bridge engineers want to make their structures robust, but don't want to waste time, money, and materials making them stronger than necessary. The Tacoma Narrows Bridge was the first to use carbon steel girders, an optimization that reduced the amount of concrete needed, and thus the overall weight. However, the engineers miscalculated how wind would interact with this new design, resulting in the bridge tearing apart in 40 mph winds. The video of its divergent oscillation is an invaluable lesson in humility, and a reminder that models may not predict all behaviors, and that people can be slow to respond to early warnings (see Tony C, 2006).

Achieving resilience in a data science application requires attention to at least nine issues:

1. Resilient systems need to prepare for **known-unknowns**. These are out-of-the-ordinary but understood events whose timing or implications are not understood. They must also prepare for **unknown-unknowns**, which have never before been seen. Even though, by definition, unknown-unknowns are unknowable, we can set forth their general categories and include those in resilience considerations.
2. Applications with many users tend to change the world in which they operate, and we need to think ahead to that changed world. For example, consider how the post-Twitter world is different from the world before Twitter. This poses a problem for machine learning algorithms trained on past data, but which operate in the present. For example, combating click fraud is more than eliminating current scam operations. It also involves thinking about what a scammer's next moves will be, how to respond to those moves, how they will respond to the response, etc.
3. We can only trust solutions we understand sufficiently well. To achieve a non-resilient success, we could gather some data, train a model to achieve high accuracy, and stop there. But to be guaranteed resilience, we need enough understanding to know how and when the model will work, and how it might fail. If the problem is a control loop, we probably need to understand the problem's underlying physics. A working program is evidence of a good

solution, but to achieve resilience, we want not just evidence but something closer to a proof.

4. We gain trust through verification and validation. There are standard software engineering practices to achieve this, and they should be applied to data science applications. But verifying data science algorithms is more challenging because of inherent uncertainty in their input data as well as their deployment environment (Wing, 2021).
5. Resilient systems must have good neighbors. We can make sure the core algorithms are correct, but a system has many peripheral parts: user interfaces, sensors, servers, networks, operating systems, and miscellaneous software. All of these should be verified and validated. Attention should be paid to staffing and training of people working with the system. Any imported technology should be equally scrutinized.
6. Applications of data science are likely to use many subcomponents, often constructed by different organizations, making it hard to assure their reliability. This also leads to complex forensics problems if it is ever needed to determine what went wrong. The SolarWinds hack and the Log4j vulnerability are examples of the far-reaching, harmful implications of a security flaw in a commonly used subcomponent (Raponi et al., 2021). While most software depends on embedded components, it is much more common in data science for those components to operate with only probabilistic correctness. This makes it harder to determine if they are fit for the intended purpose. As noted earlier, speech recognition may work fine in some applications, but not in others.
7. Resilient systems must be maintained and operated, perhaps over decades. Systems almost always require some operational management and maintenance. Operational personnel make mistakes that are often the cause of failures. Ironically, systems that work really well are at risk of mismanagement because operators have lowered vigilance and less experience with correcting errors.
8. When a machine learning technique is used, it should exhibit **robustness**, such that the technique produces similar outputs despite perturbations of the input. For example, we would want an image classifier to work robustly if images are darkened or rotated. A classifier for road signs used by self-driving cars should still correctly classify an image of a stop sign even if the sign is discolored or bent, or if parts of the image are obscured (Carter et al., 2021). Robustness is of special importance in countering the adversarial machine learning attacks discussed in the previous section.
9. Finally, data science applications do so much so well that they can lull data science professionals and user communities alike into a false sense of complacency. It is hard to remember what can go wrong when things are working.

All engineering approaches to resilient systems need to consider these issues. The needed level of perfection depends on the data science application, and not all aspects of each application are equally important or require equal analysis.

We end this section with a discussion of **humility**. Designers of critical systems must understand that things can go wrong, due to unimagined factors they have no control over. Just as computer security engineers argue for "Defense in Depth" (Schneier, 2006), data scientists should design resilient systems that can quickly respond as problems happen.

In summary, this chapter covered systems' need to be privacy- and security-focused, abuse-tolerant, and resilient. Achieving these goals can be harder than the underlying data science algorithms due to heightened dependence on the availability of data, algorithms, and related infrastructure. Sometimes quick results can be obtained while ignoring these topics, but there will often be a significant price to pay.

Chapter 11

Understandability

In Chapter 1 we said that data science is concerned with both *conclusions* and *insights*. We want our algorithms to make accurate predictions, but we also want to *understand* what is going on. Understandability is important for five stakeholders:

- The *developers* of a data science application need to validate that it is working properly, and, if not, understand how to improve it. They will look at the whole pipeline and ask: Do we have the right data? Have we chosen the right machine learning model and found the best hyperparameters? Is the model performing well?
- The *users* of an application need to trust its recommendations. They are mostly interested in their own particular case. For example, when a machine learning banking application denies a loan, the customer wants to know what financial matters they should change before reapplying.
- The *general public*, even if they are not users, want assurance that the application is not causing harm to society or acting unfairly.
- The *regulators* want to understand if an application complies with laws and regulations, discriminates against a protected class, or exhibits signs of unfairness or potential harm to society at large. They need to know if the application was developed with reasonable standards of diligence, and, if not, who is accountable.
- The *scientific community* will wish to have access to the data and model so it can reproduce results to confirm their validity or extend them.

This chapter's first three sections mirror the Analysis Rubric's understandability element, explaining how a conclusion was reached, dealing with causation, and having reproducible results. The fourth section is about communicating data science findings without being misleading.

11.1 Interpretability, Explainability, and Auditability

For many toddlers, "why?" is a favorite retort to any new information. The same is true for consumers of data science applications: "Why did the system recommend this movie?" "Why was I denied a loan?" "Why was this disease diagnosed?" The reason matters; we are taught in school that the reasoning, or showing your work, is as important as the conclusion itself. Thus, data science applications that cannot show their reasoning are at a disadvantage. We say that a system is:

- **interpretable**, if experts can determine, by examining its inner workings, why it came to a conclusion;
- **explainable**, if the system can give the reasons for its conclusion; and
- **auditable**, if we can tell how the system got to a state, produced an output, what was responsible for each step, and who is accountable.

For machine learning system developers, understanding is crucial for modifying and improving the system. Toolkits such as IBM's AI Explainability 360, Facebook's Captum, and Google's What-If Tool help with understanding by letting developers have a conversation with their models, asking questions including:

- How do an example's results change if some features changed?
- How would the model's aggregate results change if some of the hyperparameters changed?
- Which input features contribute the most to the results?
- What do typical data points look like on a histogram?
- What do outlier data points look like on a scatter plot?

For a machine learning system's users, understanding provides insight and builds trust:

- In portfolio optimization, investors prefer to understand why trades are made. While long-term success might be more important than explanation quality, investors still want to know the reasons behind trades. This is particularly the case for disappointing trades for which reassurance would be comforting.
- In recommendation systems, users may wonder "Why should I watch this movie?" An explanation – "You liked other films by this director" – makes it more likely they will accept the recommendation, and less likely that they will have a bad reaction to a poor recommendation.
- In medicine, a physician is far more likely to accept a diagnosis with potentially risky treatments if there were a believable explanation to justify it.

We have been told – by Aristotle, William of Occam, Kant, Einstein, and others – that a good explanation should be simple. Good explanations are also relevant, believable, thoroughly cover known evidence, and tell the truth. Such explanations are of great value, as we learn by paying attention to explanations.

However, our learned preference for simple, general explanations can be counter-productive in complex domains with few general rules and variability for each case

(Williams et al., 2013). In complex domains, no simple explanation can tell the whole truth and nothing but the truth. This lack holds true when dealing with any of a simple regression model, a sophisticated deep learning network, or a human analyst.

Sometimes we place too much trust in explanations. At the end of every trading day, stock analysts provide explanations such as "The Dow closed lower as traders worried the Federal Reserve could start raising rates sooner than expected" or "Stocks charged higher as investors focused on strengths in the US economy." These explanations sound plausible, but are less impressive when we realize they are post-hoc. When these same analysts make binary predictions about the future, they are wrong about half the time, thus casting doubt on their explanations.

What is an explanation's correct level of detail? Consider a deep neural network designed to predict what type of bacteria is present in a patient. When given a specific case, the system might diagnose Enterobacteriaceae, with this opaque explanation:

> A series of matrix multiplications of the input feature vector and the millions of model parameters resulted in a vector of numbers which, when operated on by the softmax function, produced a peak in the position for Enterobacteriaceae. Would you like to see the exact values of the millions of parameters? Or the intermediate-level sums?

This low-level "explanation" is not helpful. How can we do better?

Visualization aids, as discussed in Section 1.2.1, can help with understanding (Chatzimparmpas et al., 2020). They work well when a problem has a small number of important features. Two-dimensional plots are easy to understand. There are other techniques to help with a small number of additional dimensions – utilizing perspective or animation to visualize the third dimension; showing multiple two-dimensional plots side by side; or representing additional dimensions with the color, size, or shape of points in the plot.

But what if there are many more features, say 14? The human visual system is not equipped to handle them all at once. Geoff Hinton's advice: "Visualize a 3D space and say 'fourteen' to yourself very loudly. Everyone does it."

Work has been done on explanation facilities that examine a neural network model's state and generate an explanation such as this:

> The gram stain is positive, and the portal of entry is gastrointestinal tract, and the locus of infection is the abdomen; therefore there is strongly suggestive evidence (85%) that Enterobacteriaceae is the class of organism.

Note this is a **story** that emphasizes part of the situation. So are all other explanations, whether from machines or humans. Doctors can produce a story like that one, but they probably first subconsciously come to a decision, then recall facts supporting the decision and de-emphasize less relevant facts.

Some researchers suggest that, rather than have one system optimized to make the best predictions, and a second, separate, system to generate explanations, it would be better to have a single machine learning system that is inherently interpretable (Rudin, 2019). The advantage is the direct correspondence between the prediction system and the explanation. Simpler machine learning models, such as classification and regression trees (CART), produce outputs similar to the above Enterobacteriaceae explanation. Humans find these easier to interpret.

The disadvantage is that such systems often sacrifice accuracy. One study of bioinformatics data (Lee et al., 2004) is typical; a difficult-to-explain neural net model had 74% accuracy, while a more explainable decision tree model had only 57%. The moral is that complex problems usually demand complex solutions. If a problem were amenable to a simple explanation, then we probably wouldn't need a complex machine learning model. Trading off decision accuracy for understandability remains a challenge (Knight, 2017).

There are also trade-offs between explanations and privacy. We can't explain a medical case by saying "Your symptoms are just like patient Alex Doe, who had anaplasmosis," which compromises Alex's privacy. This tension leads to contradictions, such as in the French *Loi pour une République numérique*, which has heavy penalties for companies violating digital privacy. It also says that citizens subject to "a decision taken on the basis of an algorithmic treatment" have the right to ask for an explanation. It should include "the data processed and its source." Note that the law does not say how a company can both provide "the data processed" and keep it private.

Providing explanations can compromise a model's integrity. The US Equal Credit Opportunity Act provides a right to explanation. A creditor that denies a loan must "indicate the principal reason(s) for the adverse action." This applies whether the decision was made by a human or an algorithm.

Suppose a bank customer gets the explanation, "The loan would have been approved if you had four more months of debt-free credit card payment." If the customer comes back in four months with a credit card payment record, should they be approved? Not necessarily, because the decision was predicated on a model of customers paying off their debts on their own accord, not ones who were told to do so.

While the right to an explanation is valuable, sometimes an audit is more important. If an individual suspects a creditor is biased against her due to race, religion, or gender, the explanation about needing more debt-free months won't resolve my suspicions. But an audit breaking down the decisions for similar cases by protected class will help.

Explanations can help a company accused of negligent behavior. Legal liabilities are often based on the care with which a decision was made. While many have written about the Trolley Problem's complex ethics when a self-driving car might be forced to decide between the lesser of two evils (Roff, 2018), a court of law might want the vehicle's software to explain the rationale for its choice. A system may even need to show that it has been applying a regulator-approved algorithm. Section 14.1 has more on legal issues.

We regularly use systems that cannot thoroughly explain themselves. We humans make decisions and only post-facto rationalize our decision-making with plausible, possibly self-serving, explanations. But understanding through interpretability, explanation, and audits helps build trust. Regulatory regimes may limit data science's use if it cannot provide this trust (Madiega, 2019).

11.2 Causality

Determining a domain's causal structure is a crucial part of understandability. As we defined in Table I.2, **causality** means that an intervention on one variable contributes to a change in another. From a scientific point of view, a model is incomplete unless it can explain what happens "if I do X rather than Y" – in other words, it can make predictions about the **counterfactual**. From a practical point of view, we want to use a model to find an optimal action. One way is to predict the causal effect of each possible action.

Suppose an ice cream company's data scientist observes data on ice cream sales and the local monthly average temperature, as shown in Figure 11.1. We see that temperature and ice cream sales are correlated; they rise and fall together. The correlation can be quantified: the Pearson correlation coefficient is 0.90, indicating a strong positive correlation. But the correlation does not tell us about causation. It could be high temperatures cause high ice cream sales, or high sales cause high temperatures, or some other unobserved variable causes both. We can't tell just from looking at the numbers.

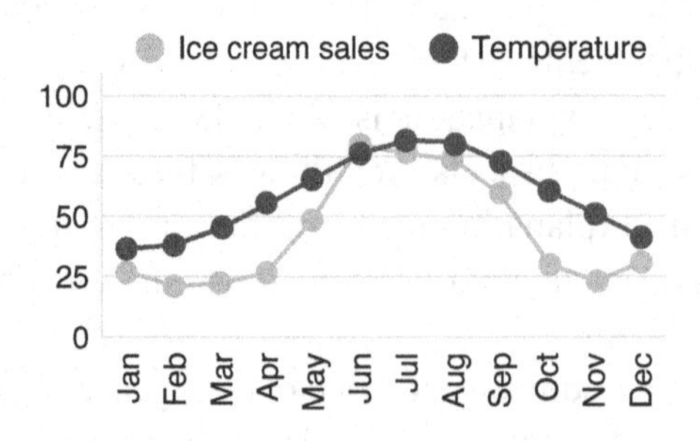

Figure 11.1 Ice cream sales and temperature by month (hypothetical data by the authors).

Statistics lets us estimate a joint probability model, such as *P*(*Temperature*, *Sales*, *Price*), that says how probable it is for a given temperature to co-occur with a given sales level and a given price. In the language of *potential outcomes*, we could attempt to model what the sales would be were we to get the price. A complementary framing is that of probability modeling, which differentiates outcomes caused by "doing" an action rather than those observing how outcome and action were correlated.[14] We could make either of two similar-looking but distinct queries:

1. *P*(*Temperature*, *Sales*, *Price* = $3)
2. *P*(*Temperature*, *Sales*, do(*Price* = $3))

Query 1 asks: Given past data, what is the distribution of likely temperatures and sales levels for when the price was $3. A joint probability learned from observational data answers this. Query 2 asks: If we set the price at $3, what effect would that have on the temperature and sales. To answer this query, we need a causal model. A joint probability learned from observational data is not enough.

In this context the price setting action is an **intervention**. We are not just observing the world – we are intervening to change it. We know from experience that setting a price can affect sales (the law of supply and demand) and that setting a price does not change the weather. Each of these is an example of a causal assumption.

We formalize this intuition with a **structural causal model**, consisting of a directed acyclic graph with random variable nodes, causal influence arrows, and probability distributions associated with each variable. Each variable's value depends only on its parents' values (the nodes with arrows pointing to it). The variables can be classified as:

- *intervention variables*, which we have the option of changing;
- *outcome variables*, which we hope to change via intervention;
- *observed variables*, which we can observe but not change; and
- *unobserved or hidden variables*, which we have no measurements for, but know play a role in the causal effects.

The structural causal model for ice cream sales shown on the left in Figure 11.2 is sensible (the model's arrows indicate sales is a function of price, temperature, and other factors, but temperature cannot be altered by a change in any model variable); and the one shown on the right in Figure 11.2 is folly (the arrows incorrectly say temperature is determined by sales and price).

We have to be especially careful of **confounding variables**. These are variables causally related to the outcome variable, and also correlated with an intervention

[14] See the book *Counterfactuals and Causal Inference* for an excellent discussion of how Pearl's "do calculus" relates to potential outcomes and other technical frameworks for modeling and learning causality (Morgan & Winship, 2014).

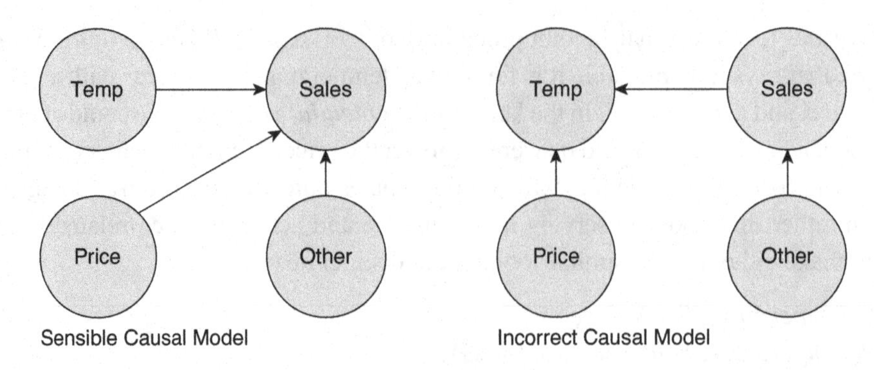

Figure 11.2 Sensible and incorrect causal models.

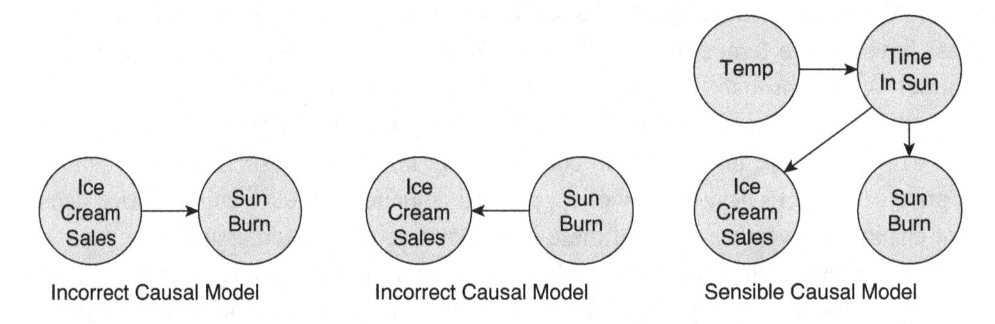

Figure 11.3 Incorrect and sensible models: illustration of hidden variables.

variable (the correlation can be causal or not). For example, consider the correlation between ice cream consumption and sunburn cases. The data shows the two are highly correlated, but neither causes the other (as shown in the two incorrect models on the left and in the middle in Figure 11.3). A better causal explanation is that higher temperatures lead to increased time outside in the sun, which in turn leads to both increased ice cream consumption and more sunburns, as shown on the right in Figure 11.3.

So far, we have considered simple causation examples, where one or two variables are the direct cause of another. But there can be complex multi-step chains of causation, and side influences that block or enhance the causation. See *The Book of Why* (Pearl & Mackenzie, 2020) for a complete catalog of causal inference graph topologies.

Getting causation right is a key way that data science leads to understanding. Don't be distracted by strong yet spurious correlations, such as the one in Figure 11.4 (Vigen, n.d.).

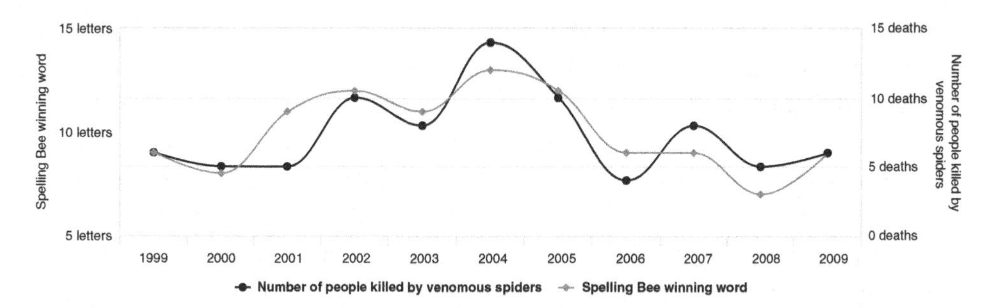

Figure 11.4 There is a close but spurious correlation between the number of letters in the winning Spelling Bee word and the number of people killed by venomous spiders, by year. Figure from tylervigen.com, based on National Spelling Bee and Centers for Disease Control and Prevention data sources.

11.2.1 Design of Experiments

With the enhanced interest in vaccine testing during the COVID-19 pandemic, the public learned something statisticians and epidemiologists long knew. The "gold standard" for discovering cause and effect is the **randomized controlled trial (RCT)**. In a randomized controlled trial, a subject population is randomly chosen from a population of interest and then further randomly divided into two groups, a **control group** and a **treatment group** (also called the intervention group). Then a treatment (also called a stimulus) is applied to the treatment group. If there is a significantly different outcome between the two groups, we can infer the treatment likely caused the outcome.

A well-designed randomized controlled trial takes into account:

1. **Outcome measure.** For many COVID-19 vaccine studies, a well-defined outcome measure was whether human subjects developed virologically confirmed (PCR-positive) symptomatic COVID-19 cases.
2. **Sufficient power.** The experiment should be designed so that it will have a good chance of detecting the effect. Given an estimate of the variance in the population, and the size of the effect to be detected, one can calculate the number of subjects needed.
3. **Recruitment.** In 1936 *Literary Digest* magazine polled 10 million people and predicted that Alf Landon would win the presidential election. With 10 million subjects, they certainly had sufficient power, but nobody remembers President Landon because he in fact lost 46 of 48 states to Franklin Delano Roosevelt. Where did *Literary Digest* go wrong? They got their subjects from three sources: their own readers, automobile registrations, and telephone subscribers. But in 1936 many people could not afford literary magazines, nor cars, nor telephones, and those who could not were more likely to vote for

Roosevelt. *Literary Digest* failed because the subjects they recruited differed from the population of voters they intended to sample.

4. **Retention and attrition controls.** When an experiment recruits human subjects who will be tracked over months or years, there must be a plan to encourage them to stay with the experiment. However, some subjects will inevitably drop out; they move away, or lose interest in participating. If the attrition pattern is random, then care is needed to choose a statistical technique that gives an unbiased estimate of the missing data. If it is non-random for unknown reasons (e.g., subjects with a bad reaction drop out more, and there are more bad reactions in the treatment group), there is no unbiased data recovery method.
5. **Stopping criteria.** Either the number of subjects is calculated ahead of time (using a power analysis) or there is a well-defined procedure for deciding when to stop recruiting new subjects. This is so experimenters won't keep the experiment going until the results start looking good and then decide to stop, exaggerating the benefit.
6. **Early stopping criteria.** If preliminary results show a strong treatment benefit, experimenters may feel ethically obligated to stop and give the treatment to the entire population. Alternatively, if the treatment group fares worse than the control group, they may feel obligated to abort the trial altogether. This ethical obligation to the subjects must be balanced against the potential harm of publishing a truncated study, which might overestimate the treatment's effect.
7. **Pair-matching.** The population of n subjects can be divided into $n/2$ closely matched pairs on baseline variables such as age, sex, weight, and economic status. Then one is randomly assigned to the control group and the other to the treatment group. The matching guarantees the two groups are similar for the known variables. The randomization gives a good chance that they will be similar on any unknown variables.
8. **Restriction.** If there might be unknown confounding variables that pair-matching would miss, a study can be modified to have more homogeneous subjects. For example, many studies are restricted to 18–25-year-old college students. The findings of the study will be less widely applicable, but the chances for confounders will be reduced.
9. **Double-blinding.** Neither the subjects nor the health workers know which group the subjects are in. For example, all subjects get a shot with an identical syringe. The injection is either the treatment drug or a placebo, which is not revealed to either the health workers or subjects until the end of the trial. That way, there is no preconception of the expected outcome to influence the results. Double-blinding may not be feasible in some trials; for example, surgical ones.

10. **Baseline treatment.** As proven treatments become available, studies may substitute a known, existing treatment for the control group's placebo. This is both to test the new treatment's relative improvement versus the old, and because it is unethical to withhold a known working treatment.
11. **Reversion.** In some experiments, on observing a positive outcome in the treatment group, the experimenters stop giving them the treatment. They then observe that the group reverts to being similar to the control group. This serves as further confirmation of the treatment. Note that this would not be possible for a vaccine study, but could be used in, say, an ongoing study of a weight-loss program.

RCTs are best known for their use in high-stakes medical studies. However, companies that do A/B experimentation perform thousands of prosaic randomized controlled trials every day, as described in Section 1.2.4. These experiments try to answer questions such as "What font causes users to click on the link more often?" or "What menu design makes it faster for users to find the right command?" It is easy to randomly assign subjects and gather outcome data, so these questions can be answered quickly.

Testing multiple factors at once (e.g., fonts, sizes, colors, and menu designs) is called **multivariate testing**. A **full factorial test** tries every combination of possible choices for all the variables. If there are too many combinations, a **fractional factorial test** can be used. It considers only some combinations, trying to pick the ones that will yield the most information. When the test is over, researchers can start to show the combination that performed best in the test to every user.

The problem is that there can be a lot of different experimental combinations, and it takes time to sort through them all. Researchers have to weigh the risk of potentially giving a small number of users a temporarily worse experience against the benefits of discovering a better experience for all users over a longer time. They also have to decide when the test is over; that is, when the diminishing returns of more data are no longer worth continuing.

An alternative approach with the colorful name **multi-armed bandit experiment** uses the metaphor of a row of slot machines, each with a different, but unknown, average payoff. Deciding which slot machine to play next is like deciding which experimental condition to try next; in each case you may get a payoff, and you gain some information about the payoff rate.

A good strategy is to experiment with the different machines, keeping track of the payoff rate estimate for each machine and also the estimate's uncertainty. If machine A has an average payoff of $2 per trial over 100 trials and machine B has an average of $1 over 80 trials, then we may want to stop trying B. But if machine

C averages $1 over just two trials, then there is a good chance that the estimate is faulty and C might actually pay off more than $2 on average. We should try C some more to check. We can do a calculation so that on each trial we choose the machine that maximizes the sum of the machine's current expected payout plus the value of information of getting a more precise payout estimate and later using that information.

Online services such as Amazon SageMaker RL, Optimizely Web Experimentation, and Google Optimize make it easy to automatically run multi-armed bandit experiments and see reports on the results.

On the other hand, too much experimentation can lead to disappointment. Suppose a company has a new algorithm to improve their spelling-correction program. They run experiments with 30 slightly different algorithm versions, and find that the best improves performance by 4%. They launch that version and monitor its performance, only to find it actually only improves performance by a disappointing 2%. What went wrong? In a similar case at Google, researchers observed this phenomenon early on and recognized it as some form of regression to the mean. It took a while to understand the problem well enough to be able to predict the precise amount of disappointment (i.e., lesser performance improvement).

In statistical language, the problem is that the expectation of the maximum is not equal to the maximum of the expectations. In plain language, the problem is called the **optimizer's curse**. The chosen version was judged best in part because it really was a good version, but also in part because of random variation in the experiment. The lesson is that, as more versions are tried, the best version's results will tend to improve, but also the disappointment of the actual results versus the expected results will be greater. One way to control for this is to use a Bayesian calculation to correct the estimated improvement (Smith & Winkler, 2006).

Randomized controlled trials are the gold standard, but they can be expensive and time-consuming. Sometimes an RCT is completely impractical or unethical. We can't randomly split subjects into two groups, and tell one group to smoke a pack of cigarettes every day and the other to abstain. Fortunately, data collected for other purposes can sometimes be used to derive a causal model. It is often considered the genius of data science that data acquired from normal activity, rather than a planned experiment, can yield useful results.

When an RCT is not feasible, one alternative is a **single-subject experiment**, in which each subject is both given a treatment and serves as a control, but at different times. These are popular in education studies. You can't take two classrooms and tell one "we're not going to teach you to read." But you can teach different things to each classroom at different times of the year, and measure performance at regular time intervals. In effect, each student serves as their own control group.

Another alternative is an **observational study**, in which we gather and analyze data but don't assign subjects to groups. Suppose we want to determine the extent to which affordable low-income housing positively affects families. We can't assign families to a control and treatment group. However, we could take existing data and select matched pairs of similar families, one that received the treatment and one that did not, and observe the outcome variables. This approach could be used for some of the studies described in Section 5.5.

The problem is that even if the two groups are balanced on observable variables (e.g., number of children, age, previous year's income), they might systematically differ on unobserved variables. Perhaps families who are resourceful enough to seek out affordable housing assistance were also resourceful in other ways, giving them improved outcome measures.

To get around this problem, we look for a **natural experiment** (also called a **quasi-experiment**) that partitions groups similarly to an RCT. Suppose there is a lottery for affordable housing slots. All applicants demonstrate an equal level of resourcefulness by virtue of entering the lottery, and the winners are chosen at random. Comparing the winners' and losers' outcomes is almost like an RCT.

Policy changes enable other natural experiments. If two nearby cities have similar demographics, and one institutes a mask mandate and the other does not, they serve as treatment and control groups in a natural experiment. When there are many cities in the no-treatment category, a statistical technique called the **synthetic control method** (Abadie, 2021) is a principled way of choosing a balanced control group.

Another type of natural experiment, **regression discontinuity analysis** (Thistlethwaite & Campbell, 1960), occurs when a policy imposes an arbitrary treatment cutoff point on a continuous-valued variable. Suppose a state enacts a new law offering housing assistance to any family with an income under \$30,000. A family making \$20,000 receives the "treatment" of assistance, and a family making \$200,000 does not. These families will have many differences, so tracking their outcomes won't tell us much about the assistance's causal effect. But, on average, families making \$29,000 are probably very similar to families making \$31,000, except for the assistance. So a trial considering only families who fall just below or just above the cutoff point is almost like an RCT.

In another example, researchers wanted to understand the effects of alcohol purchases on motor vehicle accidents (McMillan & Lapham, 2006). They couldn't assign people to two groups – this one buys alcohol and this one doesn't. But they could compare New Mexico drivers before and after July 1, 1995, when it became legal to buy alcohol on Sundays there. After that date, fatal crashes on Sundays increased by 42%. While there may be confounding variables that also changed on or about July 1, 1995, this is strong evidence of a causal link between alcohol purchase and fatal crashes. Regression discontinuity analysis has also been used to study the causal effects of school classroom size, unionization, anti-discrimination laws, limits on unemployment insurance, and many other factors (Jacob et al., 2012).

We conclude this section by discussing two complex topics: **global warming** and **hormone replacement therapy**.

RCTs cannot investigate anthropogenic **global warming**, because we only have one planet and can't split it into two groups. It is easy to observe a correlation between temperature and increasing greenhouse gas levels. However, it took a long time to gather enough data and do enough analysis to create a convincing causal model that can answer a wide range of questions.

Historically, does climate respond to gas levels rather than the other way? Yes, as demonstrated by ice cores from Greenland and Antarctica. Why has the lower stratosphere cooled since 1979? That is largely attributable to major volcanic eruptions, ozone depletion, and increased greenhouse gases. Could temperature be driven by solar irradiance cycles? Irradiance was largely aligned with temperature from 1880 to 1950, but since then it has declined while global temperatures have increased. There are still a few skeptics unswayed by the evidence. In this instance, data science can motivate and assist in the debate, but not settle it.

For post-menopausal women, **hormone replacement therapy** is probably the best real-world, medical example of the difficulties of determining causal relationships. A careful, long-term retrospective study showed that estrogen replacement therapy did lower the risk of heart disease in post-menopausal women on whom data was collected. The conclusion seemed to make sense. First, it seemed plausible that a change in estrogen could be implicated in post-menopausal heart disease. Second, the data showed that women who had estrogen replacement did indeed have fewer heart problems.

But numerous later studies, including prospective ones, had different results. Perhaps, in the initial study, there was a correlation between women who took hormone replacement and a group who did other, somehow protective, things? The evidence remains somewhat contradictory, but doctors no longer recommend hormone replacement therapy to reduce heart disease. This is illustrative of data science's risks, and the advantages of prospective studies. Randomly dividing a population into groups and treating the groups differently greatly reduces the risk of confounders.

There are many more examples of where prospective studies fall short, but most of us have noticed that dietary recommendations have a history of contradictory advice. One study claims that coffee or eggs or wine is beneficial in moderation, and the next study will claim it is harmful.

11.2.2 Variable Selection for Causal Inference

One of the biggest problems in ascertaining causality is the combination of the sheer number of possible causal variables and the expense of running randomized experiments on each of them. As a concrete example, we return to the genome-wide association studies (GWAS) discussed in Section 6.3, which aim to discover which mutations cause a particular disease. Given a specific mutation, scientists often can perform an individual randomized experiment to test a mutation's effect on biological processes. However, running millions of experiments on many different mutations is prohibitively expensive.

Another example involves detecting **heterogeneous treatment effects** in clinical trials. This means finding out when a treatment works better or worse for certain people. For example, pharmaceutical companies may want to know if a drug is more or less effective for certain subpopulations. However, to prove such claims to regulators, researchers need to specify the particular subpopulations before running a clinical trial, and there are millions of possible subpopulations. A particular drug may be more effective based on a subject's gender, weight, age, or other combination of demographic factors. While we have provided biomedical examples, this is a problem in many other domains.

All of these examples help motivate an important problem. Before running lab tests or randomized experiments, it is often necessary to **pre-screen** potential causal hypotheses to identify likely causal factors. Such pre-screening is often known as **variable selection**. After selecting relevant variables, domain experts may then run a randomized experiment to verify that the selected variables are causally important. For example, in GWAS, variable selection techniques let researchers sift through millions of mutations to find a few key seemingly causal mutations. When done well, variable selection methods reduce the cost of identifying causal factors by many orders of magnitude.

The success of variable selection methods depends on the precise criterion for "selection." For example, GWAS' initial techniques screened for mutations highly correlated with a disease of interest. While very computationally efficient and privacy-preserving, it can also lead to many false positives and wasted resources.

Modern approaches apply more stringent standards (Wang et al., 2020). One approach is to select mutations if still correlated with a disease even after accounting for all of the other mutations as possible confounders. A mutation giving unique information about a disease is not a guarantee it *causes* the disease. However, in the context of genetic analyses, it is likely, as there is a low probability of reverse causality because the disease is unlikely to cause the mutation. By accounting for all other mutations, variable selection methods account for a huge number of potential cofounders. As a result, biologists may have a strong hunch that these GWAS-selected mutations have some causal effect. In some fields, depending on the context and expert knowledge, RCT experiments may not be required to verify causal findings.

Biologists, statisticians, and computer scientists have developed a wealth of variable selection methods. Many methods simply fit a linear regression between potential causal variables and the outcome of interest (Tibshirani, 1996). Some modern methods flexibly incorporate arbitrary machine learning models while still provably controlling the false positive rate (Candès et al., 2018). Other methods leverage the many causal variables, along with unsupervised machine learning, to learn about and correct for some of the confounders (Wang & Blei, 2019).

Variable selection methods are a useful tool throughout data science. They aid in interpreting complex machine learning models as well as improving their predictive performance. They are not a panacea, and their causality determinations cannot be confirmed without explicit interventions.

11.3 Reproducibility in Scientific Applications

Science makes progress by formulating theories and verifying them by analyzing experimental data. But the scientific community won't accept a theory based on just one scientist's say-so. As Robert Boyle argued in the 17th century, others should reproduce experiments to have the opportunity to uncover errors and thus generate confidence (Bishop & Gill, 2019). Or as written in *The Economist* in 2013, "A simple idea underpins science: 'trust, but verify.' Results should always be subject to challenge from experiment" (*The Economist*, 2013).

Unfortunately, many published scientific studies fail to replicate successfully for reasons that include the following (Baker, 2016; Ioannidis, 2005):

- The heterogeneity of subjects, especially in the biological and social sciences (Bryan et al., 2021). A study may reach the conclusion that a drug is an effective treatment for a disease, but a replication study may draw subjects from a different population that responds differently to the drug. Not everyone is alike.
- The unprecedented rise in available data, the relative ease of doing studies, and the convenience of a wide variety of statistical tools, making it more likely that *some* analysis of the data will yield a finding that appears to be statistically significant.

- The expansion of science into subject areas where there are thousands of potential hypotheses, some of which will yield false positives. For example, gene chips contain hundreds of thousands of cells, and one can use them to simultaneously run experiments on thousands of genes.
- A preference by journals for novel findings, and a lack of insistence on robust experimental design and validation. Experiments would be more likely to replicate if journals required pre-registration of experiments, larger sample sizes, and smaller (stricter) p-values. Many experiments are designed to have statistical power of just 80%, meaning that they leave a 20% chance that a true effect will not be detected. If the experiment is replicated with an independent identical setup, there will be an $80\% \times 80\% = 64\%$ chance that both experiments detect the effect with a significant p-value, but a $2 \times 20\% \times 80\% = 32\%$ chance that one will and one won't (and a 4% chance that they will both miss it).
- The ever-present competition for researchers to publish or perish.

This has been called a "replication crisis," but others say that the important and interesting findings do replicate, and it is only the minor findings for which there is uncertainty (Nisbett, 2021).

Not all data science uses demand reproducibility. A product manager whose data science application met its user satisfaction goals need not do additional experiments to prove or disprove its broader usefulness. A company making movie recommendations isn't proposing a scientific theory of the best recommendations. They are merely saying these are *our* recommendations: take them or leave them.

But when data scientists act like scientists – creating predictive models, generating hypotheses, and determining underlying causal mechanisms – confidence in their conclusions matters greatly. They have the same need for reproducibility as other scientists. A model's initial proposers should clearly and comprehensively explain its details, their data, their experiment, their assumptions, and their results. (See Section 11.4.2 for more on this.) They should strive to inspire others to replicate, validate, and extend their work (Donoho, 2017).

This is not always easy. Some companies want to maintain a competitive advantage by keeping their datasets and/or software as trade secrets. Even when the software is freely shared, software packages undergo frequent updates and it may be hard to exactly replicate the original versions. Data science is often a trial-and-error process, a "garden of forking paths" (Gelman & Loken, 2013), so it is not clear exactly what it means to replicate a study. Do data scientists replicate the final procedure arrived at by the original authors? Or do they instead follow the original process, perhaps making different choices because the world and available data have changed?

Many factors can prevent replication. It could be the cost, as some computations require a prohibitively large hardware investment. Some data requires licensing fees, or the size is so large that transmission to another team is expensive. In the future, this could be mitigated if we shared data and software in a globally accessible, cloud-based file system with access controls, but this is not the case today.

Often a dataset cannot be shared for privacy reasons. Clearly this is true for medical and census information. Additionally, companies can offer to share data only to those who agree to strict terms of usage, but they can be violated. In retrospect we see that Facebook erred in 2014 when they relied on a contractual commitment and allowed academic researcher Aleksandr Kogan to build an app that gathered personal data. The data was then acquired by Cambridge Analytica, which improperly used it to build voter profiles for the 2016 election (Wong et al., 2018). Companies can take steps to anonymize or aggregate data before release (see Section 10.1), but there may be no solution that provides enough data to allow replication while preserving privacy.

Releasing information about a model might give attackers a way to abuse it. As an example, if political opinion pollsters released their complete methodology – the websites they track, the locations where they survey potential voters – political candidates would concentrate their efforts on targeting exactly those websites and locations. The data would no longer reflect the broader population.

A dataset may be so large and complex that it is difficult to understand and process, particularly after undergoing extensive data wrangling. For example, multi-site medical studies may need meticulous preprocessing to make their data compatible since providers use many different encodings. All these details need to be clearly described if we are to validate and understand our data science results. The World Health Organization advertises the ICD-11 (International Statistical Classification of Diseases and Related Health Problems) standard as having "17,000 categories, 80,000 concepts, 130,000 terms, >1.6 million clinical terms interpreted" (World Health Organization, n.d.)!

We finish with two examples of the trade-off between privacy and reproducibility.

Co-author Alfred had many uncomfortable experiences explaining why Google would not release search logs and other data to universities for research use. It became second nature to recite the list of reasons: the distribution costs and challenges, anonymization difficulties, the reputational risk due to a suspicious public not accepting privacy assurances, the risk of a malicious or inadvertent data leak, the economic value of the data, and cautionary experiences from companies that released data and saw a negative result. While keeping the data private appears to have been the right decision, the scientific community lost the opportunity to reap the potential benefits of using it for research.

Google Flu Trends was a service launched in 2008 that created a map of flu prevalence in different areas based on the frequency of certain search terms. Epidemiologists continually pressed Google to release the methodology and raw data for external validation. Google decided not to for two reasons:

1. The raw search data absolutely could not be released because it was private.
2. If the key search terms were known, abusers could spam the system with these searches and distort the data.

Eventually, Google found a way to release aggregate search data to scientists, but it was not enough to provide for reproducible system validation. Maintenance of the service proved to be difficult. Also, over time, users changed their habits; for example, they started getting an increasing amount of their information on local trends from Twitter rather than from Google searches. In 2015 the Flu Trends service shut down because it no longer met its goals.

These issues are not unique to Flu Trends. Scientific theories about human behavior are more ephemeral than theories about physics or chemistry. Theories expressed as equations such as $F = ma$ or $E = mc^2$ have stood the test of time, but human preferences are fickle.

In summary, scientific theories need to be reproduced to be believed. Theories arrived at through large data science experiments face challenges of privacy, software and data availability, replication complexity and cost, and abuse potential. On the other hand, many internal uses of data science applications by an organization justify themselves by their success, without needing to prove anything to the outside world.

11.4 Communicating Data Science Results

Portraying data in perspective is of particular importance. For example, with vast data collection, it is easy to locate and highlight outliers and make unsound arguments based on them. Erroneous, incomplete, one-sided, or misrepresented data can lead to misunderstanding and confusion. Data scientists must always be cognizant of the power of data, because humans tend to attribute great validity to a number, a graph, or a model output, and be overly confident of conclusions. It is hard to express ambiguity, and it is relatively uncommon to do it well (Hullman, 2020).

A major challenge for both the data science community and the public at large is the ease with which insights, conclusions, or data, whether truthful, misleading, or downright erroneous, can widely propagate. The marginal cost of publication today is near zero, so almost anyone can create a tweet, blog, chart, database, or video and then publicize it.

Previous barriers, such as finding a publisher, passing an editorial bar, or paying for printing and postage, are gone. Tools make it quite easy to create deceptive derivatives, such as the deep fakes discussed in Section 10.3. The Internet's long support for anonymity increases the likelihood of deliberate falsehoods, by reducing both data creators' responsibility and the likelihood of detecting and punishing bad actors. This problem further illustrates the delicate balance needed between providing privacy and preventing abuse, as previously mentioned in Section 10.1. These problems have grown larger as the Internet's ever-growing use and reach adds to the motivations for abuse.

Data can appear to have a veneer of objectiveness and certainty that is not always warranted. When presenting results, practitioners must be careful to include contextual information, such as the size of a sampled population, the method of collecting data, and the resulting uncertainty (e.g., error bars) in the results. The tools that simplify data analysis and visualizations can be problematic if not used with care. Programs from Tableau Software (now acquired by Salesforce), SAP, and Microsoft make it easy to perform analysis and create visualizations that are so compelling that audiences may see the numbers and ignore the uncertainty around them.

For example, it is easy to show the breakdown of students in elite colleges stratified by parental wealth or high school attended, but it is hard to draw conclusions as to the reasons behind the data. Similarly, we frequently read that those individuals who exercise live longer, but rarely is there a discussion that those already in better health are likelier to exercise. If done well, measuring and reporting is illuminating, but it also can easily inspire disagreement and shed more heat than light.

Internet search engines allow anyone to find information on any topic. However, some of the information may be out of date, or come from an unreliable source, or represent a biased point of view. Searchers need to take care to avoid cherry-picking just the results they would like to see, rather than getting the full story. Everyone is subject to cognitive biases that influence how we react to data. For example:

- **Availability bias** means that people rely on examples that come readily to mind when evaluating a situation. For example, when asked about the likelihood of various causes of death, people overestimate the risk of shark attacks and homicide, which are rarer than other causes, but receive a great deal of coverage in the news (Kahneman & Tversky, 1996).
- **Recency bias** means that people give greater credence to events they heard of recently. This is why constantly repeating yourself can be an effective strategy.

Lists of the greatest movies/athletes/musicians of all time are often dominated by contemporary entries because of recency bias (Chatfield, n.d.).

- **Confirmation bias** means that people tend to search for and interpret information in ways consistent with what they already believe or want to prove true, and ignore evidence contradicting their prior beliefs (Wason, 1960).

Remembering these biases is important for those planning to communicate or consume analyses based on data. We cover additional biases in Section 11.4.4.

Finally, we note that computer programs (or bots) masquerading as humans can contribute misinformation. For example, Twitter bots frequently retweet political messages, in order to give those messages undue credence. With automation, the adage of "garbage in [leading to] garbage out" becomes even more problematic.

11.4.1 Examples

More recently, individuals have had to decide if they would accept COVID-19 vaccines. The incredibly detailed record keeping on side effects, occasional adverse reactions, and occasional inefficacy highlighted outlier cases. This both reinforced anti-vaxers' opinions and even created sufficient controversy to reduce the rate of vaccinations.

Quantitative researchers, elected officials, and data journalists all rely on statistics to help inform decisions and estimate risks. However, abundant research by computer scientists and behavioral economists has shown how presenting the same fact expressed differently, or with and without perspectives, can have a significant effect on the way readers interpret that fact. As one example, blood clotting was linked to 73 deaths in the UK among people who received the AstraZeneca vaccine. Presented this way, without a denominator, "73 deaths" seemed like a lot and contributed to vaccine hesitancy.

However, 73 deaths out of 50 million doses of the vaccine in the UK (Gallagher, 2021) is just 1.46 micromorts, to use the terminology popularized by statistician David Spiegelhalter (Spiegelhalter, 2014). The average person faces a threat of 24 micromorts from other causes every single day, so the vaccine poses at most a small additional threat. Studies showed that, overall, despite the clotting issue, those taking the vaccine actually had lower rates of non-COVID mortality than the unvaccinated (Xu et al., 2021). And the rate of COVID mortality is about 50 times lower for the vaccinated versus the unvaccinated (Johnson et al., 2022).

Presenting a number without any perspective, such as neglecting to include a denominator or a comparable number, can contribute to misunderstandings even while presenting something factually sound. The lack of a denominator is called "denominator neglect," which psychologist Gerd Gigerenzer and colleagues define as "the focus on the number of times a target event has happened . . . without considering the overall number of opportunities for it to happen" (Garcia-Retamero et al., 2010).

Similarly, researchers from Microsoft and Columbia have shown experimentally how different choices of perspectives – comparing one number to another – can improve reader understanding (Barrio et al., 2016) of numerical measurements from front page articles in *The New York Times*. Crowdsourcing both the generation and the scoring of "perspectives," they tested the effect of adding, for example, the perspective "300 million firearms is about 1 firearm for every person in the United States" to the factual but less contextual "Americans own almost 300 million firearms." Such perspectives were shown to improve both recall, estimation, and error detection among readers.

At a minimum, data scientists must ensure relevant information on population sizes (i.e., the denominator) is well known and use presentation tools to tell the right story. This lets others assess probabilities and helps the public compare one risk against others. Having identified a problem, data scientists must also guard against their own natural tendency to make a forceful statement instead of being extremely rigorous and balanced. They must also recognize that most people are unlikely to understand statistics very well.

In the run-up to the 2016 US Presidential election, many cable news channels incessantly focused on post-presidential debate *poll results*. At times, there seemed to be almost no discussion about candidate experience, policy, or truthfulness. Political polling has been an industry since the 1950s (Lepore, 2020). But modern data science makes it so easy to gather, process, and present data that news coverage can skew towards shallow polls, rather than matters of deeper substance.

Certainly, we can all be taken in by leaderboards and statistics, so perhaps this data science application has led to some modern opiate of the masses. Even within organizations, polling ability has grown so rapidly that it can be a crutch replacing leadership and creativity. This example is one of many showing that data doesn't necessarily generate understanding.

11.4.2 The Role of Scientists

Scientists play a formative role in generating and disseminating new knowledge and have a particular duty to use data science carefully. In particular, they must be aware of the esteem the public holds in them. Polling shows that scientists, along with the military, are the most-trusted groups, beating out financial institutions, the press, and politicians (Public Face of Science Initiative, 2018).

Thus, scientists must be exceedingly careful in both drawing and expressing conclusions from data science. The uncertainty that frequently arises from its application makes communication particularly challenging, as summarized in a survey by van der Bles et al. (2019). While scientists and their institutions desire fast publication and credit for great ideas, they must exercise caution.

First, scientists need to use language that will not be misunderstood. For example, when a scientist asserts that something "may imply" something else, or they "hypothesize" something as true, the public may not understand that this means there is some uncertainty in the data, and may interpret it as meaning the result is definitely true. Alternatively, some members of the public might interpret the uncertainty as meaning it is definitely false. It is a great challenge for scientists and their institutions to help the press and public understand the shades of meaning and degree of uncertainty in their work.

Second, although scientists strive to be objective, they often have a preferred hypothesis and would rather prove its validity than negate it, making them subject to confirmation bias. It is tempting to ask the question that gives the answer you want, not the answer that is most revealing of the truth. In 1987, John Cannell surveyed the results of school testing and found that 50 out of 50 US states reported their children were above average (Cannell, 2006). He called this the "Lake Woebegone effect."

How was it achieved? First, it turns out that when a state contracts to have its students take a standardized test, they also purchase rights to the scores of a "comparison group," and test vendors compete on just how low a comparison group they can offer.

Second, in many cases the teachers, who were more invested in seeing their students score well than in accurately assessing their performance, drilled the students using last year's test questions, and the test did not change from year to year. They were guilty of training on the testing data.

Third, scientists must remember that correlation should not substitute for causation, particularly given the previously mentioned risk of confirmation bias.

Fourth, scientists must realize that journals have a bias towards publishing studies that produce affirmative results. A scientist might reference a positive study result without knowing of the many unpublished results tending to negate it. Published meta-analysis studies are also vulnerable to this problem. Policy efforts are underway to partially rectify this, such as the operation of the ClinicalTrials.gov website (US National Library of Medicine, n.d.), which aims to record all clinical trials whether or not they were successful.

Fifth, scientists need to be clear about where their hypotheses came from, and apply statistical techniques that are appropriate to the hypotheses' origin.

A long-standing practice in statistics, going back to the work of R. A. Fisher in the 1930s (Fisher, 1935), is to summarize experimental results with a *p*-value. This says how likely it is that an experiment would obtain results at least as extreme as those observed, under the null hypothesis that there is no difference between the control group and the treatment group.

In the social sciences, experimenters look for $p < 0.05$, which ensures that there is only a one in 20 chance of making a false discovery under the assumption that there is no difference between the treatment and control groups. Physical sciences often look for the stricter $p < 0.01$, and confirming a new elementary particle requires $p < 0.0000003$. The use of *p*-values came into practice in an era when an experiment was typically used to test a single hypothesis that was reasonably likely to be true.

However, data science techniques now enable the generation of hypotheses at unprecedented scale. Biologists run experiments on 20,000 genes in parallel on a gene chip – in effect making 20,000 hypotheses at once. Suppose a gene chip experiment's results suggest two particular genes are associated with a disease, each with an individual statistical *p*-value of 0.0001. In a traditional experiment, a *p*-value of 0.0001 is considered strong and evidence that the null hypothesis (no association) is false. But in the gene chip experiment, two out of 20,000 genes could reach the 0.0001 level just due to random noise. Instead of rejoicing at finding a significant *p*-value result, the scientist in this scenario should apply an appropriate statistical technique such as the Bonferroni correction, or should treat the two positive results of the gene chip test as suggesting two new hypotheses that need to be tested in a follow-up experiment.

The inappropriate use of *p*-values is known as *p-hacking* or *data dredging* or *data fishing* or *HARKing* (hypothesizing after results are known).

Some critics argue researchers should supplement, or even replace, *p*-values with confidence intervals and fragility indices. Researchers should use robust estimation techniques to mitigate against unusual probability distributions and outliers in the data.

Sixth, scientists need to be clear and consistent about what caused their experiment to end. A separate path to *p*-hacking lies in the previously mentioned "garden of forking paths" (Gelman & Loken, 2013). This is the innumerable small changes in data collection, data preprocessing, data analysis, and other subjective design choices in an experiment. Suppose a researcher has the hypothesis that a certain coin is more likely to come up tails than heads when flipped. The researcher flips it 100 times, records the results, and finds that the hypothesis is not confirmed. The researcher then thinks "perhaps I didn't collect enough data" and flips some more. Assuming the coin is in fact completely fair, eventually there will be a time when significantly more tails than heads are recorded, but that's only because the researcher chose the stopping point. More subtle versions of this problem occur even when researchers are well intentioned and not deliberately trying to be deceptive. Gelman and Loken further describe the paths to abusing the "$p < 0.05$" heuristic (Gelman & Loken, 2013, 2016).

11.4.3 The Role of Journalists

The press and journalism play a critical role in informing the public and influencing society. In 1787, Edmund Burke emphasized the importance of the press, referring to it as *The Fourth Estate*, assigning the press a power similar to that wielded by the Church, the Nobility, and the Townspeople (Carlyle, 1841). In the US, the term has come to mean the independent body that balances the three branches of government. Unfortunately, at a time when trustworthy journalism is sorely needed, the "public [holds] a deep suspicion of the press," according to The Trust Project (The Trust Project, n.d.).

Data science provides both opportunities and challenges for improvement. Journalists have ever more information available to them, including fine-grained data on human beliefs, actions, and processes of all forms. Data-science-powered search engines, social networks, and new communication channels reduce the difficulty of finding that information, though they also influence society in new ways that journalists must seek to understand. Analytical tools provide journalists with powerful capabilities to help them counterbalance those who may wish to bend a narrative to suit their own needs. Data science tools increase the speed at which journalists can operate, but they also enable competitors that pressure journalists to publish ever more quickly. Graphical tools empower journalists to convey information more clearly, if used well.

The abundance of easily available online information increases the possibility of finding misleading statistics that misrepresent a complex story. Search engines return such a diversity of online opinions and interpretations that journalists, if fixated on advocating for a position, will almost surely be able to find supporting evidence.

The specific availability of fine-grained data also bears risks. Journalists share many of the challenges from Chapter 8 in processing the data they receive. They must avoid having the cognitive biases described at the beginning and end of this chapter; remember that correlation does not imply causation; and always put data in context.

Joseph Pulitzer, founder of Columbia's College of Journalism, addressed both data's allures and risks in a 1904 piece that remains relevant today: "It is said that nothing lies like figures – except facts. You want statistics to tell you the truth. You can find truth there if you know how to get at it, and romance, human interest, humor and fascinating revelations as well. The journalist must know how to find all these things – truth, of course, first. His figures must bear examination." The Web has exacerbated these risks, and we refer the reader to educational texts and the BBC's excellent list of guidelines to avoid so doing (BBC, n.d.; Harford, 2021; Huff, 1993; Levitin, 2019).

To address the volume of both information and misinformation and perform thoughtful analyses, journalists are increasingly learning to use advanced analytical tools in data journalism classes. Data science education also helps journalists to understand the impact of data-science-driven applications on society. According to Journalism Professor Mark Hansen, "Data, code, and algorithms and all manner of computing technology wield real power in our society and journalists need to see and then interrogate that power" (Hansen, 2019).

Twitter, 24-hour cable news, and other sources have forced journalists to contend with the relentless time pressure of a 24/7 news cycle that values timeliness. The enormous shift of news to the Web has also provided a variety of nearly instantaneous, web-based performance metrics that add to the pressure on journalists and their editors (Whipple & Shermak, 2018). These incentives may cause journalists and editors to balance the types of competing objectives that we discuss in the next chapter.

The graphics that journalists can use are packed with power. Some newsrooms even develop their own visualization software to help them quickly produce creative charts. However, using voluminous data to illustrate meaningful information and compelling conclusions is still challenging. Visual data journalist Sarah Leo states on *The Economist*'s blog that presenting data in a misleading way is "the worst of crimes in data visualization." She further notes that, "We never do this on purpose. But it does happen every now and then" (Leo, 2019). While there is an explosion of new techniques for analysis, presentation, and dissemination, they require extremely careful use. Leo's self-critical piece is a service to her profession and provides instructive examples to advance quality visualization.

In the summer of 2021, the COVID-19 pandemic coverage illustrated these challenges. After more than a year and with vast amounts of data, there should have been consistent, easily accessible data on the pandemic's health impact. But it was maddeningly difficult to draw conclusions from popular media which had (mainly) two different approaches to gathering and reporting data:

- Some reporting used official COVID-19 data, *as reported by governmental bodies*. While there was a lot of it, it was challenging to interpret. Different governments had widely varying standards of measurement and accuracy as well as differing capabilities and desires to be truthful. Even within a region, data was not comparable over time because the quality of disease and mortality counting varied dramatically. For example, many areas vastly undercounted COVID-19 cases due to a shortage of tests and testing sites.

- Some reporting was based on the number of excess deaths (the number of deaths during the COVID-19 pandemic compared to those in previous periods) (*The Economist*, 2021a). Reports also estimated infection rates not based on government data, but rather using seroprevalence surveys and working backward from deaths. While this data had many advantages, there were risks similar to those discussed in Section 8.4 relating to data quality and the statistical techniques used to infer infection rates.

Depending on the data used, readers got very different ideas of what transpired:

- *The Economist*'s tables used the "excess" deaths methodology for reporting COVID-19 mortality rates (*The Economist*, 2021a). For example, they showed Russian mortality rates through spring of 2021 to be about four times what Russia reported, or about twice that of the US as of that time. Were one to have looked only at the official COVID-19 death numbers, they would have shown the reverse – the US then reported two-fold worse outcomes than Russia. Reports presenting the official COVID-19 death data were in a sense "accurate," but more nuanced reporting of excess deaths provided better information to readers[15] (Troianovski, 2021).
- As the pandemic continued, some journalists moved away from data unadjusted for early disease undercounting. Initially, reports of the US summer 2020 COVID-19 resurgence showed it as higher than the initial spike, but *The Economist*, using seroprevalence and mortality data, showed the reverse.

Superb visualizations sometimes compounded the problems of understanding. Their professionalism and precision made data appear more meaningful than it actually was and encouraged unwarranted comparisons. Perhaps, unsurprisingly, even in late 2021, there were still problems with COVID-19 data. US vaccination data may have been miscalculated, and that required us to modify the data insight example in Section 1.1.1.

It is important to note that differences in data portrayal are not only of academic interest. These data presentations and visualizations inform both policy makers and electorates. Without careful reconciliation and analysis, COVID-19 reporting could excessively divide an electorate based on which news they read.

11.4.4 The Role of Information Consumers

This chapter describes the challenges of clearly conveying information – a challenge for the scientists who do experiments, the data scientists who analyze and present the results of the experiments, and the journalists who report on them.

[15] December 2021 reported numbers continued to show a wide disparity.

Consumers of information are also challenged to think clearly, apply basic numerical and statistical literacy, and put the information into context. Consumers need to question the motivations and biases of the sources providing them with data and analyses of data, and to acknowledge their own human biases and frailties.

With practice, we can learn to counter our biases, to come to a more thorough and accurate understanding of the data and information that is presented to us, and to make better decisions. In high-stakes scenarios such as stock trading and military operations, training with simulations has been shown to improve decision-making and mitigate biases.

At the start of this chapter we mentioned **availability**, **recency**, and **confirmation bias**, and in Section 8.4 we covered **selection bias**. These may seem like topics in cognitive science, not data science, but an awareness of them and the other cognitive biases and fallacies listed below is actually crucial to the success of data science. No matter how comprehensive the data, no matter how accurate the analysis, it all goes for naught if stakeholders' biases cause them to reject the findings. Here are some biases that data scientists need to check for their own reasoning and for that of their audience:

1. **Framing bias.** People react differently when different words are used to describe the same thing. For example, people support a program that is described as resulting in 90% employment, but oppose the same program when it is described as resulting in 10% unemployment (Druckman, 2001).
   To mitigate this bias, consider different ways of thinking about the problem, and ask for advice from experts in the field.
2. **Anchoring bias.** People often fixate on the first number they see. Stores take advantage of this by advertising discounts: "was $10; now $5." They do that because they know that when potential buyers start to consider whether the product is worth $10, they will be more likely to then decide that it must be worth $5. Restaurants put a $200 bottle on their wine lists, not because they expect to sell a lot of them, but because the $30 bottle now seems like a bargain.
   The anchoring number doesn't have to be in any way relevant to the decision at hand. In an experiment, subjects watched the random fall of a roulette ball into a number and were then asked to estimate some quantity, such as the number of countries in Africa. The higher the roulette number, the higher their guess (Tversky & Kahneman, 1974).
   To counter anchoring bias, do research to set your own anchor point, and take your time making a decision; the power of an anchor diminishes over time.
3. **Base rate fallacy.** Suppose a patient undergoes a routine screening and tests positive for a disease. Separately, we know the test has a 5% false positive rate

and the disease affects one in 1,000 people in the population. What is the probability that the patient actually has the disease?

One might be tempted to say 95%, because there is only a 5% chance of a false positive. This would be correct if the base rate were 1/2; a person is equally likely to have or not have the disease. With a base rate of 1/1,000, the correct way to reason is that, out of every 1,000 people, one will have the disease and test as a true positive, but 50 out of the 999 who do not have the disease will be false positives, so the probability of true positive given a positive test result is 1/(50 + 1) or about 2% (see Table 11.1).

It is not just lay people who have difficulty reasoning about base rates; a survey of medical doctors showed that only 20% of them answered this question correctly (Taleb, 2004).

This is true even though doctors are taught to discount the likelihood of rare diseases; Dr. Theodore Woodward coined the phrase "when you hear hoof-beats, think horses not zebras." Presenting patients with medical test results without proper education on base rates can cause real harm. *The New York Times* (Kliff & Bhatia, 2022) reports that, in prenatal screening for Prader–Willi syndrome, a positive result is wrong 93% of the time. The syndrome occurs once in 20,000 births, so the test is more than 99.9% accurate, but the marketing material from the testing company stresses that accuracy without mentioning that most positive results will be wrong. An FDA official found this "problematic."

The best way to avoid base rate mistakes is to work through an example with concrete numbers as was done here: imagine 1,000 (or 20,000) people, and see how many fall into each category.

4. **Prosecutor's fallacy.** A prosecutor argues that DNA from the crime scene was a match to the defendant, and because DNA matching has a false positive rate of only one in a 1,000, the jury should convict the defendant.

   That's a valid argument if there were two suspects apprehended at the scene of the crime and the DNA evidence matches one of them. However, if the defendant was brought in simply because they were the one person in a pool of thousands of DNA records that happened to match, and there is no other

Table 11.1 *Tabular description of base rate fallacy.*

	Base rate 1/1000		Base rate 1/2	
	Diseased	Healthy	Diseased	Healthy
Positive test	1	50	475	25
Negative test	0	949	25	475

evidence pointed towards the defendant, then the argument is invalid – it is a version of the base rate fallacy. A prosecutor could similarly argue that winning the lottery without cheating is a very low-probability event, and therefore whoever wins must have cheated.

To avoid falling for this fallacy, we again advise working through an example.

5. **Lack of introspection.** We prefer machine learning systems that can explain their reasoning, but it turns out humans also have difficulty doing this. Our unconscious mind has processes that the conscious mind is unaware of. In one experiment, shoppers were asked which of four products on a table they preferred. The order of the products was permuted for each trial. It turned out that on each trial shoppers were four times more likely to pick the product on the far right than the one on the far left. Order was the most important factor in determining preference, yet not a single subject admitted to the possibility that order could have anything at all to do with it (Nisbett, 2021).

   It is difficult to counter this issue, but it is always good practice to check whether your holistic first impression matches the results of your calculations. If the two approaches disagree, consider why there is a conflict and try to resolve it.

6. **Representativeness and the conjunction fallacy.** In a famous experiment (Tversky & Kahneman, 1982), Kahneman and Tversky gave subjects the following description: "Linda is 31 years old, single, outspoken, and very bright. She majored in philosophy. As a student, she was deeply concerned with issues of discrimination and social justice, and also participated in anti-nuclear demonstrations." They then asked which was more likely?
   - Event B: "Linda is a bank teller."
   - Event F: "Linda is a bank teller and is active in the feminist movement."

   Some 85% of subjects said F was more probable. But that's a logical impossibility; regardless of any knowledge about Linda, the conjunction of the two events B and F can't be more likely than the single event B alone. It seems that subjects confused probability with representativeness, and chose F because, as a story, it fit with the rest of Linda's description better than B.

   To avoid this trap, it helps to work things through quantitatively. When told "There are 100 people who fit the description of Linda," and asked to estimate "How many out of 100 are bank tellers" and "How many out of 100 are bank tellers and active in the feminist movement," none of the subjects commit the conjunction fallacy.

7. **Gambler's fallacy.** A gambler will reason "I know that in the long run a roulette ball will land on black half the time. It just landed on red five times

in a row. That means that black must be due next." The fallacy is believing that independent events keep track of or are influenced by their predecessors. If events are truly independent, they don't. The long run will eventually even out, but not because the short term has a proclivity to catch up.

To avoid this fallacy, we need to think carefully about whether events are truly independent. If they are, then we need only consider the next event, not previous ones.

8. **Sunk cost fallacy.** A poker player who has invested a lot of money in the pot may be reluctant to fold, even though the current reading of the cards and betting indicates they are likely to lose even more by staying in. A company that has invested in an advertising campaign may be reluctant to abandon it, even when data shows it is performing poorly.

   To avoid this fallacy, remember that rational decision-making means surveying available actions and considering the possible outcomes of each action and the differences between them. In all possible outcomes, you've already invested the sunk cost, so it should not be a factor in a rational decision.

9. ***Clustering illusion.*** Humans are always looking for meaning in the world. When we detect a pattern, we assume there is a reason for it. That ability to detect patterns has led to all the technological advances described in this book and elsewhere, but it also leads to a lot of false positives. In 2007, the UK's *Sunday Times* published an article titled "Cancer clusters at phone masts." There were higher-than-normal rates of cancer near seven different mobile phone masts. Concerned residents saw this as evidence that the masts were responsible for the cancers; if not, they reasoned, the cancers would be spread homogeneously, not clustered.

   But random events are not homogenous (that would be un-random), and out of 47,000 masts, one would expect to see seven or more clusters by random chance. The bias to see patterns is more widespread than just clusters; *pareidolia* is the phenomenon of seeing familiar objects in random images, such as spotting animals in clouds or faces on slices of toast.

   To avoid this, remember that things that may seem out of the ordinary may not actually be so. Regrettably, certain probabilities are sometimes counterintuitive.

10. **Appeal to authority.** A useful shortcut in analyzing a situation is to trust the opinions of experts in the field. But we should count these opinions as evidence because they are sound arguments, not solely because of the credentials of their authors. Computers are often mistakenly seen as the ultimate authorities. A customer service representative may say, "It seems like you have a legitimate argument, but the computer said this is the answer, so there's nothing I can do about it."

To counter this bias, question authority. Don't dismiss authority, and don't prefer uninformed opinions over informed ones, but rather weigh all the actual evidence.

11. **McNamara's Fallacy and Goodhart's Law.** Data can be valuable, but focusing too much on the data that is available to you can cause you to ignore important information that is not in the data. During the Vietnam War, US Secretary of Defense Robert McNamara concentrated on hard quantitative statistics (such as body counts) that indicated his side was winning, but erred by ignoring qualitative assessments that gave a different picture. As we said in Section 9.2, the key to finding an accurate model and making good decisions "is not contained only in the data points themselves; it is also in what we know about the data," including non-quantitative impressions. Another issue, known as Goodhart's Law, says that, once people are aware that data is being used to guide a model, the data becomes subject to manipulation: proponents and adversaries alike want the model to go their way, and may manipulate the data to get the results they want (Wikipedia contributors, 2022).
    Continuously monitor the performance of your model to see if it is tracking what you really want it to track, and if it is degrading over time. Think hard about your model and your decision-making process; decisions should be guided by available data and models, but can also be informed by factors that are not captured in quantitative data.
12. **Information cascades.** Often the initial pieces of information have an unwarranted effect on a decision, coloring subsequent information. Consider a group meeting to decide whether to hire a candidate. If the first interviewer declares "the candidate is cunning and highly intelligent" and the second adds "the candidate is hard-working and ambitious," the group will be forming a positive mental model of the candidate. When the third says "the candidate is prone to cut ethical corners," it will be easier to dismiss that as a necessary byproduct of moving fast, and stick with the overall positive mental model.
    But if the "cuts ethical corners" remark had been first, the mental model would start off being negative, and the "cunning" and "ambitious" remarks would become negatives. They would be perceived as qualities that would enable the candidate to cause more damage.
    To protect against information cascades, have everyone separately write down their feedback. Then present all the feedback at once before starting to consider how to assimilate it.
13. **Survivorship bias.** When Richard Doll and Austin Bradford Hill studied the effect of cigarettes on lung cancer in 1950 – the first major study to prove the

link – they had to choose a cohort of subjects to follow. They decided to ask all 60,000 doctors in the UK if they could be followed in the study.

This was a wise choice for several reasons. Doctors could be expected to provide reliable reports on their health and smoking habits. When they die, it is likely that it will be in a hospital that will provide an accurate cause of death. But most importantly, the names and addresses of doctors appear in a registry, so they will be easy to find and survey even years later.

Survivorship bias is a major problem in long-term studies. If subjects drop out, no data on them is collected, but subjects suffering ill effects are more likely to drop out, hence the bias. Survivorship bias occurs in informal non-experimental settings as well. We hear the stories of the champion athlete or the CEO of a unicorn company. However, care should be taken to consider how their stories compare to the many also-rans whose stories we don't hear, lest we falsely believe their success is due to the factors in their stories (Lifchits et al., 2021). It is true that Gates, Jobs, Madonna, Winfrey, and Zuckerberg dropped out of college and became rich, but that may not work for everyone. Of the many people we don't hear about, college dropouts earn 50% less than graduates on average.

To avoid this, pay careful attention to studies that extend over a long period of time, and consider carefully what would happen if there was data on all the initial participants.

14. **Bias for action.** Many companies promote a "bias for action." As Amazon puts it, "Speed matters in business. Many decisions and actions are reversible and do not need extensive study. We value calculated risk taking." It is important to get products to market quickly and to avoid being paralyzed by over-analysis, so this is an appropriate strategy for an e-commerce company in an expanding economy. But a bias for action is not always appropriate in high-stakes scenarios. Brain surgeons plan before they cut. And in the front-line trenches of World War I, those with a bias for inaction fared much better. As Auguste Rodin said, "Patience is also a form of action."

    Co-author Peter remembers two crucial times when the start-ups he was involved with had to decide whether to move to a larger building. Both times the decision was not to move, and despite some grumbling about overcrowding, both times it turned out to be the correct choice.

    Waiting for the moment should be considered in the space of possible actions.

15. **Bias for addition.** Why is everything so complicated these days? One factor is a natural tendency to fix things by *adding* something, even when a better solution would be to *subtract* something. An experiment involving Lego blocks shows that, when subjects are asked to stabilize a structure, they do so

by adding support pieces. Even when there is a simpler solution of removing the piece that caused the instability in the first place (Adams et al., 2021). *The research suggests that subtractive ideas require more cognitive effort (they have less availability). A good practice is to remind ourselves to take the time to look for a simpler solution, and in particular for subtractive ones.*

We could add even more items to this list, but instead will point to our first recommendation of Part IV: Broaden education in data science. Better education can help us all become better consumers of data and information.

This chapter's key message is that *data science does not automatically lead to more understanding*. In fact, Harvard Professor of History, Jill Lepore, who has written and talked extensively about data, has expressed the provocation that "Data killed facts" (Lepore, 2018), implying that data may obscure truth. There is much to what Lepore says, but this book argues that only data science done poorly obfuscates facts and truth. Every dataset has a story to tell, but we need to tease out that story by clearly explaining where the data came from and what it says, putting it in the context of other studies of the same phenomenon, making sure we distinguish correlation and causation, and presenting the story in a way that is not prone to cognitive biases and will not lead to misunderstanding.

Chapter 12
Setting the Right Objectives

The fifth Analysis Rubric element is setting clear objectives, an obvious necessity when our goals are to predict, optimize, or recommend. But clear objectives are also needed to focus data science efforts in classification, transformation, or clustering. Even projects seeking insights need clear objectives to help focus and make their explorations more efficient.

Having observed many data science projects start to finish, the authors note that objectives initially seem clear, be they decreased delays, increased revenue, improved consumer engagement, increased clicks, or otherwise. Occasionally, they might actually be as obvious as they are in Part II's speech recognition, traffic speed estimation, copyright identification, and earthquake prediction examples. However, often team members learn that objectives are not as clear as they first seemed. Perhaps the goal is ill-defined. Perhaps it is hard to weigh the relative importance of multiple subgoals or to balance conflicting ones. Perhaps there are problematic and unintended consequences.

On the one hand, it might seem that teams should try to specify early in a project *exactly* what they want to achieve, to minimize wasted effort, and so those using or relying on the data science applications receive their full benefit and suffer no harm. On the other hand, problems may not become clear until a project's engineering is well underway, or it has garnered data from early users. Expressions such as "release early, release often" capture this latter notion by suggesting that project engineering be iterative and responsive. We recommend that objectives should be clear at every stage, but objectives may change.

It is also difficult to take the time upfront to think deeply about objectives. Teams are anxious to dive into the project's guts and work on difficult programming issues, machine learning, statistics, etc. Data scientists may feel elbow grease and (their own!) genius are the main ingredients of success.

This is particularly true since projects almost always have aggressive completion dates. Just "diving in" is consistent with Mark Zuckerberg's aphorism that

Facebook used in its early years: "move fast and break things." However, many feel Facebook's speed focus led to preventable mistakes. Getting the correct balance between careful upfront thought and rapid iteration is a necessary challenge in many projects.

This section focuses on the challenges in setting a project's objectives:

- The clarity of the objectives
- The balance of benefits across affected parties
- Fairness, a specific topic within the topic of balance
- The impact of the objectives on an individual: manipulation, filter bubbles (though these affect society as well), privacy, and being human
- Transparency

We will do our best to organize our discussion under these headings, but we acknowledge some challenges sit astride a few. Also, some topics will be further revisited in Section 14.3, which overlays an ethical lens on them.

12.1 Clarity of Objectives

It is surprisingly difficult to determine objectives, as shown in these six project examples:

1. Self-driving cars
2. Spam filtering
3. Search engines
4. Image classification
5. Monitoring city noise levels
6. Weighing response time versus accuracy

1. Consider the problem of setting the speed of a **self-driving car**. Perhaps the car can determine the legal speed limit, the speed of surrounding traffic, and the passengers' desires, and can predict how fast it can safely drive given traction and reaction times. But how does the team set the right speed objective? The objective "Travel as fast as safety permits, but stay under the speed limit" might be:

- unclear, because it doesn't quantify the risk threshold;
- frustrating to passengers, and dangerous, if most traffic is above the speed limit; and
- overly simplistic, since speed limits were never really intended literally.

On the other hand, should one ever create a data science application that deliberately aims to break a law, even just a posted speed limit?

2. Consider weighing false positives versus false negatives in **spam filtering**. There is always a trade-off: How many spam messages should we accept in our inbox to avoid having a valid email relegated to the spam folder? This application must set a reasonable threshold, which could vary for different email uses or users.

3. Consider setting the objectives of a **search engine**. In one sense the objective is clear: give good answers, not bad ones. But there are many complications:

- There is a trade-off between **precision** (the percentage of relevant results among all retrieved results) and **recall** (the percentage of all relevant results retrieved). This can be summarized with a single score (termed F_1), a weighted average of precision and recall, or by measuring precision among, say, the top 10 results.
- The relevance of a page to a particular query is determined by a match between words, but the implicit concepts behind the words and the user's intent must also be factored in.
- Personalization is less important in search than in song recommendation; everyone gets the same result for the query, "capital of France." But there are individual and regional differences in search results, and search engines must decide which to cater to.
- In classic information retrieval, the answer is a list of references to works published by others. Search engines give a list of links, but also present answers directly on the result page ("capital of France: Paris") and present information in pictures, maps, and other formats. They must decide how much to prioritize each format for each query.
- To be a good result, a page should be relevant to the query, and should also demonstrate expertise, authoritativeness, and trustworthiness on the topic. As a proxy for authority, search engines can use the Web's link structure and the pattern of traffic of who clicks on what links.
- Some queries, such as "what is the meaning of life" or "best ice cream flavor" have no objective ground truth response. Different people may prefer different responses, and search engines need to decide whether to give people what they prefer, or to give them a more balanced portfolio of responses.
- No matter how carefully a metric is crafted, search engines still employ human search quality raters who evaluate experimental results and give guidance on what works (Sullivan, 2021).

4. Next, **image classification** might seem to have an obvious objective of maximizing the correctness percentage, but that is not sufficient. Rather than being binary right or wrong when searching for, say, a Boston Terrier, there should be a small penalty for retrieving a French Bulldog, a larger penalty for a Saint Bernard, and a huge penalty for a cow or a pornographic image.

5. NYU's SONYC (Sounds of New York City) uses big data and machine learning to monitor and report on **city noise levels** and improve quality of life (NYU, n.d.). While this seems like a good idea, the danger is if reports of noise level are enforced mechanistically, "The system said you exceeded the allowed decibel level, so I'm going to have to write a citation," rather than with nuance, "The system said you exceeded the allowed decibel level, but I can see you're celebrating a special occasion, so just don't let it get out of hand, ok."
6. In any application, what should the balance be between **response time versus accuracy**? Perhaps some transformation gains 1% accuracy for each one second increase in latency. What is the right balance point between crisp responsiveness and accuracy? The monetary cost of computation or even its power consumption may also enter into the objective. More generally, within operations research there is a well-developed theory of multi-objective optimization, which recognizes that in all but the most trivial problems there will be multiple possible solutions that form a **Pareto frontier** where no solution is better than the others on all objectives.

One particularly challenging problem is the "tyranny of the easily measurable," which we previously covered when describing McNamara's Fallacy. We find a proxy measurement and try to optimize it, even if the proxy is not exactly what we really want to optimize. Often this ends up prioritizing easily measured short-term objectives over difficult-to-measure long-term ones. For example, it is easier to establish and achieve the goal of maximizing user clicks per day than it is to maximize long-term customer satisfaction.

Even when using a good proxy metric, as we noted in Section 11.4.4, Goodhart's Law says "When a measure becomes a target, it ceases to be a good measure" (Wikipedia contributors, 2022). People may end up optimizing the metric without regard to the underlying activity it is supposed to reflect. When a company sets the goal of minimizing the length of customer service calls, the call center agents may respond to customers with "Sorry, our systems are down – hang up now and call back later." Yet another aphorism is that "you get what you measure." The book *System Error* (Reich et al., 2021) contains many examples of situations where there has been excessive focus on optimization using insufficient proxies.

Let's look at the particularly pernicious example of a video distribution site that rewards content uploaders solely with advertising click-based revenue. However, this motivates the uploading of popular, but problematic, content to gain views, clicks, and the associated revenue. At first, that might seem okay, but the practice may lead to divisive political content, outright falsehoods, or other forms of clickbait. Not only might this be harmful to a site's reputation, it could lead to societal problems. In fact, with similar motivation, groups have uploaded problematic content and used its revenue to support harmful causes. Video hosting sites have responded to this by demonetizing controversial videos. This is not censorship – the videos can still be viewed – but it eliminates the incentive to do it for monetary gain. It is not clear what other steps should be taken.

If simple objectives don't work, there is a slippery slope to when content distribution sites need to become "arbiters of truth," again quoting Mark Zuckerberg. Determining truth or quality is a difficult objective, particularly in countries that have expectations of freedom of speech. Even human raters frequently disagree (Bhuiyan et al., 2020).

We finish by illustrating the problems of using averages to set objectives. Fantastic average outcomes may not be sufficient if some cases have egregious outcomes. Bad outcomes may be due to exceptions to the more general objectives, known as **corner cases**. Or, they may be due to data science's frequent probabilistic nature:

- A few truly bad outcomes in a classification problem have a disproportionate impact on people's views, even with high average quality.
- High average investment returns are insufficient if disastrous losses bankrupt clients or destabilize an economic system.
- Outcomes may vary by subpopulations or even individual users. If five users are 80% satisfied, that's the same average score as if four users are 100% satisfied and one is 0% satisfied. The latter may be a very serious problem.
- Outcomes that vary by subpopulation are more serious problems if they lead to fairness issues, which we discuss in Section 12.3 specifically and in Chapter 13.

12.2 Balancing Benefit Across Parties

Data science applications must often balance their impact across multiple institutions or subpopulations. This is especially evident in advertising-related applications. We touched on this in Section 6.2's advertising example, but we revisit it here.

Our previous summary listed the involved parties as consumer, publisher, advertiser, and the advertising platform. However, the public-at-large can be considered a fifth party because of policy concerns. These include what is advertised (e.g., cigarettes), truth in advertising regulations (e.g., very strong regulatory requirements on advertising prescription drugs), or, alternatively, wanting a growing, consumer-driven economy.

Many techniques have evolved to address some of these issues. Advertising space may be auctioned so as to encourage clicked-on ads, better aligning the interests of the advertiser, advertising platform, and user. Ad auctions where payment is due only on a click or on a sale are even better at balancing incentives.

However, these techniques still have challenges, including possibly over-promoting certain types of advertising or inviting clickbait. Short-term/long-term considerations must balance near-term clicks (and corresponding revenue) at the expense of:

- a reduction in a publisher's or advertiser's reputation;
- users clicking on fewer ads in the long term, perhaps, fueling the growth of ad blockers);
- regulatory scrutiny, perhaps from the US Federal Trade Commission; and/or
- harmful society-wide behaviors.

Thus, an advertising system must manage many competing objectives. Some evolve only over a long period and are hard to measure. Ads even encourage consumers to buy things they don't want, a topic we return to in Section 12.4.1.

As another example, a navigation system's objective to minimize travel time or distance traveled might usually be fine. However, there are balance issues in setting the objectives. A traffic-directing system may need to balance pedestrian and resident objections to increasing traffic on certain streets. It isn't far-fetched to believe systems might need to make more far-reaching and complex prioritization decisions, akin to high-occupancy vehicle lanes, which prioritize cars with multiple occupants. They might also want to prioritize ambulances. Certainly, these latter issues arise more with self-driving cars which presumably *will* actually follow the navigation system's directives.

Another difficult category of data science applications arises from needing to set objective functions under conditions of scarcity. All too often, optimization problems are essentially zero-sum games. One achieves an objective only by leaving another objective wanting.

For example, a school district with a relatively fixed budget can vote funding to programs either for advanced students or for remedial reading and mathematical education. Even if data science could optimize precisely the best educational intervention and predict its effectiveness, it's essentially impossible to make the broader educational policy decision because there are too many unspecified societal objectives.

If the different educational outcomes could be precisely characterized, a school committee's detailed policy analyses might be more informed. Counterintuitively, providing fine-grained predictive data could be more disruptive than having a less informed judgment call. Very possibly, the more detailed the data, the sharper the fight.

Similar trade-offs occur when applying data science to economics. Is the goal to maximize average GDP growth per capita, or to also include distribution objectives? With greater concern over planetary limits and sustainability, maximizing production and consumption might or might not be the most important objectives.

12.3 Fairness

While the previous section discussed balance among different constituencies, this section turns to the related topic of fairness across different societal subgroups. There is concern if data science generates "fair" results or answers, a difficult term to fully define. However, it certainly relates to the balance of benefits and harms defined in Chapter 3's ethical framework. Abstractly, fairness strives to eliminate disparate treatment or impact:

- **Disparate treatment** is when a decision-making process bases its decisions on a subgroup's protected attribute (such as gender or race). This is conscious, intentional discrimination.
- **Disparate impact** is when the outcome of a decision-making process disproportionately harms (or benefits) a group defined by the value of some protected attribute. Data scientists who intend to remove bias by leaving out protected attributes may still inflict disparate impact, for example, if the attribute is correlated with some other attribute.

In the US, disparate treatment is legally proscribed, whereas disparate impact is only legally proscribed when not accompanied by an adequate defense on the grounds of business necessity (Kleinberg et al., 2019).

This concern in data science research is relatively new, but interest has grown rapidly since 2015. Chouldechova et al. survey the topic and write (Chouldechova & Roth, 2020):

> The last decade has seen a vast increase both in the diversity of applications to which machine learning is applied, and to the import of those applications. Machine learning is no longer just the engine behind ad placements and spam filters; it is now used to filter loan applicants, deploy police officers, and inform bail and parole decisions, among other things. The result has been a major concern for the potential for data-driven methods to introduce and perpetuate discriminatory practices, and to otherwise be unfair.

We first observe that there are two ways an analysis of fairness concerns needs to be done:

1. Data science applications must faithfully implement their designers' objectives. Getting this right is a technical challenge, similar to the data and modeling challenges in Chapter 8 and Chapter 9.

2. A system's fairness objectives must be well considered and carefully specified. Fairness goals are not so easily stated.

The technical challenges are the clearer ones. For example, if law enforcement uses facial recognition software to identify criminal suspects, and it performs materially worse when classifying people of color, it results in unfair enforcement. If such systems had many false positives, people of color would be more likely to be inaccurately recognized, resulting in their being prosecuted more often. If systems had more false negatives, the opposite would happen.

Machine learning-based system quality may depend on how many samples they learn from as well as that data's biases (e.g., when trained on decisions resulting from unfair policies or by biased individuals). Unless carefully addressed, technical problems due to those biases are likely.

The same care is needed when doing clinical trials. Over time, more effort has been made to ensure trials include many subgroups so drug approvals take their results into account (Kost et al., 2015).

There are many other technical challenges, as Chouldechova et al. discuss:

- Not only might there be a sparsity of data from some subgroup, the data from it could be differentially poor.
- Data science applications can have a multi-stage impact on the world by impacting other parties that then respond to changing conditions. Such applications may need to have models of long-term behavior. For example, when modeling college admissions policies, not only the first stage (or present) but also the impact on the next generation may need to be modeled. This is because future college admissions may be impacted by whether a parent was college educated.
- Data science applications are frequently combined (e.g., a multi-stage selection process). But even if all the subcomponents are fair, it can be hard to show that an aggregate system is fair. For example, a hiring pipeline's first stage might be fair in and of itself, but it could still select candidates that are differentially rejected in an otherwise fair second stage.

Mehrabi et al. taxonomize many of these data- and modeling-related issues (Mehrabi et al., 2021), but, difficult as these technical challenges are, there are perhaps even *greater* fairness challenges in setting a particular application's objectives.

The criminal sentencing and parole decision-making example is a good one to consider, as fairness is central, and there has been a particularly serious debate on whether such algorithms exhibit bias. Much discussion has centered around applications of COMPAS (Correctional Offender Management Profiling for Alternative Sanctions), which has been "used at each step in the prison system, from sentencing to parole," according to a well-publicized May 2016 *ProPublica* article (Angwin et al., 2016). There are two different fairness metrics against which COMPAS could be measured:

- The *ProPublica* article deemed the use in US courts of COMPAS to be unfair when measured against a notion of fairness later called "equalized odds" in the technical fairness literature. It takes into consideration not only the protected attribute, e.g., race, but also the outcome, e.g., whether a person reoffended or not (Hardt et al., 2016).
  The authors showed it was twice as likely for black parole applicants who did not reoffend to receive high risk scores as non-reoffending white applicants (false positives). Similarly, the likelihood of a non-reoffending black applicant receiving a low risk score was about half that of a non-reoffending white defendant (false negative rate). In summary, black applicants suffered a negative disparate impact.
- COMPAS's creator, Northpointe, replied in July 2016 with an analysis arguing that the tool satisfies the classical fairness notion of "calibration" or "predictive parity" (Dieterich et al., 2016). This is defined as conditional independence of the outcome and the attribute given the prediction of the model. In the case of COMPAS, this meant that, within the separate groups of those who scored "high" or "low" risk, there was no correlation between the race and the actual recidivism. In other words, black and white defendants assigned approximately the same score by the algorithm did indeed have approximately equal recidivism rates.

This disparity led academics to show the impossibility of simultaneously satisfying two different, but reasonable, notions of fairness (Chouldechova, 2017; Kleinberg et al., 2017). Practically, data scientists have the ethical necessity of considering societal fairness, despite there not being universal consensus on what that means. They need to consider the impact on all society's subgroups. In commercial settings, that may even require ignoring whether or not some subgroups are revenue-bearing customers.

More broadly, given that all systems have some degree of imperfection and that almost nothing can satisfy all possible constraints, how good is good enough? We may become frozen by analysis paralysis or forget the popular adage, oft attributed to Voltaire: "the best is the enemy of the good." A legal precedent for a balance, dating back to a 1971 California State guideline, is the so-called "80% rule" of the US Equal Employment Opportunity Commission. This sets a 20% impact as an evidentiary standard to make a case for disparate impact.

However, the law may be a low bar for such a central question. As we emphasized in Chapter 3, an ethical approach recognizes the tensions among principles and interests. It requires a clear decision-making process within a community rather than a one-size-fits-all cutoff.

12.4 Concerns to the Individual

Recommendation systems can help cut through the thicket of choices to find good matches for our interests. But they may also lead us to make bad choices, ones benefiting others but neither us nor society. They may amplify feedback loops, creating filter bubbles reinforcing a single interest rather than a broader range of balanced choices.

In the best case, data science automates tasks, letting us instead solve harder problems, find better solutions, free up time, and improve safety. In the worst case, data science reduces our satisfaction from doing tasks, leaving us to perform only ones they cannot.

12.4.1 Personalization or Manipulation

Advertising or recommendation personalization certainly can be beneficial. In 2000, co-author Alfred's younger son was born and became their third infant in 17 months. The new parents were definitively uninterested in ads for cool cars. Minivan ads were the order of the day or, perhaps, decade.

Furthermore, personalization is not a new concept. Long before he was buying minivans, Alfred learned sales from his druggist father, who recommended customers spend more for a larger tube of toothpaste (at a lower cost per ounce), but also used his personal knowledge to suggest that a customer should buy a gift of chocolates or cologne to smooth over a marital dispute.

On the one hand, manufacturers, providers, and salespeople have reaped great benefits from data-science-based personalization informing potential customers of new products. It has created new markets, rewarded innovation, facilitated previously non-existent competition, and had significant economic benefits.

On the other hand, behavioral targeting can tempt us in ways that are counter to our best interests. The book *Phishing for Phools* (Akerlof & Shiller, 2015) argues that, while the free market is designed to bring buyers and sellers together to the benefit of both, sellers can use tricks to exploit the buyer's irrational side. This has been the case since the advent of modern advertising in the 1920s up till the current day, where candy is conveniently located next to supermarket checkouts despite the buyer's best interest of avoiding obesity. But online targeting enables an even higher level of manipulation.

In the political realm, many wonder if big data perniciously influences people's views, polarizing subgroups via reinforcing and hardening viewpoints. While perhaps true, in the US, concerns pre-date data science and the internet-wide use, going back to the advent of cable TV and its expansion of available TV channels. Since TV channels were no longer a scarce commodity, there was then room for a free market in presenting differing points of view. This led the US Federal Communications Commission (FCC) to revoke the Fairness Doctrine for TV news in 1987. Unsurprisingly, the combination of more news channels and reduced regulation led to more differentiated viewpoints, just as later happened on the Internet.

Even earlier, in the 1890s, "yellow journalism" by both the Hearst and Pulitzer newspaper chains used sensationalism to appeal to and influence their audiences. Their promulgation of what is now called fake news inflamed anti-Spanish public opinion. In particular, they both published an unfounded rumor alleging an explosion that sank the USS Maine was a Spanish attack (Kennedy, 2019). While this may not have caused the Spanish–American war, it made it easier for President McKinley to prosecute it.

Despite earlier precedents, online news recommendations are different due to the following:

- Reduced barriers to publication, letting anyone instantly disseminate anything at very low cost.
- The scale at which systems operate.
- Individual customization of a story based on the reader's characteristics.
- Lessening of restrictive societal norms that temper speech, particularly given the Internet's cross-border nature.
- A system's ability to quantify impacts and to tune itself and thus become ever more effective.

A well-publicized 2012 Facebook experiment was an example of the power to influence. Facebook wanted to determine if seeing friends' happy posts would make people happier (due to empathy) or sadder (due to envy) (Kramer, 2012). Researchers manipulated 0.04% of users' feeds so that some got more posts with more happy words, some with more sad words, and some an unaltered feed. They then measured how many happy or sad words users put in their own posts. Reducing the number of negative words users saw caused them to include more positive words in their own posts – but only by about one word in 2,000.

This had a negligible impact on any particular user, but it was statistically significant given a sample size of 700,000 users. Quantifying the impact somehow makes this experiment seem more manipulative than a newspaper choosing scandalous headline words to sell more copies, and this experiment was ill-received. Section 14.3 discusses incentives and organizational challenges from balancing research objectives and ethical principles.

Unsurprisingly, creators of recommendation systems try very hard to provide recommendations on which users click or engage. Users appear more satisfied and the content provider gets more revenue. Seemingly, this is a win–win situation, but there are multiple embedded challenges:

- First, there are challenges within the recommendation system's domain of operation (such as videos). Should recommendations be for content a user is sure to like or should the system suggest new items that might or might not be pleasing? If recommendation systems only show us what we like, they will not expose us to new ideas, they may reinforce our existing preferences, and they may reduce our understanding of different ideas or points of view. (We discuss filter bubbles a little later.) On the other hand, we humans are creatures of habit, and we do like the familiar.
- Second, assume a recommendation system was somehow "perfect" within a particular domain such as videos. How could it have sufficient perspective to maximize a user's overall satisfaction or utility across that user's many activities (e.g., books or sleep)? Should a recommendation system suggest a user exit from its domain and do something else?

People vary a lot in what they want to do at any moment, so this would be very hard to get right. It's hard even for parents to decide when to tell a child, "Stop goofing off and study." So we probably shouldn't expect a recommendation system to tell us we cannot afford something or should go to bed. On the other hand, ethical considerations would suggest that data scientists consider this issue.

After the US Surgeon General's 1964 report that smoking caused cancer and heart disease, many societies developed a consensus to reduce smoking. Most people believe it worthwhile to nudge people towards healthy objectives (Thaler & Sunstein, 2009). Environmentalists want to nudge people to use less fossil fuel or bottled water. Companies nudge consumers to like them and their products.

China nudges people to have beliefs and take actions that contribute to societal and state harmony. Most Western readers might be pleased to encourage reducing plastic waste but not be so pleased at society-wide recommendation systems trying to influence politics. Deciding if a societal nudge is beneficial or harmful is a challenge.

Let's look at video games with respect to user customization. The industry is huge, with three million customers and revenue of $86 billion in 2021 (more than double that of the movie industry). Game designers use data science to analyze player reaction and engagement. Games obtain user feedback when played and may use it to shape game play to maintain a player's interest. For example, an ad-supported poker game might recognize a player's boredom and deal them a few strong hands. On the other hand, games could become too compelling.

As these examples show, there is immense power in using data science to customize individual experiences. In the limit, one could conceive of a dystopian society with overly persuasive machines selling us things we shouldn't buy or distracting us so we get nothing done.

Companies have recognized this challenge, at least to a degree. Both Apple and Google can now track how long we use mobile devices and remind us to cut down. The Tencent video game company uses facial recognition and other technologies to force users off of a game after a certain period. In August 2021, the Chinese National Press and Publication Administration limited video game usage for players under 18 to one hour per week and only on Fridays, weekends, and public holidays. Beyond China, there is increasing desire to enforce age-related restrictions, but this might require strong authentication when accounts are created (e.g., with a photo and birth certificate), creating more privacy-related dilemmas.

Professionals are researching these issues. The first dedicated scientific conference on recommender systems was in 2007 (ACM, 2007), and there are now sessions focused on responsible recommendations in major conferences, such as the International Web Conference (Beutel et al., 2020).

Some questions to ask include these:

- What do we mean by a good recommendation? Is engagement (clicking) enough, or are other metrics of deeper user satisfaction needed?
- How does a system ensure it has no undesirable biases that perturb its recommendations?
- How do we benefit from self-reinforcing recommendations but not reinforce partisanship and reduce acceptance of other points of view?
- Given a recommendation system's power, how does it recognize heterogenous needs of individuals?

12.4.2 Filter Bubbles

People naturally gravitate towards views with which they agree. Some prefer conservative editorial pages from the *Wall Street Journal* in the US or *The Telegraph* in the UK. Others prefer more liberal viewpoints from the *New York Times* or *The Guardian*. People self-select information sources by buying a newspaper or, increasingly, visiting a website.

However, recommendation systems using data science algorithms "pre-select" what users will see. Given the vast amount of available material, such algorithmic selection is necessary. Users are no longer in a small-town library where they look at 10 or 20 book spines and choose one. They depend on automated assistance to wade through so much material.

As described by Pariser (2011), **filter bubbles** are when the algorithmic preselection of materials is consistent with an individual's demonstrated point of view. This can be based on the group to which they belong or certain actions they have taken; clicking on links, visiting sites, or buying related merchandise. As with advertising, personalization is valuable, but too much personalization seems manipulative and restricts what viewpoints one might be exposed to. The "filter bubble" term connotes excessive personalization that engenders harm.

Many people are concerned about societal polarization in the Internet era and recommendation system effects . The capability for almost anyone to publish on the Web at very low cost has created a system with a tremendous number of different content creators, some of which are polarizing by design. Furthermore, as of 2022, social media platforms in the US are generally not responsible for the content they propagate due to Section 230 of the Communications Decency Act.

In Section 12.4.1, we observed that there are multiple reasons for increased polarization in the US, and the importance of filter bubbles is contentious:

- "Your filter bubble is destroying democracy," a 2016 *Wired* magazine editorial (El-Bermawy, 2016), argued that recommendation systems cause polarization. The author reflected on the innate likelihood of self-reinforcing systems and his own experiences. The correlation of increasing social media use with increasing societal polarization was seen as supporting evidence.
- Richard Fletcher of Oxford University showed that people who use social media, search engines, and news aggregators have more diverse news diets than people who go directly to news websites (Fletcher, 2020; Fletcher et al., 2021). Work by Zuiderveen et al. concludes that "at present there is little empirical evidence that warrants any worries about filter bubbles" (Zuiderveen Borgesius et al., 2016). We return to this topic in Part IV.

Recommendation systems also face the challenge in providing perspective to users, particularly but not exclusively with respect to news. Lots of clicks are rewarding from a monetary or user engagement perspective, but focusing only on that goal may result in one-sided recommendations that reinforce viewing patterns. Many also acknowledge that filter bubbles arise, at least in part, due to the use of clicks as imperfect proxies of user interest. For example, users sometimes click on an article out of curiosity but have no long-term interest.

Some believe that filter bubbles can be "burst" by diversifying the content that is shown to users, but content diversity may come at the cost of a lower click rate. On the other hand, increasing the dispersion of results may also benefit information platforms, as they can learn the applicability of new information and better understand the tail of click distributions.

12.4.3 Individual's Privacy Concerns

Consumers are concerned about their privacy. They wonder how their data is being used for personalization and advertising, and whether their data is being shared in ways they don't know about and wouldn't approve of.

In some cases, these concerns are well justified. In February 2020, the FCC imposed over $200 million in fines for cell phone carriers who sold customer location data to data aggregators without the customer's permission. In this data, the identity of phones is anonymized in the sense that each phone is assigned a random ID tag.

However, it is possible to de-anonymize the ID tags, as in the case of the General Secretary of the US Conference of Catholic Bishops, who resigned after reporters legally obtained phone records and discovered that a certain ID tag was correlated with his home location, his office location, his vacation home location, and also with activity on the gay dating app Grindr. Consumers would be better served if selling data like this was more tightly regulated, and the risks better explained. Privacy would be enhanced if no individual ID tags were allowed, just aggregate data.

In other cases, even if personal data is actually secure, the use cases are confusing to consumers, so they still have concerns. The common practice of **behavioral retargeting** is particularly confusing to consumers. Suppose a user visits company A and browses a product, but decides not to buy. Later, the user is on news site N and sees an ad for the same product. The user assumes that A and N have colluded to share their private information and identity and may feel betrayed. Actually what happens is that company A contracts with an advertising broker B to show ads to users who meet a behavioral profile (such as browsing a specific product). When the user comes to site N, a cookie on the user's computer determines what ad is shown, but neither A, B, nor N retains any personal information about the user. Only aggregated information, such as the number of impressions, is reported for payment purposes.

However, users may find these ad placements or recommendations to be creepy. Creepiness is hard to specify ("I know it when I see it"), so companies need to be careful to avoid alienating users.

Companies such as search engines and social networks may have a large enough network that they can serve as their own ad broker. These sites are, in effect, **walled gardens** of personal information, which contractually protect user data while using it to do personalization. They usually succeed in protecting user data. Cases such as Facebook's error with Cambridge Analytica are the exception, not the common case. That said, companies are realizing that holding personal data can be a liability, and are investing in technologies, such as federated learning (discussed in Section 10.1.3), that keep data only on a user's personal device.

12.4.4 Impact of Data Science on Being Human

In addition to impacts on choice, data-science-based recommendations and, more generally, automation can have broad effects on us as humans. Data science is at the center of many innovations that modify our everyday lives.

As mentioned in Section 5.1, Nicholas Carr ponders the impacts of automation on humans. In his book, *The Glass Cage: How Our Computers Are Changing Us* (Carr, 2014), he wonders whether technology somehow ensnares us, perhaps taking away joys of life. But despite this question, no one argues we should risk human life if a robot can remediate a hazardous waste situation.

Automobile safety systems, with highly detailed road maps, detailed situational awareness, and adaptive response algorithms, reduce traffic accidents. More broadly, despite transitional effects that caused harm, automation of human labor was responsible for great benefits from the Industrial Revolution onward.

On the other hand, data science applications change what people actually do and learn. A colleague who started a job in Hartford said he would never really learn the lay of the land; he just followed his mapping system's directions. These systems do the cognitively difficult task of finding the best route, even in complex traffic, reducing us to piloting the car and following directions.

The sports community has had similar concerns about data science changing the game, as shown by stories on data-driven analytics/automation in auto racing (Wolkin, 2020), baseball (Diamond, 2020; Lewis, 2004), and golf (Costa, 2016). For example, in baseball, analytics has shown that the traditional hitting strategy of "just make contact with the ball" is inferior to a strategy based on power hitting. The result is that batters wait longer for a good pitch to hit, and games take more pitches and more time to complete, necessitating rule changes to try to speed the game up. Additionally, if higher-level sports judgments become more automated, sporting results may still be based on the strength, coordination, and training of athletes, but data science will have an increasing role in strategy.

While we may rebel against automation in some circumstances, we may not mind it in others. We will thus be challenged to develop those applications of data science that best benefit our long-term welfare. Despite Socrates's admonition that "the unexamined life is not worth leading," in modern parlance, we will need to establish ground rules on how we are to be examined, measured, and optimized.

The many Future of Work conferences in the mid-2010s, for example the Shift Commission workshop (Shift, n.d.), considered job automation concerns. Some think today's situation is different than in the Industrial Revolution, and automation will result in longer-term disruption and unemployment. Others think data science will unlock human potential, pointing to vast new markets, industries, and new unanticipated jobs. Only in the fullness of time will it become clear how society will set objectives for data science applications that affect employment. However, there is little doubt this will challenge policy makers and data scientists in new ways. Section 14.2 on economic impacts touches again on this topic.

12.5 Transparency

Designers of data science applications benefit from disclosing their goals to the relevant audiences. To quote Benjamin Franklin, "honesty is the best policy." In the data science world, transparency serves three benefits:

- It forces a team to have broadly acceptable objectives.
- It forces the team to make them clear and succinct.
- It helps gain trust.

But it is also challenging for four reasons:

- Teams that feel their objectives may be misunderstood do not want to call attention to them.
- Teams don't want competitors to duplicate their "secret sauce."
- Teams don't want adversaries to be able to easily defeat their systems.
- Lawyers may not want teams to publicly commit to goals.

This is similar to Chapter 11's understandability discussions, but with a focus on the ends, not the means. Like many of the challenges, this is a delicate balance.

Finally, in selecting any specific objective, we must consider the risk/reward ratio. Some projects have limited risk, so a mistaken objective won't matter much. Other life-critical systems have great risks, and their objectives must be set far more carefully. Chapter 13 has more to say on this.

12.6 Objectives Recap

For convenience, the following summarizes our objectives-related challenges. They illustrate the considerations needed when embarking on or maintaining a data science application. We acknowledge some items overlap and – thankfully – not all challenges apply to every data science application.
From Chapter 12 introductory matter

- **Pre-specified or evolutionary.** To what degree must objectives be specified up front versus arrived at iteratively? If determined iteratively, will initial incompleteness or errors lead to harm? How are objectives modified to meet changing circumstances?

From Section 12.1 Clarity of objectives

- **Clarity.** Are the objectives well specified? Are they understandable to implementation teams, users, and other stakeholders?
- **Balancing across competing objectives.** Do the objectives capture and properly balance what the application is trying to achieve across competing goals?
- **Balancing across time horizons.** Do objectives balance near- and long-term benefits? Does the objective function consider and try to minimize long-term negative consequences?
- **Relation to the law.** Are the objectives legal? Should, or can, data science applications follow the law or is the law too ambiguous? If data science applications enforce law, are there negative consequences to unanticipated literal and overzealous enforcement?
- **Acceptability of variable results.** Is the objective tolerant of results of varying quality and will it recognize that some results may be better for some inputs and users than they are for others? We more fully address this in Chapter 13.

From Section 12.2 Balancing benefit across parties

- **Balancing across the breadth considerations.** Do the objectives take all stakeholders into account? Will stakeholders agree that the objectives consider their needs?
- **Societal harmony.** Do the objectives lead to societal coherence or antagonism? Will there be agreement that scarce resources will be well allocated?

From Section 12.3 Fairness

- **Fairness.** Do the objectives ensure different societal subgroups are treated fairly, especially traditionally underserved groups? Are fairness objectives achievable given the available data and technical approaches? If not, can valid, achievable objectives be found?

From Section 12.4 Concerns to the individual

- **Breadth of results.** Do the objectives specify the results should represent different points of view? Will the application attempt to minimize echo chamber-like phenomena?
- **Dependability.** Will the objectives meet the necessary privacy, security, and abuse requirements? While resilience is an implementation concept, are the objectives matched to application's capabilities? This is discussed more in Chapter 13.
- **Creepiness.** Will the system exhibit creepy behavior? Even if legal and arguably beneficial, will people accept such behavior?

- **Manipulation.** Does the system coerce people against their best interests? Does the system meet the need for humans to be in control?
- **Being human.** Do the objectives properly specify what data science should do and what should be left to humans? In other words, do they render unto data science only that which is data science and leave the rest to humans?

From Section 12.5 Other considerations

- **Transparency.** Are the objectives public or is there a good reason for them not to be? Are the objectives acceptable, at least to the relevant subcommunities? If published on the front page of a newspaper, would readers accept them?
- **Risk/reward ratio.** Do the objectives balance risk and reward? Including unintended consequences, will the application be beneficial?

We have three closing thoughts that apply to all objectives.

First, are they reasonably achievable? If not, can they be modified and still result in a useful data science application? Trying to build an application with unmeetable objectives is a self-deceiving waste of time and resources, and it is likely harmful.

Second, objectives must take ethics into account, as discussed in Chapter 3 and Chapter 7. We'll say more about how organizations can operationalize this in Section 14.3 on acting ethically.

Finally, we acknowledge that the most subtle force behind the difficulty in establishing objectives arises from data science being applied to really complex and hard problems. Individuals, organizations, and societies have to confront issues they previously had not reckoned with. The applications of data science are important, and that importance leads to pragmatic difficulties and new ethical quandaries.

Chapter 13

Toleration of Failures

In traditional software, the challenge is to eliminate bugs and achieve certainty that the software correctly implements the appropriate algorithm and computes the right answer. But data science has additional challenges:

- Data science problems often have no unambiguously correct answers. For example, there is no 100% agreed-upon best path for a self-driving car to take. For image recognition tasks, there may be no definitive answer ("is that a dog or a wolf; I can't tell"), and no agreed-upon theory about how to verify answers.
- Statistical analyses often yield confidence intervals, not definitive answers. Machine learning approaches may return poor answers due to an incomplete training set, an imperfect model, or a lack of clarity in setting objectives.

Data scientists should also humbly factor in dependability risks. This is particularly important in safety-critical (e.g., autonomous vehicles) or very large-scale systems (e.g., recommendations provided to billions of people). Chapter 10 discussed dependability in significant detail, and we won't repeat that material.

The Analysis Rubric specifically calls out toleration of failures to remind data scientists to determine explicitly if a problem is amenable to a data science solution. If not, they need to figure out how to make it so or else conclude data science may not be the answer. As of mid-2021, image recognition works for tagging people in personal photo albums, as that is very failure-tolerant and there are no significant security issues. However, in court, image recognition cannot be the sole indicator of a person's identity. Disease diagnosis applications aid medical practitioners but do not yet operate on their own.

There may even be problems that are just too difficult to ever expect solutions – in chaotic systems or where sufficient data is unattainable. We should try to solve important problems, but some applications may be innately failure-intolerant.

This chapter looks at how to characterize uncertainty. How to minimize risks entailed by that uncertainty while balancing risks against rewards? How to assess liability for any residual harms that may occur, despite the best efforts to minimize them?

13.1 Uncertainty Quantification

A fundamental responsibility of any data science application is to clearly explain the uncertainty associated with its conclusions or outcomes. That way, users will have an idea of the level of risk they face. The field of uncertainty quantification has a vast literature, including its own journal (SIAM/ASA, n.d.). Uncertainty can appear in many forms:

- The data may be **noisy**, resulting in a model that has high **variance** – sampling a slightly different set of data points results in a surprisingly different model.
- There may be limits to the **accuracy** of the data. We might have a near-perfect model of the situation, but be unable to gather the data we need with the accuracy required.
- The model might **extrapolate** or **generalize** poorly when queried with novel inputs.
- The model may be **biased** – a flaw makes the model consistently wrong.
- The computer implementation may have flaws – either outright bugs, or subtle **numerical errors** resulting from arithmetic with approximate numbers.
- The computer implementation may intentionally include some **randomness** and give different results when run twice with the exact same inputs.

These practices can clarify the uncertainty in data science systems:

- Don't report an output prediction as a single number. Instead, specify the prediction as a range with a mean and a **confidence interval**, or possibly a complete probability distribution. Monte Carlo simulations are often used to create this range of predictions.
- Clarify the sources of uncertainty in this confidence interval. Is the uncertainty due to inherent noisiness in the underlying process in the real world? Is it due to limitations of measurements or of the model's expressiveness? Or is it due to flaws in the implementation?
- Be ready to update the model's parameters. In some cases, after calibrating the uncertainty on a number of experimental trials, it is possible to feed that error back so as to minimize the amount of uncertainty. This is called **inverse uncertainty quantification**.
- Be aware that a material change in the world, leading to a change in the input data, will usually lead to an increase in uncertainty. See the discussion of non-stationarity and concept drift in Section 9.1. Not only will predictions be worse, the confidence intervals will be larger.

Much of data science is understandably focused on the accuracy of predictions. But quantification of uncertainty is often even more important than quantification of accuracy. For example, the real estate site Zillow uses a machine learning model to estimate house prices. In 2018 they started buying houses that their model predicted would appreciate in value.

In 2021 they abandoned this effort after a $300 million loss. Two problems contributed to their loss. First, they had a lot of objective data on each house: address, school district, square footage, number of bedrooms, comparable sales in the area, etc. But the individual homeowner had subjective insider data that Zillow lacked: Did the house have a persistent leaking roof? Was it aesthetically above or below average? In a rising market that was okay; there was still plenty of profit available for both the homeowner and Zillow. But the second problem was that Zillow underestimated the overall uncertainty and volatility in the housing market, including factors like the difficulty of renovating houses under supply chain constraints.

13.2 Risk

When applying the toleration of failures Analysis Rubric element, data science applications must balance benefits against the possible harms arising from failures. Data scientists must explicitly consider how to mitigate harms such as:

- a poor recommendation;
- undesired, but perhaps subtle, built-in biases;
- outright errors in the transformation of information;
- analyses that disseminate incorrect conclusions; and
- other expense, reputational, financial liability, and ethical consequences.

Even when systems work as intended, there may also be reputational costs to consider. Hotels and airlines use historical data to optimize their revenue by knowing some travelers are no-shows, and overbook. In effect, they sell several rooms or seats twice. This benefits them by using their capacity more efficiently, but at the cost of customer frustration and compensation when it is overbooked.

Determining the optimization's correct set point is very challenging, particularly if systems need resilience to deal with unusual events, such as bad weather or some other event that makes a flight or location more desirable. As another example, consider Section 6.2's discussion of the reputational challenge to a web search company if even a tiny percentage of search results are really bad.

Generally, the specific *application* of data science dictates the reliability properties it must meet. The standards are highest when human life is at stake, as when data science is applied to medical diagnosis. Society generally holds automated systems to a higher standard than human judgment.

As a non-life-critical example, in the early 2010s the New York Department of Health asked co-author Alfred whether Google Translate could help the city's multilingual population understand drug labels. Since these were provided in only a few languages, their translation would be valuable to many non-English speakers. Google ultimately declined because it felt its translations were not accurate enough to provide human health advice, and great harm could result. (Google also knew training data on drug advice translation was sparse, so the system would likely be less accurate than on normal text.) Since then, automatic translation systems have become much more accurate. However, there is no definitive answer as to what constitutes sufficient accuracy for this application.

13.3 Liability

Liability for failures focuses organizations and teams on deterring unwarranted errors and, perhaps, partially compensates victims for harm. However, data science applications make liability considerations complex. It may be difficult to determine (1) whether there is a failure, (2) what were the circumstances leading up to the failure, and (3) who is at fault.

In uncertain environments, the first step is to set a threshold for failure. Is 99% accurate speech recognition a success or a failure? Is five minutes of downtime a month a failure? Terms-of-service agreements try to define these points.

To determine liability, evaluators must establish a correctness baseline, which is not necessarily easy to do. Returning to the example of how fast an autonomous vehicle should go, if almost everyone drives 10% over the speed limit, matching that speed may be safer. However, a police officer might disagree with this logic. The "everybody else is doing it" argument would seem simultaneously both a valid reason to go faster, but an invalid legal defense. As another example, many social networks moderate their content. Action or inaction on certain content is often politically charged, and there may not be consensus on what a failure is.

A common issue with a semi-automated system is whether the system or the human operator is at fault. If a car manufacturer warns drivers that its automation system is not for completely autonomous driving, what liability does the manufacturer have if a human driver neglects to take control when the system commands them to? In 2021 a driver of a (non-automated) Amazon delivery truck caused a serious accident. The victim's family sued Amazon, alleging that the company's driver-monitoring software system, not the human driver, was ultimately responsible for the vehicle. As of early 2022, the case has not yet been decided.

The more parties involved, the harder it is to ascertain fault. Researchers create techniques, software engineers instantiate them into programs, data scientists collect and wrangle the data, other engineers may combine the algorithms and data, and yet others may own, use, license, and operate the resultant systems. These systems include software and hardware. While not wholly unique to data science, the problem's complexity does make attribution more difficult.

Self-driving cars or medical treatments are good domains to illustrate the attribution of liability in complex systems. Autonomous vehicles gather data from many sources to accurately model road networks, traffic signals, traffic patterns, vehicular and pedestrian traffic, and regulatory rules. Algorithms use this data to produce the logic to operate vehicles. The logic is bundled by manufacturers into cars, which are sold to consumers who drive them – sometimes in accordance with guidelines, sometimes not.

Medical systems increasingly provide valuable, but imperfect, diagnostic and treatment information to physicians. How will our legal system assign liability and allocate damages for these complex, multi-stage systems? And how will insurance work to both protect and properly incentivize safety?

Regarding the circumstances leading to error, whether the error was due to gross negligence, negligence, or anticipated behavior is also important. Gross negligence (a legal term of art) is more odious, and usually results in far greater penalties. On the other hand, certain data science applications may fail expectedly, yet still usually produce great benefits.

Liability issues are likely to become more significant as applications become increasingly valuable, with a higher potential to cause significant economic harm or loss of life if they fail. Large data-science-based utilities serving vast numbers of applications and customers, possibly in healthcare, transportation, or other essential tasks, could have societal-scale risks. Any large-scale failure would simultaneously impact many people. We alluded to this problem in some of the examples of Chapter 6, such as the route-finding application. However, there could be far worse outages than this one.

We close with both an organizational and societal lens on liability:

As three examples of organizational reactions to liability, we note again the prudent delay in releasing Google Health's first application. This reduced Google's risk of liability if it had a data breach. Second, when he was CTO of Two Sigma, co-author Alfred considered the risks of a data breach of intellectual property or personally identifiable information as the hardest issue he had. This was due to the potential consequences being so reputationally and economically destructive. Finally, data science applications often use cloud computing vendors, so risk and liability determination require challenging decisions about trust in computing infrastructure. Some organizations are willing to trust cloud vendors for almost all their operations, but others are more cautious.

At a societal level, liability issues may make it very difficult to deploy applications that have truly real risks, yet make fewer mistakes than humans and are thus a net positive. If deep-pocketed enterprises develop these systems, penalties for failures could be so large to prevent their deployment. To be specific, with Level 5 (fully automated) self-driving cars, one can imagine achieving a factor of 10 reduction in fatalities in the US. But what would the liability be for those remaining approximately 4,000 deaths per year?

When a new office building is constructed, the architects and civil engineers are certified, licensed, insured, and operate under strict rules of liability. If a defect develops, there is a well-defined process for adjudicating responsibility. Not so with software. There is not comparable licensing for software engineers or the companies that hire them.

This difference makes sense when we consider that constructing a new building leverages a huge history of experience and established practices, but creating a new software app is largely a novel act of invention, and thus a poor fit for strict, predefined rules. In addition, the harm from a building collapsing is great, while the harm from, say, a game app crashing is small.

However, as software in general and data science in particular play an increasing role in life-critical applications, there will be calls for increased scrutiny and regulation. This should be done in a way that balances risks with innovation. In the case of COVID-19, countries needed a vaccine so much that they granted drug companies immunity from liability for unintentional harm, while providing a Countermeasures Injury Compensation Program to cover cases such as people who lost pay due to sick days after taking the vaccine.

Chapter 14

Ethical, Legal, and Societal Challenges

This chapter begins with data science's broad legal issues and continues with some previously undiscussed societal (primarily economic) implications of data science. It ends by discussing the challenges of internalizing ethical considerations into data science practices.

14.1 Legal Issues

As technology and data science have ever greater societal impact, the number and diversity of laws regulating them has also grown. Historically, there are legal precedents on many relevant topics, such as the following:

- **Scale concerns.** In the 1930s, IBM's economic power in the punch card marketplace led to antitrust concerns.
- **National security.** Nations have long restricted the export of weapons, and from the 1950s on, the US and other countries heavily restricted the export of encryption technology and computers.
- **Regulation of content.** Nations have long had libel laws and regulated publication of certain types of information, for example, publications relating to national security or violating broadly accepted norms.

We won't attempt to review the historical bases, but instead look into the future, first considering data science from a governmental perspective and then from the perspective of individuals and institutions.

14.1.1 Legal Challenges – A Governmental Perspective

Table 14.1 lists many of the most pertinent legal/regulatory areas. One of the most universal problems in these regulations is the question of balance:

- National security and societal protection argue for strong rights for government subpoena, while strong limitations best serve privacy.

Table 14.1 *Representative areas of government interest in regulation of data-science-related activities*.*

Area	Examples: *Laws*
Protection of the individual	• Privacy: *EU's GDPR, California's CCPA, EU's Right to be Forgotten, US Federal Trade Commission Authority under Section 5 of the FTC Act* • Libel and misinformation: *Ancient English common law, US state laws, US False Information and Hoaxes Law* • Security: *Notification of breach under US state laws* and *HIPAA (see below)* • Children: *US Children's Online Privacy Protection Act, many laws against their exploitation*
Protection of society	• Content: *German Volksverhetzung laws against incitement of populated hatred* • Subpoena of data: *Chinese cybersecurity law* • Rules of international data transmission: *EU's Schrems II*
Regulation of the business landscape	• Antitrust regulations: *Tying, pricing, mergers, and acquisitions* • Credit card transactions*: US Payment Card Industry Data Security Standard* • Copyright: *Fair use* • Other intellectual property: *Patent, trade secret* • Best practices: *SOC 2 to reduce risk*
Taxation across national boundaries	• Sales and value-added taxes • Corporate taxation
Liability	• Liability and liability limitations: *California CCPA's private right of action with statutory damages for security breaches, US Section 230* • Attribution of liability • Standards of culpability
National security and sovereignty	• Rules on disputed borders • Import/export regulation of technology • Regulation of elections: *Canadian Elections Modernization Act, US federal campaign finance law* • Data residency: *Many countries have barriers to cross-border data flows*
Application-specific	• Advertising: *US truth in advertising, US regulation of drug advertising* • Health: *HIPAA (Health Insurance Portability and Accountability Act of 1996)* • Financial: *US Gramm–Leach–Bliley Act, requirements for record keeping, use of social media, truth in lending* • Education: *US federal Family Educational Rights and Privacy Act*

* This table lists a collection of government regulations that affect enterprises doing data science, particularly those deploying data science applications internationally.

- Complex regulations can favor large organizations. They have the resources to understand and follow them, while smaller organizations might not.
- Rules protecting individuals or societies from harmful effects of certain expressions of speech may conflict with legal or even constitutionally mandated protections.

Another major challenge occurs because data science applications are often supra-jurisdictional, that is, operating across multiple jurisdictional entities of countries or federated states. US privacy law, in the absence of a comprehensive national approach, is growing increasingly complex as some states, such as California, Virginia and Colorado, enact their own robust consumer privacy laws. Similarly, a national government will have difficulty legislating desired limits if they require international agreements or if extra-territorial entities just ignore its rules. Taken to extremes, such issues could cause a country to assert its sovereignty by partitioning its internet to exclude foreign impact – something Russia is implementing, and China has substantially accomplished. Jurisdictional issues are why taxation is listed in Table 14.1. It is a highly complex topic for data-science-based entities that operate across borders.

Our final topic relates to complexity. Both the specification and enforcement of laws is difficult, requiring complex political decisions, highly competent staff, and other enforcement mechanisms. They may be equally complex for both for-profit and not-for-profit institutions to follow, which increases costs and reduces agility. Complexity may result in ineffective or untimely laws, poor enforcement, and reduced innovation. While governments unquestionably have an interest in regulating harms to their countries or population, they must also recognize they may reduce the agility of the technical sector if regulation is not done well, particularly given the complexity and dynamism of data science domains.

14.1.2 Legal Challenges – Applying Data Science

Organizations face many challenges in interpreting the regulations on data science applications, and then faithfully abiding by the intent and letter of the law:

- If data science applications operate across jurisdictions, the multiple bodies of laws may be in conflict. Governmental rights or limits of subpoena of data may be different for people who store their data in a different jurisdiction. Data storage and access mandates may be in direct conflict. For example, Apple has accommodated laws in its Chinese market, despite their negative impact on individual privacy, while taking a more protective approach to privacy in the US (Nicas et al., 2021). In areas of contested borders, map providers show different borders based on the user's location (Bensinger, 2020).

- Privacy regulations on data from a multi-site research study might require sites to maintain an arms-length relationship, so the overall study must meet differing legal requirements. Even a single jurisdiction may have conflicting legal requirements. As mentioned, privacy concerns could impact competition, so companies have to balance conflicting objectives.
- An organization experiencing a security breach involving personal information of individuals from multiple nations and US states may have to craft an approach to breach notification that is consistent with both GDPR and the laws of 50 states.

Some laws are particularly hard to interpret or follow. The EU Right to Be Forgotten legislation requires search engine companies to determine if certain search results should be delisted, with decisions based on EU guidelines reduced to practice by the companies. As discussed in Section 10.1, GDPR is another example of a regulatory framework that is complex to interpret. Societal laws (and expectations) on content moderation force social networks and content sites to make similar determinations. While laws prohibiting foreign payments for political advertising may be clear, it can be very difficult to truly know who ultimately paid for the ads. Many complex rules regulating advertising vary by the product advertised and the locale where the ad is shown.

Laws and regulations require detailed disclosure of policies and actions by data science products and projects. Yet it is extremely challenging to write end-user licenses or policies that both meet legal requirements and are comprehensible to people with different educational backgrounds. The complex disclosures on many commercial websites show the challenge, but complex disclosures also extend to participants in scientific studies (and even car rentals). Moreover, privacy requirements – for example, transparency – become more challenging with respect to the proliferation of Internet of Things devices. Many of these do not even include a user interface where a privacy policy could be readily displayed.

While needed for safety or security, legal requirements can be at odds with the most elegant or efficient way of implementing data science applications. The legal requirements might force complex, expensive, and voluminous record keeping to show organizations are in compliance. Differences between national requirements may prevent cross-border access to global data stores which would allow for more efficient operational and analytical approaches.

Understanding legal requirements and complying with them may be expensive, and the added costs might make otherwise worthy projects unfeasible. To minimize expense and maximize compliance, developers can apply data science to continually monitor operations and help applications[16] meet legally mandated requirements, but this too leads to challenges. Data science typically operates

[16] This can become recursive as data science applications monitor the operations of other ones, etc.

probabilistically, and the law and public opinion may not accept imperfect results. For example, a 99.99% accurate content moderation system's one in 10,000 error may generate severe ill-will and be the source of legal violations.

Although regulations may be designed to promote fairness and strengthen the competitive landscape, complex regulations can cause even greater problems by advantaging larger firms that have developed the capacity to follow them. Paradoxically, this often makes it harder for new firms to challenge incumbents. Thus, while regulations are an important governmental responsibility, it is complex to craft the right ones.

A 2021 survey of tech policy experts by Clifford Chance LLP concludes (Clifford Chance & Milltown Partners, 2021):

> The regulatory landscape for AI will likely emerge gradually, with a mixture of AI-specific and non-AI-specific binding rules, non-binding codes of practice, and sets of regulatory guidance. As more pieces are added to the puzzle, there is a risk of both geographical fragmentation and runaway regulatory hyperinflation, with multiple similar or overlapping sets of rules being generated by different bodies.

Readers interested in the current US legal framework can begin with this overview of US privacy laws given by Swire & Kennedy-Mayo (2020).

14.2 Economic Impacts

Chapter 12 discussed data science's complex impacts on *individuals* and *groups*, and illustrated challenges in misleading information, manipulation, fairness, and more. This section examines the economic impacts data science may have on firms, individuals, and markets:

- **Benefits of scale.** The quantity of data gathered and used in analysis, the vast capabilities for storing and processing data, and the size of technical design and engineering teams needed to develop large systems.
- **Benefits of technical sophistication.** The ability to apply statistics, optimization, and computer science to important domains with significant impact.
- **Ability to optimize.** The ability to use scale and technical approaches to optimize results in ways that have far-reaching impacts on marketplaces and consumer behavior.

14.2.1 Scale Effects

Throughout history, economies of scale effects have benefited many industries. They have been particularly important to the technology sector. Hardware and software systems are expensive and difficult to create, but marginal costs are low and profit margins per unit are high. Commonly used interfaces benefit consumers, but also help maintain a company's place in the market. Scale effects are very prevalent, particularly in large-scale software and cloud services, globally used communications infrastructure, and semiconductors. However, there are also forces that reduce the need for scale. These include open-source software, standard interfaces and protocols that allow for competitive implementations, better programming methodologies, and sophisticated design tools.

Data science adds a second dimension to the benefit of scale; many applications benefit from the virtuous cycle. Their data needs can only be met via many commercial relationships and/or significantly engaged users.[17] While there are certainly "small" straightforward data science applications, many important applications require great scale. Some may also require complex and expensive systems for data acquisition, storage, analysis, model operation, and more.

Non-technical drivers of scale may further encourage enterprises to grow. As the Internet provides unparalleled customer access, its international reach may require global workforces. Additionally, for applications relating to the physical world, large scale may require concomitantly scaled logistics and distribution networks. As shown in the previous section, the complexity of legal regulations can favor larger organizations with the resources to understand and meet complex mandates.

Users may benefit from scale due to both better-quality applications and increased connectivity to other applications. Data science requires scale to build things like search engines, social networks, shared content sites, large-scale online stores, or self-driving cars that work well and mitigate dependability perils. Scale can provide the resources to enterprises to do bold R&D and to enter new markets.

Also, Metcalfe's Law claims that a network's value is proportional to the number of its users squared (Wikipedia contributors, 2021). While neither a true law nor a fully justified numerical relationship,[18] it does give another reason why some large organizations keep growing larger.

Thus, scale effects are at least part of the cause of a landscape having large, albeit changing, enterprises.[19] One result has been increased market concentration (notably in the US and China), causing many constituencies to have concerns about large enterprises' economic power and influence. Scale motivates antitrust regulators and policy makers to scrutinize the behavior of large organizations, and

[17] As an anecdote on scale, many of us have used our organization's own internal search, and found that it does not perform as well as web search. This is a scale phenomenon, since even a huge organization of 100,000 employees has about four orders of magnitude less data than a web search engine.

[18] The true value of a network is proportional to the number of users times the average number of other users they want to connect to, times the average value of the connection.

[19] Most of the early computer and software companies no longer exist; IBM is a much smaller force in computing, and Intel, which more recently looked dominant, is challenged by new processor architectures and, as of 2021, semiconductor leadership by others.

their continual interest and investigation may make them less agile and more bureaucratic.

It is a challenge to balance scale issues that enable technology and data science to support valuable innovation against winner-take-most outcomes. There are clear echoes of this in ongoing regulatory discussions in many regions.

14.2.2 Economic Effects on Individuals

Building a successful data science application requires people with particular skills:

- **Data science skills.** Analytical skills from statistics, operations research, mathematics, certain engineering disciplines, and computer science.
- **Software engineering skills.** The largest technical systems require huge amounts of computer software. In 2016, Google's main repository had over two billion lines of code (Potvin & Levenberg, 2016). It takes a very sophisticated technical staff to make data-science-based systems work. Requisite skills include intricate knowledge of computers and networks' smallest details.
- **Management skills.** Coordinating the work of data scientists, product managers, software engineers, reliability engineers, security professionals, ethicists, and more.
- **Leadership skills**. Extending data science into new domains requires visionary entrepreneurs with the desire, energy, and creativity to do new things, and the perspective to do them well.

People with such skills are highly sought after. Data science's automation and optimization capabilities may enable relatively few people with the right skills to generate great value. A recommendation system can span a huge corpus and signals, doing the work of many human curators. Partial or total automation of truck driving could improve a huge sector's efficiency, but change aspects of the jobs of more than three million workers in the US alone.

Based on Michael Young's 1958 book, *The Rise of Meritocracy* (Young, 1958), he would term data scientists and those who use their work as being meritorious. He says merit arises from "intelligence plus effort," though today we would more neutrally say "*skill* and effort."

However, despite having coined the term **meritocracy**, Young's book was actually a satire. He was concerned with what happens if meritocracy is pushed too far – in particular, if meritocracy provided excessive benefit to some. Data science may need to be considered in that light, given its outsized rewards.

It is true that the founders and designers of a hot new tech giant have created something of value and deserve rewards. It is also true that society at large created the global network and marketplace that made it all possible, so society deserves a share of the rewards. Currently everyone who uses the technology gets some benefit from their use, and many people and institutions are invested in a pension, endowment, or index fund that benefits them when tech stocks go up. However, there have been calls to spread the value more equally, via taxation and other policies.

Data science's leverage creates a related benefit to those who use it to gain fame and customers. **Superstar effects**, according to Koenig, "arise when technologies open up bigger markets and make it possible to reach consumers in larger, perhaps even global markets" (Koenig, 2020). Koenig shows demonstrable impacts of broadcast TV on entertainment industry salaries, and relays the concern that new technologies may create more winner-takes-all labor markets. For example, recommendation engines can accelerate an individual's rise to fame, and sharing sites enable global markets. Korinek provides a fuller discussion of superstar effects (Korinek & Ng, 2017).

Before concluding this section, we return briefly to automation's societal impact on employment levels. This topic first arose in Section 12.4.4, where it was a byproduct of discussing data science's impact on being human.

While automation has raised and will continue to raise aggregate standards of living, data-driven approaches will also change work and employment.

- The tasks that humans do will change, just as the task of bank tellers changed with the introduction of ATMs.
- However, it is not clear how this will affect employment. There are just too many open questions, ranging from the rate at which automation progresses, to the invention rate of new productive activities that require human contributions, to increasing educational opportunities, to birth and death rates, and more. For example, in contrast to experts' angst in the early 2010s, unemployment numbers dropped to record lows.

Thus, we humbly (or timidly) refer the reader to the many future-of-work publications, including that of the previously mentioned Shift Commission (Shift, n.d.) or the MIT Task Force on the Work of the Future (Autor et al., 2020).

14.2.3 Impact of Optimization

Data science, paired with the Internet's global reach, has created new markets, made existing ones far more global, and lowered economic friction. Purchasers can more easily find specialized products and compare prices and terms from multiple competing products or distributors, often without regard to proximity. Producers have benefited by having access to much larger markets.

Optimization, a core data science goal, contributes to economic efficiency, guiding opportunity and human activity to meet important objectives. The flip side is that data science may reduce the roles of the friendships, business relationships, or other norms that previously held sway. It does this by enabling highly optimized decisions, rather than just "satisficing," a term and practice that Herb Simon introduced and described. He noted that optimization is frequently too difficult and perhaps too risky, so decisions are often made by finding a choice that meets some acceptability threshold (Mintrom, 2015). But that was before data science made optimization easier.

Shopping is a great example of how things have changed. For specialized items, consumers used only to have easy access to (mostly) geographically close businesses. For many products, these businesses may have had little nearby competition. Thus, consumers might shop around a bit and make a few phone calls, but ultimately they satisficed. They may have made their choice based on the friendliness of a salesperson, not a product's detailed attributes or absolute minimal price.

Information technologies (database management systems and parameterized search), data science (automated recommendation systems and optimized pricing), and sophisticated logistics and delivery systems have all made markets more competitive. Companies need to compete more aggressively on quantifiable metrics. The market rewards superior products or services and exposes inferior and more expensive ones. Modern systems focus on optimization and have created situations where different types of institutions or certain regions may flourish. As observed previously, scale effects sometimes lead to "winner-takes-most" outcomes, at least in the short term.

The Internet's global nature and data science's ability to cross international borders allows for global optimization and competition. Manufacturing products in the developing world is often of significantly lower cost than doing so in wealthier countries, so data science and information technology direct and facilitate the flow of global goods and services there. Technology has contributed to greatly reducing global poverty levels, but the benefits of per capita GDP growth have not accrued uniformly.

Finally, we note that successful optimization often requires organizational scale, as discussed in Section 14.2.1.

14.3 Acting Ethically

Throughout Part III of the book, we have described numerous challenges in the application of data science. We have argued that practitioners need to have ethical principles in mind as they consider the techniques they use and the decisions they make. As stated previously, continual reflection forces data scientists to consider difficult challenges, acts as a check on significant errors, and motivates practical improvements.

The clearest obligation of data scientists and their organizations is adherence to professional codes of ethics covering truthfulness, integrity, and similar issues.

Addressing the broader and more varied socio-technical complexities in developing and deploying data science is more challenging. This is true even if organizations have realized the benefits of acting ethically, whether from altruism, the desire to gain long-term customer trust, to minimize regulatory oversight, or to recruit and retain talent. These challenges include the following:

- Potential tensions between individual incentives and organizational goals, particularly when framed in terms of optimization.
- Uncertainty of *how* an organization motivates itself to achieve ethical standards and *who* in the organization is directly accountable and able to ensure it follows ethical processes.
- The gap between general, shared principles and specific, actionable policies.

Each of these may seem abstract, but we will elaborate below and discuss some representative problem cases.

14.3.1 Incentives: Organizational and Individual

Organizations advance by breaking complex missions into simpler goals. Within a university, this can mean well-defined but separate goals for its research, teaching, and university administration functions. Within a company, some teams are primarily motivated by engineering goals, some by revenue, some by employee happiness, etc.

This separation of concerns risks an unintended consequence if individuals successfully optimize their group's objectives in a way that is ultimately inconsistent with the larger mission or its ethical objectives. In academia, individual researchers have, among other incentives, the incentive to maximize their publications and grant dollars. Sales team commission-based incentives may motivate different behavior than quality-assurance team reliability-based ones.

The risk of scientific or ethical misconduct is why universities create conflict-of-interest offices and **institutional review boards (IRBs)**. The process of peer review (whether within a department or at a journal) is another check on maximizing individual success metrics (more publications) at an overall mission's expense. Companies also have resolution mechanisms for balancing different team objectives.

For example, a data science application could have a development team divided into subteams that focus on only a part of a complex user journey (e.g., configuring an app, using an app frequently, or clicking on in-app purchases). Individuals in the teams are then charged with meeting distinct metrics, sometimes termed key performance indicators (KPIs). This divide-and-conquer approach comes naturally to technologists and the quantitatively minded. However, the challenges of constructing subtasks whose optima coincide with the best overall organizational strategy are daunting. Notably, this challenge is an organizational analog of some of the competing objectives challenges raised in Section 12.2.

In the case of a digital app's user journey, premature optimization of in-app purchases could drive down long-term customer retention. This may be especially true if it was achieved via so-called **dark patterns** of manipulative design choices, such as misleading button descriptions or a "purchase" button placed so near to "close popup" as to cause inadvertent purchases. When goals are divided among teams, this can lead to suboptimal solutions as well as inter-team rivalries that destabilize an organization. Challenges are even more formidable when they include difficult-to-quantify goals such as a commitment to an ethical process.

The Belmont Commissioners recognized the need to align individuals' goals with mission and ethics. They ensured that both the Belmont Report authors and members of the report's proposed IRBs included not just researchers but individuals representing a variety of views, including law, philosophy, and policy. In Part IV, we discuss the careful planning and process needed to maintain individuals' alignment with an organizational mission, including ethical considerations.

14.3.2 Governance: Locating Ethics Within an Organizational Chart

A CEO, university president, or other top leader has the ultimate responsibility for an organization's ethics, particularly for balancing the competing incentives raised in the previous section. But no one person can ensure that *all* of the organization's actions will be ethical – an awareness of ethics must be infused throughout.

Particularly in data science, many teams make highly technical decisions on data quality, dependability, and balancing objectives. These decisions are often local to a particular technique, technology, or sub-business, yet have broad implications.

But if everyone "owns ethics," it is challenging to ensure that:

- Employees are informed of all ethical principles and processes.
- Employees begin with a shared ethical consensus.
- Employees take their responsibility to apply these principles seriously and do not fall into the trap of assuming that "someone else will worry about the issue at hand."

The cultural and educational challenges are very real. Making ethics everyone's equal responsibility gives everyone a sense of agency in defining ethical practice. An emphasis on ethical responsibility may also benefit an organization's ability to recruit and retain talented people for whom ethics are a priority. However, merely stating broad responsibility does not define a process for resolving individual disputes or ensure that ethics are prioritized uniformly.

Distributing ethical agency and accountability works better in organizations operating with enlightened self-interest. This is when most individuals realize what's best for the community is also best for themselves or their team, at least in the long term. However, not every organization enjoys such universal enlightenment. Also, there is an efficiency concern. Organizations are not usually democracies, and even democracies require that decisions be delegated so they can be made expeditiously.

To address both of these shortcomings, organizations sometimes create an ethics group to "own" the more integrative ethical objectives. This group takes responsibility for defining, communicating, and ensuring a high standard for ethical processes. Such a group can guide analysis of ethical decisions, ensure ethical processes are applied, and adjudicate disputes. While this can be a valuable addition, there is a downside: the group's existence could provide the rest of an organization with a convenient excuse to ignore ethical concerns.

For example, a university with a separate IRB (which, by design, applies only to human subjects research) facilitates researchers focusing on publication and grant writing goals while only considering ethics when a study must go through IRB review. This may also prevent others from developing the "habit" of analyzing decisions about their ethical impact; individuals may reason they can just leave ethics to the ethics review.

Note that challenges with an ethical focal point occur whether ethical responsibilities are given to a new subgroup or an existing team, e.g., legal or compliance. Assigning ethics to an existing team also risks conflation of the ideas (e.g., blurring the lines between ethical questions and legal ones) and prevents developing ethics expertise as a separate skill.

Despite the complexity, organizations often arrange themselves such that:

- A president or CEO takes ultimate responsibility for ethics by setting policy and being responsible.
- Each individual or team is informed of and expected to abide by the relevant ethical principles and processes.
- A designated ethics group is empowered to make certain decisions, particularly when individuals disagree.

Coordinating this multifaceted strategy is also complex; we return briefly to this point in Section 19.2.

14.3.3 From Principles to Policies

Connecting high-level principles to policies and decisions takes great effort. The principlist approach to ethics requires that an organization first commits to stating principles. They must be sufficiently general to be useful in a wide variety of contexts. Both internal and external stakeholders must understand them as legitimate goals.

However, the principles must also be sufficiently clear and specific that a community can use them to guide decisions, constrain bad outcomes, and reach a consensus about the decision-making process's integrity. Moreover, these principles, particularly with changing technology and norms, periodically need to be re-evaluated and possibly updated. Just as some countries have evolving case law that results from detailed and evolving court decisions, organizational experience can lead to more prescriptive rules that make ethical principles easier to apply.

As an engineering example, in summer 2021 Facebook's Reality Labs tried to set a responsible course for future augmented and virtual reality work. They enumerated four high-level principles, but the true challenge is the difficulty of applying them to good effect:

- "Never surprise people" (transparency)
- "Provide controls that matter" (informed consent)
- "Consider everyone" (justice)
- "Put people first" (community above individuals or business)

Their website states, "Everyone at Reality Labs is responsible for upholding these principles, with dedicated teams focused on ethics, safety, security and privacy. These principles will continue to evolve as we seek and receive feedback on our principles and products" (Reality Labs, n.d.).

Research and product development teams must take different steps to bridge the gap between stated, commonly agreed general principles and individual decisions. For product development, this includes specifying questions teams can review during a digital product's life-cycle. At different data life-cycle stages, different ethical questions are most appropriate. Privacy is more apropos to a data-gathering phase, while objective setting is more relevant to modeling and product design.

As for academic research, its ethical process happens at two different scales:

- Infrequent formal review, as by the IRB.
- Frequent informal peer review, including funding proposals, research publications, and individual promotions.

Integrating ethical principles into the career development process, including hiring and promotion decisions, helps keep incentives aligned between organizations and individuals.

As emphasized above, data science presents particular challenges in applying ethical principles. Companies developing automated decision systems must deal with how they can be complex and opaque in ways that obscure potential harms and biases. Every organization has a responsibility to build, refine, and improve their habitual critical inquiry into ethical issues. Their inquiries must take place both across an organization and throughout data science product life-cycles.

14.3.4 Example Challenges in Ensuring Ethical Consideration

Content recommendations, whether as a news feed or a "recommended for you" feature, illustrate the above challenges. An engineering organization with separate teams for maximizing engagement (e.g., clicks), maximizing revenue, and surveying user satisfaction might see them optimize for contradictory goals.

There needs to be shared principles of sufficient specificity, or an organizational structure which maintains alignment. Otherwise, such disharmony can frustrate data scientists and increase the risk of ethical harms to users. These harms include addictive or coercive design choices and algorithms which maximize clicks by promoting disinformation from user-generated content.

As discussed in Section 6.6, automated decision-making tools in the criminal justice system present ethical challenges in achieving fairness while aiming to reduce crime. They could optimize for accuracy on training data yet not achieve fairness (technically) or justice (societally). Investigative journalism can also provide an important check on misalignments.

Also consider an application that uses personal GPS data to recommend workout regimens. Team members that produce it are aligned in thinking engagement metrics are a win–win. Higher engagement benefits clients by encouraging more exercise and is also good for business. Presumably, employees do not want to harm their users.

Even such a simple application produced by a well-meaning company has at least two challenges: First, how do they ensure techniques that increase engagement do not encourage risky behavior? Second, how much more data analysis and engineering should the company do to make work regimens safer and better? For example, engineers could gather and apply additional data such as outdoor temperature, humidity, pulse rate, heart rhythm, etc. It's hard to know how much is needed and when to stop.

Our final example is about the complex incentives that science communicators deal with. These could include organizational productivity goals, which aim to maximize publications, research grant dollars, and mentions in popular press. In the long term, peer review aligns these with research excellence, but short-term goals often incentivize publishing too quickly or interpreting results too broadly. The latter can be particularly easy when researchers publish outside their expertise or cannot fully evaluate the breadth of their results' potential impact.

All of the above were on clear display during the rush of COVID-19-related publications. Of course, public health policy needed excellent research done quickly. However, the many retractions at RetractionWatch.com are evidence that scientists were indeed both moving fast and sometimes breaking things (Retraction Watch, 2020). Additionally, as discussed in Section 4.6, the predictive power of mortality modeling was sufficiently limited that interpreting it as *prescriptive* to public health policy was a leap of faith.

Communicating uncertainty is difficult for data journalists and data scientists, but is necessary to keep incentives aligned in the long term. In epidemiological emergencies and similar events, it is also needed to protect the public from harm. We remind the reader of Mosteller's warning that "It is easy to lie with statistics; it is easier to lie without them." Nonetheless, individual and organizational incentives must not override scientists' responsibility to accurately represent results, warts and all.

These examples showed the complexity of balancing teams with different incentives. Multiple teams need an organizational structure that can adjudicate disagreements and ensure someone assumes ultimate responsibility. Finally, team members need coherent ethical views and defined processes that ensure ethics are a factor in decision-making.

Recap of Part III: Challenges in Applying Data Science

Part III has addressed challenges motivated by the Analysis Rubric:

- Chapter 8, Chapter 9, and Chapter 10 addressed the technical issues of gathering good data, developing a model providing the needed insights or conclusions, and sufficiently considering privacy, security, abuse, and resilience.
- Chapter 11, Chapter 12, and Chapter 13 addressed the requirements-focused issues of providing understanding, setting proper objectives, and being appropriately tolerant of failures.
- Chapter 14 addressed a collection of ethical, legal, and societal issues.

Notably, all of this part's chapters address ethical issues, either implicitly or explicitly. For example, data collection raises questions on proper bounds for personal data gathering and retention; setting objectives raises issues of fairness or manipulation; and the difficulty of providing understanding raises issues of integrity. Chapter 14's explicit ethics discussion focused on the meta-topic of how to have the right organizational incentives and structures to best achieve ethical principles.

We hope our list of challenges motivated many difficult questions and illustrated that their answers are nuanced. Here are some examples:

- How do we balance data's enormous value with the risks from its collection and storage?
- What are the limits to data-driven models?
- How can we avoid applying data-driven models in ill-suited domains where they are likely to yield poor answers and be counterproductive?
- Can we meet data science's increasing dependability (privacy, security, abuse-resistance, and resilience) needs as we address ever more important problems?
- How can we educate data scientists, prospective data science users, and the public to exercise care with data science's powerful, but risky, capabilities?
- For every data science application, what objectives achieve our primary goals (educational, health, economic, entertainment, etc.) while minimizing risks (polarization, dissemination of falsehoods, or unfairness)?

- Does a government using big data and clever optimization yield a better society, or does it enable ever more creative strategies to sustain and enrich itself? How can we minimize the latter's chances?
- Will data science lead to a beneficial growth in wealth or will it lead to excessive wealth concentration?

We could write pages of additional questions. In fact, we plan to have them on the book's website, DataScienceInContext.com. We hope we have catalyzed our readers to ask more, given the challenges and ambiguities of data science.

Let us end similarly to how we started, noting our primary goals of providing a broad and coherent survey of the field and motivating a consideration of the needed balance of the opportunities and challenges of data science. We also hope our framework is useful for readers who wish to delve deeper.

Part IV

Addressing Concerns

Data science has been successfully applied in many applications, and it will be applied to many more. New techniques, greater computational power, and creativity will combine to make currently impossible and impractical applications feasible. Individuals and institutions dependent on data science for their success are likely to become even more so. Growth indications such as new products, attendance at research conferences, and job opportunities all confirm the opportunity.

However, there are very significant societal concerns about some of its impacts, which arise in part from Part III's challenges. While these concerns were minimal a few decades ago, when data science usage was in its infancy, they have grown substantially in recent years. This could be due to increased public awareness of data science applications, their use in more important domains, perceived or actual harms, the availability of larger and more complex datasets (in both the private and public sector), or expectations of increased future risks. Data science's societal issues are now at the top of mind in many business, economic, political, and ethical circles.

Chapter 15 summarizes these concerns. Later chapters then make recommendations in areas relating to:

- Education and intelligent discourse (Chapter 16)
- Regulation (Chapter 17)
- Research and development (Chapter 18)
- Quality and ethical governance (Chapter 19)

Our recommendations are pragmatic so as to avoid unintended, negative consequences. However, we humbly admit we are not politicians, political scientists, lawyers, or seers, and acknowledge our recommendations may be narrower than some might prefer. They are also our own views and not that of any institutions with which we are affiliated.

Chapter 15

Societal Concerns

There are several reasons why the stakes for data science and its related information technology have grown:

- Usage communities have become very large and, in many cases, global. Users both contribute data and are positively or negatively impacted by its use. Even individuals who are not users of systems may be indirectly affected due to societal impacts.
- Data science and its applications affect nearly every facet of our lives in increasingly serious ways. They have progressed from recommending cat videos to recommending news that drives voters' decisions; from translating language as a curiosity to translations affecting vast populations; from personalizing advertising to personalizing medicine; and many more.
- Changes arising from data science are often disruptive, advantaging some and disadvantaging others. Also, harm may occur because data science can provide powerful benefits to individuals or institutions, which in aggregate lead to problematic societal impacts.
- Data science is not always applied well. Sometimes, this is due to a lack of care in its application, but other times it is being applied in unanticipated, unwanted, and perhaps illegal ways. There are problems from plain thievery, nation-state goals of influence or spying, or bad actors intent on creating mayhem. The potential for financial gain or other power attracts very well-funded manipulators, including individuals, companies, political parties, and nation states.
- People aren't well informed about the conclusions data science presents to them or how they were derived.
- Many societies are increasingly sensitive to issues of fairness and expect data science applications to contribute to solutions, not to only maintain the status quo. This is even more challenging because there may not be broad agreement as to what the goals should be.

This chapter's goal is to summarize these concerns, informed not only by what we in the field read and hear but also by Part III's challenges. For example, we regularly hear about societal concerns over the influence of very large, data-science-oriented companies – concerns that arise in part from both the economic benefits of scale and the complexity of solving hard problems. We also understand societal concerns over social network-induced divisiveness, which arise in part from challenges in setting competing objectives and in controlling abuse.

15.1 Enumerating the Concerns

Table 15.1 summarizes the issues, with the following prose explaining its rows in greater detail.

Table 15.1 *Societal concerns and relevant major technical challenges**.

Societal concerns		
General	Specific	Most relevant challenges from Part III
Economic and fairness impacts on people and institutions	Institutional scale and competitive playing field	ELSI/societal optimization and differentiated gain, ELSI/legal
	Differentiated individual benefit: income and employment	ELSI/societal/individual gain on merit, objectives/concerns to the individual, impact on being human
	Broader questions of fairness	Objectives/fairness, models, toleration of failures
Personal implications to data	Confidentiality of information	Dependability/privacy, dependability/security, toleration of failures
	Individual concerns of manipulation	Objectives/concerns to the individual/manipulation, dependability/privacy, models
	Data deluge, concerns regarding mis- or imbalanced information	Understandability/deserving trust, objectives, toleration of failures
Institutional and societal operation and governance	Divisiveness/freedom of expression	Objectives, ELSI/legal, toleration of failures
	National governance and sovereignty	ELSI/legal, dependability/security
	Other security risks	Dependability/security, ELSI/legal
Environment	Power consumption	Models
Trust	Quality/trustworthiness of data science applications	All

* This table shows six categories of societal concerns about data science. The degree of data science's impact varies greatly. The second column adds a little more specificity to the concerns. The third column lists *some* of Part III's challenges which contribute to the concern; the data ELSI/ethics thread underlies all of them.

The first group, labeled *Economic and fairness impacts on people and institutions*, addresses the balance of rewards and harms that accrue from the application of data science:

- *Institutional scale and competitive playing field.* Both the virtuous cycle phenomenon and economies of scale may encourage market concentration and advantage large institutions. Additionally, the hyper-optimization that data science facilitates may benefit firms that can win on quantifiable metrics. These are often the firms large enough to amass both the necessary data and economies of scale to be effective. This topic is motivated not just by antitrust discussions, but also from multiple sections of Chapter 14 on legal, societal, and ethical challenges.
- *Differentiated individual benefit: income and employment.* Optimizations and automation made possible by data science may change the nature and availability of jobs and provide economic leverage to individuals who can effectively employ it. As automation reduces opportunities in some sectors and increases them in others, it may also result in more job churn and associated economic instability.

  A major concern is whether education and retraining can happen fast enough to "smooth the hump," allowing affected individuals to move to new jobs in growth areas. In the fullness of time, there are concerns about the aggregate impact of automation on unemployment, though more automation may benefit many societies given the decline in working age populations, the growth of elderly needing care, and the likely increase in aggregate productivity. Most generally, there are concerns that data science may contribute to inequality and economic security issues for some individuals or groups, as discussed in Section 14.2.2.
- *Broader questions of fairness.* Many societies' increased focus on fairness has caused increased scrutiny on whether data science's benefits and harms are balanced across different subgroups. Given the breadth of exceedingly important applications data science now powers, data scientists must focus on this issue, as highlighted in the challenges of Section 12.3 on fairness objectives and Chapter 9 on technical approaches to models.

The second group, labeled *Personal implications to data*, addresses concerns individuals may have with increasing use of their data:

- *Confidentiality of information.* Individuals are concerned that captured and recorded information is often lost or otherwise divulged to others. Whether due to confusing or flawed privacy policies or implementations, or due to security break-ins, individuals are concerned about the release of geographical, financial, medical, and other data. The challenges of loss of confidentiality were addressed in Chapter 10's privacy and security sections.

- *Individual concerns of manipulation.* Individuals are concerned about economic, location, health, interpersonal, and other sensitive data being used in possibly manipulative ways against their long-term interest. These concerns are related to the challenges relating to personalization and manipulation of Section 12.4 and, of course, privacy in Section 10.1.
- *Data deluge, concerns regarding mis- or imbalanced information.* The proliferation of data paradoxically may make finding underlying truths harder. A general lack of understanding of data, causality, and potential errors may be leading to less understanding. Many are also concerned about the proliferation of fake news and echo chamber effects. Related challenges arose from Section 11.4 on deserving trust and Chapter 12 on setting objectives.

The third group, *Institutional and societal operation and governance*, addresses concerns that data science may impede the operation and governance of societies:

- *Divisiveness/freedom of expression.* Despite the importance of freedom of expression and its legal protection in some countries, many are concerned about the potential divisive and destabilizing effects of algorithmic approaches to information dissemination. These include over-amplification of certain points of view, suppression of others, and promotion of outright falsehoods.
  Data science can inadvertently facilitate bad actors who use scams or misinformation to harm society. It may also be used to promote good; but what some think of as good, others may consider to be manipulative or even tyrannical. These issues were discussed in Chapter 12 relating to the challenges in setting objectives and Section 14.1 on legal challenges.
- *National governance and sovereignty.* Technology itself operates without regard to national borders, so nation states have concerns regarding their ability to establish norms, rules, and protections for their own territories. Specific concerns relate to protection and mandates for storage and cross-border flows of personal data, rules on promulgation and presentation of information, regulation of commerce including political advertising, and taxation.
  While not an entirely new problem, data science's growth has made it more prevalent and significant. It has grown as technology and data science have become central to everyday life. Discussions of related challenges were presented in Section 10.2 on security (a source of many international risks) and Section 14.1 on legal issues.
- *Other security risks.* Data science provides new attack vectors against important societal systems, such as leveraging vulnerabilities triggered by data manipulation. Attacks could affect healthcare, transportation networks, utilities, financial systems, and more. As in the previous concern, the discussions of related challenges were covered in Section 10.2 and Section 14.1 on security and legal issues, respectively.

The fourth, labeled *Environment*, addresses the concern that the *power consumption* of data science applications may contribute to climate change, as mentioned in Section 9.3. It is beyond our scope to attempt to balance the energy ledger resulting from the benefits and harms of substituting online shopping, virtual meetings, e-books, etc., against physical goods and travel. But there is no doubt that they (in particular, certain types of computationally intensive machine learning) consume significant power and are hence an increasing concern.

The last and very broad category is *Trust*. With so many now dependent on data science's proper application, people cannot help but be concerned by widely differing viewpoints on some applications' value and on well-publicized problems or failures. The latter occur for many reasons, but they include insufficient care in specification and engineering, difficulty in balancing commercial and ethical objectives, and even the lack of clarity of governing laws. Many may have decreased trust because they do not understand the complex landscapes that data science powers.

15.2 Perspective Behind our Recommendations

A blunt approach to addressing data science concerns would be to try to slow or stop its adoption. As previously mentioned, some might take comfort in a more leisurely pace of advances. However, dampening innovation will not happen. If anything, the pace will more likely accelerate. Some reasons follow:

- Data science and its technological underpinnings now provide too many present and near-term benefits to reverse course. There continue to be high hopes and even demands for the future.
- Countries and regions are aggressively competing with each other to "win" data science competitive races so they gain economic, geopolitical, and military advantages. As in all races, speed is of the essence. For example, China is proceeding at full speed towards its goal of being the global leader in artificial intelligence by 2030 (Robles, 2018). Many other countries, the US included, have taken notice and are increasing their data science efforts.[20]
- This competition among nations cannot be controlled, and treaties to suppress science and technology rarely work. Even rules fostering nuclear non-proliferation have barely hung on, despite nuclear warfare's overwhelmingly worse risk profile and the much greater ease of detecting cheating.

Co-author Alfred attended the February 2020 Ditchley Conference on Technology, Society, and the State. This was a meeting of an international group of government

[20] In mid-2022, the US Congress authorized an 80% increase in the National Science Foundation's five-year science and technology spending.

and military officials, academics, technologists, and business and labor leaders concerned with the broad impacts of technology, particularly data science (Brill, 2020). Even among that diverse group, there was no support for going backward or slowing innovation, despite amorphous concerns that technology may just be moving too fast (Brand, 2000) or concrete ones of changing employment opportunities. Instead, there was general agreement that technology and data science need to progress rapidly, but with the proviso that we must make progress on government and other societal structures to address problems that will inevitably be created.

Our recommendations are thus guided by the twin needs to retain a creative environment that supports the vast investments in time, capital, and human creativity to increase data science's benefits, while simultaneously reducing its risks. In the following chapters, we discuss what we can do to sufficiently educate ourselves. This includes crafting rational policies, norms, and regulatory regimes as well as establishing enlightened agendas for research and engineering. Importantly, it emphasizes including quality and ethics in all we do. Our recommendations represent what we believe is reasonable today, though circumstances may change over time and be different in different regions.

Chapter 16

Education and Intelligent Discourse

Your authors, who have substantial background as academicians, unsurprisingly believe in the importance of education and rigor in the definition and use of vocabulary. More education helps individuals by enhancing their ability to understand data and data science's growing impact, and to both contribute to and benefit from the field. A more knowledgeable public and a clear vocabulary for discourse would permit better communication and debate.

16.1 More Data Science in the Curriculum

The prevalence of data science and the diversity of its impacts, from personal/social life to school/work life to politics/international relations, argue for increased educational focus on data science at all levels. A National Academies 2018 study strongly makes this case, and, while focused primarily on undergraduate education, it also argued for increasing focus in K-12 (National Academies of Sciences, Engineering, and Medicine, 2018).

Recommendation 1 Broaden Educational Opportunities in Data Science

16.1.1 Primary and Secondary Education

To educate all members of the public about data science, the topic must be covered in primary and secondary schools. We recognize the problems with fitting new material into an already constrained curriculum and suggest two approaches.

First, many data science topics can and should be taught alongside the sciences and social sciences for mutual benefit. We call this teaching DS+X (data science in conjunction with other fields, X), a modest expansion of CS+X, a term that co-author Alfred has used to express the importance of fusing computer science with almost every other discipline (Spector, 2004). For example, we might teach simple statistical techniques in physics laboratories, demonstrate the power of visualization in history or social studies classes, and provide programming tools to allow hands-on data manipulation of datasets relevant to a specific curriculum. In very early grades, we could expose students to data – collecting it, doing simple analysis, and even raising ethical questions about its use. The integration of data science topics with traditional subject matter would improve education in both.

Second, we also think that many students should take a specific, rigorous data science class, which should replace calculus (despite its pre-eminence as one of the most beautiful modeling tools) or possibly some other parts of the high-school mathematics curriculum. While we have resisted giving this advice for years, there is clearly enough accessible, yet intellectually deep, material for a course. Furthermore, data-science- and technology-related material is likely to be much more useful than calculus for most. Of course, many students who continue to higher-level study in many disciplines, including data science, will still need to learn calculus. Steven Levitt makes many of these arguments in his podcast, *America's Math Curriculum Doesn't Add Up* (Levitt, 2021).

In high school, a specific data science course would likely be grounded in computing and statistics. If not a requirement for college tracked students, such a course should at least be widely available.

We believe the growing awareness of data science's ubiquity will motivate many to consider this proposal strongly. However, we also recognize the many challenges of changing school curricula:

- Responsibilities for establishing new curricula are decentralized.
- Curriculum mandates change slowly.
- Curricula must be in accord with college admissions expectations.
- Courses must prepare students for first-year-level college courses.
- Where data science needs more computing equipment, it must be provided.

There is also a need for teachers well trained in data science. We note that well-engineered data science and technology platforms might be able to augment teachers and help achieve broad and cost-effective education.

It is beyond our scope to specify the precise topics to teach, but we suggest consideration be given to the definition of data science from Part I, some of the more important application areas in Part II, and the more important challenges in Part III, in particular the need for understanding explained in Chapter 11 (see Table 16.1).

16.1.2 Post-Secondary Education

Higher education must also broadly educate all its students in data science. Curriculum differences across institutions will certainly be typical, given goals (e.g., an engineering versus a liberal arts focus). While difficult to implement,

Table 16.1 *Suggested general education topics for data science**.

Area	Explanation
Mathematical and statistical skills	Explanation of the notion of models. Ability to analyze data and perform the necessary mathematics. Probability and statistical knowledge. Correlation and causality. Introduction to optimization
Algorithms, abstractions, and programming	Understanding algorithms, computational abstractions, and simple programming based on application to data-science-related issues
Examples of data science applications	Knowledge of data science's challenges, uses, and potential in a variety of domains. Examples would be used in the above rows
Critical reading and analysis	Critical reading and analysis of important contemporary data science applications to show both the exposition of truth and the promulgation of falsehood. Use of historical and contemporary examples should be a significant part of the curriculum
Humanist, societal, and ethical challenges of data science	Understanding the implications of data science and technology's growth on economic, political, and social systems, as well as everyday life, and teaching an ethical lens

* The first three rows build off of co-author Jeannette's "Computational Thinking" viewpoint (Wing, 2006), extended with a more specific focus on data science. The fourth and fifth rows relate, respectively, to critical reading of case studies, and to humanist, societal, and ethical issues.

colleges will need to have courses accessible to students with varying K-12 levels of student preparation and attainment.

Higher education also has a critical role in training true experts in data science and fields where it plays a significant role. In the former category, there may be many different courses and tracks of study due to the field's breadth with differing focus on engineering and computer science, statistics or mathematical optimization, application areas, or policy-related topics. Some students may end up seeking advanced degrees in data science, but many are likely to become well versed in data science but receive degrees in related fields.

As with technology, the union of data science and other disciplines often produces a sweet spot for great amounts of innovation. To provide the needed interdisciplinary background, many disciplines must offer appropriate courses, perhaps using cross-departmental teachers. In some cases, the courses may vary primarily in their use of examples from different application areas (e.g., biology versus economics).

There are different models for achieving this interdisciplinary approach, as shown by these examples:

- Berkeley's wide collection of "connector courses" from data science to other disciplines (Adhikari et al., 2021).
- Columbia's jointly designed and jointly taught "collaboratory" courses (Zaugg et al., 2021).
- MIT's Common Ground classes, which are specially designed to integrate computing and data science concepts with various disciplines (MIT Schwarzman College of Computing, 2021).

We acknowledge there are many more such approaches and classes than we can list here.

In some cases, data science and computing have become so linked with another discipline that a new field of study has arisen. Medical informatics and computational biology are early examples, respectively dating from the 1970s and 2000s. MIT's much more recent undergraduate major, "Computer Science, Economics, and Data Science," is another emerging example.

The breadth of these topics will necessarily engage faculty in the humanities and social sciences. Data science is a new opportunity for technologists and humanists to co-design courses and ensure students understand they must consider societal consequences.

At the same time, data science and technology add greater importance to the humanities and social sciences. It seems counterintuitive, but data science's great changes add to the importance of studying deep aspects of humanity and society. Humanists and social scientists are even more critical to our future.

Finally, we emphasize the importance of teaching data science's societal and ethical considerations in order to remind students of the field's power, the importance of quality work, and the value, yet complexity, of setting ethical objectives. The introduction of these topics will aid students, and hence society at large, in promoting data science for true benefit.

16.2 Improve Education by Using More Data Science and Technology

We feel that hands-on, immersive instruction makes data science education more effective, helps maintain students' interest, reduces drop-out rates, and possibly provides teachers with increased leverage that helps a limited number of professionals teach more students. Much more can be done to broadly infuse technology into education, but data science has a particular advantage due to the availability of hands-on technology.

Recommendation 2 Use Data Science and Technology in Teaching Data Science

There are excellent programming tools ranging from Scratch for beginners to Python programming environments for older students, and finally to custom tools, such as the R language. There are magnificent visualization libraries, all manners of simulation environments, and platforms tailored to particular application domains. Because students are continually interacting with a computer, to express themselves (or, more formally, code), to experiment, and to validate their work, online tools innately provide immersive education and adapt to different learning rates and styles.

In addition to immersive education's direct benefits, data science and technology may help to reduce high education costs, which reduce access to education. This efficiency-focused motivation coupled with COVID-19's acceleration of technology adoption should prod educational institutions to find ways to utilize technology and data science to make their core educational missions more efficient and effective. While not a new idea (Won, n.d.) and certainly complex for many reasons (which become clear when applying the Analysis Rubric), we speculate there should be ways to use student background and real-time attainment to provide personalized education in accordance with students' learning styles. Such adaptive approaches could help retain student interest and help them to more rapidly achieve their educational goals.

16.3 Vocabulary/Definitions

We suspect that many readers have had many informal discussions on privacy, fairness, fake news, and other related topics. We also suspect many of these discussions were unsatisfying. We hypothesize a major reason is that participants do not have clear terminology for expressing themselves on the topics. In fact, we have wrestled with this problem while writing this book.

Even if parties agree on some points, issues aren't clearly decomposed into subtopics that can be analyzed. For example, when someone says, "I'm concerned over privacy," the topic is often so amorphous that a discussion must wait until specific concerns are stated and labeled. Narrower topics are easier to define, and they admit to clearer, perhaps even mathematical, analyses.

Recommendation 3 Promote Clear Vocabulary

The field should establish and use a clear vocabulary for discussing topics of critical concern. It's beyond this book's scope to specify *all* the needed terms, but this section provides examples of terms where discourse would benefit from precise terminology with defined meanings.

Data science's lack of sufficient agreed-upon terminology is unsurprising due to the field's explosive growth. It takes time to decompose a field into the right subfields and to create the right ontologies, particularly given data science's wide breadth. It also takes time to promulgate and popularize the vocabulary. This effort needs to be a coalition of academic, government, and business experts, and regrettably done without the efforts of Samuel Johnson or Daniel Webster (see Table 16.2).

Table 16.2 *Examples of terms and categories of terms needing clarification**.

	Example terminology
Privacy	Many are concerned about privacy, but the term has so many potential meanings, even some formalized (e.g., differential privacy) that discussions are often at cross-purposes. Clarity would benefit by having terms or modifiers that specify whether we are referring to data's collection, storage, confidentiality, usage for self, or usage for others, as in Section 10.1, and perhaps other meanings
Fairness	There are many fairness measurements based on the specific application and desired outcomes. Thus, individuals discussing whether an application is fair or not need to know the specific fairness criteria being used. Perhaps "fairness" could often have a modifier, such as "with respect to" a specific scale
Trust	This term comes up frequently, but it has so many connotations (reliability, privacy, etc.) that discussions involving it are often amorphous
	Example categories of terminology
Statistical	Statistics' long history has resulted in it having a broad and clear vocabulary. However, its terms are insufficiently understood or commonly used outside the field. Few know even the most basic terms, such as standard deviation, variance, mean, correlation, etc. Knowledge and usage of these terms by data scientists and the public would increase the understanding of results and reduce misinformation
Risk	We need terminology and metrics to define the impact of failures (outright system failures, less well-understood resilience risks, security attacks, etc.) so we can have crisper discussions of risk/reward ratios
Uncertainty characterization	Simple, understandable terminology to express degrees of certainty or skepticism about results might help the public better understand how certain a scientist or journalist is about a data science result. For example, the Intergovernmental Panel on Climate Change (IPCC) has created clear terminology to characterize the confidence in their predictions (Mastrandrea et al., 2010). Even simple color coding would be beneficial

* These lists provide examples of a few terms and categories of terms where we need clarification and precise definition to facilitate discourse and analysis.

We close this section by quoting Aristophanes: “By words, the mind is winged” (Aristophanes, 414 BC). William Chomsky, father of well-known linguist Noam Chomsky, said, “we think in words, by means of words” (Wise, 2011). With the right words, we could have much greater understanding, far better debate with less noise, and more rapid progress.

Chapter 17
Regulation

Given data science's wide use, the broad acceptance of its potential, and international competition for rapid invention and deployment, we have argued that coarse regulation to prevent data science progress is highly unlikely. We have also noted that any regulation is complicated by many factors, including the Internet's cross-border aspects and that existing legal frameworks were not written with data science in mind.

On the other hand, as societies and their processes become more complex, there is much precedent for highly specific regulation mechanisms. Some are legally mandated, some are established by voluntary trade groups, others arise due to business rationales (e.g., to minimize insurance costs), and some just become de facto societal norms. We focus on just a few topics and refer the reader to a vast and growing literature on regulation coming from public policy, economic, technology, and legal perspectives.

17.1 Regulation: De Jure

This section includes recommendations for de jure, or legally mandated, regulation.

Recommendations 4 and 5 address new regulations that might be made to data science applications. Recommendation 6 addresses issues with current laws and regulations that could make it difficult to deploy some data science applications. Recommendation 7 addresses the impacts of data science and technology on the scale of enterprises.

Recommendation 4 Regulate Uses, Not Technology

How well technology works in a particular application varies greatly. This means regulatory approaches must focus on a situation's specifics. Below, we present examples showing that regulatory regimes must attend to situational details.

For example, facial recognition's varying accuracy in different populations has been clearly and publicly stated, even though work is underway to rectify its shortcomings. This means if it is used to screen for crime, some people may be unfairly subjected to more false positives than others. In some applications, facial recognition may reduce our feelings of privacy and freedom, open us up to snooping by criminals, or allow increased extra-judicial government monitoring of populations.

However, there are also many applications where facial recognition is useful and uncontroversial. For example, unlocking cell phones or helping us search our photo collections for friends or loved ones are innocuous.

As another example, fears of warfare driven by machine learning make some suggest a blanket prohibition on using data science for autonomous military targeting. There are use cases where it would be unethical, destabilizing, or just militarily dubious to deploy autonomous weaponry. But it is hard to make a clear definition of "autonomous operation." The autocannon made its first appearance in 1903, and there are certainly use cases where data science and autonomous control would fulfill military objectives with less damage to human life and property than conventional systems. Moreover, prohibiting military technology requires major powers to agree, which has proven very challenging even with chemical weapons that all claim to abhor.

Closer to home, we have discussed using data science in parole/incarceration decisions and the complexity of setting, implementing, and meeting objectives relating to fairness, societal safety, and even efficiency. One could ban its use in these settings, but perhaps it would be best to subject systems to very specific regulatory standards, taking into account the ethical issues we discussed in Section 6.6 and Chapter 7. This definitely requires robust checks and balances, great care in deployment, and ultimately great and open debate. Whether any existing technologies meet the necessary requirements is an important topic with views on both sides (Miller, 2018; O'Neil, 2016).

The same type of argument also applies to self-driving vehicles. There is a great opportunity to save lives, reduce transportation delays, increase highway utilization, and more. However, getting standards and regulations exactly right will be very challenging. While the underlying technology has elements usable in other domains (e.g., computer vision or route optimization), regulatory approaches have traditionally been **sectoral**. This means that they are specific to a particular, typically, economic sector and regulated with that sector in mind. Regulation would thus be applied to cars as means of transportation, rather than to their specific data science advances.

Nowhere is this need for specificity clearer than with respect to privacy. Blanket prohibitions could be legislated on the collection, storage, and use of private data.

However, few actions could hamstring future data science applications more than certain types of bans. There are just too many potentially valuable use cases that could be proscribed.

For example, large-scale genetic data has great potential to detect, prevent, and treat disease. Clearly, this type of information requires high privacy standards, and the topic is very complex. Even opt-in promulgation of one's own genetic code will divulge information about blood relatives. But blanket restrictions would be counterproductive.

Beyond sectoral approaches, we understand that there may also be substantive differentiation by particular technology application within a sector. However, many aspects of contemporary society are this way. For example, technology and data science can look to the financial industry, which regularly adds new rules to address new technologies' potential harms (e.g., data-driven, high-speed trading) without prohibiting them. Despite their complexity, these regulatory frameworks are generally accepted as useful.

Recommendation 5 Regulate Clear, Not Potential, Problems[21]

The obvious risk of regulation is that complexity will become so great as to be stultifying. Also, some who suggest regulatory regimes may do so with the conscious or unconscious motivation to help *their* organization at a competitor's expense. We thus suggest that problems should be *clear* and *broadly agreed upon* before we attempt regulation.

Another risk is over-anticipating problems that are not yet significant or clear. However, we should quickly address certain problems, because they may become ingrained and very expensive to remediate. The clearest examples arise outside data science; e.g., toxic waste sites, where the solution is far more expensive than the cost of having had sound waste disposal standards.

We must remember that, however well intentioned, early regulation may significantly suppress innovation at its most vulnerable stage. It may establish overly broad regulatory solutions for amorphous problems that ultimately never occur. Regulations also have many unintended and unexpected side effects. For example, regulations frequently make corporate operations more expensive. As discussed above, this favors larger incumbents at the expense of new and creative market entrants, reducing competition. Finally, once created, regulatory regimes tend not to be revoked but to grow. Thus, it is better, if at all possible, to wait until needed regulatory requirements become clear and then react with precision.

[21] This derives from Eric Schmidt's presentation to the Columbia Data Science Initiative on September 14, 2020 (Schmidt, 2020).

Our next recommendation is based on the likelihood that data science will increasingly lead to machines performing activities or making decisions now done by humans. However, the laws and regulations for those activities were written with humans in mind.

Recommendation 6 Update Laws with Data Science and Technology in Mind

Legal scholars recognize that defining laws requires a mixture of approaches (Solum, 2009). Some laws or judicial precedents are highly specific and directive to law enforcement and the judicial system. Others allow some degree of prosecutorial or judicial interpretation. There are also established general principles that judges take into account. Laws often establish regulators and grant them the authority to create detailed binding rules. This complexity makes it difficult for data-science-based applications to not run afoul of the law.

Consider these examples:

- While traffic laws reference "safety" as a principle that overrides speed limits, clarification is needed given the still abundant focus on speed limits. Should self-driving cars break speed limits or risk driving too slowly relative to other vehicles?
- In the insurance realm, some US regions ban the use of certain types of data (e.g., zip codes or credit scores) in insurance pricing decisions. What is the legality of machine learning algorithms that do *not* use such data but behave in some ways as if they did?
- Liability laws must also be written to account for the increasing operation of autonomous and semi-autonomous agents. Will the current system make it too easy to deploy negligent technologies or practically impossible to deploy good ones because everything has some risk?

A different type of problem arises if laws are written so that their mechanistic enforcement becomes mis- or over-enforcement. As example, applying increased sensing and data science together could result in over-enforcement of noise limits, jaywalking, parking violations, minor zoning violations, violations of terms of service, etc. This could be particularly problematic if enforcement tended to single out particular groups.

In particular, excess enforcement could result in those least able to navigate or afford the legal system having to deal with an endless number of minor infractions. Thus, laws may need to be revised to take into account they may be enforced literally, rather than just serving as deterrents or assuming that law enforcement officers will be sensitive as to their application.

As so many of this book's topics, the relationship of data science (and technology) and the law is the subject of intense focus in academic circles, as evidenced by many new university research centers around the world.

Recommendation 7 Consider the Impact of Economies of Scale and the Virtuous Cycle

As we argued in Section 14.2.1, some firms built on data science benefit from both technology's economies of scale and the virtuous cycle phenomena. Some firms, particularly ones with social network or communication components, are further advantaged by Metcalfe's Law. Finally, since regulatory scrutiny adds to the complexity of creating a new business, regulation may tend to "favor the incumbents," some of whom may be large.

Scale has its pros and cons, which we do our best to show. The ambiguity is why our Recommendation 7 is more along the lines of suggesting thoughtful focus than proposing a simple answer.

17.1.1 Pros to Scale

Many large companies based on data science provide innovative and often free services to consumers worldwide. By many measures, they have benefited the broader economy by eliminating market rigidities, increasing consumer choice, and creating competitive marketplaces for new products. Data science and technology have also enabled increased global trade, which most economists believe has benefited many by allowing each economy to do what it does best.

Large companies' scale has enabled them to do the sophisticated engineering to build mature and scalable applications. Windows 10 reportedly had at least 50 million lines of code. A crude analysis of Google engineering employment data would indicate that Google has devoted upwards of 100,000 engineer years to bring web search to its current state. Some data science applications require a scale similar to well-known efforts like landing a human on the Moon or engineering a new commercial jet. In some instances, the business models enabled by data science also necessitated the scale-out of traditional operations such as warehousing and logistics.

The long-term investment needed to achieve certain advances also benefits from scale. Co-author Alfred helped create the first large-scale file sharing systems (like Google Drive, or Microsoft OneDrive) that would scale around the world. The team's basic work was done in the 1980s, but the technology only came to broad realization about 30 years later through vast amounts of engineering work. Even smaller firms, such as Box and Dropbox, have deployed hundreds of engineers on their systems. Yet these file systems are but one small contribution to data science's growth.

Sometimes, scale is needed to enter and disrupt existing markets. Amazon challenged Google and Facebook and became the third largest online advertiser, and Google is challenging US cloud leaders Amazon and Microsoft in their space (*The Economist*, 2022a).

Furthermore, large technology companies have contributed to many scientific and engineering advances. While credit for the advances that make this book topical goes to both academia[22] and industry (with a multitude of philanthropic, government, and industrial funding sources), the technology sector made very strong contributions.

Economic measures show the research and development impact of the big technology companies. According to Wikipedia, as of 2018, seven of the top 10 companies in R&D spending were technology companies: Amazon, Samsung, Alphabet, Microsoft, Huawei, Intel, and Apple.

While by no means an apples-to-apples comparison, those firms' R&D budgets are 100 times larger than the circa 2020 US National Science Foundation's budget for computer science and electrical engineering. Even if development (not research) expenses were subtracted, the corporate research budgets are still considerably larger in aggregate. Finally, most of these companies contribute broadly to the general technology ecosystem through open-source software, university funding, etc.

As a result of these benefits, US policy views have been somewhat unclear. While there is concern about corporate size, there is pressure to not distribute profits, but instead invest them to produce more economic activity, more jobs, and, yes, further growth (Schumer & Sanders, 2019).

17.1.2 Cons to Scale

From a company's perspective, increasing scale is a two-edged sword. Balancing the previous section's benefits, scale may also lead to more regulatory scrutiny (e.g., concern over control of highly used information channels) or reduced freedom of action (e.g., greater restrictions on acquisitions).

Scale may also challenge a company's ability to maintain its strategic focus and workforce commitment. Employees of larger firms often grumble about the bureaucracy keeping them from getting things done, taking risks, and being innovative. When he was CEO of IBM, Lou Gerstner said, "Every little company wants to be big, and every big company wants to be little."[23]

From society's perspective, scale has many potential problems, in particular, if scale leads to market concentration. Companies with reduced competition may

[22] The 2009 Computing Research that Changed the World symposium highlighted many critical research advances from academe that contributed to the success of the technology industry (Lazowska, 2009).

[23] Gerstner made this statement to a group of his top executives in the late 1990s, responding to criticism that the company wasn't moving fast enough.

have increased pricing power and a lessened pressure to innovate.[24] Fewer firms also means fewer consumer choices.

In related realms of societal governance, large companies may have increased power due to their large value, workforce size, and economic importance. Many are concerned with that power; for example, this has triggered debates about social network recommendation policies. There may be even increased societal risk or inconvenience if a large company's essential services fail. Many large cloud vendors and consumer-facing sites have had outages, which, while rare, affect many all at once.

Some argue that even if today's negative consequences are minimal, we need to consider regulatory regimes to mitigate data science's scale-oriented downsides – if only to be prepared for the worst.

17.1.3 Perspective

While many of the previous points argue that scale may give too much advantage to firms, there are certainly counterexamples. Historically, the tech sector has many examples of small companies defeating mighty incumbents. Netflix completely displaced Blockbuster. Microsoft overcame IBM in operating systems. Small companies Zoom and TikTok rapidly gained share in video conferencing and video distribution due to innovative services and user experiences. Over the longer term, all the initial US computer manufacturers now have greatly diminished, if any, remaining market presence.

Galbraith in his 1967 book, *The New Industrial State*, wrote about a diversity of forces that moderate harmful impacts of large firms (Galbraith, 1967). However, Galbraith, who died in 2006, could not know about data science's virtuous cycle. Nor that, in mid-2021, the top five US firms by market capitalization would be built on data science and related technologies.

Without question, it will take a multidisciplinary team of economists, policy experts, business experts, and technologists to fully understand the scale-related effects that data science has unleashed.

17.2 Other Guiding Forces

While traditional forms of governmental regulation are effective in many domains, there are some where it is challenged:

- As observed in Section 14.1.1, regulating a data science application in one jurisdiction might just result in it being hosted elsewhere. Consequently, if

[24] Nobel Laureate Sir John Hicks commented, "the best of all monopoly profits is a quiet life" (Hicks, 1935).

a political entity truly wants to ban certain applications, it may need to make their use illegal and/or be willing to block internet traffic to where they are hosted. Relatedly, we note the European Union's Court of Justice ruled that the EU cannot require other countries to enforce its Right to be Forgotten law. Under it, individuals have the right to have certain personal results removed from web search. Thus, European nationals could circumvent it by connecting to search engines through unaffected areas. International regulation or treaty might seem an answer to some above-country issues, but it would be very difficult to reach wide agreement on forums for discussion, objectives, or approaches to enforcement.
- Political institutions may have neither the trust to regulate certain activities (e.g., due to the potential for abuse of power, political vicissitudes, and insufficient technical expertise) nor the legal authority (perhaps due to constitutional restrictions such as the US First Amendment). These concerns particularly center on issues such as control of content; regulating search results, fake news, hate speech, or distribution of material on social networks.

An obvious alternative is self-regulation by firms, which can have many positive benefits for those with proper incentives and operational mechanisms.

- One downside is that companies may also be insufficiently trusted. While their actions may be guided by a long-term, ethical point of view, many may feel their concerns are primarily for managers, employees, and shareholders. Furthermore, some are also concerned on how companies might behave if their business performance is challenged.
- Another risk is that self-regulation by some firms may lead others to attempt to capitalize on their forbearance. For example, if some firms moderate content to temper the impact of false information, these very actions could provide an impetus for creating new platforms catering to extreme positions. In the social network realm, this could lead to greater challenges.

Finally, one could imagine a role for existing non-governmental institutions. However, universities, by themselves, cannot solve these types of issues, and other, existing, non-profits with the needed expertise are not really focused on the right missions. Thus, we surmise that new trusted institutions may be needed.

Recommendation 8 Create Independent, Consensus-Building Institutions for Difficult Problems

There are many consensus-building institutions throughout the world; Wikipedia lists about 100 standards organizations, some of which are about 150 years old. For example, Underwriters Laboratories sets safety standards and then tests products to certify they meet those standards. It is in the mutual interest of consumers to have safe products, manufacturers to have consumers know their products meet safety standards, and insurance companies to minimize payout risk. While it might seem these groups might have difficulty reaching agreements, there is a sweet spot of commonality motivated by safety and economic efficiency.

Many bodies manage to bridge competing interests to create definitive policies and standards in medicine, all forms of engineering, accounting, and other areas. The Internet and World Wide Web would not function without largely volunteer organizations like the IETF and the W3C. While the governance of internet domain names and IP addresses has had a tortuous history, its current organizational structures seem to be working. In data-related realms, as just two of a vast number of examples, the WHO has created the ICD-11 International Classification of Diseases, and Schema.org has created the standard for labeling web page content.

Outside of traditional standards bodies, open-source initiatives have marshaled the talents of many competing organizations to produce valuable consensus bodies of work. Because users trust it as a reliable source of information, Wikipedia has become one of the top 10 most visited sites on the Web. In software, the Linux Foundation convenes and coordinates the work of technology professionals around the world to produce some of the most critical software underlying modern computer systems.

The Partnership in AI was founded in 2016 by seven technology companies, in part to share best practices and to build consensus on ethical principles of AI usage. It has grown to over 100 organizations worldwide.

The financial sector contributes ideas on structure, particularly on partnerships between industry and government. As two examples, FASB (FASB, n.d.) does financial accounting regulation, and FINRA (FINRA, n.d.) is responsible for broker–dealer regulation.

This book hypothesizes that a fairly wide variety of consensus-building institutions could provide a diverse set of standard definitions, policies, and content. They could make products and services more comprehensible and provide transparency that might make them better. They may help create societal expectations and norms that seem lacking today. Here is a partial set of ideas:

- As we argued in Recommendation 3, we believe that certain terminology would benefit from clear and commonly used definitions. This is a natural activity for a consensus-building institution. Perhaps there could also be a small set of clear, well-defined privacy and ownership standards, making it easier for firms to introduce products and for consumers to use them. This is in contrast to the ubiquitous lengthy and rarely read terms-of-use statements, and similar to creative commons licenses. As an example, the notion of "Privacy Seals" was explored and once used to assert that a website abided by privacy standards (Rifon et al., 2005). Perhaps renewed focus could make them a success.

- Recommendation system policy standards could include standard, transparent disclosures on objectives and goals, results dispersion measures, other fairness guarantees, policies relating to fact checking, and more. Consumers might prefer using systems that adhere to recognized standards.
- Data publication norms, for journalists and others who promulgate data, could include tenets to encourage data to be placed into perspective:
  - Labeling on sample sizes and positive-outcome biases.
  - Clear terminology to label association studies.
  - Error bars on data (as in scientific publications).
  - Including denominators representing population size so readers can place specific data in perspective.

  If such norms became widely applied, they would reduce the dangers of mis- and imbalanced information described in Chapter 11. Principles for journalism are by no means a new idea, as evidenced by AP's ethics statement (Associated Press, 2021), but they could be augmented to address data science challenges and more widely promoted.
- Science communication standards should temper research organizations' and scientists' enthusiasm on overly definitive or optimistic results. Also they should use terminology that could be better calibrated by the press and public. These could create a culture of humility in science announcements, helping scientists to be guided by the Belmont Principles.
- There could even be standardized templates that could serve as a basis for organizations to adopt and consider ethical guidelines. (See Section 19.2 for more on this.)

Once started, the list of topics would naturally grow based on the creativity of involved teams and evolving societal needs. Some consensus-building institutions would be international, but some would be tailored to the needs of particular nations and cultures. Some would have a strong technology orientation; others would be more focused on a particular application domain.

Results from these bodies could impact the world in these three ways:

1. They could create societal consensus around reasonable practices.
2. In some circumstances, governments could codify definitions and standards in law.
3. Institutions that adopted these standards could advertise their doing so, gaining reputational, ease-of-use, and other advantages. Institutions that declared their

adoption would need to take it very seriously, as consumer protection rules would legally obligate them.

The third point could be a powerful marketing benefit and might also provide a force for societal agreement. While some institutions may still refuse to be party to new standards, presumably they would have much less acceptance.

In a related thought, consensus-building institutions could develop standardized content in some domains. While not feasible in all areas due to difficulty of attaining unassailable truths (e.g., "arbiter of truth" argument), it is in some. For example, the American Association for the Advancement of Science (AAAS) sponsors https://SciLine.org/ (SciLine, 2017), a site that (among other things) produces scientific, consensus-driven materials for journalists.

In addition to standardization and consensus content organizations, there could be organizations which monitor and grade sites on predefined metrics. They would build on and extend the US NIST mission, which is to advance "measurement science, standards, and technology in ways that enhance economic security and improve our quality of life."

Fact checking is a challenge because of biases that can easily influence the fact checker policies and even which facts are checked. But there are clearly objective measurements that would serve to influence compliance with standards and to temper poor behavior. Proper measurement could be used to provide "official" seals of approval for organizations in compliance with certain standards, thus providing added benefits to the organization and consumer alike. The Poynter Institute, for example, has defined the International Fact-Checking Network code of principles to promote excellence in fact checking, and also provides a verification process for fact checkers (Poynter Institute, n.d.).

Chapter 18
Research and Development

We make two R&D recommendations to address Chapter 15's concerns.

Recommendation 9 Increase Focused and Transdisciplinary Research

During data science's rapid growth period, it has seen enormous progress as a field. Part of this was due to research breakthroughs in many fields. Advances in computer vision, speech recognition, natural language processing, and robotics graduated from the laboratory to become important industries. The research community responded to bias concerns in computer vision systems by developing tools to identify bias and fairness issues, such as IBM's AI Fairness 360 toolkit and Google's What-If Tool. There are countless more examples.

Table 18.1 and Table 18.2 illustrate opportunities in technical and non-technical areas that combine data science with other disciplines. Co-author Jeannette gives

Table 18.1 *Suggested research in core areas*.*

Domain	Suggested research areas
Statistics, operations research, machine learning	Causality, reduced training time, resistance to adversarial attack, explanation, returning distributions, optimization in game theoretic environments, reducing trial-and-error characteristics of machine learning, inferring from noisy or heterogenous data from possibly many sources, experimental replicability, scale issues
Computing	Computer security, reliability, privacy, resilience, data streaming and processing at scale, scalable computer architectures for performance and reduced power consumption, advancing visualization in traditional and virtual reality environments, uncovering fake information, data provenance, quantum and optical computing, probabilistic programming, formal methods in software engineering to ensure quality

* This table lists fertile areas of research at data science's core. We tried to make the topics in this table sufficiently detailed to be meaningful, but this detail makes it hard to also be complete.

Table 18.2 *Select transdisciplinary research areas**.

Domain	Suggested research areas – data science opportunities
Education	Efficient and inclusive education
Science	Astronomy, biology, climate, materials discovery, neuroscience
Humanities	Literature, history, language, archaeology, art
Philosophy, ethics, and law	Considerations of privacy, manipulation, fairness, data ownership, liability, the role of the nation state in a world of global data
Economics and finance	Economic prediction, regulatory issues, mitigating economic inequality, dealing with noisy data
Political science	Prediction, explanation, and analysis of political phenomena, regulation, politics and governance
Journalism	Tools to enable better journalism, better news aggregation
Medicine	Improved application to epidemiology, reduced friction in applications of data science, enhanced diagnosis, phase IV drug monitoring, precision medicine, drug design

* This table lists some fertile areas of research which combine data science and other disciplines. We acknowledge we have listed only a subset of the areas where data science is applicable.

another descriptive formulation of many of these and divides them into 10 categories (Wing, 2020).

As many challenges exist in data science's core subfields, there are even more in the broader universe outside its core.

Universities will play an important role in advancing data science, particularly exploratory and transdisciplinary research. Fortunately, they are seizing the opportunity, as evidenced by the worldwide explosion of data science initiatives, institutes, centers, and schools. In 2012, only a handful of universities had data science entities; nine years later, there were over 100 worldwide.

Reports on data science's effect on universities discuss the challenges universities face in embracing data science (Katz, 2019; Wing et al., 2018). However, there is no question they have realized data science has been valuable for most departments, facilitating their efficient operation and increasing their research productivity. Many further realize that data science is not just a tool but rather a catalyst adding to many fields' research agendas. Technology and data science make some older research topics and problems tractable, while providing new, previously unencountered problems.

Recommendation 10 Foster Innovation

Throughout history, further innovation has been a powerful resolver of problems, even those problems caused by previous technological generations. For example, personal computers, microprocessors, cell phones, and modern cloud computing solved more of the concentration issues in 1960s/1970s mainframe and 1990s personal computing markets than did regulation. In automobile safety, vehicle technology advances have reduced fatality rates per mile driven to less than 1% of early 1920s rates. In the future, even if Level 5 self-driving cars are not on the near-term horizon, their spin-off technologies will increase automobile safety.

How will new innovations let us benefit from data science with fewer of the disadvantages? We can't know for sure, but we see many opportunities:

1. Just as music services resolved much of the music copyright infringement problem by providing low-cost, low-friction, easily used services worthy of people's roughly $10 monthly fees, new services and business models in other domains might prove worthy of subscription revenue. This would reduce some of the negative incentives related to the solicitation of click revenue.
   Benefit: Moving objective setting to the individual.
2. Alternative business models where users purchase clear and vetted policies that govern their search, social network, or streaming application results, thereby obtaining recommendations that meet their long-term objectives. Relatedly, recommendation systems could become user agents, instead of agents of the organization that has users as their customers.
   Benefit: Moving objective setting to the individual.
3. Innovations in the power of personal devices and machine learning may continue to reduce the need for data aggregation on central sites.
   Benefit: Reducing security and privacy risks.
4. As machine learning continues to become more capable, automated systems can better resist bad actors and provide truly better information to individuals and society. On the other hand, this is partially balanced by the use of increasingly powerful adversarial techniques to generate fake data.
   Benefit: Reducing mis-information.
5. New scientific publication mechanisms could have faster peer review, quicker publication, and add continued revision to scientific papers, reducing the need for endless republication.
   Benefit: More accurate, up-to-date information for both scientists and journalists.
6. Systems with more knowledge of cognitive psychology could assist people in focusing on their most important problems.
   Benefit: Reduced manipulation and improved focus on humanness.
7. New uses of technology in education could increase student attainment and reduce costs in ways that better keep students' attention.
   Benefit: Education solves many problems.

8. Ongoing efforts to apply data science to medicine, education, government, transportation, and more could alleviate many ills and provide broad improvements to societal infrastructure and inclusivity.
   Benefit: Manifold.

Innovation cannot solve all data science challenges. However, looking back, we could not have guessed how combined creativity and immense effort would make data science applications so central to the world. We believe that great data science and technology will continue to combine in unanticipated ways, rectifying many of society's concerns, particularly with the continuing trillion-fold-plus effects of Moore's Law as a tailwind.

Chapter 19

Quality and Ethical Governance

19.1 Quality and Care

A central theme of this book is that data science must be applied with quality and care, because it can do more harm than good when poorly executed. The world has moved beyond needing toy, incomplete, or risky applications. This is in contrast to the field's earliest days when practitioners were sometimes satisfied just to build proof points for approaches holding novelty and promise. Broadly, those applying data science must consider the plethora of Part III's challenges, choose good techniques, and then implement them with care.

This need to exercise great care is the main reason we crafted the Analysis Rubric. We briefly summarize its elements as these seven questions data scientists should ask and answer:

1. Is there **Tractable Data**?
2. Does a valid **Technical Approach** exist?
3. Can the **Dependability** properties of privacy, security, resilience, and abuse-resistance be met?
4. To provide **Understandability**, will the result be sufficiently explainable, will it shed sufficient light on the causal chain underlying its conclusions, and/or will it be reproducible by others?
5. Are there **Clear Objectives** specifying what we want to achieve, taking unintended consequences and stakeholders into account?
6. Given their likely occurrence, will there be the necessary **Toleration of Failures**.
7. Is the application of data science appropriate given its **Ethical, Legal, and Societal** implications?

If any of these questions does not have a good answer, data scientists should take caution. This discussion motivates our eleventh recommendation.

Recommendation 11 Apply the Analysis Rubric to Improve Data Science Results

We hope it is now self-explanatory why we feel the holistic consideration of all Analysis Rubric items is needed to have data science applications of sufficient quality. *Quality only emerges when the myriad challenges are considered and met.*

19.2 Ethics, Expertise, and Organizations

The variety of data science application areas and their increasing impact point to a future in which data scientists will have greater responsibility. With that, they must also consider the ethical consequences of their actions. However, these considerations will change greatly from field to field and from era to era.

Thus, beyond the relatively clear items in the traditional professional codes of ethics to which we referred in Chapter 3, we cannot reduce ethics to a precise list of detailed rules. Instead, we have advocated for a principlist approach, building on a tested applied ethical tradition. This, in turn, requires deliberation and, when data science takes place within organizations, discussion among colleagues with a shared vocabulary and values.

Despite the difficulty of addressing the many application-specific ethical concerns, we can still make three important recommendations.

Recommendation 12 Scrutinize Results and Be Truthful

Data scientists use highly technical means to arrive at important conclusions. Also, they often advocate for a particular world view with their research and development. Their results may receive little critical skepticism for two reasons:

- Perception that results are more certain than they actually are, perhaps due to seemingly high numerical precision.
- Insufficient understanding that data scientists may be making subjective design choices in their data analysis and algorithm development.

Therefore data scientists have an ethical obligation to carefully apply the tools of their trade and engage in self-critical inquiry before communicating or publishing results.

In particular, data scientists are best equipped to understand the complexities and potential consequences of their applications and research. For that reason, they are also best suited to provide critical reviews before deployment and publication of results. In short, as with other experts in medicine, engineering, or science, data scientists benefit from others' trust, and must conduct themselves in ways that merit, rather than exploit, that trust – with honesty in their craft and humility as to their claims.

Recommendation 13 Use Data Science to Explain Alternatives

Data scientists have unique insight into their research. They should avail themselves of their expertise not just to state technical results and performance, but also to communicate their work's consequences and potential risks. They cannot assume others will easily understand these implications. Just as health practitioners provide alternative choices and communicate the risks of a recommended treatment, so should data scientists communicate alternative approaches and the risks associated with their recommendations.

While our principlist approach to ethics is a start for ensuring ethical policies, achieving them also requires the right organizational structure. Without question, it is difficult to overlay ethical considerations onto already complex individual and institutional motivations. So for this aspect of ethical governance, we suggest a focus on the structures and processes in which principled decision-making occurs.

Recommendation 14 Create Organizational Approaches for Principled Decision-Making

Section 14.3 discussed the limitations of different organizational structures and their impact on policy, both in universities and in corporations. Appropriate organizational structures include:

- Leadership which values ethics, communicates this as a value, and is accountable when these values are challenged or undermined.
- A community in which individuals understand and commit to these shared values and principles.
- An organizational structure which surfaces and resolves deliberative disputes when ethical consensus cannot be reached among individuals and teams. Due attention must be paid to ensuring its appropriate evolution as an organization and its challenges evolve.

Ethical principles define the framework, but organizational design provides the mechanism for applying it.

Recap of Part IV: Addressing Concerns

This part began by describing some of society's concerns about data science, most of which are motivated by the challenges we laid out in Part III. We recognize there are probably more concerns than we have included, so we hope we have stimulated readers to consider additional topics. We then proposed some resolutions, as we felt obliged not just to illustrate problems but also to attempt to propose paths towards solutions. As with our list of concerns, we know our list of recommendations is likely incomplete.

We admit that we authors have differing degrees of certainty on some and/or the importance or practicality of others. While we are united on promoting data science education, we have nuanced views on the balance between the over-regulation of data science applications versus the importance of protecting the public against risk. Just as many of the Part III chapters could be books unto themselves, there are policy tomes on almost all of the subjects. The Appendix puts our recommendations in one place, while Table IV.1 shows which recommendations connect to which societal concerns.

Table IV.1 *Top-level concerns and recommendations to address*.*

		Societal concerns				
#	Recommendation	Economic and fairness impacts on people and institutions	Personal implications to data	Institutional and societal operation and governance	Environment	Trust
1	Broaden educational opportunities in data science	✓	✓	✓		✓
2	Use data science and technology in teaching data science	✓	✓	✓		✓

Table IV.1 (*cont.*)

#	Recommendation	Societal concerns				
		Economic and fairness impacts on people and institutions	Personal implications to data	Institutional and societal operation and governance	Environment	Trust
3	Promote clear vocabulary		✓	✓		✓
4	Regulate uses, not technology	✓	✓	✓		✓
5	Regulate clear, not potential, problems	✓	✓	✓		✓
6	Update laws with data science and technology in mind	✓	✓	✓		✓
7	Consider the impacts of economies of scale and the virtuous cycle	✓		✓		
8	Create independent, consensus-building institutions for difficult problems	✓	✓	✓		✓
9	Increase focused and transdisciplinary research	✓	✓	✓	✓	
10	Foster innovation	✓	✓	✓	✓	
11	Apply the Analysis Rubric to improve data science results		✓	✓		✓
12	Scrutinize results and be truthful		✓			✓
13	Use data science to explain alternatives		✓			✓
14	Create organizational approaches for principled decision-making					✓

* The columns represent the categories of concerns listed in Chapter 15. The rows represent recommendations, as summarized in the Appendix. A "tick" means the recommendation at least partially addresses the concern.

Chapter 20
Concluding Thoughts

We had several goals in writing *Data Science in Context*:

- We wanted to introduce data science as a *coherent field*, while illustrating the need to balance *its opportunities and challenges*.
- We wanted to advise our readers on how both to *apply data science* and to *critically understand* its uses in the world.
- We wanted to emphasize ethical considerations, through both the *ethics framework* and a large collection of *ethics-related challenges*.
- We wanted to summarize *societal concerns* about data science and make recommendations to address them.

This chapter briefly summarizes these points and concludes with a few lessons we learned while writing this book.

20.1 Data Science – A Coherent Field

Our explanation of this field began with a definition: "Data science is the study of extracting value from data – value in the form of **insights** or **conclusions**." We then made more explicit what we mean by insights and specified six types of conclusions: **prediction**, **recommendation**, **clustering**, **classification**, **transformation**, and **optimization**.

As we described, data science's intellectual origins lie mostly in statistics, operations research, and computing. We find the story of the forces that combined to form data science over the decades prior to the term's breakout in around 2010 to be a compelling one, replete with visionaries, breakthroughs, the march of technology, and economic incentives. We illustrated data science's broad and growing impact, complex challenges, and powerful future with many examples. We used the term "transdisciplinary" to emphasize its integration of many forms of knowledge, techniques, and modes of thought.

The **Analysis Rubric** and associated discussions of challenges completed this theme by showing data science's breadth of problems and methods for addressing them.

20.2 Data Science – Opportunities and Challenges

One of our main aims has been to accurately and comprehensively cover both data science's positive benefits and its potential harms when misused.

- The domains where data science is proving applicable are already important and are growing rapidly. They affect almost everyone's day-to-day life. As co-author Jeannette says, "Data science provides the 21st-century methods to tackle 21st-century problems," meaning climate, public health, education, and more.
- Applying data science well is difficult. We discussed many challenges in Part III relating to data, modeling, dependability, supporting understandability, setting objectives, tolerating failures, and meeting ELSI objectives. They are mathematical, engineering, epistemological, societal, and political in nature. Because of them, society has developed concerns over data science's actual and perceived harms, as we summarized in Chapter 15.

20.3 Understanding and Applying the Analysis Rubric

We have aimed to instruct students and practitioners on how to approach new data science problems by offering the Analysis Rubric with its seven elements and implied questions:

- Is there **data**?
- If the goal is to provide a conclusion, is there a **model** that will do so?
- Will the project be **dependable**?
- Can the project provide sufficient **understandability**?
- Are there clear and beneficial **objectives**?
- Can the application **tolerate failures?**
- Are the needed **ethical, legal, and societal** implications met?

A priori, the Analysis Rubric helps determine if a proposed project is feasible. A posteriori, it can be used to see if it addressed needed issues. We do not advocate a particular top-down or bottom-up methodology, and we recognize that different project teams will use the Analysis Rubric in different ways. We feel that the benefits of a rubric or checklist are well documented (Gawande, 2009), and that our Analysis Rubric is a good starting point for most teams.

This book presents many examples of applying the Analysis Rubric. Some showed data science works naturally; others showed great challenges. The examples informed us not only as practitioners, but also as people who interact with uses of data science on a daily basis. We acknowledge that some of our examples will become stale and that future readers will be surprised we omitted others of then-current contemporary importance.

As previously noted, we readily admit that aspiring data science practitioners need to augment our discussions with technical material from statistical, optimization, and computational texts.

20.4 Ethics

We believe a data science project is only a complete success when it satisfies an actual human need and doesn't merely meet a statistical measure. To that end, a successful data scientist considers not only design constraints and statistical goals but also the context that defines success. Framed this way, and with a nod to our title, *Data Science in Context*, a data science project's success clearly depends on the human and societal context in which it exists.

By no means do we argue that it's easy to balance ethical and other objectives, but we do argue that the act of trying to do so results in better outcomes. Ethical consideration is not just for philosophers – it is a necessary and useful exercise that is the responsibility of all data science practitioners.

We recommend the Belmont Principles of **respect for persons**, **beneficence**, and **justice** (Chapter 3) as a concrete framework for thinking about ethics in data science. We also emphasized that ethical uses of technology necessitate scientists and engineers to successfully navigate all of Part III's challenges. We then discussed the organizational and governance challenges that make it hard to balance incentives and achieve good outcomes. Chapter 19 concluded the ethics discussion with recommendations on quality and organization.

20.5 Addressing Concerns

In Part IV, we divided societal concerns on data science into five categories. Summarized in Table 15.1, they are the data science implications on *Economic and fairness impacts on people and institutions*, *Personal implications to data*, *Institutional and societal operation and governance*, the *Environment*, and *Trust*. We then proposed some recommendations of varying specificity and complexity:

- Some are straightforward and relatively short-term. For example, some of our recommended technology improvements can occur quickly. As one example, we are seeing rapidly increased uses of federated learning to reduce privacy risks.

Also, we could quickly define and use more precise vocabulary (e.g., for specific privacy concerns) and thus have clearer and more thoughtful policy debates.
- Some are clear to us but take time. A focus on education is of the utmost importance, as individuals with data science knowledge will gain leverage in their vocation and better understand their rapidly changing world. More practitioners will also speed progress. We want to emphasize that humanities and social science education provides data scientists with valuable perspectives.
- Others are complex. Regulation requires care due to negative, unintended consequences. Issues such as content moderation or the implications of scale are complex and require significant thought and consensus-building.

20.6 Reflections from Your Authors

We have each written a brief essay, representing our own individual interests and concerns.

Jeannette M. Wing: Where Does Data Science Fit in Academia?

"Will data science evolve as an academic field like computer science or like computational science?" This insightful and probing question asked by Ed Lazowska, renowned computer scientist at the University of Washington, at the inaugural Academic Data Science Leadership Summit in 2018, still has no answer – it is too early to tell. And maybe it doesn't matter.

Computer science as a field of study emerged from its roots of electrical engineering, mathematics, and business in the 1960s. Within two decades, one could major in computer science, get a Ph.D. in computer science, be a faculty member in a computer science department, be a dean of a computer science school, publish in computer science journals and conference proceedings, buy computer science textbooks, attend computer science conferences, get a job as a computer scientist, join computer science professional organizations, and win the equivalent of the Nobel Prize in computing (i.e., the Turing Award).

Funding agencies, such as the National Science Foundation and the Defense Research Projects Agency, had created directorates or offices dedicated to computer science. The information technology sector grew quickly on the shoulders of computer science giants. To date, industry demand for computer scientists continues to outstrip the supply. It took only a couple of decades, but computer science is now an established and accepted field of study worldwide. No question.

Computational science, in contrast, refers to the use of computational methods, tools, and thinking in the sciences. For the most part, it is not considered a single field of study. Rather, one can specialize or even major in computational astrophysics, computational biology, computational chemistry, computational materials science, computational neuroscience, computational physics, and more. But most universities do not have a computational science degree program or a computational science department.

Data science, like computer science, has its roots in other disciplines. Data science, also like computer science, has nearly universal applicability. So, will the foundations of data science solidify and evolve, much like they did for computer science, and lead to data science being its own discipline? Or will data science be so integral to each domain, where eventually each domain's repertoire of methods necessarily includes data science?

Here are two other suggestive analogies: On the one hand, mathematics is the language of science, yet it remains an independent field of study. On the other hand, software engineering is typically studied as part of computer science, yet one of the first jobs a computer scientist might land in industry is titled "software engineer."

Universities today are embracing data science but in different ways. In some schools, it is a part of the computer science department or college (e.g., University of Southern California, and University of Massachusetts, Amherst) or part of the statistics department (e.g., Carnegie Mellon University, and Yale University). In some, data science is its own school (e.g., University of Virginia), alongside its computer science and statistics departments. At some schools, there is an independent data science institute (e.g., Columbia University, Georgia Tech, Harvard University, University of Chicago, University of Michigan, and University of Washington), cutting across schools, and thus across disciplines; however, degree programs and joint faculty have homes in an academic department. And some schools have a hybrid approach: at MIT, the Institute for Data, Systems, and Society serves the entire university, cutting across all schools and disciplines, but, organizationally, it is housed in the Schwarzman College of Computing; at New York University, the Center for Data Science serves the entire university but offers its own degree programs and hires joint faculty; and at UC Berkeley, the Division of Computing, Data Science, and Society is a new academic entity, incorporating its computer science faculty, who are part of the School of Engineering, and Berkeley's School of Information.

Watching these multiple models emerge is not surprising, as data science builds on core strengths in computer science, statistics, and operations research. How a university embraces data science is related to its organization of these and other related disciplines. Universities understand the value of data science in the future of all academic pursuits, and thus to their own future, but today there is no one right answer to the question when the president asks "Where do I tuck data science in the org chart at my university?"

At the same time, interest in data science continues to skyrocket. The 2018 Academic Data Science Leadership Summit led to the creation of the Academic Data Science Alliance, a non-profit organization initially funded by the Gordon and Betty Moore Foundation, the Alfred P. Sloan Foundation, and the National Science Foundation. As of 2021 it had 40 founding member institutions. It convenes annual meetings, already engaging over 100 organizations from academia, industry, and government to share best practices in education, research, and the ethics of data science.

And the next generation is voting with their feet. In late 2020, the NSF-funded Northeast Big Data Innovation Hub, headquartered at Columbia University, started an effort in the nine northeastern states to engage directly with students interested in data science. This effort blossomed into the National Data Science Student Data Corps, which by January 2022 had 1922 student members (including high-school students) from 348 colleges and universities, 40 states, and seven countries. Twenty-four percent of the members are from minority-serving institutions. Students from over 40 academic institutions are asking to create their own NDSC chapters.

Regardless of how data science fits into an academic organizational structure, data science is here to stay. If your child asks you "Should I study data science?," reply "Yes!," because data science students learn techniques useful for any future profession – and useful for life.

Chris Wiggins: Rethinking Responsibility and Success

In May of 2017, I asked the scholar danah boyd how we engineering educators could convince students and practitioners that context was worth studying. Her suggestion was to push data scientists to think more deeply about what it means for data science research and data science products to be "successful": success does not simply mean meeting a statistical goal (for example, low generalization error) but rather that the research or product aims to actually improve lives.

Much of this book has been about the promise of data science. Certainly, in the last decade, it has become clear that computational advances for making sense of the world through data have vastly increased its impact. Arguably, the mindset of data science goes back to work by John Tukey, who split his career between industry and academia (Bell Labs and Princeton). A slightly earlier point of origin is the dawn of digital computation at Bletchley Park, where computing with data and the combined statistical and engineering mindset has been credited with shortening World War II by two to four years. However, as Spider Man's uncle once warned him, "With great power comes great responsibility."

For most of us raised as technologists, the idea that a technical subject can have "politics," meaning it can change the dynamics of power, is unfamiliar and sometimes unbelievable. Like many earlier researchers in machine learning, my personal training was in physics, a field in which the potential politics of one's work has been inescapable since August of 1945. One of many significant differences from data science today is that the technical and financial barriers are lower than ever before to having a wide impact on a large number of people.

Part of our goal in this book, implicit in the title *Data Science in Context*, is to illustrate how data science as a technical field is built from and shares techniques with many adjacent fields of the last 50 to 100 years. A second meaning to "data science in context" is to remind practitioners that, particularly in industry, data science powers products – that is, things that real people use and which impact their lives. A similar sentiment guides our treatment of ethics. We hope that this book not only convinces you, our reader, that the context is worth thinking about, but also that it gives you the conceptual tools for thinking through this context and the difficult responsibilities data science practitioners now bear.

We hope that by introducing you not only to the fundamental technical concepts of data science, but also to fundamental concepts such as the Belmont Principles, we will help you expand and ground your conception of what constitutes a successful data science project and a successful career in data science.

Peter Norvig: From Algorithms to Data to Needs

When I started work in artificial intelligence in 1980, researchers were focused on inventing new algorithms to solve problems more effectively. By 1990 it became clear that the field of AI was changing, in three ways:

- The canonical approach shifted from an expert system (a program designed to mimic the thinking processes of human experts) to an intelligent assistant (designed not to imitate humans, but rather to optimize performance on some task – to do the right thing).
- Researchers, notably Pearl (Pearl, 1988), along with Cheeseman (Cheeseman, 1985), Heckerman, Horvitz, and Nathwani (Heckerman et al., 1992), convincingly argued that reasoning with probabilities and decision theory was superior to reasoning with logic for the types of problems AI faced – problems where uncertainty is a key component.
- Machine learning grew from a subfield to the dominant approach within AI, and the emphasis of the field shifted from *algorithms* to *data*. No longer were knowledge

> bases carefully hand-crafted and curated by graduate students; instead we could appeal directly to the data. Researchers such as Banko and Brill (Banko & Brill, 2001) showed learning curves that continued to improve as the amount of data went from thousands to millions to billions of unlabeled examples. There was plenty of room at the top for more data, and the phrase "big data" came into vogue.

Stuart Russell and I were able to chronicle these changes in a mid-1990s textbook (Russell & Norvig, 2021), and we had good luck in our timing; professors and students were eager to embrace this newly evolving picture of AI. Later, Alon Halevy, Fernando Pereira, and I were also able to put down some thoughts on the effectiveness of data (Halevy et al., 2009).

With the frontier of AI shifting from algorithms to data, I swapped my .edu address for .com to get the resources – computing power and teammates – necessary to harness big data. It was an exciting time and we created applications that were used by millions, and then billions, of people. Before anyone codified AI principles, I learned to embrace the principles of the World Wide Web Consortium: "Put user needs first," and "The Web should not cause harm to society." I'm proud of the dedication and hard work that my teammates put in towards achieving these goals.

One day in 2012 I was sitting by myself, contemplating what project to focus on next, when Geoff Hinton approached, very excited, and said "You've got to see this. It finally works!" He showed me the image classification network that was to win the ImageNet ILSVRC competition. I immediately realized that this would mark another significant change in the field, but I underestimated just how widespread the influence of deep neural networks would become in vision, speech recognition, natural language, robotics, and other fields.

By 2020, it looked like the field had changed again. This time it was a change in how we look at problems. We still had to answer "What's the right algorithm?" and "What data should we use?," but most often the hardest question to answer was "What is the goal?" or "What do we want to optimize?," and the related questions of "What is fair?" and "Who is this for?"

Underlying all this is the deeper question "What context are we operating under?" I spent a lot of my time in college and grad school playing Ultimate Frisbee, and in 1982 I was called upon to serve on the committee to write the eighth edition of the rules. My experience with rule-based systems, both in AI and in sports, told me that when there is a specific set of rules, competitors look for loopholes in the rules. For example, in basketball, sometimes a player will intentionally foul an opponent, because doing so gives their team an advantage. To counter this, the rules are constantly updated with new penalties (e.g., the "clear path" rule and the "Hack-a-Shaq" rule).

I realized that it would never be possible to foresee all situations and codify all penalties, so instead the eighth edition rules state that "Ultimate has traditionally relied upon a spirit of sportsmanship which places the responsibility for fair play on the player" and "Such actions as taunting, dangerous aggression, intentional fouling, or other 'win-at-all-costs' behavior are contrary to the *spirit of the game* and must be avoided by all players." In effect, we told players that their first responsibility was not merely to optimize their chance of winning the game under a set of rules; their primary goal was to conscientiously contribute to the betterment of the community of players, and only secondarily to win the game.

I saw these lessons as both a challenge and an opportunity for machine learning systems. The challenge: any system that is described by a set of rules may have exploitable loopholes. The opportunity: it is easier to describe the boundaries of acceptable behavior with a set of examples than with rules, and machine learning systems are good at learning from examples. If we model things correctly, we can build machine learning systems that learn to act like conscientious members of a community, not like win-at-all-costs exploiters. We want to make it easier to create systems that are creative enough to, for example, come up with "move 37" in Go, yet are ethical enough to know that cheating is not the right way to win, and that turning the whole world into one big paper clip factory is not the right thing. I believe that a major area of research will be in finding better ways to communicate with machine learning systems, to have more effective ways of describing to them the bounds of what we want them to do, and to help us discover for ourselves what we really want.

To date, the computer industry does not have the best record of protecting the community from win-at-all-costs exploiters. The Web is a global marketplace, for products, ideas, and attention; and we have made it all too easy to harvest user's attention (Center for Humane Technology, n.d.).

The 20th-century British philosophers Michael Philip Jagger and Keith Richards wrote that "you can't always get what you want" but "you get what you need." However, when it comes to the Web, they got it exactly backwards. We have constructed a very efficient feedback mechanism to say what you *want* – a system that encourages you to consume the latest amusing game, meme, or video, and then uses collaborative filtering to make recommendations to others as well. But we don't have a good system for saying what we really *need* – equality, justice, health, safety – and we don't have good feedback systems to make sure everyone gets them.

The challenge for machine learning and data science is to build systems that align with society's real needs, and work for everyone. I hope this book will inspire researchers to develop ideas that contribute to this; will enable developers to build systems that work for the betterment of all; and will empower consumers to know what they can ask for.

Alfred Z. Spector: Post-Modern Prometheus

I recently came upon an article arguing that data science had hit "Peak Metaphor."[25] This is no surprise given the contemporary importance of the field, and the need for many of us to find an apt turn of phrase to summarize some point of view. On my mind is this message:

Data Science: Powerful Technology. Great and Increasing Value. Handle with Care

I realize this is hardly new. It's been repeated countless times, perhaps beginning with the Greek Myth of Prometheus, who delivered fire, a technology of unarguable value and lasting impact. However, Prometheus suffered acutely for pilfering the gods' trade secret, and we are still dealing with fire's disadvantages some twenty-eight hundred years after the Greek poet Hesiod's writing. So:

- **Fire.** It's easy to start, diversely useful, but it's risky and has harmful side effects. The harms have been relatively evolutionary and, despite repeated catastrophes, we've found ways to deal with them. Concerns over CO_2 will curtail bulk use, but otherwise fire will remain.
- **Data science.** It's ever easier to gather data and create great insights or conclusions. Like fire, it is astoundingly useful. It's also a risky endeavor with subtle problems that have harmful effects. It may even be with us for twenty-eight hundred years more.

The really big question we don't answer in this book is whether data science (and the overlapping field of artificial intelligence) will have a gradually increasing impact or whether it will catalyze fundamentally extreme and discontinuous change. Addressing this topic from the vantage point of AI, Nick Bostrom wrote in 2014 that the time is near when we have "superintelligence," which he defines as "any intellect that greatly exceeds the cognitive performance of humans in virtually all domains of interest" (Bostrom, 2014). Kissinger et al. wrote in 2021 about AI causing "a new epoch" and an "alteration of human identity and the human experience of reality at levels not experienced since the dawn of the modern age" (Kissinger et al., 2021).

Nearer term, pragmatists like me will be focused on what to learn and do now. While I strongly endorse deep thinking about the longer-term issues, our work is mostly to solve the challenges we perceive today. I see these as dividing into ones that are primarily technical and others that relate to application or use:

- **Technical concerns.** Research already underway will solve many of data science's technical challenges, though some breakthroughs are needed. In particular,

[25] Paul Sonderegger used this phrase, perhaps sarcastically, to note the recent spate of metaphors for data science (Sonderegger, 2021).

we can't yet replicate the type of transfer learning that enables humans to quickly learn from books. We also don't have a good handle on how to combine common sense knowledge with machine-learned models. Modeling applications with concept drift seems almost impossible, particularly if there is sudden change. I also don't see how we will solve the interpretability problems discussed in Section 11.1. Finally, resilience in the face of adversarial attacks seems like it will be a long-term challenge.

- **Application concerns.** As we have said, when data science is used incorrectly, there are negative consequences.
  - Data science exacerbates the problem of misaligned incentives. It is too easy to tune systems to meet a narrow goal (optimizing an overly simplistic objective) that is not to the long-term benefit of individuals, organizations, or society. The problems of incentives may be greater if they are created by a government or a small number of large organizations, potentially reducing a society's pluralistic voices.
  - Data science methods coupled with the sheer quantity of fine-grained data can lead to compelling but false insights. In particular, our book warns against confusing correlation and causation. Creators and consumers of information should practice the greatest care in communicating and understanding data science results, and should pay particular heed to the list of cognitive biases co-author Peter has assembled in Section 11.4.
  - Data science makes it harder to agree on reasonable, but imperfect, solutions to difficult problems. Even though it may be possible to quantify mathematical trade-offs between different solutions, this analysis may only serve to highlight the inevitable limitations of each and prevent pragmatic action. Many systems are zero-sum games, and data science can be used to highlight each loss. It's hard to remember "The great is the enemy of the good" when confronted with quantified objections.
  - Data science solutions are often insufficiently tolerant of errors or abuse. Some errors naturally occur because of the probabilistic nature of data science solutions or the innate difficulty of solving certain types of problems. Security vulnerabilities also play a big role, and they are extremely hard to prevent. Risks are heightened because many of us, myself included, were late in realizing that nation states would engage in attacks on non-military applications. These challenges are not solely technical, because they often arise because of interactions between people and computers. We thus need to think carefully about where we are applying data science.

Many of these challenges will require the transdisciplinary efforts of the diverse coalitions we referred to in Chapter 2. We surely need to apply an ethical lens as we make important decisions, and societal norms may also change. As with the control of fire, we will also require sensible laws and regulations, though we must take care to avoid negative regulatory consequences. Solutions will take time, and, as with fire (and all good inventions), there will inevitably be residual risks that we learn to live with.

In her 1818 novel *Frankenstein*, Mary Shelley explored the consequences of a powerful and groundbreaking technology – in this case, one that created a living creature. In recognition of the parallel between Frankenstein's delivery of a synthetic life and Prometheus's delivery of fire, she subtitled her book *The Modern Prometheus*. We data scientists are perhaps, collectively, a "post-modern Prometheus," who can and should strive to minimize the risks of our own fire, for the well-being of ourselves and our societies.

However, we should receive encouragement to pursue our dreams from the words of Percy Shelley, her husband, who also wrote about Prometheus. He concluded his play, *Prometheus Unbound*, in an uplifting manner (Shelley, 1898):

> To defy Power, which seems omnipotent;
> To love, and bear; to hope till Hope creates
> From its own wreck the thing it contemplates;
> Neither to change, nor falter, nor repent;
> This, like thy glory, Titan, is to be
> Good, great and joyous, beautiful and free;
> This is alone Life, Joy, Empire, and Victory.

20.7 Final Thoughts

Data science practitioners have employed enormous effort and creativity to create applications of great value. They have addressed many difficult challenges to deliver results embraced by billions of people every day. Data science has brought increased understanding, economic growth, and new tools and entertainment.

We believe that data science will continue to thrive and extend its reach in important areas such as healthcare, education, climate, transportation and logistics, commerce, sports and games, and economic development, to name but a few. We should proactively encourage and engage in data science, while also addressing its pitfalls. The increasing international competition in data science means nation states will very likely reach the same conclusion.

There are indeed very hard foundational questions underlying data science: How do we deal with missing or differentially sampled data? What does it mean to be fair?

How do we distinguish correlation and causation? How do we explain conclusions? Some real-world applications may continue to elude data science solutions, due to the sparsity of data, complexity of the problem, or cleverness of adversaries. We reiterate that an application of data science has not provided a complete solution if it does not meet the breadth of the Analysis Rubric considerations.

Some problems are particularly hard to set proper objectives for, as discussed in Chapter 12. Simple metrics, such as maximizing clicks or counting near-term revenue, are unlikely to suffice from either a business or ethical perspective. When data science is asked to provide solutions where people have not agreed on the preferred outcomes, the solutions will not please everyone. Gaining a consensus requires advice from ethicists, governments, economists, political scientists, other experts, and the general public.

Data science is being asked to provide solutions to very difficult problems. For example, it is plainly difficult to optimize complex systems that exhibit non-stationarity and which have adversarial responses, as we discussed in the country-wide economic prediction example of Section 6.5. In recognition of this and the difficulty of establishing consensus objectives, these problems have been called **wicked**, and are acknowledged to be very difficult (Churchman, 1967).

Finally, we admit the field's breadth and speed make it hard to keep up with everything. We ourselves are confronted with the rapid changes in application areas, technical approaches, and problems, though we find that this book's frameworks allow us to put these changes in perspective. We are less sure about all of the details, and we know we have probably made errors or provided overly shallow discussions of some topics so that we could cover the full scope of the challenges and opportunities we see. In recognition, we expect to put updates on our book's website, DataScienceInContext.com. We also acknowledge that some of our examples will become stale.

This book has not covered three topics that may have practical implications in the future:

- The application of quantum computing to solve currently intractable problems.
- The widespread deployment of capable robots throughout society.
- The development of artificial general intelligence, rather than AI for specific applications.

We close by stressing that data science is important to society – too important to be done poorly. We thus hope this book stimulates more of us – data scientists and humanists, ethicists, social scientists of all types, scientists, politicians, jurists, and more – to study data science's opportunities and challenges and work together to better our world.

Appendix

Summary of Recommendations from Part IV

Recommendation	Comment
1. Broaden educational opportunities in data science	Broad education in data science, including at the boundaries of other disciplines, provides increased opportunity to all and is important for the field
2. Use data science and technology in teaching data science	Immersing students in data science tools will improve educational outcomes and leverage skilled teachers
3. Promote clear vocabulary	Our vocabulary for discussing data science challenges is often imprecise, so discussions are meandering. Policies with standardized definitions would benefit both service providers and consumers
4. Regulate uses, not technology	Harms arise more from the application of technology in particular circumstances, not the technology itself
5. Regulate clear, not potential, problems	There are places where regulation will benefit both the regulated entities and the consumer, though it is challenging to mitigate unintended consequences
6. Update laws with data science and technology in mind	Data science applications may be challenged to interpret existing laws. Also, existing laws may not be intended to be mechanistically applied
7. Consider the impact of economies of scale and the virtuous cycle	Recognizing that data science and technology catalyze scale, careful thought is needed to balance benefits and risks
8. Create independent, consensus-building institutions for difficult problems	New organizations to lead the standardization of terminology, technology, and policy, to create repositories of trusted, reusable content, and to do measurement and compliance testing. They might help organizations self-regulate and help achieve societal consensus
9. Increase focused and transdisciplinary research	Based on its track record, many of data science's challenges will be solved by great research
10. Foster innovation	Continuing innovation will bring many valuable data science capabilities to fruition

(*cont.*)

Recommendation	Comment
11. Apply the Analysis Rubric to improve data science results	Careful attention to the breadth of data science problems will make for better-quality solutions
12. Scrutinize results and be truthful	Data scientists must be self-critical and very careful to tell the truth
13. Use data science to explain alternatives	Given that the technical aspect of a new product addresses only a part of a human need, and that a new technical research result provides only a part of a larger answer, data scientists should illustrate alternatives so that decision makers can weigh alternatives
14. Create organizational approaches for principled decision-making	Practicing ethical decision-making is difficult; organizations should create structures and mechanisms that foster the application of ethical principles

About the Authors

Alfred Z. Spector is a technologist and research leader. His career has led him from innovation in large-scale, networked computing systems (at Stanford University, Carnegie Mellon University, and his company, Transarc) to broad research leadership: first leading IBM Software Research and then Google Research. Following Google, he was the CTO at Two Sigma Investments, and he is presently a Visiting Scholar at MIT. In addition to his managerial career, Dr. Spector has lectured widely on the growing importance of computer science across all disciplines (CS+X) and on the societal implications of data science. He is a fellow of the ACM, IEEE, and the American Academy of Arts and Sciences, and a member of the National Academy of Engineering. Dr. Spector won the 2001 IEEE Kanai Award for Distributed Computing, was co-awarded the 2016 ACM Software Systems Award, and was a Phi Beta Kappa Visiting Scholar. He received a Ph.D. in Computer Science from Stanford and an A.B. in Applied Mathematics from Harvard.

Peter Norvig is a Distinguished Education Fellow at Stanford's Human-Centered Artificial Intelligence Institute and a research director at Google; previously he directed Google's core search algorithms group and Google's research group. He has taught at the University of Southern California, Stanford University, and the University of California at Berkeley, from which he received a Ph.D. in 1986 and the distinguished alumni award in 2006. He was co-teacher of an Artificial Intelligence class that signed up 160,000 students, helping to kick off the current round of massive open online classes. His books include *Artificial Intelligence: A Modern Approach* (the leading textbook in the field) and *Paradigms of AI Programming: Case Studies in Common Lisp*. He is also the author of the Gettysburg PowerPoint Presentation and the world's longest palindromic sentence. He is a fellow of the AAAI, ACM, California Academy of Science, and the American Academy of Arts and Sciences.

Chris Wiggins is an Associate Professor of Applied Mathematics at Columbia University and the Chief Data Scientist at *The New York Times*. At Columbia he is a founding member of the executive committee of the Data Science Institute, and a member of the Department of Applied Physics and Applied Mathematics as well as the Department of Systems Biology, and is affiliated faculty in Statistics. He is a co-founder and co-organizer of hackNY (http://hackNY.org), a non-profit which since 2010 has organized once-a-semester student hackathons, and the hackNY Fellows Program, a structured summer internship at NYC startups. Prior to joining the faculty at Columbia, he was a Courant Instructor at New York University (1998–2001) and earned his Ph.D. at Princeton University (1993–98) in theoretical physics. He is a Fellow of the American Physical Society and is a recipient of Columbia's Avanessians Diversity Award.

Jeannette M. Wing is the Executive Vice President for Research and Professor of Computer Science at Columbia University. She joined Columbia in 2017 as the inaugural

Avanessians Director of the Data Science Institute. From 2013 to 2017, she was a Corporate Vice President of Microsoft Research. She twice served as the Head of the Computer Science Department at Carnegie Mellon University, where she had been on the faculty since 1985. From 2007 to 2010 she was the Assistant Director of the Computer and Information Science and Engineering Directorate at the National Science Foundation. Professor Wing's current research focus is on trustworthy AI. She is known for her research contributions in security and privacy, programming languages, and concurrent and distributed systems. Her 2006 seminal essay, titled "Computational Thinking," is credited with helping to establish the centrality of computer science to problem-solving in fields where previously it had not been embraced. She received the Computing Research Association Distinguished Service Award in 2011 and the ACM Distinguished Service Award in 2014. She is a Fellow of the American Academy of Arts and Sciences, the American Association for the Advancement of Science, ACM, and IEEE. She received her S.B., S.M., and Ph.D. degrees in Computer Science from MIT.

References

Abadie, A. (2021). Using Synthetic Controls: Feasibility, Data Requirements, and Methodological Aspects. *Journal of Economic Literature*, 59(2), 391–425. https://doi.org/10.1257/jel.20191450

ACM. (2007). *ACM RECSYS 2007. 1st ACM Conference on Recommender Systems*, Minneapolis, MN. https://recsys.acm.org/recsys07/

ACM CIGCHI. (n.d.). Conference History – ACM CIGCHI. Retrieved January 8, 2022, from https://sigchi.org/conferences/conference-history/CHI/

Adams, G. S., Converse, B. A., Hales, A. H., & Klotz, L. E. (2021). People Systematically Overlook Subtractive Changes. *Nature*, 592(7853), 258–261. https://doi.org/10.1038/s41586-021-03380-y

Adhikari, A., Denero, J., & Jordan, M. I. (2021). Interleaving Computational and Inferential Thinking in an Undergraduate Data Science Curriculum. *Harvard Data Science Review*, 3(2). https://doi.org/10.1162/99608f92.cb0fa8d2

Akerlof, G. A. & Shiller, R. J. (2015). *Phishing for Phools: The Economics of Manipulation and Deception*. Princeton University Press. https://press.princeton.edu/books/hardcover/9780691168319/phishing-for-phools

Aktay, A., Bavadekar, S., Cossoul, G., et al. (2020). Google COVID-19 Community Mobility Reports: Anonymization Process Description (version 1.1). arXiv [cs.CR]. https://arxiv.org/pdf/2004.04145v4

Alfano, M., Carter, J. A., & Cheong, M. (2018). Technological Seduction and Self-Radicalization. *Journal of the American Philosophical Association*, 4(3), 298–322. https://doi.org/10.1017/apa.2018.27

Amazon Web Services (2006). Announcing Amazon Elastic Compute Cloud (Amazon EC2) – Beta, August 24. https://aws.amazon.com/about-aws/whats-new/2006/08/24/announcing-amazon-elastic-compute-cloud-amazon-ec2—beta/

American Statistical Association (ASA). (n.d.). Ethical Guidelines for Statistical Practice. American Statistical Association. Retrieved December 11, 2021, from www.amstat.org/ASA/Your-Career/Ethical-Guidelines-for-Statistical-Practice.aspx

Amershi, S., Begel, A., Bird, C., et al. (2019). Software Engineering for Machine Learning: A Case Study. *2019 IEEE/ACM 41st International Conference on Software Engineering: Software Engineering in Practice (ICSE-SEIP)*, pp. 291–300. https://doi.org/10.1109/ICSE-SEIP.2019.00042

Andrews, R. J. (2019). Florence Nightingale is a Design Hero. *Nightingale*. https://medium.com/nightingale/florence-nightingale-is-a-design-hero-8bf6e5f2147

Anfinsen, C. B. (1973). Principles That Govern the Folding of Protein Chains. *Science*, 181 (4096), 223–230. https://doi.org/10.1126/science.181.4096.223

Angwin, J., Larson, J., Kirchner, L., & Mattu, S. (2016). Machine Bias, May 23. ProPublica. www.propublica.org/article/machine-bias-risk-assessments-in-criminal-sentencing
Apache. (n.d.). Apache Log4j 2. The Apache Software Foundation. Retrieved January 7, 2022, from https://logging.apache.org/log4j/2.x/
Apple Inc. (2021). Expanded Protections for Children: Frequently Asked Questions, August. Apple Inc. www.apple.com/child-safety/
Apple Support. (2019). Get a Copy of the Data Associated With Your Apple ID Account, May 16. Apple Inc. https://support.apple.com/en-us/HT208502
Aristophanes. (414 BC). The Birds. In E. O'Neill Jr, ed., unknown transl. See www .perseus.tufts.edu/hopper/text?doc=urn:cts:greekLit:tlg0019.tlg006.perseus-eng1:1-48
Associated Press. (2021). News Values and Principles, December 14. Associated Press. www.ap.org/about/news-values-and-principles/
Association for Computing Machinery (ACM). (2018). ACM Code of Ethics and Professional Conduct, June 22. Association for Computing Machinery (ACM). www.acm.org/code-of-ethics
AT&T. (2022). Transparency Report. AT&T. https://about.att.com/content/dam/csr/2019/transparency/2022/2022-February-Transparency-Report.pdf
Autor, D., Mindell, D., & Reynolds, E. (2020). The Work of the Future: Building Better Jobs in an Age of Intelligent Machines. Massachusetts Institute of Technology. https://workofthefuture.mit.edu/research-post/the-work-of-the-future-building-better-jobs-in-an-age-of-intelligent-machines/
Baek, M., DiMaio, F., Anishchenko, I., et al. (2021). Accurate Prediction of Protein Structures and Interactions Using a Three-Track Neural Network. *Science*, 373 (6557), 871–876. https://doi.org/10.1126/science.abj8754
Baker, M. (2016). 1,500 Scientists Lift the Lid on Reproducibility. *Nature*, 533(7604), 452–454. https://doi.org/10.1038/533452a
Banko, M. & Brill, E. (2001). Scaling to Very Very Large Corpora for Natural Language Disambiguation. *Proceedings of the 39th Annual Meeting on Association for Computational Linguistics*, pp. 26–33. https://doi.org/10.3115/1073012.1073017
Barocas, S. & Nissenbaum, H. (2014). Big Data's End Run Around Procedural Privacy Protections. *Communications of the ACM*, 57(11), 31–33. https://doi.org/10.1145/2668897
Barrio, P. J., Goldstein, D. G., & Hofman, J. M. (2016). Improving Comprehension of Numbers in the News. *Proceedings of the 2016 CHI Conference on Human Factors in Computing Systems*, pp. 2729–2739. https://doi.org/10.1145/2858036.2858510
BBC. (n.d.). Guidance: Reporting Statistics. Retrieved December 20, 2021, from www .bbc.com/editorialguidelines/guidance/reporting-statistics/
Bendavid, E., Mulaney, B., Sood, N., et al. (2020). COVID-19 Antibody Seroprevalence in Santa Clara County, California. Preprint. https://doi.org/10.1101/2020.04.14.20062463
Bendavid, E., Mulaney, B., Sood, N., et al. (2021). COVID-19 Antibody Seroprevalence in Santa Clara County, California. *International Journal of Epidemiology*, 50(2), 410–419. https://doi.org/10.1093/ije/dyab010
Bensinger, G. (2020). Google Redraws the Borders on Maps Depending on Who's Looking. *Washington Post*, February 14. www.washingtonpost.com/technology/2020/02/14/google-maps-political-borders/
Berners-Lee, T. (1990). Information Management: A Proposal. www.w3.org/History/1989/proposal.html
Beutel, A., Chi, E. H., Diaz, F., & Burke, R. (2020). Responsible Recommendation and Search Systems. *WWW 2020*, April 19, Taipei. http://alexbeutel.com/www2020_resprecs/
Bhuiyan, M. M., Zhang, A. X., Sehat, C. M., & Mitra, T. (2020). Investigating Differences in Crowdsourced News Credibility Assessment: Raters, Tasks, and Expert Criteria.

Proceedings of the ACM on Human–Computer Interaction, vol. 4 (CSCW2), New York, October. Association for Computing Machinery, Art. 93, pp. 1–26. https://doi.org/10.1145/3415164

Bishop, D. & Gill, E. (2019). Robert Boyle on the Importance of Reporting and Replicating Experiments. *Illustrating the Development of Fair Tests of Treatments in Health Care*. The James Lind Library. www.jameslindlibrary.org/articles/robert-boyle-on-the-importance-of-reporting-and-replicating-experiments/

Blackbaud. (2020). Security Incident. Blackbaud, September 29. See www.blackbaud.com/securityincident

Bloom, B. S. (1984). The 2 Sigma Problem: The Search for Methods of Group Instruction as Effective as One-to-One Tutoring. *Educational Researcher*, 13(6), 4–16. https://doi.org/10.3102/0013189X013006004

Bogetoft, P., Christensen, D. L., Damgård, I., et al. (2009). Secure Multiparty Computation Goes Live. In R. Dingledine & P. Golle, eds., *Financial Cryptography and Data Security, Revised Selected Papers, 13th International Conference, FC 2009*, Accra Beach, Barbados, February 23–26, 2009 (Lecture Notes in Computer Science, 5628), Springer, pp. 325–343. https://doi.org/10.1007/978-3-642-03549-4_20

Bonifacic, I. (2020). Artist Creates Traffic Jams in Google Maps With a Wagon Full of Phones. *Engadget*, February 3. www.engadget.com/2020-02-03-google-maps-traffic-jams-art-project.html

Boston University School of Public Health. (2016). John Snow – The Father of Epidemiology. MPH Online Learning Modules. https://sphweb.bumc.bu.edu/otlt/mph-modules/ph/publichealthhistory/publichealthhistory6.html

Bostrom, N. (2014). *Superintelligence: Paths, Dangers, Strategies*. Oxford University Press. https://global.oup.com/academic/product/superintelligence-9780199678112?cc=us&lang=en&

Box, G. E. P. (1979). Robustness in the Strategy of Scientific Model Building. In R. L. Launer & G. N. Wilkinson, eds., *Robustness in Statistics*, Academic Press, pp. 201–236. https://doi.org/10.1016/C2013-0-11050-1

Box, G. E. P., Hunter, J. S., & Hunter, W. G. (2005). *Statistics for Experimenters: Design, Innovation, and Discovery*. Wiley-Interscience. www.worldcat.org/title/statistics-for-experimenters-design-innovation-and-discovery/oclc/474755360

boyd, d. m. & Ellison, N. B. (2007). Social Network Sites: Definition, History, and Scholarship. *Journal of Computer-Mediated Communication: JCMC*, 13(1), 210–230. https://doi.org/10.1111/j.1083-6101.2007.00393.x

Brand, S. (2000). *Is Technology Moving Too Fast?* The Long Now Foundation, June 19. https://longnow.org/essays/technology-moving-too-fast/

Breiman, L. (2001). Statistical Modeling: The Two Cultures (With Comments and a Rejoinder by the Author). *Statistical Science*, 16(3), 199–231. https://doi.org/10.1214/ss/1009213726

Brill, J. (2020). *Technology, Society and the State: How Do We Remain Competitive, and True to Our Values, as the Technological Revolution Unfolds and Accelerates? The Ditchley Foundation Meeting on Technology, Society and the State*, Chipping Norton, UK. www.ditchley.com/programme/past-events/2020/technology-society-and-state-how-do-we-remain-competitive-and-true-our

Brin, S. & Page, L. (1998). The Anatomy of a Large-Scale Hypertextual Web Search Engine. *Computer Networks and ISDN Systems*, 30(1–7), 107–117. https://doi.org/10.1016/s0169-7552(98)00110-x

Broder, A. (2002). A Taxonomy of Web Search. *ACM SIGIR Forum*, 36(2), 3–10. https://doi.org/10.1145/792550.792552

Brown, T. B., Mann, B., Ryder, N., et al. (2020). Language Models Are Few-Shot Learners. arXiv [cs.CL]. http://arxiv.org/abs/2005.14165

Bryan, C. J., Tipton, E., & Yeager, D. S. (2021). Behavioural Science Is Unlikely to Change the World Without a Heterogeneity Revolution. *Nature Human Behaviour*, 5(8), 980–989. https://doi.org/10.1038/s41562-021-01143-3

Brynjolfsson, E., Eggers, F., & Gannamaneni, A. (2018). *Using Massive Online Choice Experiments to Measure Changes in Well-being* (Working Paper Series No. 24514). National Bureau of Economic Research. https://doi.org/10.3386/w24514

Bryson, S. (1996). Virtual Reality in Scientific Visualization. *Communications of the ACM*, 39(5), 62–71. https://doi.org/10.1145/229459.229467

Bubar, K. M., Reinholt, K., Kissler, S. M., et al. (2021). Model-Informed COVID-19 Vaccine Prioritization Strategies by Age and Serostatus. *Science*, 371(6532), 916–921. https://doi.org/10.1126/science.abe6959

Bunnik, E. M., Janssens, A. C. J. W., & Schermer, M. H. N. (2013). A Tiered-Layered-Staged Model for Informed Consent in Personal Genome Testing. *European Journal of Human Genetics*, 21(6), 596–601. https://doi.org/10.1038/ejhg.2012.237

Candès, E., Fan, Y., Janson, L., & Lv, J. (2018). Panning for Gold: "Model-X" Knockoffs for High Dimensional Controlled Variable Selection. *Journal of the Royal Statistical Society. Series B, Statistical Methodology*, 80(3), 551–577. https://doi.org/10.1111/rssb.12265

Cannell, J. J. (2006). "Lake Woebegone," Twenty Years Later. *Independent Education Review*, 2(1). www.researchgate.net/publication/24089508_Lake_Woebegone_Twenty_Years_Later

Card, S. K., Mackinlay, J., & Shneiderman, B. (1999). *Readings in Information Visualization: Using Vision to Think*. Morgan Kaufmann. https://books.google.com/books/about/Readings_in_Information_Visualization.html?hl=&id=wdh2gqWfQmgC

Carlyle, T. (1841). *On Heroes, Hero-Worship, & the Heroic in History: Six Lectures; Reported, With Emendations and Additions*. James Fraser. www.worldcat.org/title/on-heroes-hero-worship-the-heroic-in-history-six-lectures-reported-with-emendations-and-additions/oclc/2158602

Carr, N. (2008). Is Google Making Us Stupid? *The Atlantic*, July. www.theatlantic.com/magazine/archive/2008/07/is-google-making-us-stupid/306868/

Carr, N. (2014). *The Glass Cage: How Our Computers Are Changing Us*. W. W. Norton. https://wwnorton.com/books/the-glass-cage/

Carter, B., Jain, S., Mueller, J., & Gifford, D. (2021). Overinterpretation Reveals Image Classification Model Pathologies. arXiv [cs.LG]. https://arxiv.org/pdf/2003.08907v3

CCC (Computer Community Consortium). (n.d.). CCC/ACM SIGAI/INFORMS Workshop 1 Report Out – Artificial Intelligence & Operations Research (November 2021). *Artificial Intelligence/Operations Research Workshop*, September 23–24, 2021. https://cra.org/crn/2021/11/ccc-acm-sigai-informs-workshop-1-report-out-artificial-intelligence-operations-research/

CDC. (2020). COVID Data Tracker. Centers for Disease Control and Prevention (CDC), March 28. https://covid.cdc.gov/covid-data-tracker/

CDC. (2021). V-safe After Vaccination Health Checker. Centers for Disease Control and Prevention (CDC), November 10. www.cdc.gov/coronavirus/2019-ncov/vaccines/safety/vsafe.html

Center for Humane Technology. (n.d.). How Social Media Hacks Our Brains. *Brain Science*. Retrieved January 17, 2022, from www.humanetech.com/brain-science

Chatfield, T. (n.d.). The Trouble With Big Data? It's Called the "Recency Bias." BBC. Retrieved December 20, 2021, from www.bbc.com/future/article/20160605-the-trouble-with-big-data-its-called-the-recency-bias

Chatzimparmpas, A., Martins, R. M., Jusufi, I., & Kerren, A. (2020). A Survey of Surveys on the Use of Visualization for Interpreting Machine Learning Models. *Information Visualization*, 19(3), 207–233. https://doi.org/10.1177/1473871620904671

Cheeseman, P. (1985). In Defense of Probability. *Proceedings of the 9th International Joint Conference on Artificial Intelligence*, vol. 2, pp. 1002–1009. https://dl.acm.org/doi/abs/10.5555/1623611.1623677

Chen, J. (2021). Risk-Adjusted Return Definition. Investopedia, November 30. www.investopedia.com/terms/r/riskadjustedreturn.asp

Chen, M., Tworek, J., Jun, H., et al. (2021). Evaluating Large Language Models Trained on Code. arXiv [cs.LG]. http://arxiv.org/abs/2107.03374

Chen, M. X., Lee, B. N., Bansal, G., et al. (2019). Gmail Smart Compose: Real-Time Assisted Writing. arXiv [cs.CL]. http://arxiv.org/abs/1906.00080

Chiang, Y.-K., Makiya, R., Ménard, B., & Komatsu, E. (2020). The Cosmic Thermal History Probed by Sunyaev–Zeldovich Effect Tomography. *Astrophysical Journal*, 902(1), 56. https://doi.org/10.3847/1538-4357/abb403

Choi, H. & Varian, H. (2012). Predicting the Present With Google Trends. *Economic Record*, 88, 2–9. https://doi.org/10.1111/j.1475-4932.2012.00809.x

Chouldechova, A. (2017). Fair Prediction with Disparate Impact: A Study of Bias in Recidivism Prediction Instruments. *Big Data*, 5(2), 153–163. https://doi.org/10.1089/big.2016.0047

Chouldechova, A. & Roth, A. (2020). A Snapshot of the Frontiers of Fairness in Machine Learning. *Communications of the ACM*, 63(5), 82–89. https://doi.org/10.1145/3376898

Churchman, C. (1967). Free for All – Wicked Problems. *Management Science*, 14(4), B141–B146. https://doi.org/10.1287/mnsc.14.4.B141

Cicero. (n.d.). *Cicero: On the Orator*, Books I–II (English and Latin Edition), E. W. Sutton & H. Rackham, transl. (Loeb Classical Library No. 348), 1948. Harvard University Press. www.amazon.com/Cicero-Orator-Classical-Library-English/dp/0674993837

Claussnitzer, M., Dankel, S. N., Kim, K.-H., et al. (2015). FTO Obesity Variant Circuitry and Adipocyte Browning in Humans. *New England Journal of Medicine*, 373(10), 895–907. https://doi.org/10.1056/NEJMoa1502214

Clifford Chance & Milltown Partners. (2021). Our Relationship With AI: Friend or Foe? Summary of Our Global Study, November 9. Clifford Chance. www.cliffordchance.com/briefings/2021/11/our-relationship-with-ai–friend-or-foe–summary-of-our-global-s.html

Coenen, A. (2019). How The New York Times is Experimenting with Recommendation Algorithms. *NYT Open*, October 17. https://open.nytimes.com/how-the-new-york-times-is-experimenting-with-recommendation-algorithms-562f78624d26

Collins, F. S. (n.d.). Genome-Wide Association Studies (GWAS). Retrieved December 14, 2021, from www.genome.gov/genetics-glossary/Genome-Wide-Association-Studies

Concorde. (n.d.). Concorde TSP Solver (The Traveling Salesman Problem). Retrieved December 27, 2021, from www.math.uwaterloo.ca/tsp/concorde/index.html

Connelly, M. J., Hicks, R., Jervis, R., Spirling, A., & Suong, C. H. (2021). Diplomatic Documents Data for International Relations: The Freedom of Information Archive Database. *Conflict Management and Peace Science*, 38(6), 762–781. https://doi.org/10.1177/0738894220930326

Cook, W. (2012). *In Pursuit of the Traveling Salesman: Mathematics at the Limits of Computation*. Princeton University Press. https://press.princeton.edu/books/paperback/9780691163529/in-pursuit-of-the-traveling-salesman

Corrigan, J. R., Alhabash, S., Rousu, M., & Cash, S. B. (2018). How Much is Social Media Worth? Estimating the Value of Facebook by Paying Users to Stop Using It. *PloS One*, 13(12), e0207101. https://doi.org/10.1371/journal.pone.0207101

Costa, B. (2016). Golfers Join the Rest of World, Use Data. *Wall Street Journal (Eastern Edn.)*, May 16. www.wsj.com/articles/golfers-join-rest-of-world-use-data-1463434676

COVID-19 Forecast Hub. (n.d.). COVID19 Forecast Hub Home page. Retrieved December 13, 2021, from http://covid19forecasthub.org

Cox, M. & Ellsworth, D. (1997). Managing Big Data for Scientific Visualization. *ACM Siggraph '97 Course #4, Exploring Gigabyte Datasets in Real-Time: Algorithms, Data Management, and Time-Critical Design*, pp. 21–38. www.researchgate.net/profile/David-Ellsworth-2/publication/238704525_Managing_big_data_for_scientific_visualization/links/54ad79d20cf2213c5fe4081a/Managing-big-data-for-scientific-visualization.pdf

Cramer, E. Y., Ray, E. L., Lopez, V. K., et al. (2021). Evaluation of Individual and Ensemble Probabilistic Forecasts of COVID-19 Mortality in the US. medRxiv. www.medrxiv.org/content/10.1101/2021.02.03.21250974v3

Dartmouth. (2018). Artificial Intelligence (AI) Coined at Dartmouth – Celebrate Our 250th, October 12. Dartmouth College. https://250.dartmouth.edu/highlights/artificial-intelligence-ai-coined-dartmouth

Data Transfer Project. (n.d.). About Us. Retrieved March 9, 2022, from https://datatransfer project.dev/

Datta, A., Tschantz, M. C., & Datta, A. (2015). Automated Experiments on Ad Privacy Settings: A Tale of Opacity, Choice, and Discrimination. arXiv [cs.CR]. https://arxiv.org/abs/1408.6491v2

Davis, J. (2020). *Blackbaud Confirms Hackers Stole Some SSNs, as Lawsuits Increase*, September 30. HealthITSecurity. https://healthitsecurity.com/news/blackbaud-confirms-hackers-stole-some-ssns-as-lawsuits-increase

DeMarco, T. (2002). *Slack: Getting Past Burnout, Busywork, and the Myth of Total Efficiency*. Broadway Books.

Deng, L., Hinton, G., & Kingsbury, B. (2013, May). New Types of Deep Neural Network Learning for Speech Recognition and Related Applications: An Overview. *2013 IEEE International Conference on Acoustics, Speech and Signal Processing, ICASSP 2013*, Vancouver, BC, Canada. https://doi.org/10.1109/icassp.2013.6639344

Devlin, J., Chang, M.-W., Lee, K., & Toutanova, K. (2019). BERT: Pre-Training of Deep Bidirectional Transformers for Language Understanding. arXiv [cs.CL]. http://arxiv.org/abs/1810.04805

DHS Privacy Office. (2017). *Handbook for Safeguarding Sensitive PII* (Privacy Policy Directive 047-01-007, Revision 3). US Department of Homeland Security (DHS). www.dhs.gov/sites/default/files/publications/dhs%20policy%20directive%20047-01-007%20handbook%20for%20safeguarding%20sensitive%20PII%2012-4-2017.pdf

Diamond, J. (2020). The World Series-Bound Rays Epitomize Baseball in 2020 – For Better or for Worse. *Wall Street Journal (Eastern Edn.)*, October 18. www.wsj.com/articles/the-world-series-bound-rays-epitomize-baseball-in-2020for-better-or-for-worse-11603022401

Dieterich, W., Mendoza, C., & Brennan, T. (2016). *COMPAS Risk Scales: Demonstrating Accuracy Equity and Predictive Parity Performance of the COMPAS Risk Scales in Broward County*. Northpointe Inc. Research Department. http://go.volarisgroup.com/rs/430-MBX-989/images/ProPublica_Commentary_Final_070616.pdf

Dietz, K. & Heesterbeek, J. A. P. (2002). Daniel Bernoulli's Epidemiological Model Revisited. *Mathematical Biosciences*, 180(1–2), 1–21. https://doi.org/10.1016/s0025-5564(02)00122-0

Donoho, D. (2017). 50 Years of Data Science. *Journal of Computational and Graphical Statistics*, 26(4), 745–766. https://doi.org/10.1080/10618600.2017.1384734

Dorman, C. (2018). Building the Next Generation of Personalized Themed Playlists. *Algorithm and Blues*, May 23. https://engineering.pandora.com/building-the-next-generation-of-personalized-themed-playlists-43f567b964f9

Druckman, J. N. (2001). Using Credible Advice to Overcome Framing Effects. *Journal of Law, Economics, & Organization*, 17(1), 62–82. https://doi.org/10.1093/jleo/17.1.62

Ducato, R. (2020). Data Protection, Scientific Research, and the Role of Information. *Computer Law & Security Review*, 37, 105412. https://doi.org/10.1016/j.clsr.2020.105412

Duhigg, C. (2012). How Companies Learn Your Secrets. *The New York Times*, February 16. www.nytimes.com/2012/02/19/magazine/shopping-habits.html

Dwork, C. (2008). Differential Privacy: A Survey of Results. In M. Agrawal, D. Du, Z. Duan, & A. Li, eds., *Theory and Applications of Models of Computation* (Lecture Notes in Computer Science, 4978), Springer, pp. 1–19. https://doi.org/10.1007/978-3-540-79228-4_1

Dwork, C. & Roth, A. (2014). The Algorithmic Foundations of Differential Privacy. *Foundations and Trends in Theoretical Computer Science*, 9(3–4), 211–407. https://doi.org/10.1561/0400000042

Dwork, C., Hardt, M., Pitassi, T., Reingold, O., & Zemel, R. (2012). Fairness Through Awareness. *Proceedings of the 3rd Innovations in Theoretical Computer Science Conference – ITCS '12*, pp. 214–226. https://doi.org/10.1145/2090236.2090255

Eckhouse, L., Lum, K., Conti-Cook, C., & Ciccolini, J. (2019). Layers of Bias: A Unified Approach for Understanding Problems With Risk Assessment. *Criminal Justice and Behavior*, 46(2), 185–209. https://doi.org/10.1177/0093854818811379

Economist, The. (2013). How Science Goes Wrong. *The Economist*, October 17. www.economist.com/leaders/2013/10/21/how-science-goes-wrong

Economist, The. (2021a). Tracking Covid-19 Excess Deaths Across Countries. *The Economist*, October 20. www.economist.com/graphic-detail/coronavirus-excess-deaths-tracker

Economist, The. (2021b). Instant Economics: The Real-Time Revolution. *The Economist*, October 23. www.economist.com/weeklyedition/2021-10-23

Economist, The. (2022a). The Growing Demand for More Vigorous Antitrust Action. *The Economist*, January 7. www.economist.com/special-report/2022/01/10/the-growing-demand-for-more-vigorous-antitrust-action

Economist, The. (2022b). Predicting Earthquakes Is Not Possible. Yet. *The Economist*, January 12. www.economist.com/science-and-technology/predicting-earthquakes-is-not-possible-yet/21807129

Einav, L. & Levin, J. (2014). Economics in the Age of Big Data. *Science*, 346(6210), 1243089. https://doi.org/10.1126/science.1243089

Eisenstadt, L. (2017). *After a Decade of Genome-Wide Association Studies, a New Phase of Discovery Pushes On*, August 14. Broad Institute. www.broadinstitute.org/news/after-decade-genome-wide-association-studies-new-phase-discovery-pushes

El-Bermawy, M. M. (2016). Your Filter Bubble is Destroying Democracy. *Wired*, November 18. www.wired.com/2016/11/filter-bubble-destroying-democracy/

Ellison, A. M., Boose, E. R., Lerner, B. S., Fong, E., & Seltzer, M. (2020). The End-to-End Provenance Project. *Patterns*, 1(2), 100016. https://doi.org/10.1016/j.patter.2020.100016

Engineers Yukon. (n.d.). Code of Ethics. Engineers Canada. Retrieved April 7, 2022, from https://engineerscanada.ca/sites/default/files/Yukon/APEY_Code_Of_Ethics.pdf

Eriksson, J., Girod, L., Hull, B., et al. (2008). The Pothole Patrol: Using a Mobile Sensor Network for Road Surface Monitoring, *Proceedings of the 6th International*

Conference on Mobile Systems, Applications, and Services, pp. 29–39. https://doi.org/10.1145/1378600.1378605

Esteva, A., Kuprel, B., Novoa, R. A., et al. (2017). Dermatologist-Level Classification of Skin Cancer with Deep Neural Networks. *Nature*, 542(7639), 115–118. https://doi.org/10.1038/nature21056

European Commission High-Level Expert Group on AI. (2019). *Ethics Guidelines for Trustworthy AI*. European Commission. https://digital-strategy.ec.europa.eu/en/library/ethics-guidelines-trustworthy-ai

European Parliament and Council of the European Union. (2016). Regulation EU 2016/679 of the European Parliament and of the Council of 27 April 2016 (General Data Protection Regulation). *Official Journal of the European Union*. https://eur-lex.europa.eu/legal-content/EN/TXT/PDF/?uri=CELEX:32016R0679

Facebook Help Center. (n.d.). What Categories of My Facebook Data Are Available to Me? Facebook. Retrieved December 16, 2021, from www.facebook.com/help/930396167085762

FASB. (n.d.). FASB Home page. Financial Accounting Standards Board. Retrieved December 23, 2021, from www.fasb.org/home

Fiesler, C., Young, A., Peyton, T., et al. (2015). Ethics for Studying Online Sociotechnical Systems in a Big Data World. *Proceedings of the 18th ACM Conference Companion on Computer Supported Cooperative Work & Social Computing, CSCW '15*, February 28, Vancouver, BC, Canada. https://doi.org/10.1145/2685553.2685558

FINRA. (n.d.). Rules & Guidance. FINRA Financial Industry Regulatory Authority, Inc. Retrieved December 23, 2021, from www.finra.org/rules-guidance

Fisher, R. A. (1935). *The Design of Experiments*. Oliver and Boyd. www.worldcat.org/title/design-of-experiments/oclc/905516590

Fletcher, R. (2020). *The Truth Behind Filter Bubbles: Bursting Some Myths*, January 24. Reuters Institute for the Study of Journalism. https://reutersinstitute.politics.ox.ac.uk/news/truth-behind-filter-bubbles-bursting-some-myths

Fletcher, R., Kalogeropoulos, A., & Nielsen, R. K. (2021). More Diverse, More Politically Varied: How Social Media, Search Engines and Aggregators Shape News Repertoires in the United Kingdom. *New Media & Society*, 22. https://doi.org/10.1177/14614448211027393

Frazier, P. I. (2022). Fighting the Pandemic With Mathematical Modeling: A Case Study at Cornell University. *The Bridge – Linking Engineering and Society*, 51(4), 18–22. www.nae.edu/266395/Fighting-the-Pandemic-with-Mathematical-Modeling-A-Case-Study-at-Cornell-University

Galbraith, J. K. (1967). *The New Industrial State*. Houghton Mifflin. www.google.com/books/edition/_/gH1eAAAAIAAJ?hl=en&sa=X&ved=2ahUKEwi2vbLD98P1AhUjIkQIHbV1DjgQre8FegQIAxBC

Gallagher, J. (2021). Covid: Trigger of Rare Blood Clots With AstraZeneca Jab Found by Scientists, December 2. BBC. www.bbc.com/news/health-59418123

Garcia-Retamero, R., Galesic, M., & Gigerenzer, G. (2010). Do Icon Arrays Help Reduce Denominator Neglect? *Medical Decision Making*, 30(6), 672–684. https://doi.org/10.1177/0272989X10369000

Gawande, A. (2009). *The Checklist Manifesto: How to Get Things Right*. Picador. https://us.macmillan.com/books/9780312430009/thechecklistmanifesto

Gebru, T., Morgenstern, J., Vecchione, B., et al. (2021). Datasheets for Datasets. *Communications of the ACM*, 64(12), 86–92. https://doi.org/10.1145/3458723

Gee, J., Marquez, P., Su, J., et al. (2021). First Month of COVID-19 Vaccine Safety Monitoring – United States, December 14, 2020–January 13, 2021. *Morbidity and*

Mortality Weekly Report (MMWR), 70(8), 283–288. https://doi.org/10.15585/mmwr.mm7008e3

Gelman, A. & Carpenter, B. (2020). Bayesian Analysis of Tests with Unknown Specificity and Sensitivity. *Journal of the Royal Statistical Society. Series C, Applied Statistics*, 69(5), 1269–1283. https://doi.org/10.1111/rssc.12435

Gelman, A. & Loken, E. (2013). The Garden of Forking Paths: Why Multiple Comparisons Can Be a Problem, Even When There is no "Fishing Expedition" or "p-hacking" and The Research Hypothesis Was Posited Ahead of Time. www.stat.columbia.edu/~gelman/research/unpublished/p_hacking.pdf

Gelman, A. & Loken, E. (2016). The Statistical Crisis in Science. In M. Pitici, ed., *The Best Writing on Mathematics 2015*, Princeton University Press, pp. 305–318. https://doi.org/10.1515/9781400873371-028

Gentry, C. (2009). Fully Homomorphic Encryption Using Ideal Lattices. *Proceedings of the Forty-First Annual ACM Symposium on Theory of Computing*, pp. 169–178. https://doi.org/10.1145/1536414.1536440

Ginsberg, J., Mohebbi, M. H., Patel, R. S., et al. (2009). Detecting Influenza Epidemics Using Search Engine Query Data. *Nature*, 457(7232), 1012–1014. https://doi.org/10.1038/nature07634

Gitlin, J. M. (2017). Hacking Street Signs With Stickers Could Confuse Self-Driving Cars. Ars Technica. https://arstechnica.com/cars/2017/09/hacking-street-signs-with-stickers-could-confuse-self-driving-cars/

Global Change Data Lab. (n.d.). Our World in Data. Retrieved December 10, 2021, from https://ourworldindata.org/

Goodfellow, I. J., Shlens, J., & Szegedy, C. (2015). Explaining and Harnessing Adversarial Examples. arXiv [stat.ML]. http://arxiv.org/abs/1412.6572

Google. (n.d.-a). COVID-19 Community Mobility Reports [Dataset]. Retrieved December 14, 2021, from www.google.com/covid19/mobility/

Google. (n.d.-b). How Google Anonymizes Data – Privacy & Terms – Google. Retrieved December 15, 2021, from https://policies.google.com/technologies/anonymization

Google. (n.d.-c). Google Transparency Report. Retrieved December 16, 2021, from https://transparencyreport.google.com/user-data/overview

Google Books. (2010). Google Ngram Viewer. https://books.google.com/ngrams

Google, Inc. (n.d.). Google Takeout. Google Account. Retrieved December 16, 2021, from https://takeout.google.com/

Gootman, S. (2016). OPM Hack: The Most Dangerous Threat to the Federal Government Today. *Journal of Applied Security Research*, 11(4), 517–525. https://doi.org/10.1080/19361610.2016.1211876

Gostin, L. O., Salmon, D. A., & Larson, H. J. (2021). Mandating COVID-19 Vaccines. *Journal of the American Medical Association*, 325(6), 532–533. https://doi.org/10.1001/jama.2020.26553

Gotterbarn, D., Brinkman, B., Flick, C., et al. (2018). *A Guide for Positive Action*. Association for Computing Machinery. https://doi.org/10.1145/3274591

Gray, J. (2009). Jim Gray on eScience: A Transformed Scientific Method. In A. Hey, S. Tansley, & K. Tolle, eds., *The Fourth Paradigm: Data-Intensive Scientific Discovery*, Microsoft Research, pp. xvii–xxxi. www.microsoft.com/en-us/research/publication/fourth-paradigm-data-intensive-scientific-discovery/

Greengard, S. (2019). Will Deepfakes Do Deep Damage? *Communications of the ACM*, 63(1), 17–19. https://doi.org/10.1145/3371409

Hale, J. (2019). More Than 500 Hours of Content Are Now Being Uploaded to YouTube Every Minute, May 7. Tubefilter. www.tubefilter.com/2019/05/07/number-hours-video-uploaded-to-youtube-per-minute/

Halevy, A., Norvig, P., & Pereira, F. (2009). The Unreasonable Effectiveness of Data. *IEEE Intelligent Systems*, 24(2), 8–12. https://doi.org/10.1109/mis.2009.36

Hansen, M. (2019). The Reporter's Notebook, *Jupytercon 2018*, New York, March 21. Youtube. www.youtube.com/watch?v=IzUEWgC7-Ls

Hardt, M., Price, E., & Srebro, N. (2016). Equality of Opportunity in Supervised Learning. arXiv [cs.LG]. http://arxiv.org/abs/1610.02413

Harford, T. (2021). *The Data Detective: Ten Easy Rules to Make Sense of Statistics*. Riverhead Books. www.penguinrandomhouse.com/books/610963/the-data-detective-by-tim-harford/

He, X., Madigan, D., Yu, B., & Wellner, J. (2019). *Statistics at a Crossroads: Who Is for the Challenge?* National Science Foundation. www.nsf.gov/mps/dms/documents/Statistics_at_a_Crossroads_Workshop_Report_2019.pdf

Heckerman, D. E., Horvitz, E. J., & Nathwani, B. N. (1992). Toward Normative Expert Systems: Part I. The Pathfinder Project. *Methods of Information in Medicine*, 31(2), 90–105. www.ncbi.nlm.nih.gov/pubmed/1635470

Held, M. & Karp, R. M. (1962). A Dynamic Programming Approach to Sequencing Problems. *Journal of the Society for Industrial and Applied Mathematics*, 10(1), 196–210. https://doi.org/10.1137/0110015

Hicks, J. R. (1935). Annual Survey of Economic Theory: The Theory of Monopoly. *Econometrica*, 3(1), 1–20. https://doi.org/10.2307/1907343

Hinton, G. E., Osindero, S., & Teh, Y.-W. (2006). A Fast Learning Algorithm for Deep Belief Nets. *Neural Computation*, 18(7), 1527–1554. https://doi.org/10.1162/neco.2006.18.7.1527

Hinton, G., Deng, L., Yu, D., et al. (2012). Deep Neural Networks for Acoustic Modeling in Speech Recognition: The Shared Views of Four Research Groups. *IEEE Signal Processing Magazine*, 29(6), 82–97. https://doi.org/10.1109/MSP.2012.2205597

Hripcsak, G., Duke, J. D., Shah, N. H., et al. (2015). Observational Health Data Sciences and Informatics (OHDSI): Opportunities for Observational Researchers. *Studies in Health Technology and Informatics*, 216, 574–578. www.ncbi.nlm.nih.gov/pmc/articles/PMC4815923/

Hripcsak, G., Ryan, P. B., Duke, J. D., et al. (2016). Characterizing Treatment Pathways at Scale Using the OHDSI Network. *Proceedings of the National Academy of Sciences of the United States of America*, 113(27), 7329–7336. https://doi.org/10.1073/pnas.1510502113

Hripcsak, G., Suchard, M. A., Shea, S., et al. (2020). Comparison of Cardiovascular and Safety Outcomes of Chlorthalidone vs Hydrochlorothiazide to Treat Hypertension. *JAMA Internal Medicine*, 180(4), 542–551. https://doi.org/10.1001/jamainternmed.2019.7454

Huff, D. (1993). *How to Lie With Statistics* (Reissue edition; original work published 1954). W. W. Norton. https://wwnorton.com/books/How-to-Lie-with-Statistics/

Hullman, J. (2020). Why Authors Don't Visualize Uncertainty. *IEEE Transactions on Visualization and Computer Graphics*, 26(1), 130–139. https://doi.org/10.1109/TVCG.2019.2934287

Institute for Operations Research and the Management Sciences (INFORMS). (n.d.). INFORMS Ethics Guidelines. INFORMS. Retrieved December 11, 2021, from www.informs.org/About-INFORMS/Governance/INFORMS-Ethics-Guidelines

Institute of Medicine of the National Academies. (2009). *Beyond the HIPAA Privacy Rule: Enhancing Privacy, Improving Health Through Research*. S. J. Nass, L. A. Levit, & L. O. Gostin, eds., National Academies Press. https://doi.org/10.17226/12458

Ioannidis, J. P. A. (2005). Why Most Published Research Findings Are False. *PLoS Medicine*, 2(8), e124. https://doi.org/10.1371/journal.pmed.0020124

Ion, M., Kreuter, B., Nergiz, E., et al. (2017). Private Intersection-Sum Protocol with Applications to Attributing Aggregate Ad Conversions. *Cryptology ePrint Archive*, Report 2017/738. https://eprint.iacr.org/2017/738.pdf

Jacob, R., Zhu, P., Somers, M.-A., & Bloom, H. (2012). A Practical Guide to Regression Discontinuity. MDRC. https://eric.ed.gov/?id=ED565862

Johnson, A. G., Amin, A. B., Ali, A. R., et al. (2022). COVID-19 Incidence and Death Rates Among Unvaccinated and Fully Vaccinated Adults With and Without Booster Doses During Periods of Delta and Omicron Variant Emergence – 25 U.S. Jurisdictions, April 4–December 25, 2021. *Morbidity and Mortality Weekly Report (MMWR)*, 71(4), 132–138. https://doi.org/10.15585/mmwr.mm7104e2

Jouppi, N. P., Young, C., Patil, N., et al. (2017). In-Datacenter Performance Analysis of a Tensor Processing Unit. *Proceedings of the 44th Annual International Symposium on Computer Architecture*, pp. 1–12. https://doi.org/10.1145/3079856.3080246

Juang, B. H. & Rabiner, L. R. (2005). Automatic Speech Recognition – A Brief History of the Technology Development. https://web.ece.ucsb.edu/Faculty/Rabiner/ece259/Reprints/354_LALI-ASRHistory-final-10-8.pdf

Jumper, J., Evans, R., Pritzel, A., et al. (2021). Highly Accurate Protein Structure Prediction with AlphaFold. *Nature*, 596(7873), 583–589. https://doi.org/10.1038/s41586-021-03819-2

Jurafsky, D. & Martin, J. H. (2009). *Speech and Language Processing*, 2nd edn. Pearson. www.pearson.com/us/higher-education/program/Jurafsky-Speech-and-Language-Processing-2nd-Edition/PGM181706.html

Kahneman, D. & Tversky, A. (1996). On the Reality of Cognitive Illusions. *Psychological Review*, 103(3),582–591; Discussion 592–596. https://doi.org/10.1037/0033-295x.103.3.582

Kamara, S., Mohassel, P., Raykova, M., & Sadeghian, S. (2014). Scaling Private Set Intersection to Billion-Element Sets. In *Financial Cryptography and Data Security*, Springer, pp. 195–215. https://doi.org/10.1007/978-3-662-45472-5_13

Katz, L. (2019). *Evaluation of the Moore–Sloan Data Science Environments*. Alfred P. Sloan Foundation; Gordon and Betty Moore Foundation. http://msdse.org/files/MSDSE_Eval_Final_Report_Feb_2019_v2.pdf

Kennedy, L. (2019). Did Yellow Journalism Fuel the Outbreak of the Spanish–American War? *History*, August 21. www.history.com/news/spanish-american-war-yellow-journalism-hearst-pulitzer

Kirschenbaum, M. (2012). What is Digital Humanities and What's It Doing in English Departments? In M. K. Gold, ed., *Debates in the Digital Humanities*, University of Minnesota Press, pp. 3–11. https://doi.org/10.5749/minnesota/9780816677948.003.0001

Kissinger, H. A., Schmidt, E., & Huttenlocher, D. (2021). *The Age of AI: And Our Human Future*. Little, Brown. www.littlebrown.com/titles/henry-a-kissinger/the-age-of-ai/9780316273800/

Kleinberg, J., Mullainathan, S., & Raghavan, M. (2017). Inherent Trade-offs in the Fair Determination of Risk Scores. In C. H. Papadimitriou, ed., *8th Innovations in Theoretical Computer Science Conference (ITCS 2017)* (Leibniz International Proceedings in Informatics, vol. 67), Schloss Dagstuhl, pp. 43:1–43:23. https://doi.org/10.4230/LIPIcs.ITCS.2017.43

Kleinberg, J., Lakkaraju, H., Leskovec, J., Ludwig, J., & Mullainathan, S. (2018). Human Decisions and Machine Predictions. *Quarterly Journal of Economics*, 133(1), 287–293. https://doi.org/10.3386/w23180

Kleinberg, J., Ludwig, J., Mullainathan, S., & Sunstein, C. R. (2019). Discrimination in the Age of Algorithms. *Journal of Legal Analysis*, 10, 113–174. https://doi.org/10.1093/jla/laz001

Kliff, S. & Bhatia, A. (2022). These Prenatal Tests Are Usually Wrong When Warning of Rare Disorders. *The New York Times*, January 1. www.nytimes.com/2022/01/01/upshot/pregnancy-birth-genetic-testing.html

Knight, W. (2017). The Dark Secret at the Heart of AI. *Technology Review*, 120(3), 54–61. www.technologyreview.com/2017/04/11/5113/the-dark-secret-at-the-heart-of-ai/

Knight, W. (2021). Clearview AI Has New Tools to Identify You in Photos. *Wired*, October 4. www.wired.com/story/clearview-ai-new-tools-identify-you-photos/

Knorr, E. (2021). CSO Global Intelligence Report: The State of Cybersecurity in 2021, July 30. CSO Online. www.csoonline.com/article/3627274/cso-global-intelligence-report-the-state-of-cybersecurity-in-2021.html

Koenig, F. (2020). Technology Can Benefit a Few Superstar Workers, at the Expense of Everyone Else. *LSE Business Review*, February 29. https://blogs.lse.ac.uk/businessreview/2020/02/29/technology-can-benefit-a-few-superstar-workers-at-the-expense-of-everyone-else/

Kohavi, R., Tang, D., & Xu, Y. (2020). *Trustworthy Online Controlled Experiments: A Practical Guide to A/B Testing*. Cambridge University Press. https://doi.org/10.1017/9781108653985

Korinek, A. & Ng, D. X. (2017). The Macroeconomics of Superstars. *5th IMF Statistical Forum*, November, Washington, DC. www.imf.org/-/media/Files/Conferences/2017-stats-forum/session-3-korinek.ashx

Kost, R. G., Corregano, L. M., Rainer, T.-L., Melendez, C., & Coller, B. S. (2015). A Data-Rich Recruitment Core to Support Translational Clinical Research. *Clinical and Translational Science*, 8(2), 91–99. https://doi.org/10.1111/cts.12240

Kozyrkov, C. (2018). What on Earth is Data Science? HackerNoon, August. https://medium.com/hackernoon/what-on-earth-is-data-science-eb1237d8cb37

Kramer, A. D. I. (2012). The Spread of Emotion via Facebook. *Proceedings of the SIGCHI Conference on Human Factors in Computing Systems*, Austin, Texas, USA. https://doi.org/10.1145/2207676.2207787

Krizhevsky, A., Sutskever, I., & Hinton, G. E. (2012). ImageNet Classification With Deep Convolutional Neural Networks. In P. Bartlett, ed., *Advances in Neural Information Processing Systems*, pp. 1097–1105. https://doi.org/10.1.1.299.205

Lane, J. C. E., Weaver, J., Kostka, K., et al. (2020). Risk of Hydroxychloroquine Alone and in Combination With Azithromycin in the Treatment of Rheumatoid Arthritis: A Multinational, Retrospective Study. *The Lancet. Rheumatology*, 2(11), E698–E711. https://doi.org/10.1016/S2665-9913(20)30276-9

Lapets, A., Volgushev, N., Bestavros, A., Jansen, F., & Varia, M. (2016). Secure MPC for Analytics as a Web Application. *2016 IEEE Cybersecurity Development (SecDev)*, Boston, MA, USA, November. https://doi.org/10.1109/secdev.2016.027

Layton, R. (2019). The 10 Problems of the GDPR. Statement before the Senate Judiciary Committee, March 12. www.judiciary.senate.gov/imo/media/doc/Layton%20Testimony1.pdf

Lazer, D. & Kennedy, R. (2015). What We Can Learn From the Epic Failure of Google Flu Trends. *Wired*, October 1. www.wired.com/2015/10/can-learn-epic-failure-google-flu-trends/

Lazowska, E. (2009). Computing Research That Changed the World – VIDEOS! *Computer Community Consortium Catalyst*, June 7. https://cccblog.org/2009/06/07/computing-research-that-changed-the-world-videos/

Lee, K.-F. (2018). *AI Superpowers: China, Silicon Valley, and the New World Order*. Houghton Mifflin Harcourt. https://books.google.co.uk/books/about/AI_Superpowers.html?id=g7JvtAEACAAJ&redir_esc=y

Lee, P. (2016). Learning from Tay's Introduction. Official Microsoft Blog, March. https://blogs.microsoft.com/blog/2016/03/25/learning-tays-introduction/

Lee, S.-M., Kang, J.-O., & Suh, Y.-M. (2004). Comparison of Hospital Charge Prediction Models for Colorectal Cancer Patients: Neural Network vs. Decision Tree Models. *Journal of Korean Medical Science*, 19(5), 677–681. https://doi.org/10.3346/jkms.2004.19.5.677

Leo, S. (2019). Mistakes, We've Drawn a Few. *The Economist*, March 27. https://medium.economist.com/mistakes-weve-drawn-a-few-8cdd8a42d368

Lepore, J. (2018). MLTalks: How Data Killed Facts (A. Lippman, Interviewer), April 24, ML Talks, MIT Media Lab, Cambridge, MA. www.media.mit.edu/videos/ml-talks-2018-04-23/

Lepore, J. (2020). *If Then: How the Simulmatics Corporation Invented the Future*. Liveright Publishing. https://wwnorton.com/books/9781324091127

Levitin, D. J. (2019). *A Field Guide to Lies: Critical Thinking With Statistics and the Scientific Method*. Dutton. www.penguinrandomhouse.com/books/318650/a-field-guide-to-lies-by-daniel-j-levitin/9780593182512

Levitt, S. D. (2021). America's Math Curriculum Doesn't Add Up [Podcast]. In *Freakonomics*, No. 42. Freakonomics Radio. August 27 https://freakonomics.com/podcast/americas-math-curriculum-doesnt-add-up/

Lewis, M. (2004). *Moneyball: The Art of Winning an Unfair Game*. W. W. Norton. https://play.google.com/store/books/details?id=oIYNBodW-ZEC

Li, L., Chu, W., Langford, J., & Wang, X. (2011). Unbiased Offline Evaluation of Contextual-Bandit-Based News Article Recommendation Algorithms. *Proceedings of the Fourth ACM International Conference on Web Search and Data Mining – WSDM '11*, Hong Kong, China. https://doi.org/10.1145/1935826.1935878

Liebman, B. L., Roberts, M. E., Stern, R. E., & Wang, A. Z. (2020). Mass Digitization of Chinese Court Decisions: How to Use Text as Data in the Field of Chinese Law. *Journal of Law and Courts*, 8(2), 177–201. https://doi.org/10.1086/709916

Lifchits, G., Anderson, A., Goldstein, D. G., Hofman, J. M., & Watts, D. J. (2021). Success Stories Cause False Beliefs About Success. *Judgment and Decision Making*, 16(6), 1439–1463. http://journal.sjdm.org/21/210225/jdm210225.pdf

Lohr, S. (2013). The Origins of "Big Data": An Etymological Detective Story. *New York Times*, February 1. https://bits.blogs.nytimes.com/2013/02/01/the-origins-of-big-data-an-etymological-detective-story/

Lohr, S. L. (2021). *Sampling: Design and Analysis*. Chapman and Hall/CRC. https://doi.org/10.1201/9780429298899

Loukides, M. (2011). *What Is Data Science?* O'Reilly Media. www.oreilly.com/library/view/what-is-data/9781449336080/

Madiega, T. (2019). EU Guidelines on Ethics in Artificial Intelligence: Context and Implementation (PE 640.163). European Parliamentary Research Service. www.europarl.europa.eu/RegData/etudes/BRIE/2019/640163/EPRS_BRI(2019)640163_EN.pdf

Marcus, J. L., Hurley, L. B., Krakower, D. S., et al. (2019). Use of Electronic Health Record Data and Machine Learning to Identify Potential Candidates for HIV Preexposure Prophylaxis: A Modelling Study. *The Lancet HIV*, 6(10), E688–E695. https://doi.org/10.1016/S2352-3018(19)30137-7

Markoff, J. (2011). Computer Wins on "Jeopardy!": Trivial, It's Not. *The New York Times*, February 16. www.nytimes.com/2011/02/17/science/17jeopardy-watson.html

Mastrandrea, M. D., Field, C. B., Stocker, T. F., et al. (2010). *Guidance Note for Lead Authors of the IPCC Fifth Assessment Report on Consistent Treatment of*

Uncertainties. Intergovernmental Panel on Climate Change. www.ipcc.ch/publication/ipcc-cross-working-group-meeting-on-consistent-treatment-of-uncertainties/

McCulloch, W. S. & Pitts, W. (1943). A Logical Calculus of the Ideas Immanent in Nervous Activity. *Bulletin of Mathematical Biology*, 5(4), 115–133. https://doi.org/10.1007/BF02478259

McMillan, G. P. & Lapham, S. (2006). Effectiveness of Bans and Laws in Reducing Traffic Deaths: Legalized Sunday Packaged Alcohol Sales and Alcohol-Related Traffic Crashes and Crash Fatalities in New Mexico. *American Journal of Public Health*, 96(11), 1944–1948. https://doi.org/10.2105/AJPH.2005.069153

Mehrabi, N., Morstatter, F., Saxena, N., Lerman, K., & Galstyan, A. (2021). A Survey on Bias and Fairness in Machine Learning. *ACM Computing Surveys*, 54(6), 1–35. https://doi.org/10.1145/3457607

Michel, J.-B., Shen, Y. K., Aiden, A. P., et al. (2011). Quantitative Analysis of Culture Using Millions of Digitized Books. *Science*, 331(6014), 176–182. https://doi.org/10.1126/science.1199644

Microsoft. (n.d.). Law Enforcement Request Report. Retrieved December 16, 2021, from www.microsoft.com/en-us/corporate-responsibility/law-enforcement-requests-report

Miller, A. P. (2018). Want Less-Biased Decisions? Use Algorithms. *Harvard Business Review*, July 26. https://hbr.org/2018/07/want-less-biased-decisions-use-algorithms

Mintrom, M. (2015). Herbert A. Simon, *Administrative Behavior: A Study of Decision-Making Processes in Administrative Organization*. In M. Lodge, E. C. Page, & S. J. Balla, eds., *The Oxford Handbook of Classics in Public Policy and Administration*, Oxford University Press, pp. 12–21. https://doi.org/10.1093/oxfordhb/9780199646135.001.0001

Mirhoseini, A., Goldie, A., Yazgan, M., et al. (2021). A Graph Placement Methodology for Fast Chip Design. *Nature*, 594(7862), 207–212. https://doi.org/10.1038/s41586-021-03544-w

MIT Schwarzman College of Computing. (2021). Common Ground Subjects. MIT, February 9. See https://computing.mit.edu/cross-cutting/common-ground-for-computing-education/common-ground-subjects/

Mohamed, A.-R., Dahl, G., & Hinton, G. (2009). Deep Belief Networks for Phone Recognition. *Proceedings of the NIPS Workshop on Deep Learning for Speech Recognition and Related Applications*. https://nips.cc/Conferences/2009/Schedule?showEvent=1512

Moore, G. E. (1965). Cramming More Components onto Integrated Circuits. *Electronics*, 38(8), 114–117. For reprint, see https://doi.org/10.1109/n-ssc.2006.4785860

Morgan, S. L. & Winship, C. (2014). *Counterfactuals and Causal Inference*, 2nd edn. Cambridge University Press. https://play.google.com/store/books/details?id=Q6YaBQAAQBAJ

Morris, R. G. (1999). D.O. Hebb: *The Organization of Behavior*, Wiley: New York; 1949. *Brain Research Bulletin*, 50(5–6), 437. https://doi.org/10.1016/s0361-9230(99)00182-3

Moseley, A. (n.d.). Just War Theory. *Internet Encyclopedia of Philosophy*. Retrieved May 20, 2022, from https://iep.utm.edu/justwar/

Mullard, A. (2021). What Does AlphaFold Mean for Drug Discovery? *Nature Reviews. Drug Discovery*, 20(10), 725–727. https://doi.org/10.1038/d41573-021-00161-0

Nabulsi, Z., Sellergren, A., Jamshy, S., et al. (2021). Deep Learning for Distinguishing Normal Versus Abnormal Chest Radiographs and Generalization to Two Unseen Diseases Tuberculosis and COVID-19. *Scientific Reports*, 11(1), 15523. https://doi.org/10.1038/s41598-021-93967-2

Narang, R. K. (2013). *Inside the Black Box: A Simple Guide to Quantitative and High-Frequency Trading*, 2nd edn. John Wiley & Sons. https://onlinelibrary.wiley.com/doi/book/10.1002/9781118662717

Narayanan, A. (2018). 21 Fairness Definitions and Their Politics. *Machine Learning Research Conference on Fairness, Accountability, and Transparency (FAT)*, New York University, February 23 and 24. YouTube. www.youtube.com/watch?v=jIXIuYdnyyk

Narayanan, A. & Shmatikov, V. (2007). How To Break Anonymity of the Netflix Prize Dataset. arXiv [cs.CR]. https://arxiv.org/pdf/cs/0610105v2.pdf

Narayanan, A. & Shmatikov, V. (2008). Robust De-anonymization of Large Sparse Datasets. *2008 IEEE Symposium on Security and Privacy (SP 2008)*, Oakland, CA, USA, May. https://doi.org/10.1109/sp.2008.33

National Academies of Sciences, Engineering, and Medicine. (2018). *Data Science for Undergraduates: Opportunities and Options*. National Academies Press. https://doi.org /10.17226/25104

National Cancer Institute. (2022). Surveillance, Epidemiology and End Results Program. ICD-0-3 SEER Site/Histology Validation List [dataset]. See www.datascienceincontext /seer

National Commission for the Protection of Human Subjects of Biomedical and Behavioral Research. (1978). *The Belmont Report: Ethical Principles and Guidelines for the Protection of Human Subjects of Research*. Department of Health, Education, and Welfare. www.hhs.gov/ohrp/regulations-and-policy/belmont-report/read-the-belmont-report/index.html

National Institutes of Health, Office of Science Policy. (n.d.). Significant Research Advances Enabled by HeLa Cells. National Institutes of Health. Retrieved December 16, 2021, from https://osp.od.nih.gov/scientific-sharing/hela-cells-timeline/

National Research Council. (2007). *Toward a Safer and More Secure Cyberspace*, S. E. Goodman & H. S. Lin, eds., National Academies Press. https://doi.org/10.17226/11925

National Science Board. (2005). *Long-Lived Digital Data Collections: Enabling Research and Education in the 21st Century* (NSB-O5-40). National Science Foundation. www.nsf.gov/pubs/2005/nsb0540/

Naur, P. (1974). *Concise Survey of Computer Methods*. Studentlitteratur, Lund, Sweden. www.google.com/books/edition/Concise_Survey_of_Computer_Methods/ 0KEpAQAAIAAJ?hl=en&gbpv=0

Navalpakkam, V. & Churchill, E. (2012). Mouse Tracking: Measuring and Predicting Users' Experience of Web-Based Content. *Proceedings of the SIGCHI Conference on Human Factors in Computing Systems*, pp. 2963–2972. https://doi.org/10.1145 /2207676.2208705

NCSL. (2021). Differential Privacy for Census Data Explained. *National Conference of State Legislatures*, November 10. NCSL. www.ncsl.org/research/redistricting/differential-privacy-for-census-data-explained.aspx

New York Times. (2020). Coronavirus in the U.S.: Latest Map and Case Count. *The New York Times*, March 3. www.nytimes.com/interactive/2021/us/covid-cases.html

Nicas, J., Zhong, R., & Wakabayashi, D. (2021). Censorship, Surveillance and Profits: A Hard Bargain for Apple in China. *The New York Times*, June 17. www.nytimes.com /2021/05/17/technology/apple-china-censorship-data.html

Nichols, J. A. & Schneider, M. L., eds. (1982). *Proceedings of the 1982 Conference on Human Factors in Computing Systems*. ACM. https://dl.acm.org/doi/proceedings/10.1145/800049

Nickerson, D. W. & Rogers, T. (2014). Political Campaigns and Big Data. *Journal of Economic Perspectives*, 28(2), 51–74. https://doi.org/10.1257/jep.28.2.51

Nisbett, R. E. (2021). *Thinking: A Memoir.* Agora Books. www.worldcat.org/title/thinking-a-memoir/oclc/1240772815

Nissenbaum, H. (2009). *Privacy in Context*. Stanford University Press. https://doi.org/10 .1515/9780804772891

NIST. (n.d.). *Computer Security Resource Center (CSRC) – Glossary.* National Institute of Standards and Technology (NIST). Retrieved March 7, 2022, from https://csrc.nist.gov/glossary/term/infosec

Norman, D. (1993). *Things That Make Us Smart: Defending Human Attributes in the Age of the Machine.* Perseus Books, p. 43. www.perseusbooks.com/titles/don-norman/things-that-make-us-smart/9780201626957/

Norman, D. (2013). *The Design of Everyday Things*, Revised and expanded edition. Basic Books. www.basicbooks.com/titles/don-norman/the-design-of-everyday-things/9780465072996/

Norvig, P. (2009). Natural Language Corpus Data. In T. Segaran & J. Hammerbacher, eds., *Beautiful Data: The Stories Behind Elegant Data Solutions.* O'Reilly Media, pp. 219–242. www.oreilly.com/library/view/beautiful-data/9780596801656/

Nuño, B. S.-A., Vicente, G. S., & Pecherskiy, M. (2020). *Google, Apple, and Facebook: Understanding Mobility During Social Distancing With Private Sector Data*, May 11. The Development Data Partnership. https://datapartnership.org/updates/mobility-during-social-distancing/

NYU. (n.d.). About SONYC – Sounds of New York City. New York University. Retrieved December 21, 2021, from https://wp.nyu.edu/sonyc/

Office for Civil Rights (OCR). (2008). Summary of the HIPAA Privacy Rule, May 7. US Department of Health & Human Services. www.hhs.gov/hipaa/for-professionals/privacy/laws-regulations/index.html

Offord, C. (2020). The Surgisphere Scandal: What Went Wrong? *The Scientist*, October. www.the-scientist.com/features/the-surgisphere-scandal-what-went-wrong–67955

O'Neil, C. (2016). *Weapons of Math Destruction: How Big Data Increases Inequality and Threatens Democracy.* Crown. www.penguinrandomhouse.com/books/241363/weapons-of-math-destruction-by-cathy-oneil/

O'Reilly, T. (2021). Data Is the New Sand. *The Information*, February 24. www.theinformation.com/articles/data-is-the-new-sand

OpenSAFELY. (n.d.). About OpenSAFELY – Secure Analytics Platform for NHS Electronic Health Records. Retrieved December 13, 2021, from www.opensafely.org/about/

Orwant, J. (2010). Our Commitment to the Digital Humanities. Google AI Blog: The Latest from Google Research, July 14. https://doi.org/10.1097/NNE.0000000000000892

Pandya, M. & Desai, C. (2013). Compensation in Clinical Research: The Debate Continues. *Perspectives in Clinical Research*, 4(1), 70–74. https://doi.org/10.4103/2229-3485.106394

Papernot, N., Song, S., Mironov, I., et al. (2018). Scalable Private Learning with PATE. arXiv [stat.ML]. http://arxiv.org/abs/1802.08908

Pariser, E. (2011). *The Filter Bubble.* Penguin Books. www.penguinrandomhouse.com/books/309214/the-filter-bubble-by-eli-pariser/

Pearl, J. (1988). *Probabilistic Reasoning in Intelligent Systems: Networks of Plausible Inference.* Morgan Kaufmann. www.elsevier.com/books/probabilistic-reasoning-in-intelligent-systems/pearl/978-0-08-051489-5

Pearl, J. & Mackenzie, D. (2020). *The Book of Why: The New Science of Cause and Effect.* Basic Books. www.basicbooks.com/titles/judea-pearl/the-book-of-why/9781541698963/

Peirce, C. S. (1883). A Theory of Probable Inference. In C. S. Peirce, ed., *Studies in Logic by Members of the Johns Hopkins University*, vol. 203. Little, Brown, pp. 126–181. https://doi.org/10.1037/12811-007

Petruzzi, N. C. & Dada, M. (1999). Pricing and the Newsvendor Problem: A Review With Extensions. *Operations Research*, 47(2), 183–194. https://doi.org/10.1287/opre.47.2.183

Playfair, W. (1786). *The Commercial and Political Atlas: Representing, by Means of Stained Copper-Plate Charts, the Progress of the Commerce, Revenues, Expenditure and Debts of England During the Whole of the Eighteenth Century.* London. https://play.google.com/store/books/details?id=dgRdAAAAcAAJ

Pleiss, G., Raghavan, M., Wu, F., Kleinberg, J., & Weinberger, K. Q. (2017). On Fairness and Calibration. arXiv [cs.LG]. https://arxiv.org/pdf/1709.02012v2

Plonsky, O., Chen, D. L., Netzer, L., Steiner, T., & Feldman, Y. (2021). Best to Be Last: Serial Position Effects in Legal Decisions in the Field and in the Lab. Bar Ilan University Faculty of Law Research Paper No. 19-15. Bar Ilan University. See https://doi.org/10.2139/ssrn.3414155

Porter, J. (2020). Garmin Reportedly Paid Multimillion-Dollar Ransom After Suffering Cyberattack. *The Verge*, August 4. www.theverge.com/2020/8/4/21353842/garmin-ransomware-attack-wearables-wastedlocker-evil-corp

Potvin, R. & Levenberg, J. (2016). Why Google Stores Billions of Lines of Code in a Single Repository. *Communications of the ACM*, 59(7), 78–87. https://doi.org/10.1145/2854146

Poynter Institute. (n.d.). IFCN Code of Principles. International Fact Checking Network. Retrieved December 23, 2021, from www.ifcncodeofprinciples.poynter.org/

Public Face of Science Initiative. (2018). *Perceptions of Science in America.* American Academy of Arts and Sciences. www.amacad.org/publication/perceptions-science-america

Pullman, J., Thomas, K., Bursztein, E., et al. (2019). New Research: Lessons from Password Checkup in Action. Google Online Security Blog, August 15. https://security.googleblog.com/2019/08/new-research-lessons-from-password.html

Raina, R., Madhavan, A., & Ng, A. Y. (2009). Large-Scale Deep Unsupervised Learning Using Graphics Processors. *Proceedings of the 26th Annual International Conference on Machine Learning*, pp. 873–880. https://doi.org/10.1145/1553374.1553486

Raponi, S., Caprolu, M., & Di Pietro, R. (2021). Beyond SolarWinds: The Systemic Risks of Critical Infrastructures, State of Play, and Future Directions. In A. Armando & M. Colajanni, eds., *Proceedings of the Italian Conference on Cybersecurity (ITASEC 2021)* (CEUR Workshop Proceedings, vol. 2940). CEUR-WS.org. http://ceur-ws.org/Vol-2940/paper33.pdf

Reality Labs. (n.d.). Responsible Innovation Principles. Meta. Retrieved January 27, 2022, from https://about.facebook.com/realitylabs/responsible-innovation-principles/

Rees, V. (2020). Novel Antibiotic Compound Revealed Through Artificial Intelligence Screening. *Drug Target Review*, February 24. www.drugtargetreview.com/news/56448/novel-antibiotic-compound-revealed-through-artificial-intelligence-screening/

Rehmeyer, J. (2008). Florence Nightingale: The Passionate Statistician. *Science News*, November 26. www.sciencenews.org/article/florence-nightingale-passionate-statistician

Reich, R., Sahami, M., & Weinstein, J. M. (2021). *System Error: Where Big Tech Went Wrong and How We Can Reboot*. Hodder and Stoughton. www.hachette.com.au/jeremy-weinstein-rob-reich-mehran-sahami/system-error-where-big-tech-went-wrong-and-how-we-can-reboot

Retraction Watch. (2020). Retracted Coronavirus (COVID-19) Papers, April 29. See https://retractionwatch.com/retracted-coronavirus-covid-19-papers/

Rev. (2020). Big Tech Antitrust Hearing, Full Transcript, July 29. REV.com. www.rev.com/blog/transcripts/big-tech-antitrust-hearing-full-transcript-july-29

Rifon, N. J., LaRose, R., & Choi, S. M. (2005). Your Privacy Is Sealed: Effects of Web Privacy Seals on Trust and Personal Disclosures. *Journal of Consumer Affairs*, 39(2), 339–362. https://doi.org/10.1111/j.1745-6606.2005.00018.x

Robles, P. (2018). China Plans to be a World Leader in Artificial Intelligence by 2030. *South China Morning Post*, October 1. https://multimedia.scmp.com/news/china/article/2166148/china-2025-artificial-intelligence/index.html

Roff, H. M. (2018). The Folly of Trolleys: Ethical Challenges and Autonomous Vehicles, December 17. The Brookings Institution. www.brookings.edu/research/the-folly-of-trolleys-ethical-challenges-and-autonomous-vehicles/

Romeo, N. (2014). Is Google Making Students Stupid? *The Atlantic*, September. www.theatlantic.com/education/archive/2014/09/is-google-making-students-stupid/380944/

Rosenblatt, F. (1958). The Perceptron: A Probabilistic Model for Information Storage and Organization in the Brain. *Psychological Review*, 65(6), 386–408. https://doi.org/10.1037/h0042519

Rosset, C. (2020). Turing-NLG: A 17-Billion-Parameter Language Model by Microsoft, February 13. Microsoft Research. www.microsoft.com/en-us/research/blog/turing-nlg-a-17-billion-parameter-language-model-by-microsoft/

Royal Statistical Society. (2015). Data Science and Statistics: Different Worlds?, May 19. YouTube. https://youtu.be/C1zMUjHOLr4

Rubiera, C. O. (2021). AlphaFold 2 Is Here: What's Behind the Structure Prediction Miracle, July. Oxford Protein Informatics Group (OPIG). www.blopig.com/blog/2021/07/alphafold-2-is-here-whats-behind-the-structure-prediction-miracle/

Rudin, C. (2019). Stop Explaining Black Box Machine Learning Models for High Stakes Decisions and Use Interpretable Models Instead. *Nature Machine Intelligence*, 1(5), 206–215. https://doi.org/10.1038/s42256-019-0048-x

Rumelhart, D. E., Hinton, G. E., & Williams, R. J. (1986). Learning Representations by Back-Propagating Errors. *Nature*, 323(6088), 533–536. https://doi.org/10.1038/323533a0

Russell, S. & Norvig, P. (2021). *Artificial Intelligence: A Modern Approach*, 4th edn. Pearson. www.google.com/books/edition/Artificial_Intelligence/B4xczgEACAAJ?hl=en

Saey, T. H. (2015). Big Data Studies Come With Replication Challenges. *Science News*, 187(3), 22–27. www.sciencenews.org/article/big-data-studies-come-replication-challenges

Salton, G. (1971). Relevance Feedback and the Optimization of Retrieval Effectiveness. *The SMART Retrieval System – Experiments in Automatic Document Processing*. Prentice Hall.

Sambasivan, N., Kapania, S., Highfill, H., et al. (2021). "Everyone Wants to Do the Model Work, Not the Data Work": Data Cascades in High-Stakes AI. *Proceedings of the 2021 CHI Conference on Human Factors in Computing Systems*, pp. 1–15. https://doi.org/10.1145/3411764.3445518

Samuel, A. L. (1959). Some Studies in Machine Learning Using the Game of Checkers. *IBM Journal of Research and Development*, 3(3), 210–229. https://doi.org/10.1147/rd.33.0210

Samuelson, P. & Nordhaus, W. (2009). *Economics*, 19th edn. McGraw-Hill Professional. www.mhprofessional.com/9780073511290-usa-economics

Sankar, P. (2014). ELSI: Origins and Early History. *Meeting Sixteen, Presidential Commission for the Study of Bioethical Issues*, February 11, Washington, DC. https://bioethicsarchive.georgetown.edu/pcsbi/sites/default/files/Sankar%20Meeting%2016%20Presentation.pdf

Schafer, J. B., Konstan, J. A., & Riedl, J. (2001). E-Commerce Recommendation Applications. *Data Mining and Knowledge Discovery*, 5(1), 115–153. https://doi.org/10.1023/A: 1009804230409

Schiffer, Z. & Robertson, A. (2021). Watch a Police Officer Admit to Playing Taylor Swift to Keep a Video Off YouTube. *The Verge*, July 1. www.theverge.com/2021/7/1/22558292/police-officer-video-taylor-swift-youtube-copyright

Schmidt, E. (2020). Ethics & Privacy: Terms of Usage, a Data Science Day Virtual Event. Keynote Address. Columbia Data Science Institute, September 18. Youtube. See https://datascience.columbia.edu/news/2020/data-science-day-2020/

Schneier, B. (2006). Security in the Cloud. *Schneier on Security*, February 15. www.schneier.com/blog/archives/2006/02/security_in_the.html

Schuemie, M. J., Cepeda, M. S., Suchard, M. A., et al. (2020). How Confident Are We About Observational Findings in Healthcare: A Benchmark Study. *Harvard Data Science Review*, 2(1). https://doi.org/10.1162/99608f92.147cc28e

Schumer, C. & Sanders, B. (2019). Opinion: Limit Corporate Stock Buybacks. *The New York Times*, February 4. www.nytimes.com/2019/02/03/opinion/chuck-schumer-bernie-sanders.html

SciLine. (2017). SciLine home page. American Association for the Advancement of Science. See www.sciline.org/

Shaw, D. E., Maragakis, P., Lindorff-Larsen, K., et al. (2010). Atomic-Level Characterization of the Structural Dynamics of Proteins. *Science*, 330(6002), 341–346. https://doi.org/10.1126/science.1187409

Shelley, P. B. (1898). *Prometheus Unbound: A Lyrical Drama in Four Acts*, G. L. Dickinson, ed., vol. 50. J. M. Dent. www.google.com/books/edition/Prometheus_Unbound/6O6aNo60Pi0C

Shen, D., Wu, G., & Suk, H.-I. (2017). Deep Learning in Medical Image Analysis. *Annual Review of Biomedical Engineering*, 19, 221–248. https://doi.org/10.1146/annurev-bioeng-071516-044442

Shift. (n.d.). Shift: The Commission on Work, Workers, and Technology. Retrieved December 21, 2021, from https://shiftcommission.work/

SIAM/ASA. (n.d.). SIAM/ASA Journal on Uncertainty Quantification (JUQ). Retrieved December 21, 2021, from www.siam.org/publications/journals/siam-asa-journal-on-uncertainty-quantification-juq

Silver, D., Hubert, T., Schrittwieser, J., et al. (2018). A General Reinforcement Learning Algorithm that Masters Chess, Shogi, and Go Through Self-Play. *Science*, 362(6419), 1140–1144. https://doi.org/10.1126/science.aar6404

Sinclair, J. (1794). *The Statistical Account of Scotland: Drawn Up From the Communication of the Ministers of the Different Parishes*, vol. 12. Creech. www.google.com/books/edition/The_Statistical_Account_of_Scotland/_AA-AAAAcAAJ?hl=en

Skloot, R. (2010). *The Immortal Life of Henrietta Lacks*. Crown. www.penguinrandomhouse.com/books/168191/the-immortal-life-of-henrietta-lacks-by-rebecca-skloot/

Sly, L. (2018). U.S. Soldiers Are Revealing Sensitive and Dangerous Information by Jogging. *The Washington Post*, January 28. www.washingtonpost.com/world/a-map-showing-the-users-of-fitness-devices-lets-the-world-see-where-us-soldiers-are-and-what-they-are-doing/2018/01/28/86915662-0441-11e8-aa61-f3391373867e_story.html

Smith, J. E. & Winkler, R. L. (2006). The Optimizer's Curse: Skepticism and Postdecision Surprise in Decision Analysis. *Management Science*, 52(3), 311–322. https://doi.org/10.1287/mnsc.1050.0451

Smithsonian Institution. (n.d.). About – Collections Search Center, Smithsonian Institution. The Smithsonian Collections Search Center. Retrieved December 11, 2021, from https://collections.si.edu/search/about.htm

Sodhi, M. (2007). What About the "O" in O.R.? *ORMS Today*, 34(3), December. https://doi.org/10.1287/orms.2007.06.05

Solum, L. (2009). Legal Theory Lexicon: Rules, Standards, and Principles. Legal Theory Blog, September 6. https://lsolum.typepad.com/legaltheory/2009/09/legal-theory-lexicon-rules-standards-and-principles.html

Sonderegger, P. (2021). Data Hits Peak Metaphor. *Data Capital*, March 4. https://paulsonderegger.com/2021/03/04/data-hits-peak-metaphor/

Spector, A. Z. (2002). Technology Megatrends Driving the Future of e-Society. In J. Eberspächer & U. Hertz, eds., *Leben in der e-Society: Computerintelligenz für den Alltag*. Springer, pp. 35–50. https://doi.org/10.1007/978-3-642-56059-0_5

Spector, A. Z. (2004). Research on the Edge of the Expanding Sphere. AZS Services, Google Drive. https://azs-services.com/older-material/

Spector, A. Z. (2016). *Opportunities and Perils in Data Science*. Unpublished.

Spector, A. Z. (2020). Thought Experiment: Corona Virus and Tracing Contacts. LinkedIn, February 4. www.linkedin.com/pulse/thought-experiment-corona-virus-tracing-contacts-alfred-spector/

Spector, A. Z. (2021). Data Science Goals and Pragmatics. *Harvard Data Science Review*, 3 (2). https://doi.org/10.1162/99608f92.643b1bf8

Spector, A. Z. & Gifford, D. (1984). The Space Shuttle Primary Computer System. *Communications of the ACM*, 27(9), 872–900. https://doi.org/10.1145/358234.358246

Spiegelhalter, D. J. (2014). The Power of the MicroMort. *BJOG: An International Journal of Obstetrics and Gynaecology*, 121(6), 662–663. https://doi.org/10.1111/1471-0528.12663

SRI International, Network Information Center, & US Defense Communications Agency. (1978). *ARPANET Directory*. The Center. https://books.google.com/books?id=AHo-AQAAIAAJ

Statista. (n.d.). Facebook Fake Account Deletion per Quarter 2021. Retrieved December 17, 2021, from www.statista.com/statistics/1013474/facebook-fake-account-removal-quarter/

Statt, N. (2021). Slack's New DM Feature Can Be Used to Send Abuse and Harassment With Just an Invite. *The Verge*, March 24. www.theverge.com/2021/3/24/22348422/slack-connect-direct-message-abuse-harassment

Stecuła, D. & Motta, M. (2021). Unverified Reports of Vaccine Side Effects in VAERS Aren't the Smoking Guns Portrayed by Right-Wing Media Outlets – They Can Offer Insight Into Vaccine Hesitancy. *The Conversation*, August 25. http://theconversation.com/unverified-reports-of-vaccine-side-effects-in-vaers-arent-the-smoking-guns-portrayed-by-right-wing-media-outlets-they-can-offer-insight-into-vaccine-hesitancy-166401

Steele, J. & Iliinsky, N., eds. (2010). *Beautiful Visualization: Looking at Data Through the Eyes of Experts*. O'Reilly Media. www.oreilly.com/library/view/beautiful-visualization/9781449379889/

Sterne, J. (2021). Real-World Effectiveness of COVID-19 Vaccines. Vaccines and Related Biological Products Advisory Committee Meeting, September 17. www.fda.gov/media/152241/download

Stokes, J. M., Yang, K., Swanson, K., et al. (2020). A Deep Learning Approach to Antibiotic Discovery. *Cell*, 181(2), 475–483. https://doi.org/10.1016/j.cell.2020.04.001

Sullivan, D. (2021). An Overview of Our Rater Guidelines for Search, October 19. Google. https://blog.google/products/search/overview-our-rater-guidelines-search/

Sweeney, L. (2002). *k*-Anonymity: A Model for Protecting Privacy. *International Journal of Uncertainty, Fuzziness and Knowledge-Based Systems*, 10(5), 557–570. https://doi.org/10.1142/S0218488502001648

Swire, P. P. & Kennedy-Mayo, D. (2020). *U.S. Private-Sector Privacy*, 3rd edn. International Association of Privacy Professionals. https://iapp.org/resources/article/u-s-private-sector-privacy-third-edition/

Taleb, N. N. (2004). *Fooled by Randomness: The Hidden Role of Chance in Life and in the Markets*, 2nd edn. TEXERE and Random House. www.penguinrandomhouse.com/books/176225/fooled-by-randomness-by-nassim-nicholas-taleb/

Taleb, N. N. (2007). *The Black Swan: The Impact of the Highly Improbable*, 2nd edn. TEXERE and Random House. www.penguinrandomhouse.com/books/176226/the-black-swan-second-edition-by-nassim-nicholas-taleb/

Tau, B. (2020). Next Step in Government Data Tracking Is the Internet of Things. *Wall Street Journal (Eastern Edn.)*, November 27. www.wsj.com/articles/next-step-in-government-data-tracking-is-the-internet-of-things-11606478401

Thaler, R. H. & Sunstein, C. R. (2009). *Nudge: Improving Decisions About Health, Wealth, and Happiness*. Penguin. www.penguinrandomhouse.com/books/304634/nudge-by-richard-h-thaler-and-cass-r-sunstein/

Thistlethwaite, D. L. & Campbell, D. T. (1960). Regression-Discontinuity Analysis: An Alternative to the Ex Post Facto Experiment. *Journal of Educational Psychology*, 51 (6), 309–317. https://doi.org/10.1037/h0044319

Tibshirani, R. (1996). Regression Shrinkage and Selection via the Lasso. *Journal of the Royal Statistical Society*, 58(1), 267–288. https://doi.org/10.1111/j.2517-6161.1996.tb02080.x

T-Mobile. (2021). T-Mobile Shares Additional Information Regarding Ongoing Cyberattack Investigation, August 18. See https://investor.t-mobile.com/news-and-events/t-mobile-us-press-releases/press-release-details/2021/T-Mobile-Shares-Additional-Information-Regarding-Ongoing-Cyberattack-Investigation/default.aspx

Tony C. (2006). Tacoma Narrows Bridge Collapse "Gallopin' Gertie", December 9. Youtube. www.youtube.com/watch?v=j-zczJXSxnw

TOR Project. (n.d.). About The Tor Project: History. Retrieved March 16, 2022, from www.torproject.org/about/history/

Troianovski, A. (2021). "You Can't Trust Anyone": Russia's Hidden Covid Toll Is an Open Secret. *The New York Times*, April 10. www.nytimes.com/2021/04/10/world/europe/covid-russia-death.html

Trust Project, The. (n.d.). The Trust Project – News With Integrity. Retrieved December 20, 2021, from https://thetrustproject.org/

Tufte, E. R. (2001). *The Visual Display of Quantitative Information*, 2nd edn. Graphics Press. www.edwardtufte.com/tufte/books_vdqi

Tukey, J. W. (1962). The Future of Data Analysis. *Annals of Mathematical Statistics*, 33(1), 1–67. www.jstor.org/stable/2237638

Tukey, J. W. (1977). *Exploratory Data Analysis*. Addison-Wesley. http://theta.edu.pl/wp-content/uploads/2012/10/exploratorydataanalysis_tukey.pdf

Turing, A. M. (1950). I. – Computing Machinery and Intelligence. *Mind; a Quarterly Review of Psychology and Philosophy*, LIX(236), 433–460. https://doi.org/10.1093/mind/LIX.236.433

Tversky, A. & Kahneman, D. (1974). Judgment Under Uncertainty: Heuristics and Biases. *Science*, 185(4157), 1124–1131. https://doi.org/10.1126/science.185.4157.1124

Tversky, A. & Kahneman, D. (1982). Judgments of and by Representativeness. In *Judgment Under Uncertainty: Heuristics and Biases*. Cambridge University Press, pp. 84–98. https://doi.org/10.1017/CBO9780511809477.007

US Bureau of Economic Analysis. (n.d.). Interactive Access to Industry Economic Accounts Data – Value Added by Industry [Dataset]. Bureau of Economic Analysis – US Department of Commerce (BEA). Retrieved December 10, 2021, from https://apps.bea.gov/iTable/iTable.cfm?reqid=150&step=2&isuri=1&categories=gdpxind

US Census Bureau. (n.d.). North American Industry Classification System (NAICS). US Census Bureau. Retrieved December 10, 2021, from www.census.gov/naics/

US Department of Homeland Security. (2012). *The Menlo Report: Ethical Principles Guiding Information and Communication Technology Research*. US Department of Homeland Security. https://doi.org/10.2139/SSRN.2445102

US Department of Transportation. (n.d.). Automated Vehicles for Safety. National Highway Traffic Safety Administration. Retrieved December 14, 2021, from www.nhtsa.gov/technology-innovation/automated-vehicles-safety

US Federal Trade Commission. (1998). Fair Information Practice Principles. Internet Archive. https://web.archive.org/web/20131110022137/http://www.ftc.gov/reports/privacy3/fairinfo.shtm

US National Library of Medicine. (n.d.). ClinicalTrials.gov. Homepage. US National Library of Medicine. Retrieved December 20, 2021, from https://clinicaltrials.gov/

van der Bles, A. M., van der Linden, S., Freeman, A. L. J., et al. (2019). Communicating Uncertainty About Facts, Numbers and Science. *Royal Society Open Science*, 6(5), 181870. https://doi.org/10.1098/rsos.181870

Van Hoeve, W.-J. (2014). Operations Research: Opportunities and Challenges. *INFORMS IE Seminar*, University of Pittsburgh. www.andrew.cmu.edu/user/vanhoeve/papers/u_pitt_2014_OR.pdf

Vaswani, A., Shazeer, N., Parmar, N., et al. (2017). Attention Is All You Need. In I. Guyon, U. V. Luxburg, S. Bengio, et al., eds., *Advances in Neural Information Processing Systems*, vol. 30. Curran Associates, pp. 5998–6008. https://proceedings.neurips.cc/paper/2017/file/3f5ee243547dee91fbd053c1c4a845aa-Paper.pdf

Verma, I. M. (2014). Editorial Expression of Concern: Experimental Evidence of Massive-Scale Emotional Contagion Through Social Networks. *Proceedings of the National Academy of Sciences of the United States of America*, 111(29), 10779. https://doi.org/10.1073/pnas.1412469111

Vigen, T. (n.d.). 15 Insane Things That Correlate With Each Other. Tylervigen.com. Retrieved January 17, 2022, from http://tylervigen.com/spurious-correlations

Vitak, J., Shilton, K., & Ashktorab, Z. (2016). Beyond the Belmont Principles: Ethical Challenges, Practices, and Beliefs in the Online Data Research Community. *Proceedings of the 19th ACM Conference on Computer-Supported Cooperative Work & Social Computing – CSCW '16*, pp. 941–953. https://doi.org/10.1145/2818048.2820078

Vodrahalli, K., Gerstenberg, T., & Zou, J. (2022). Uncalibrated Models Can Improve Human–AI Collaboration. arXiv [cs.AI]. http://arxiv.org/abs/2202.05983

von Borzyskowski, I., Mazumder, A., Mateen, B., & Wooldridge, M., eds. (2021). *Data Science and AI in the Age of COVID-19 – Reflections on the Response of the UK's Data Science and AI Community to the COVID-19 Pandemic*. Alan Turing Institute. www.turing.ac.uk/sites/default/files/2021-06/data-science-and-ai-in-the-age-of-covid_full-report_2.pdf

Wang, G., Sarkar, A., Carbonetto, P., & Stephens, M. (2020). A Simple New Approach to Variable Selection in Regression, With Application to Genetic Fine Mapping. *Journal of the Royal Statistical Society. Series B, Statistical Methodology*, 82(5), 1273–1300. https://doi.org/10.1111/rssb.12388

Wang, P. & Johnson, C. (2018). Cybersecurity Incident Handling: A Case Study of the Equifax Data Breach. *Issues in Information Systems*, 19(3), 150–159. https://doi.org/10.48009/3_iis_2018_150-159

Wang, Y. & Blei, D. M. (2019). The Blessings of Multiple Causes. *Journal of the American Statistical Association*, 114(528), 1574–1596. https://doi.org/10.1080/01621459.2019.1686987

Wason, P. C. (1960). On the Failure to Eliminate Hypotheses in a Conceptual Task. *Quarterly Journal of Experimental Psychology*, 12(3), 129–140. https://doi.org/10.1080/17470216008416717

Wells, G., Horwitz, J., & Seetharaman, D. (2021). Facebook Knows Instagram Is Toxic for Teen Girls, Company Documents Show. *Wall Street Journal*, September 14.

www.wsj.com/articles/facebook-knows-instagram-is-toxic-for-teen-girls-company-documents-show-11631620739

Whipple, K. N. & Shermak, J. L. (2018). Quality, Quantity and Policy: How Newspaper Journalists Use Digital Metrics to Evaluate Their Performance and Their Papers' Strategies. *ISOJ (International Symposium on Online Journalism)*, 8(1), 67–88. https://isoj.org/research/quality-quantity-and-policy-how-newspaper-journalists-use-digital-metrics-to-evaluate-their-performance-and-their-papers-strategies/

White, R. W., Harpaz, R., Shah, N. H., DuMouchel, W., & Horvitz, E. (2014). Toward Enhanced Pharmacovigilance Using Patient-Generated Data on the Internet. *Clinical Pharmacology and Therapeutics*, 96(2), 239–246. https://doi.org/10.1038/clpt.2014.77

Wikipedia contributors. (n.d.). Category: Lists of Albums by Release Date [Dataset]. Wikipedia, The Free Encyclopedia. Retrieved December 14, 2021, from https://en.wikipedia.org/wiki/Category:Lists_of_albums_by_release_date

Wikipedia contributors. (2021). Metcalfe's Law. Wikipedia, The Free Encyclopedia, December 9. https://en.wikipedia.org/w/index.php?title=Metcalfe%27s_law&oldid=1059470400

Wikipedia contributors. (2022). Goodhart's Law. Wikipedia, The Free Encyclopedia, March 8. https://en.wikipedia.org/w/index.php?title=Goodhart%27s_law&oldid=1076008798

Wild Sky Media. (n.d.). Baby Names Popularity – NameVoyager: Baby Name Wizard Graph of Most Popular Baby Names. Internet Archive. See www.datascienceincontext.com/babyname

Williams, J. J., Lombrozo, T., & Rehder, B. (2013). The Hazards of Explanation: Overgeneralization in the Face of Exceptions. *Journal of Experimental Psychology, General*, 142(4), 1006–1014. https://doi.org/10.1037/a0030996

Williams, M. (2020). The Average Temperature of the Universe Has Been Getting Hotter and Hotter. *Universe Today - Space and Astronomy News*, November 14. www.universetoday.com/148794/the-average-temperature-of-the-universe-has-been-getting-hotter-and-hotter/

Wing, J. M. (2006). Computational Thinking. *Communications of the ACM*, 49(3), 33–35. https://doi.org/10.1145/1118178.1118215

Wing, J. M. (2019). The Data Life Cycle. *Harvard Data Science Review*, 1(1). https://doi.org/10.1162/99608f92.e26845b4

Wing, J. M. (2020). Ten Research Challenge Areas in Data Science. *Harvard Data Science Review*. https://doi.org/10.1162/99608f92.c6577b1f

Wing, J. M. (2021). Trustworthy AI. *Communications of the ACM*, 64(10), 64–71. https://doi.org/10.1145/3448248

Wing, J. M., Janeja, V. P., Kloefkorn, T., & Erickson, L. C. (2018). *Data Science Leadership Summit: Summary Report*. National Science Foundation. https://dl.acm.org/doi/10.5555/3293458

Wingrove, J. (2021). Vaccine Data Gaps Point to Millions More in U.S. Who Lack Shots. *Bloomberg News*, December 18. www.bloomberg.com/news/articles/2021-12-18/vaccine-data-gaps-point-to-millions-more-in-u-s-who-lack-shots

Wise, C. (2011). *Chomsky and Deconstruction: The Politics of Unconscious Knowledge*. Palgrave Macmillan US. https://doi.org/10.1057/9780230117051

Wolkin, J. (2020). Richard Childress Racing Enhances Performance With Predictive Analytics. *Forbes Magazine*, August 2. www.forbes.com/sites/josephwolkin/2020/08/02/richard-childress-racing-enhances-performance-with-predictive-analytics/

Won, M. (n.d.). PLATO (Programmed Logic for Automatic Teaching Operations) System. HistoryIT. Retrieved April 7, 2022, from https://chip.web.ischool.illinois.edu/people/projects/timeline/1960won.html

Wong, J. C., Lewis, P., & Davies, H. (2018). How Academic at Centre of Facebook Scandal Tried – and Failed – to Spin Personal Data Into Gold. *The Guardian*, April 24. www.theguardian.com/news/2018/apr/24/aleksandr-kogan-cambridge-analytica-facebook-data-business-ventures

World Health Organization. (n.d.). International Statistical Classification of Diseases and Related Health Problems (ICD). ICD-11. Retrieved December 20, 2021, from www.who.int/standards/classifications/classification-of-diseases

World Traveling Salesman Problem. (n.d.). TSP: The Traveling Salesman Problem. Retrieved December 27, 2021, from www.math.uwaterloo.ca/tsp/world/

wwPDB consortium. (2019). Protein Data Bank: The Single Global Archive for 3D Macromolecular Structure Data. *Nucleic Acids Research*, 47(D1), D520–D528. https://doi.org/10.1093/nar/gky949

Wymant, C., Ferretti, L., Tsallis, D., et al. (2021). The Epidemiological Impact of the NHS COVID-19 App. *Nature*, 594(7863), 408–412. https://doi.org/10.1038/s41586-021-03606-z

Xu, S., Huang, R., Sy, L. S., et al. (2021). COVID-19 Vaccination and Non-COVID-19 Mortality Risk – Seven Integrated Health Care Organizations, United States, December 14, 2020–July 31, 2021. *Morbidity and Mortality Weekly Report (MMWR)*, 70(43), 1520–1524. https://doi.org/10.15585/mmwr.mm7043e2

Yau, N. (n.d.). FlowingData Data Visualization and Statistics. FlowingData. Retrieved December 10, 2021, from www.flowingdata.com/

Young, M. D. (1958). *The Rise of the Meritocracy, 1870–2033: An Essay on Education and Equality.* Thames and Hudson. https://books.google.com/books?id=TdMVAAAAIAAJ

Zaugg, I. A., Culligan, P. J., Witten, R., & Zheng, T. (2021). Collaboratory at Columbia: An Aspen Grove of Data Science Education. *Harvard Data Science Review*, 3(4). https://doi.org/10.1162/99608f92.53c4a1b4

Zhang, Y. & Zhao, Y. (2015). Astronomy in the Big Data Era. *Data Science Journal*, 14, 11. https://doi.org/10.5334/dsj-2015-011

Zheng, S., Trott, A., Srinivasa, S., et al. (2020). The AI Economist: Improving Equality and Productivity with AI-Driven Tax Policies. arXiv [econ.GN]. http://arxiv.org/abs/2004.13332

Zuiderveen Borgesius, F., Trilling, D., Möller, J., et al. (2016). Should We Worry About Filter Bubbles? *Internet Policy Review*, 5(1). https://doi.org/10.14763/2016.1.401

Index

Printed in the United States
by Baker & Taylor Publisher Services